AutoCAD: Drafting and 3D Design

Mark Merickel

NRP
NEW RIDERS
PUBLISHING

New Riders Publishing, Carmel, Indiana

AutoCAD: Drafting and 3D Design

By Mark Merickel

Published by:
New Riders Publishing
11711 N. College Ave., Suite 140
Carmel, IN 46032 USA

Printed in the United States of America   2 3 4 5 6 7 8 9 0

Library of Congress Cataloging-in-Publication Data
AutoCAD: Drafting and 3D Design / Mark Merickel
     p.   cm.
     Includes index.
     ISBN 1-56205-034-6 : $29.95
     1. AutoCAD (Computer program) I. Title.
T385.M439 1991
620'.0042'02855369—dc20   91-34051
     CIP

Publisher

David P. Ewing

Managing Editor

Tim Huddleston

Production Editor

Rob Lawson

Editors

Mark Montieth

Rob Tidrow

Richard Limacher

Technical Editors

Tom Boersma

Kevin Coleman

Scott D. Pesci

Educational Consultant

Robert South

Editorial Secretary

Karen Opal

Book Design and Production

William Hartman,
Hartman Publishing

Proofreaders

Sandra Profant

George Bloom

Indexed by

Sharon Hilgenberg

**Composed in Bookman
and Courier by**

William Hartman,
Hartman Publishing

About the Author

Mark Merickel holds a B.A. in Drafting and Design, an M.A. in Industrial Technology, and a Ph.D. in Technology Education. Mr. Merickel has taught design and drafting for over 20 years. He has industrial training and hands-on experience with mainframe and microcomputer-based CAD/CAM systems. Mr. Merickel is a frequent guest lecturer and speaker on CAD/CAM, 3D modeling, and various other new technologies in industrial and educational forums.

Mr. Merickel is an active member of many CAD/CAM/CAE educational committees and professional organizations, including the Society of Manufacturing Engineers (SME), the Computer Automated Systems Association, the National Computer Graphics Association (NCGA), the National Association of Industrial and Technical Teacher Educators, the Council on Technology Teacher Education, and the American Educational Research Association.

For the past ten years, Mr. Merickel has been a pioneer and leader in bringing CAD/CAM curriculum into public education. He developed and authored the original Autodesk, Inc. Teacher Training Program. For the past three years, he has been involved in virtual reality and cyberspace research. Mr. Merickel is currently Assistant Professor of Technology in Education at Oregon State University, Corvallis.

Acknowledgments

A special thanks to my primary editor, Colleen Kay Merickel, for your input and continued support of this work.

Thanks to Autodesk, Inc., and especially Gloria Bastidas, Marketing Communications, and Dr. Joseph Oakey, the Autodesk Foundation, for their continuing support and encouragement.

Thanks to Richard Erickson of Hayward, California, and John Larson from San Joaquin Delta College, Stockton, California, for their valuable input on GDT and ANSI Y14.5 standards.

Thank you Victor Wright and Tom Boersma for your editorial contributions to this book. Victor Wright is an author, certified mechanical engineer, and Vice President of Engineering for Challenger Lifts Division of VBM Corporation of Louisville, Kentucky. Tom Boersma is a certified manufacturing engineer, an ATC trainer, and is a CAD/CAM training specialist at Grand Rapids Community College.

And a special thanks to all of those who assisted with this project at New Riders Publishing. From me to all of you . . . THANKS.

Trademark Acknowledgments

New Riders Publishing has made every attempt to supply trademark information about company names, products, and services mentioned in this book. Trademarks indicated below were derived from various sources. New Riders Publishing cannot attest to the accuracy of this information.

ANSI is a registered trademark of American National Stanards Institute.

Apollo is a registered trademark of Hewlett Packard, Co.

AutoCAD, AutoLISP, and AutoSHADE are registered trademarks of Autodesk, Inc.

dBase III is a registered trademark of Ashton-Tate Corporation.

DEC VMS is a registered trademark of Digital Equipment Corp.

IBM/PC/XT/AT, IBM PS/2, and PC DOS are registered trademarks of International Business Machines, Corp.

Macintosh is a registered trademark of Apple Computer, Inc.

MS-DOS, OS/2, and Xenix are registered trademarks of Microsoft Corp.

Norton Editor is a registered trademark of Symantec Corp.

SideKick is a registered trademark of Borland International, Inc.

UNIX is a registered trademark of AT&T.

Wordstar is a trademark of Wordstar International.

"Dimensioning and Tolerancing ANSI Y14.5-1982" is a publication of the American Society of Mechanical Engineers.

Trademarks of other products mentioned in this book are held by the companies producing them.

Warning and Disclaimer

This book is designed to provide information about the AutoCAD program. Every effort has been made to make this book as complete and as accurate as possible, but no warranty or fitness is implied.

The information is provided on an "as is" basis. The author and New Riders Publishing shall have neither liability nor responsibility to any person or entity with respect to any loss or damages arising from the information contained in this book or from the use of the disks or programs that may accompany it.

Table of Contents

INTRODUCTION

AutoCAD is a computer-aided drafting (CAD) tool with which you can design and draft virtually any object. The more you use AutoCAD, the more you appreciate its power. AutoCAD's power and your skills are two variables that lead to efficient production designing and drafting. Beginning in Chapter 3 and continuing throughout the rest of the book, *AutoCAD: Drafting and 3D Design* addresses these two variables by guiding the user through a series of both practical and manageable AutoCAD lessons.

A third variable covered in the first two chapters of this book is system management. Managing your AutoCAD working environment is also key to using AutoCAD productively. No matter how fast or creative you are, you will never realize the full potential of AutoCAD without employing good system setup and management.

Who Should Read this Book?

AutoCAD: Drafting and 3D Design serves not only students but also the engineer, designer, and technical drafter by quickly putting AutoCAD to work. With each release, AutoCAD becomes more powerful. This book is your guide to using AutoCAD's many tools, options, and techniques efficiently and productively.

Using AutoCAD for Design, Engineering, and Technical Drafting

The goal of an engineer, designer, or drafter is to communicate ideas clearly. To avoid ambiguity and resulting production errors, designers and drafters need to be able to accurately use the tools of the trade to convey design intent. AutoCAD and this book are two important tools in producing superior drawings with minimal effort.

AutoCAD: Drafting and 3D Design assists you with choosing the right tool for the job, whether you are doing traditional two-dimensional drafting or three-dimensional design and modeling.

2D versus 3D: Choosing the Right Tool for the Right Job

AutoCAD offers an extremely wide variety of commands. With a little practice, you will soon be using simple AutoCAD drafting techniques to develop projects in both two and three dimensions. Speed, efficiency, and post-CAD uses for your documentation are factors upon which the decision of whether to draw in 2D or 3D should be based.

If a simple two-dimensional drawing will do the job, why spend the time generating three-dimensional drawings? On the other hand, if three dimensional drawings are useful for interpretation or production, then use them. *AutoCAD: Drafting and 3D Design* will guide you through commands and techniques for 2D, 3D, and various combinations of both.

What You Need To Use this Book

Although *AutoCAD: Drafting and 3D Design* has been written for a wide range of AutoCAD users, there are a few considerations which should be followed.

DOS Version

We recommend that you use PC or MS-DOS 3.0, or later.

UNIX, Macintosh, and Other Operating Systems

AutoCAD is designed so that all of its drawing and support files are compatible with every system capable of running AutoCAD. No special files or preparations should be necessary if you have an operating system other than PC or MS-DOS, except you will need a DOS system to copy the files from the optional ACAD Disk. *AutoCAD: Drafting and 3D Design* has not been tested on other operating systems, but because all of AutoCAD's files are compatible with any system running AutoCAD, it should work with little trouble. The exercises are shown in DOS format; if you are working on another operating system, your prompts or file handling procedures will vary.

AutoCAD Version and Equipment

You do not need a fast and fancy system to run AutoCAD. If your system is not running at IBM-AT speed or faster, however, you may find some operations a little slower than you like. This especially applies to the 3D polygon mesh surface models. You will need 640K of RAM. A mouse or digitizing tablet is essential.

Run the following sequence in AutoCAD to check your version and to verify that AutoLISP is enabled for the setup and Y14.5 Menu System exercises.

Checking Your AutoCAD Version	
Command: **Ver**	(Type **Ver** and Press Enter.)
"AutoLISP Release 11.0"	(Or your version number.)

 If you get a bad command message, check to see if AutoLISP is disabled by insufficient memory or if AutoLISP is disabled by the AutoLISP option on the configuration menu under Configure operating parameters.

Compatibility with Earlier Versions of AutoCAD

If you have a release that is earlier than AutoCAD Release 11, don't be alarmed. Most *AutoCAD: Drafting and 3D Design* exercises are compatible with Release 10. If you are using Release 9 or earlier, you will see some discrepancies, and you will need to substitute some of the following commands and techniques:

Use VIEW and ZOOM in place of multiple viewports.

Use CHANGE instead of CHPROP commands.

Recalculate your coordinates to compensate for offset UCSs where used. (This should not be necessary for the slight offset of the BDR UCS.)

If you want to use the Y14.5 Menu System with earlier versions of AutoCAD, it may be necessary for you to edit some menu functions and revise commands such as CHPROP.

How this Book Is Organized

AutoCAD: Drafting and 3D Design is a hands-on tutorial designed to teach you how to use AutoCAD for production machine drafting, engineering drawing, and related disciplines. It is organized to guide you through operations that demonstrate the command tools and techniques you would use to complete a typical technical project.

This book has 18 chapters and three appendixes. You can work through the book from cover to cover or, if you are an experienced AutoCAD user, you may wish to skip around and choose sections containing information which is new to you.

In two-dimensional drafting, geometric dimensioning and tolerancing (GDT) is essential to communicating the design concept. Whether you will be creating 2D drawings or extracting your 2D from 3D drawings, *AutoCAD: Drafting and 3D Design* will guide you through the most efficient process to perform the operations for production design and drafting.

This book emphasizes the use of GDT according to ANSI Y14.5 standards and accepted industry practice. Our discussion of GDT includes how to use and customize AutoCAD's dimensioning according to industry standards, how to create and use GDT symbols, and how to automate the process of doing GDT with our optional menu system (more about that later).

The Optional AutoCAD: Drafting and 3D Design Drawing Disk

To help you save time and effort, we offer an optional AutoCAD: Drafting and 3D Design Disk (ACAD Disk) with this book. The disk contains both the customized ANSI Y14.5 Menu System and completed drawing files from the exercises. These drawing files can save you valuable time and enable you to get right to the heart of the exercises by eliminating repetitive or tedious setup tasks. Some exercises in later chapters depend on drawings created in earlier chapters. The ACAD Disk gives you the option of being able to do these later exercises using drawing files from its disk. You, therefore, don't have to spend time making drawings that teach you commands and techniques you may already know.

Having the disk, however, is not essential to work through the book. The book is designed so that every exercise can be performed by a new user in a step-by-step approach.

You will find an order form for the ACAD Disk in the back pages of this book. See the instructions for Installing the ACAD Disk to make the drawing files and the Y14.5 Menu System files ready to use.

How To Use the ACAD Disk's Exercise Drawings

Exercises which use pre-developed drawings from the ACAD Disk are designated at the beginning of those exercises by the following simple icons:

 Do this if you have the AutoCAD: Drafting and 3D Design Disk. This is the disk icon.

 Do this if you do not have the AutoCAD: Drafting and 3D Design Disk. This is the no-disk icon.

The Y14.5 Menu System

The ACAD Disk also contains the Y14.5 Menu System. The system's geometric dimensioning and tolerancing tools simplify drawing setup and enable you to draft and dimension according to the ANSI Y14.5 standards. The Y14.5 Menu System enables you to set decimal precision, limits, and tolerances as well as to generate ANSI Y14.5 symbols in both decimal inch and SI metric standards.

The Y14.5 Menu System uses screen menus, tablet menu, pull-down menus, or any combination of these menus. Whichever your system supports, you will increase your drafting productivity with the drafting functions and AutoLISP routines available with the ACAD Disk's Y14.5 program.

About this Book

We've made *AutoCAD: Drafting and 3D Design* as easy to use and follow as possible. To avoid errors and misunderstandings, we recommend that you read the following sections before beginning any of the book's exercises.

Things To Watch For

The printing font used in the exercises and program listings doesn't distinguish clearly between zero and the letter O, or the number one and lower case letter L. You need to watch these closely:

0   This is a zero.

O   This is an upper case letter O.

1   This is the number one.

l   This is a lower case letter L.

As you look through this book, you will notice certain conventions that show you at a glance what actions to take as you use the program. These conventions are as follows:

- AutoCAD commands begin with an uppercase letter: Line
- AutoCAD system variables and file names appear in all uppercase letters: TILEMODE and PROTO-C
- DOS and AutoCAD prompts and messages appear in a special typeface: `Command:`
- New terms are introduced in italics: *entities*
- Two special icons, one for tips and the other for notes, are used throughout the book to help keep the reader informed.
- AutoCAD commands introduced for the first time have a special command icon in the left margin. The Circle command, for example, might be introduced in the following way:

The *Circle* command enables you to draw circles. There are several ways to draw a circle; one of the most direct methods is to specify a center point on the screen and then give either the radius or diameter.

How Exercises Are Shown

Most student exercises, especially in the early chapters, are shown as though you are typing from the keyboard, rather than selecting commands from the pull-down or screen menu.

The sample exercise that follows demonstrates our format for commands and instructions. Exercises use the full width of the page, with commands, instructions, and computer feedback (prompts) positioned at the left margin. In the exercise example (taken from Chapter 3), commands or operations which you are expected to enter are shown in **this bold text**. Since commands may be entered in various ways (keyboard, screen menus, pull-down menus, and tablet menus, to name a few), the command name is shown following the `Command:` prompt as if it were entered from the keyboard. This should not restrict the way you enter commands; you may type them or access them through a menu. The approach used in *AutoCAD: Drafting and 3D Design* is only intended to provide a solid foundation from which you are expected to build your AutoCAD expertise.

Prompts which appear in the command area are shown in `this special typeface`. As you progress through the book, simple commands and repetitive sequences may be abbreviated or replaced with simple instructions.

The section to the right of the commands and prompts is reserved for comments and explanations. They are for your information in completing the command and are not intended to be entered literally. Exercise comments and explanations that appear later in the book will be replaced with more general instructions that begin in the left margin and are shown in *this italic typeface*.

Drawing the Object

`Command:` **Line**	Starts the Line command
`From point:` *Press F8 and F9 to toggle Ortho and Snap on, and then type* **14,2**	Selects first point
`To point:` *Press F6 to toggle Coords on, and then type polar point* **@11<180**	Selects second point
`To point:` *Type polar point* **@2<90**	Selects third point
`To point:` *Press F8 to toggle Ortho off, and then type polar point* **@1.41<45**	Selects fourth point
`To point:` **@2,0**	Selects fifth point
`To point:` **@0,2**	Selects sixth point
`To point:` **@2,2**	Selects seventh point
`To point:` *Press F6 to toggle Coords off. Then type absolute point* **11,9**	Selects eighth point
`To point:` **@3,-5**	Selects ninth point
`To point:` **C**	Closes drawing

All you need to do in an exercise is to follow the command sequence, refer to the in-line instructions, and input any text shown in bold. Unless directed otherwise, you are expected to press Enter after typing in commands and other responses.

Exercises are accompanied by illustrations and screen shots of what you should see on your screen at key points. Bubbles like this ① are shown in many illustrations to refer to key points or positions on the exercise drawing. An example of an illustration using two bubbles is shown in figure I.1.

Figure I.1:
Sample screen shot with two bubble points.

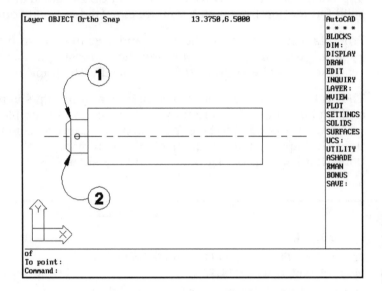

In most cases, *AutoCAD: Drafting and 3D Design* enables you to jump from chapter to chapter, especially if you have the ACAD Disk. But there are a few operations which need to be done in earlier chapters so that later exercises will work properly. These are identified in the text. In particular, you need to start with the setup sections of Chapter 3.

1

Hardware Tools for CAD

In this chapter:

- Understanding input devices
- Using disks and disk drives
- Learning about monitors
- Printing with output devices
- Networking AutoCAD

9

Overview

The computer system has become the primary hardware tool for drafting and design work. Although AutoCAD can run on a number of different hardware platforms, IBM Personal Computers and IBM-compatible computers are the most widely used computers for industrial and educational microcomputer-based computer aided drafting and design (CAD).

CAD workstation hardware includes the microcomputer and all the physical devices that are attached to it. No matter which hardware you use for your CAD system, a number of components are typically matched. These components make up what is defined as the input and output or I/O devices. Each of these components must be configured together (compatible and plugged into each other) to create the communication linkage between the hardware and the AutoCAD program.

A typical CAD workstation configuration includes a keyboard, a mouse or digitizer, a computer with disk drives, disk drive and graphic controller cards, a monitor, and a printer or plotter. This chapter introduces you to each of these components and describes its function within the CAD system.

Understanding Input Devices

Input devices provide information that goes into the computer. The most common input devices are the keyboard, a digitizer, and a mouse. You spend most of your time at a CAD workstation using one or more of these devices.

Keyboard

The keyboard is the most familiar input device. You can use the workstation's keyboard, as shown in figure 1.1, to enter drawing commands or text. You also can enter precise data, such as coordinates or dimensions. All AutoCAD commands can be input through the keyboard.

The IBM PS/2-style keyboard uses a standard typewriter key format but has additional function keys, position keys, and a numeric keypad. AutoCAD supports several shortcut toggle and function keys for quick access to frequently used features. Although the keyboard is a very efficient input device for entering text and numbers, it gives only minimum control of the cursor and cannot be used to access AutoCAD's pull-down menus.

Figure 1.1:
IBM PS/2 style keyboard.

Note

Throughout this text, you enter AutoCAD commands primarily through the keyboard in response to prompts that appear in the command area at the bottom of the screen. This textbook favors the use of the keyboard in student exercises rather than the use of pull-down or screen menus because it is considered the best way to learn how each command works; however, once you become comfortable using various commands, you should use the most direct and simple method to access those commands.

Mice and Digitizer Tablets

The *mouse*, as illustrated in figure 1.2, is a fairly inexpensive input device that controls the AutoCAD cursor. Most mice provide one to three buttons for cursor and command interaction. The left-most (or only) button is the *pick button*. By pressing (*clicking*) the mouse's pick button, you can pick a point on the AutoCAD drawing screen or select an option from an on-screen menu. The other buttons are controlled by the AutoCAD menu. Generally, the button on the right performs an Enter function just like the Enter key does; and the middle button, if available, pulls down Assist, the first pull-down menu.

Figure 1.2:
Typical mouse.

As figure 1.3 illustrates, the *digitizer* is an electronic drawing board. The digitizer's pointing device tracks positions and sends signals that direct the drawing screen's cursor. Most digitizers come with either a stylus or a puck that has three to sixteen selection buttons. Both of these pointing devices give you cursor control. The AutoCAD ACAD.MNU menu file defines the button functions.

Figure 1.3:
Typical digitizer.

AutoCAD's tablet menu overlay, as shown in figure 1.4, can be used with any digitizer tablet that supports the AutoCAD program. Menu items are assigned a box and position on the template. They are grouped into related sets of tools. You can select any item by putting your pointing device directly on top of the box and pushing the select button.

Tablet menus perform the same functions as screen and button menus. You can use the tablet to select AutoCAD drawing and editing commands. Many tablet menu selections open a corresponding screen menu page to help you select a subcommand. The tablet menu can also show graphic images that identify the selection. Tablet menus offer a few advantages over some of the other menus. Tablet menu selections provide immediate access to tools without flipping through menu pages. You can customize the entire tablet, or you can just add your own items to Tablet Area 1 at the top of AutoCAD's standard tablet menu.

As you can see in figure 1.4, one advantage of using a digitizer as a pointing device is that AutoCAD commands, as well as drawing symbols, can be selected from the tablet menu as well as from the screen drawing area. You can input your data without lifting the pointing device from the digitizer's surface. This enables you to rapidly alternate between picking coordinate points and choosing commands or symbols. Also, AutoCAD's Tablet command enables you to use the digitizer tablet to trace existing drawings. But even digitizers have their disadvantages. Digitizers require you to periodically look away from the screen and, therefore, can slow you down.

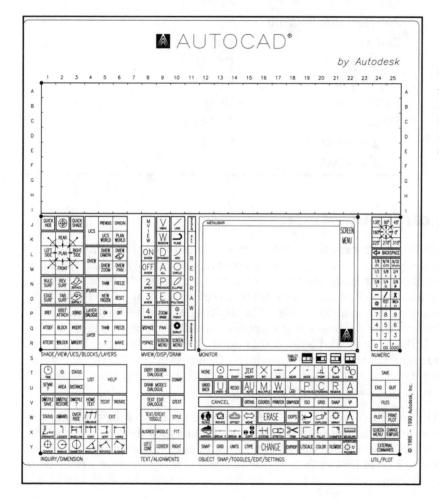

Figure 1.4:
AutoCAD Release 11 standard tablet menu, courtesy Autodesk, Inc.

Pointing devices usually have a number of buttons. A typical mouse has two or three buttons; a tablet cursor can have up to sixteen buttons. AutoCAD reserves one button as a select or pick button. The remaining buttons are predefined in the ACAD.MNU file but may be reassigned to different functions through menu customizing. The standard assignments are shown in table 1.1.

Table 1.1
ACAD.MNU Standard Button Assignments

Button	Function	Keyboard Alternative
1	Enter	Enter
2	Pull-down tools menu	
3	Cancel	Ctrl-C
4	Toggle Snap	Ctrl-B
5	Toggle Ortho	Ctrl-O
6	Toggle Grid	Ctrl-G
7	Toggle Coords	Ctrl-D
8	Toggle Isoplane	Ctrl-E
9	Toggle Tablet	Ctrl-T

Selecting an Input Device

When you select input devices, there are several points to keep in mind. First, select an input device that accommodates your own drafting style. Although the cost of a mouse is considerably below that of a digitizer, most drafters prefer a digitizer and stylus or puck. A digitizer's high degree of accuracy is recommended if you must trace drawings. Also, the digitizer supports AutoCAD's tablet menu overlay or other customized production drafting tablet overlays, such as the ANSI Y14.5 overlay available with this book. A few dollars saved up front may cost you far more in lost productivity later. If, however, you prefer a combination keyboard, screen, and pull-down menu style of input and have no need to trace, you may find a mouse perfectly suitable.

Like many CAD hardware components, digitizers and mice are now commodity items, so stick to proven brand names. Although most input devices work with AutoCAD, not all do. The one steadfast rule for acquiring AutoCAD workstation hardware is that *seeing is believing*. If you can, try out the hardware under your actual working conditions.

Using the Numeric Pad for Cursor Control

Although you usually control your drawing cursor with your mouse or digitizer pointing device, it is possible to control your drawing cursor using the keyboard. These keys are located on the numeric keypad at the right of the IBM Personal Computer keyboard:

- **Menu (Ins).** Toggles screen menu cursor control over to the arrow keys.
- **Screen (Home).** Toggles screen drawing cursor control over to the cursor movement keys on or adjacent to the numeric keypad.
- **Abort (End).** Returns cursor control to the mouse or digitizer pointing device.
- ← → ↑ ↓. Moves the cursor or highlight bar.
- **Fast** or **Slow (PgUp)** or **(PgDn).** Increases or decreases screen drawing cursor speed.

When you have positioned your cursor with these keys, use the Enter key to pick the point.

Understanding Disks and Disk Drives

Disk drives are usually housed in the same case as the CAD workstation computer. The *disk drive* reads and writes information to a magnetic disk. The computer can read the information on the disk as many times as necessary and can write new information to the disk's unused space. New information can be written over old information on the disk. When this occurs, the old information is permanently erased from the disk.

Hard Disks

The most common devices for storing data on an AutoCAD system are *hard disks*, which operate in ranges of millisecond access rates. The density and number of disks and read-write heads determine the data capacity of a hard disk unit. Hard disk capacities are measured in megabytes (1M is 1,048,576 bytes, or 1000K), and these capacities are steadily increasing. Today's technology offers hard disk storage capacities from 20 to 300 or more megabytes. This book assumes that you are running AutoCAD on a personal computer that has both a hard disk and a floppy disk drive.

Floppy Disks

Removable disks are 3 1/2-inches or 5 1/4-inches in diameter and may store data from 360K (low density) to 1.2M or 1.44M (high density). The 3 1/2-inch disks are encased in durable hard plastic, whereas the 5 1/4-inch disks are flexible and require extra care in handling.

Note It pays to handle all disks with caution. Don't bend them or expose them to heat, moisture, or magnetic forces. An individual bit (1/8 of a byte) of information occupies a very small portion of the disk. As a result, a scratch or even a fingerprint on the magnetic surface can cause major read or write errors.

Backup Systems

There are two typical ways to back up your CAD system's hard disk data. The first backup method is to copy data files from your hard disk to several floppy disks. You should periodically back up selected files either by using DOS commands or by using a commercial hard disk backup program. If you are backing up an entire hard disk, or multiple hard disks, a commercial backup program can quickly pay for itself in time saved. The second backup method is to use a streaming tape cartridge. A good streaming tape cartridge system can back up a 20M hard disk in approximately three minutes. When you compare backup programs or tapes, consider *portability* (that is, the ease with which the system can be used with different computers), speed, and whether you can retrieve individually selected files or only all the files on the disk.

Understanding Monitors

The computer's main output device is the monitor, which shows the graphics and text produced by the computer. The monitor displays your AutoCAD drawing as well as the menus from which you can select drawing commands. Figure 1.5 shows (1) the status line, (2) the screen menu, and (3) the Command: prompt.

Chapter 2 examines elements of the AutoCAD screen in detail; for now you should focus on the display hardware. The display has two components: the *video card* (often called a *video graphics controller*) that generates the image, and the *monitor* that displays the image. The system requirements of these two components must be matched.

Display Resolution

The video card's *resolution* determines the quality of the image on your system's monitor. Screen resolutions are measured in dots (pixels) along the x and y axis. AutoCAD supports video cards exceeding 1024x1024 pixel resolution. Some common resolutions are the following:

■ **EGA.** (Enhanced Graphics Adapter) Low resolution, 640x350 pixels

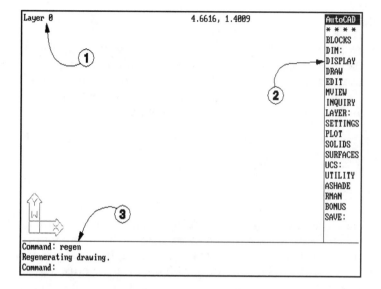

Figure 1.5:
Typical AutoCAD screen display.

- **VGA** and **PGA**. (Video Graphics Array and Professional Graphics Array) Medium resolution, 640x480 pixels

- **Enhanced** or **Super EGA/VGA**. Medium-high resolution, 800x600 pixels

- **High Resolution**. 1024x768 pixels or greater

 Note Although the EGA is the minimum resolution you should consider for production drafting and design applications, a VGA card currently costs no more and yields 37 percent greater resolution. Higher resolution increases detail, reduces the jaggedness of diagonals and curves, and eliminates many pans and zooms. Most drafters and designers prefer medium to medium-high resolution.

Video cards that use a technology known as "display list processing" provide significantly greater performance but at a higher cost. They handle Pan and Zoom commands in hardware, reducing the calculations that AutoCAD performs to magnify and reposition images.

As the types of microcomputer-produced graphics continue to increase, so do the video formats that drive these graphics. Your monitor must match the output format of your video card. The easiest way to accomplish this is to use the one-monitor-fits-all display.

Autosync Monitors

The *autosync monitor* (or multisync monitor) bypasses the need to match input bandwidths and synchronization rates. Instead, an autosync monitor analyzes the video signal received and, if the signal is within its range, adjusts to match the graphics card. Besides simplifying your choices, this device makes it possible to upgrade your video card without having to change your monitor.

If you do not use an autosync monitor, be careful to match the specifications of your monitor with those of your video card.

Ghosting or Cursor Trails

All monitors with the same display resolution are not necessarily created equal. When doing production drafting, you should make every attempt to use a monitor that minimizes eye strain. Two causes of eye strain are phosphor persistence and flickering. Unfortunately, these are conflicting problems and the cure for one often makes the other worse.

Phosphor persistence or "ghosting" occurs when a moving cursor smears or leaves a cursor trail in its wake. This can be bothersome when you spend a lot of time tracking cursor positions across the screen. You may find flicker most noticeable when you look at the monitor out of the corner of your eye. Flicker is worsened by interlaced video, a technology that increases resolution at low cost. Interlaced monitors usually increase the scan rate or use long-persistence phosphors that increase cursor smear. It is impossible to find a monitor that does not flicker, but you should try to select a display with the least amount of flicker and an acceptable amount of cursor smearing. Today, there are reasonably inexpensive non-interlaced monitors available that eliminate almost all of the flicker. Try to select a monitor within your price range with the least amount of flicker to eliminate eye strain.

AutoCAD's Advanced User Interface (AUI)

AutoCAD's AUI (Advanced User Interface) is available for Releases 10 and 11. Figure 1.6 illustrates the pull-down menu. This type of menu, as well as the icon menu and dialog box, requires AUI. The dialogue box is illustrated in figure 1.7. When using these AUI features, AutoCAD's drawing and editing commands are easier to access. The AUI, however, is not necessary when using *AutoCAD: Drafting and 3D Design*.

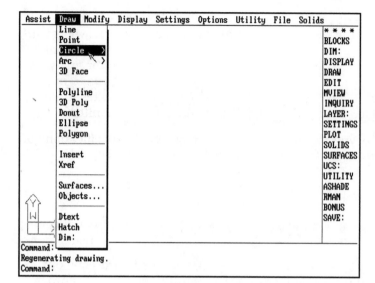

Figure 1.6:
AutoCAD's AUI pull-down menu.

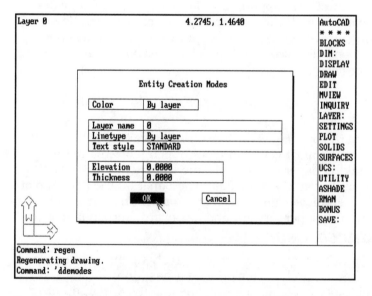

Figure 1.7:
AutoCAD's AUI dialogue box.

You can tell if your workstation supports AUI by checking the Popups command. (Simply type **POPUPS** and press Enter.) If Popups is 1, you can use AUI features; if it is 0, you need an ADI driver to get AUI. Many graphics controllers provide support for AutoCAD's AUI through ADI drivers. ADI is a generic device interface supported by AutoCAD that requires drivers supplied by the hardware manufacturer. Some third-party developers also provide ADI drivers for older video boards. If in doubt, ask your dealer for particulars. An ADI version 4.0, or later, driver also improves the performance of AutoCAD's multiple viewport windows.

 Note Some ADI drivers, particularly older ones, do not (or cannot) support AUI. You should always check before you buy. If you have AutoCAD Release 10, you can tell whether or not your system supports AUI by checking the POPUPS system variable. Type **POPUPS** at the Command: prompt. If you see a 0, you need an ADI driver. If you see a 1, you can use the AUI features.

Understanding Output Devices

In addition to the monitor (graphics display output), you need hard-copy output. Your choice of output device depends on the quantity, size, and accuracy needed for your drawings. AutoCAD supports a wide variety of hard-copy devices, ranging from pen plotters to dot-matrix printers, from electrostatic plotters to laser printers. You can use any of these output devices in connection with the exercises in this book. The sections that follow discuss some of the typical AutoCAD output devices.

Pen Plotters

Plotters output accurate hard copies of your drawings in a variety of sizes with reasonable speed and cost. The most common types of pen plotters are the *flatbed* plotters (usually taking paper up to 11x17 inches) and the *grit-wheel* plotters (taking paper beginning at 36x48 inches). The paper on the flatbed plotter is stationary while the pen moves along the x and y axis. The grit wheels of the grit-wheel plotter move the paper forward and backward, perpendicular to the pen's side-to-side movement.

The plotter, turning out hard copy after hard copy, is truly the beast of burden in the CAD industry. It pays to purchase a plotter that has a proven track record. You need to weigh plotter cost against the line quality, speed, number, and type of pens. No matter what the cost of the plotter, test your potential purchase by using the plotter to plot a benchmark drawing. Consider the following factors when you evaluate plotters:

- Accuracy
- Resolution

- Maximum pen speed
- Pen acceleration (time needed to reach maximum speed)
- Pen down delay (time needed for ink to flow before accelerating)

Pen acceleration is usually more important than maximum pen speed because most pen and media combinations do not plot well at high speeds.

Whether you are using single-pen or multiple-pen plotters, the pens you use must work properly to perform their job. Available plotter pens range from disposable to jewel-tipped. Choose pens that fit both your printer and your plotter management style. Here are some common plotter pen types:

Good-quality *ceramic disposable pens* are available at moderate cost, but are durable and perform consistently at slow plotting speeds. You can use this type of pen with either paper or mylar. Low cost *felt-tip pens* make good *check plot* pens (pens used for draft-quality output), but can be used with paper only. Also available at low cost, *fiber-tip pens* are consistent at moderate speeds, make good check plot pens, but can be used only with paper. Moderate cost *disposable liquid-ink pens*, produce very good quality output and are consistent at moderate speeds. Disposable liquid-ink pens can be used with paper or mylar. Low cost *roller-ball pens* have good quality, are consistent at moderate speeds, but can be used with paper only. Pressurized *ballpoint pens* are fast, consistent on most media, have long life, are trouble-free, but only a few kinds of plotters can use them. *Refillable liquid-ink pens* have the best quality but require user care and maintenance for consistent plots. This pen's high-initial cost (jewelled tips are preferable) is moderated with re-use. Refillable liquid ink pens can use either paper or mylar.

 Note When you configure AutoCAD for plotting, you can set pen speed to match the pen type (ink) and media used for plotting. Four inches per second (ips) is considered a slow pen speed; 16 ips is considered a moderate pen speed. Any pen speed over 20 ips is considered fast and requires pens that support rapid movement.

Printer Plotters

Printers are gaining wide acceptance in the CAD field as output devices for producing small, low-cost check plots. Because many CAD workstations also are commonly used for word processing and spreadsheet applications, printers are commonly available. AutoCAD can use dot-matrix, thermal, laser (see fig. 1.8), and ink jet printers as plotters.

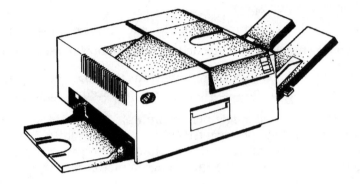

Figure 1.8:
A typical laser printer used as a printer plotter.

Dot-Matrix Printers

Dot matrix printers are low-cost and reliable. They produce printer plots that are inexpensive in per-sheet cost with reasonable speed. Their major drawback is low resolution. Low resolution printers may be acceptable for text, but they produce unacceptable jagged edges for technical drawings. Dot matrix printers vary from 60 to 360 dpi (dots per inch). Most printers exceeding 200 dpi yield satisfactory plots, but these higher resolutions generally require more time. More acceptable, are printers that can be configured as plotters using ADI (Autodesk Device Interface) drivers that yield high resolution at speeds faster than pen plotters.

Ink Jet, Thermal, and Laser Printers

Ink jet, thermal, and laser printers are all non-impact printers. Non-impact printers are more common today, and in the last few years, their price has dropped dramatically. Non-impact printers range in price from $500.00 for ink jets to up to $3000.00 for lasers. Laser printers are most commonly used, offering high resolution (300 to 400+ dpi). Because their prices are continually coming down, laser printers are excellent output devices for AutoCAD workstations. Some laser printers emulate pen plotters, reducing the time it takes to get a drawing plotted. Ink jet printers offer color, high resolution, and reasonable cost but at slower speeds. Thermal printers offer beautiful colors but at lower resolutions. Whatever printer you choose, be sure that AutoCAD supports it or that the manufacturer provides an ADI driver.

Networking AutoCAD

Networking is accomplished by electronically linking several computers together so that they can pass data to and from each other. This method of sharing information is a highly efficient means of avoiding duplication and ensuring consistency. Networks use a *server* that acts as the repository for programs, CAD drawings, and other data. The server receives requests for information and manages the requests so that they are answered in an orderly, sequential manner.

AutoCAD Release 11 may be networked. For more information on networking AutoCAD, refer to Appendix B and *Managing and Networking AutoCAD* (New Riders Publishing).

Summary

In this chapter, you learned about input and output devices that make up a typical AutoCAD workstation. In particular, you explored the advantages of such input devices as the keyboard, mice, and digitizer tablets. You investigated the working relationship of hard and floppy disks, and you learned about the importance of backup systems. You discovered that monitors, a form of "soft" output, have particular CAD considerations, including resolution, autosync, and ghosting concerns. Also, you learned about AutoCAD's Advanced User Interface and networking AutoCAD. Remember that hardware supplies the new tools of drafters and designers. Just as in the past, modern CAD tools must be cared for to ensure that they continue to operate when you need them.

At this point, your hardware and software should be configured to run AutoCAD. If not, refer to Appendix B. If AutoCAD is configured, you are ready to proceed to Chapter 2.

2

AUTOCAD COMMANDS AND COMMAND ENTRY

In this chapter:

- Booting up AutoCAD's main menu
- Understanding AutoCAD's drawing editor menus
- Using toggles and function keys
- Giving commands to the drawing editor

Overview

AutoCAD is organized into several major parts, including the main menu, the configuration menu, the plotting dialogue, the file utilities menu, and the drawing editor. Each part is typically a collection of related tools. You will spend most of your time drawing and editing in the drawing editor, but to get there (or anywhere else) you have to go through the main menu.

Think of the main menu as AutoCAD's table of contents. Once you know which part of the program you need to use, you can simply enter its corresponding number, and AutoCAD will access it. The first part of this chapter introduces you to the main menu's numbered options.

Since the AutoCAD user typically spends most of his time completing CAD projects in the drawing editor, you should become familiar with the drawing editor's organization. AutoCAD is a command-driven program, which means that once you are working in the drawing editor, you enter commands—such as those from the pull-down menu (see fig. 2.1)—to have AutoCAD perform various drafting and design functions. Each of the commands and functions is designed to simplify the tasks required to produce graphic documentation. The more familiar you are with how AutoCAD is organized, the more efficient and productive your CAD work will become.

Booting Up to AutoCAD's Main Menu

After booting the AutoCAD program, you see the program's main menu, as illustrated in figure 2.2. This menu gives you quick access to AutoCAD's entire tool chest. From the main menu, you can enter AutoCAD's drawing editor and execute several utility functions.

Using AutoCAD's Main Menu Options

To start a drafting project, choose `Begin a NEW drawing` from the main menu. To select an option from the main menu, simply type the option's number at the `Enter Selection:` prompt which appears at the bottom of the main menu screen, and then press Enter. AutoCAD either prompts you for more information or clears the main menu to open up another part of the program, such as the drawing editor. For example, to begin a new drawing, you select number 1. To call up and edit an existing drawing, you select number 2. Here is a list of all the selections:

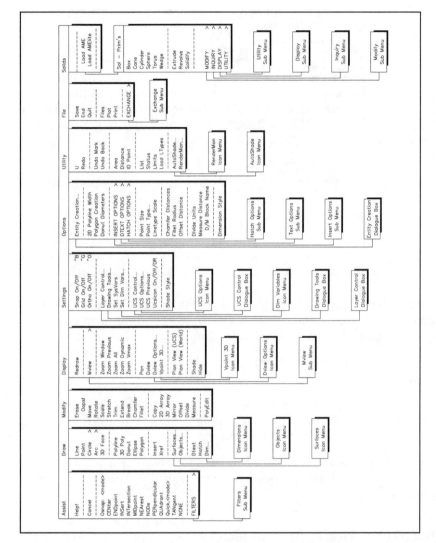

Figure 2.1:
AutoCAD's
Release 11 pull-
down menu,
courtesy
Autodesk, Inc.

0. Exit AutoCAD returns to the operating system. Use this option whenever you need to leave the AutoCAD program.

1. Begin a NEW drawing initiates AutoCAD's drawing editor for creating a new drawing. AutoCAD prompts you to name the new drawing.

2. Edit an EXISTING drawing opens AutoCAD's drawing editor for editing an existing drawing. AutoCAD prompts you for the name of the existing drawing file.

Figure 2.2:

The main menu—
AutoCAD's list of tools.

```
             A U T O C A D (R)
Copyright (c) 1982–91  Autodesk, Inc.  All Rights Reserved.
Release R11 c1 (2/24/91) 386 DOS Extender
Serial Number:  117–10012853
EVALUATION VERSION — NOT FOR RESALE
Licensed to:    Mark L. Merickel, Visualization Research, Inc.
Obtained from:  XXXX – XXXX
Current drawing: 1

Main Menu

   0.  Exit AutoCAD
   1.  Begin a NEW drawing
   2.  Edit an EXISTING drawing
   3.  Plot a drawing
   4.  Printer Plot a drawing

   5.  Configure AutoCAD
   6.  File Utilities
   7.  Compile shape/font description file
   8.  Convert old drawing file
   9.  Recover damaged drawing

Enter selection:
```

3. `Plot a drawing` makes hard copies of a drawing on a plotter without entering the drawing editor. After entering this option, AutoCAD prompts you for the drawing file name and plotting parameters. (See Chapter 3.)

4. `Printer Plot a drawing` makes hard copies of a drawing on a printer plotter without entering the drawing editor. (See Chapter 3.)

5. `Configure AutoCAD` brings up the AutoCAD configuration menu. If you install a new input or output device, or if you reinstall AutoCAD, use this selection to adjust or reset your workstation's configuration file.

6. `File Utilities` provides access to several DOS functions. AutoCAD prompts you to supply the DOS format needed for each utility. These tools are listed later in this chapter.

7. `Compile shape/font description file` enables you to use a custom shape (a type of symbol) or custom text font. AutoCAD's standard text fonts are already compiled.

8. `Convert old drawing file` converts drawings made with AutoCAD version 2.5 or earlier.

9. `Recover damaged drawing` recovers damaged or corrupted drawing files. Recovering a drawing consists of an audit that looks for damage. If the recovery is successful, the drawing is automatically loaded into the drawing editor. At this point you may edit, save, end, or quit the drawing.

With the exception of option 5, all these options require a file name.

Drawing File Names

Once you choose `Begin a NEW drawing`, `Edit an EXISTING drawing`, or `Recover damaged drawing`, AutoCAD prompts you for a drawing file name. Because the drawing's name is used as the file name, the name must conform to the DOS file-naming conventions. That is, the name can be no more than eight characters long. You can use any letter of the alphabet and include any of the following non-alphabetic characters: numerals, dollar signs ($), hyphens (-), and underscores (_). Drawing names, however, cannot contain blank spaces or periods.

DOS file names generally end with a three-character extension. Drawing files are automatically given a file extension of DWG, so you do not need to type DWG after the name. AutoCAD also accepts a subdirectory prefix attached to your drawing name, such as \DRAWINGS\PART. In this instance, AutoCAD saves the drawing named PART in the designated subdirectory named DRAWINGS.

You can use the AutoCAD file utilities menu to copy a drawing into a different subdirectory.

File Utilities Menu

The following is a list of the file utilities tools. Their DOS command counterparts are shown in square brackets.

0. `Exit File Utility Menu`

1. `List drawing files` [DIR *.DWG] This utility examines a specified disk or subdirectory and lists the drawing files the disk or directory contains.

2. `List user specified files` [DIR] This utility lists files of any type in a designated disk or subdirectory. (Specific file names or wild cards (* or ?) can be used.)

3. `Delete files` [DEL or DELETE] This utility removes unwanted files from a disk or subdirectory. (File name must match name on the disk exactly. It may include the drive or directory, but not wild cards.)

4. `Rename files` [REN or RENAME] This utility enables renaming of files. (File name must match name on the disk exactly. It may include the drive or directory, but not wild cards.)

5. `Copy file` [COPY] This utility enables copying of files from one disk or directory to another, or making a backup copy of a particular file. (No wild cards permitted.)

You also can access the file utilities menu from within AutoCAD's drawing editor by using the Files command. This command provides an alternative to DOS (or other operating systems) for managing your files.

Getting To Know AutoCAD's Drawing Editor Menus

After you activate the drawing editor, you have a whole set of menu tools at your disposal. By selecting either `Begin a NEW drawing` or `Edit an EXISTING drawing`, you activate the drawing editor, as shown by figure 2.3. The drawing editor is where you do the bulk of your CAD work.

Figure 2.3:
The typical drawing editor screen.

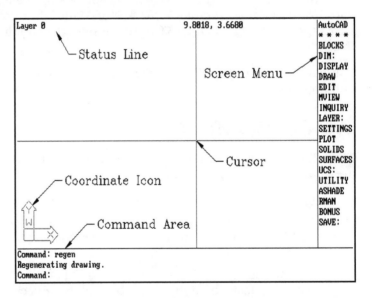

The illustrated status line (see fig. 2.3) shows that you are currently in Layer 0 and your current coordinate position is 9.8018,3.6680. The status line also hides the pull-down menu options. You can activate either the pull-down menu or the screen menu by moving the crosshair cursor up into the status line area or to the right into the screen menu area. The crosshair cursor shows your current location on the drawing editor screen. The command area at the bottom of the screen shows three lines that scroll up as you enter information at the `Command:` prompt line. The coordinate icon in the lower left corner of the drawing screen shows your current XY orientation and which coordinate system you are currently in. If the UCS icon is not on your screen, type **Ucsicon** at the `Command:` prompt, and then type **On** at the `ON/OFF/ALL/Noorigin/Origin <ON>:` prompt.

The AutoCAD program is command-driven. Commands draw lines, enter data, or add dimensions. Everything you do in the drawing editor is done by issuing one of AutoCAD's more than 140 commands. For most people that is too many commands to remember, so AutoCAD organizes commands into sets that are accessed by several menus. Because drafting and designing are personal processes and because many drafters are not used to typing commands into a computer, AutoCAD provides five alternative methods for entering drawing commands: screen menu, keyboard, tablet menu, pull-down menu, or icon menu. You can fully customize any or all of these menus, but AutoCAD starts you out by providing a standard menu with tools you can use right away. As Chapter 1 points out, the exercises in this textbook are designed to be completed mainly from the keyboard with some mouse input as well.

AutoCAD's standard menu has several hundred menu items. Most of these access scores of commands or options. Menus are a convenient way to organize and group commands so they can be easily found and selected for execution. When a menu item is selected, it sends a command, a series of commands, a subcommand, or other input to AutoCAD for execution. AutoCAD receives the command or other input in the same way, regardless of whether it is typed at the keyboard or chosen from a menu.

Accessing the Screen Menu

The most commonly used menu is the *screen menu*, which is on the right-hand side of the screen when using the drawing editor.

The *root menu* is the first group of menu items in AutoCAD's drawing editor. Most items on the root menu lead to further collections of tools. Each collection of menu items is referred to as a *menu page*. Some pages lead to still more pages, as demonstrated by figure 2.4. Draw and Edit, two of the most frequently used commands, activate tools for drawing and editing. Usually, you select a menu item by highlighting it with the pointing device and then pressing the pick button.

Applying Screen Menu Rules

Although menus can be customized, you do need to observe several conventions when you use the standard AutoCAD screen menu:

- A selection followed by a colon executes the AutoCAD command and usually presents a selection of subcommands.
- A selection without a colon following it is a key to other menu pages, but it does not execute a command by itself.

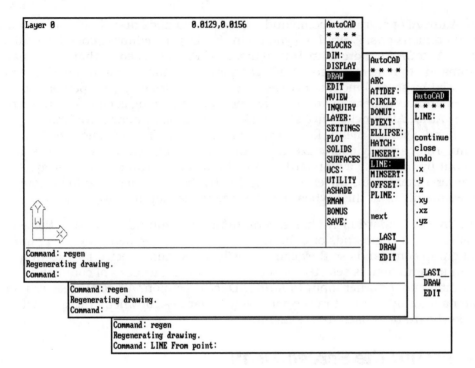

Figure 2.4:
AutoCAD's screen menu paging.

- Selecting AutoCAD at the top of a menu page always returns you to the root menu.
- Selecting **** presents object snap options.
- Shortcut key selections are at the bottom of many menu pages. They enable you to return to the LAST (preceding) menu page or to the DRAW and EDIT menu pages.
- Some groups of menu items offer more selections than can fit on one page. Use NEXT, PREVIOUS, and LAST to move forward or back to all the available selections.

If you get lost somewhere in the menu system, you always can return to the root menu by selecting AutoCAD at the top of the menu page. If you get really lost or just want to see the complete menu organization, the primary screen menu tree shown in figure 2.1 can help you find AutoCAD submenus and sets of tools. Use this menu tree to familiarize yourself with AutoCAD's screen menus and commands. Seeing the entire menu structure at one time helps you visualize AutoCAD's menu sequences.

The organization of the menu is for convenience of command access but has no effect on the AutoCAD command structure. You always can type any command at any time, regardless of the current menu page.

Selecting Menu Items from the Keyboard

You also can use the keyboard to access menu items. The keyboard offers two methods of making screen menu selections. If the screen menu is not active, press the menu cursor key (usually Ins) and an area of the menu selection is highlighted. Then use the up-arrow (↑) and down-arrow (↓) keys to move the highlight bar to your chosen item. Press Ins again or Enter to execute the selection.

The second method of making screen menu selections is to start typing the name of the menu selection at the Command: prompt. As you type, the first menu item that begins with characters matching what you have typed becomes highlighted. The desired selection should be highlighted by the time you have typed two or three characters. As a rule, you should type in the entire command or option name. Then press Ins, Enter, or the Spacebar to execute the selection.

Using Pull-Down Menus

Pull-down menus are similar to screen menus. If your video hardware supports pull-down menus (supports the AUI or Advanced User Interface feature), you see a menu bar when you move your pointing device to the top of the graphics screen. You need a mouse or some other pointing device to access the pull-down menus. You cannot access them from the keyboard. The menu bar presents a list of labels indicating the selections available in each pull-down menu.

Ten pull-down menus are available. AutoCAD's standard menu is preprogrammed to use the first eight menus. To access the options in a pull-down menu, you must first make them visible by opening the menu. To open a pull-down menu, highlight the menu bar label and press the pick button on your pointing device. This pulls the menu down over the graphics screen and presents you with a list of items that can be selected in the same manner as screen menus. Let up on the pick button in order to highlight the various choices. After you make a selection, the command is executed, and the pull-down menu is closed.

The pull-down menu illustrated in figure 2.5 helps you find submenus and sets of tools within the standard AutoCAD pull-down menu structure.

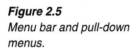

Figure 2.5
Menu bar and pull-down menus.

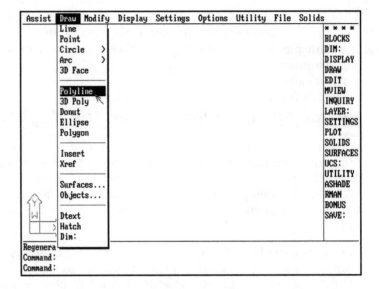

As with screen menus, you can customize pull-down menus, but standard AutoCAD pull-down menus observe several conventions:

- Many pull-down selections present dialogue boxes, icon menus, and multiple commands.

- Multiple commands repeat until they are cancelled or another command is selected.

- Many pull-down menu selections open appropriate screen menu pages that lead to subcommands.

- Screen menu selections can be made quickly because it is not necessary to flip through multiple menu pages (see fig. 2.5).

- Pull-down menus remain displayed until: items are picked, another menu is accessed, another area of the screen is accessed, the keyboard is activated, or items are picked from the tablet or button menus.

- Menu bar and pull-downs are disabled during Dtext, Sketch, Vpoint, Dview, and Zoom Dynamic commands.

- Not all AutoCAD commands are in pull-down menus. (Be sure to check the screen or tablet menus as well.)

Using Dialogue Boxes

The *dialogue box* offers you a convenient way to view and execute certain complex commands or groups of settings. You can call up a dialogue box by making a menu selection or by entering its command name. Dducs, for example, calls up the UCS dialogue box, as shown in figure 2.6.

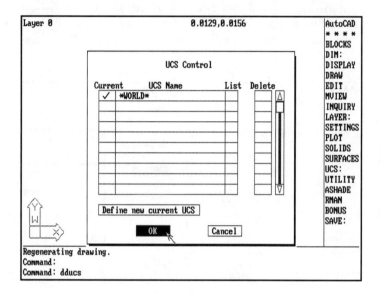

Figure 2.6:
AutoCAD's UCS dialogue box.

Dialogue boxes pop up over the graphics screen. You can make changes by pointing to a setting and pressing the pick button on your pointing device. You can then enter new values, give names, turn toggles on or off, and execute commands. Each dialogue box provides an OK and a Cancel box. When you are satisfied with the dialogue box settings, just point to OK and press your pick button. These are the dialogue commands and boxes:

- **Ddemodes.** Accesses a dialogue box that enables you to set the current layer, color, linetype, elevation, and thickness

- **Ddlmodes.** Accesses a layer dialogue box and, unlike Ddemodes, provides complete control of layers

- **Ddrmodes.** Accesses the screen drawing aids dialogue box, which contains the Snap, Grid, Axis, Ortho, Blipmode, and Isoplane drawing aids

- **Ddatte.** Accesses the attribute editing dialogue box

- **Dducs.** Accesses all settings and functions of the Ucs commands

- **Ddedit.** Accesses text editing and attribute definitions dialogue box

Dialogue boxes are a dynamic and efficient way to change settings. As with the pull-down menus, you can only access dialogue boxes if your video devices support AUI.

Using Scroll Bars

As figure 2.7 illustrates, some AutoCAD dialogue boxes contain *scroll bars*, which are used to move through lists. Each part of the scroll bar serves a function. By picking various points on the bar, you can scroll up or down a list with relative ease.

Figure 2.7:
The saving dialogue box with scroll bar.

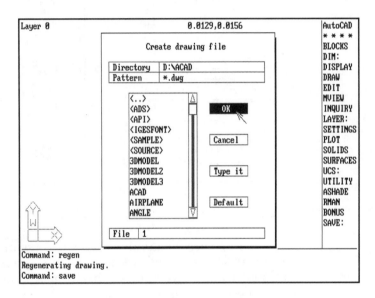

The position of the slider box inside the scroll bar shows you where a file is located in relationship to an entire list. Also, most dialogue boxes with a scroll bar and a slider box contain OK, Cancel, Type it, and Default buttons as figure 2.8 shows. You can select Type it and enter the name at the keyboard, or you can select Default and the default file name is automatically selected.

Using Icon Menus

An *icon menu*, such as the one shown in figure 2.8, displays your menu selections as graphic images on the screen. This provides visual cues to aid in selecting the correct item. Like pull-down menus, you need AUI display hardware support before you can use AutoCAD's icon menus.

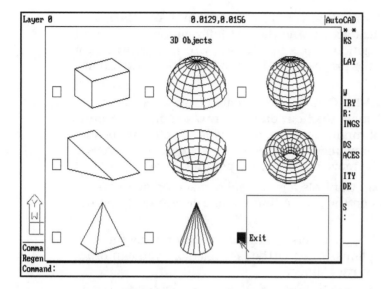

Figure 2.8:
AutoCAD's icon menu for 3D objects.

AutoCAD uses slide files (compact, quick-displaying screen image vector files) to construct icon menus. AutoCAD can display four, nine, or sixteen images, each containing one menu item. You can select an item on an icon menu by high-lighting the small square to the left of its icon image and pressing the pick button on your pointing device. AutoCAD executes the selection like any other menu selection. Icon menus can page through other icon menus the same way the screen menu pages through other menu pages. The preset icon menus showing hatch patterns and text styles are a very effective use of icon menus. The images provide more information than a brief descriptive label could.

Sometimes, however, it is useful to remember that the quickest way to issue commands or options is to type them at the keyboard.

Using Toggles and Function Keys

AutoCAD supports several shortcut toggle and function keys for quick access to frequently used features. The specific keys vary with the system; however, the IBM-style assignments are the most common. (See your *AutoCAD Installation and Performance Guide* if you do not have an IBM or compatible system.) AutoCAD has assigned certain features to the following function and control keys:

- **Flip Screen (F1).** Controls AutoCAD's flip screen function. Flip screen toggles between AutoCAD's graphics and text screens. If you need to check data that you have entered into AutoCAD, you can toggle to the text screen and the text information is displayed. This flip screen function also is handy as a screen saver when you don't need to exit the program but have to leave the workstation for awhile.

■ **Coords (F6 or Ctrl-D).** Controls coordinate display, toggling the status line's coordinate read-out on and off. When on, the coordinate read-out continually changes, displaying the current location of your crosshair drawing cursor (the two perpendicularly crossed lines that follow the movements of your pointing device).

■ **Grid (F7 or Ctrl-G).** Controls a grid display made up of an arrangement of dots on the screen that act like electronic graph paper.

■ **Ortho (F8 or Ctrl-O).** Controls the *Orthographic* drawing function, an aid for drawing lines. When Ortho is toggled on, you can draw only horizontal or vertical lines.

■ **Snap (F9 or Ctrl-B).** Controls the *Snap* drawing aid. When Snap is on, it constrains the cursor to moving in precise increments.

■ **Tablet (F10 or Ctrl-T).** Toggles the digitizing tablet between tracing mode and the normal screen-pointing drawing mode.

■ **Delete (Ctrl-X).** Cancels the current input, enabling you to re-enter your input.

■ **Cancel (Ctrl-C).** Cancels commands. Pressing Ctrl-C from one to three times gets you out of any AutoCAD command.

Giving Commands to the Drawing Editor

Once you know your way around AutoCAD's commands, it can be quicker to type them than to wade through pages of menus. You can execute any command or option in AutoCAD by simply typing the command or option name and then pressing Enter. Usually, one key letter is enough to enter an option and even some commands (typing **L** for Line, for example), but when entering a command at the keyboard, you normally want to type the entire command name. For example, try the following exercise using the Arc command.

Entering Commands from the Keyboard

Command: **Arc**	The full command name starts the Arc command
Center/<Start point>: **C**	The option's first letter
Center: *Pick a point*	Specifies the center point of the arc
Start point: *Pick a point*	Specifies the arc's starting point
Angle/Length of chord/<End point>: **A**	The first letter selects the desired option
Included angle: **45**	This number specifies the arc's included angle

---

Entering a command puts the program into a data entry mode. In this mode, you are prompted to specify the data needed to complete the command. After you input the data, AutoCAD executes the function. The command prompt line changes to reflect your data entry. After AutoCAD executes the command, it returns to the command mode and displays the Command: prompt again.

Selecting Defaults and Entering Values

Defaults are displayed at the prompt line in angle brackets < >. Defaults may be accepted by pressing the Enter key or Spacebar, or they may be overridden by entering different values or information. Other command options are separated by forward slashes and displayed with their key letters in uppercase characters. If you prefer, you can type the entire option key name, but you only need to type the character(s) displayed in uppercase. You also can type numerical data and coordinates (the X,Y,Z coordinates, for example, that are relative to the drawing's 0,0,0 base point). You also may enter points, angles, and distances by picking them with your pointer (digitizer, mouse, or keyboard cursor) as shown in the first exercise of Chapter 3.

Using Transparent Commands

You can use some commands transparently while you are in the middle of other commands. To do this, make sure an apostrophe precedes the command name (like 'Example). Transparent commands do not work while you are using the Text, Dtext, Attdef, Sketch, Plot, Prplot, Vpoint, Dview, or Dim (dimensioning) commands. You also cannot use transparent commands if the drawing requires a regeneration.

AutoCAD commands that can be used transparently are presented in the following two-column list:

Ddemodes	Redrawall
Ddlmodes	Resume
Ddrmodes	Setvar
Graphscr	Textscr
Help or ?	View
Pan	Zoom
Redraw	

The following exercise demonstrates how the transparent command works while another command is being used. Enter the following at the Command: prompt:

```
Command: Line
From point: 2.5,2.5
To point: 'Redraw
```

Now resume using the Line command by entering the following coordinates:

```
To point: @8<0
To point: @2,-6
To point: @3.5<180
To point: C
```

AutoCAD recognizes 'Redraw as a transparent command and, therefore, executes it even while the Line command is in use. Once you enter a transparent command, its operation is performed and you are signaled that AutoCAD is resuming the original command. In the case of the preceding example that utilized the Line command, you can resume the line from the last point entered before using the transparent 'Redraw command.

Correcting Data Entry Errors

If you enter some data that does not match the data type required by a command, AutoCAD generally balks and reprompts you with an error message, such as one of the following:

```
Unknown command
Point or option keyword required
*Invalid*
```

Whenever AutoCAD reprompts, you get another chance to enter the correct data. You can type '**?** or '**Help** to get help, or you can cancel the command. To cancel a command, select Cancel from the screen menu or hold down the Ctrl key while pressing C. Some commands require two or three Ctrl-Cs before they fully cancel.

Undoing Mistakes

If you enter an incorrect value, simply press Backspace to fix it. If you have already pressed Enter or you have picked a wrong point, you can select Undo or type **U** and then press Enter (in most commands). For example, in the Line command, Undo removes the last line developed; so you can then continue from that previous point. You can, of course, undo all your lines back to the original line's starting point. Once a command has been completed, you can still select Undo or type **U** at the command prompt and undo the entire previous command or selected menu item.

Summary

Menus are powerful tools within AutoCAD, and using them efficiently can increase your drafting productivity. You can execute many commands from the screen, tablet, pull-down, and icon menus, or you can type them at the command prompt line. AutoCAD offers a great deal of menu and command flexibility. After you practice all the various command entry methods, you may soon develop your own preferences.

3

STARTING A
DRAFTING PROJECT

In this chapter:

- Establishing parameters and values for PART1
- Navigating with AutoCAD's coordinate system
- Drafting a part
- Using text tools
- Using drafting inspection tools
- Using AutoCAD's built-in calculator
- Saving and exiting the drawing editor

Overview

AutoCAD is a very versatile drafting tool. It is used by a number of drafting disciplines from mechanical drafting to architectural drafting. To provide for this versatility, AutoCAD has been developed to be customizable. Every time you begin a new drawing you have the option of setting various drawing parameters to suit your drafting requirements. These parameters include the drawing units, the scale of the drawing, and the size of the drawing sheet.

AutoCAD has changed the way a drafter and designer plan and prepare a project. Although the end product is often similar, the task has been greatly simplified. AutoCAD can be an efficient drafting tool. It provides the means for developing drafting geometry such as lines, arcs, and circles with just a series of commands and responses to prompts (questions asked the user such as locations, height, etc.). AutoCAD also enables you to select and edit entities by simply pointing at them and then specifying specifically how you want them edited. You will be able to correct mistakes by editing your drawings on the graphics screen before making the hard copies.

The drafting exercises in this chapter take you on an introductory tour of AutoCAD. Participating in these exercises, you will learn how to start, quit, save, and end drawing sessions. You also will become familiar with AutoCAD's drawing editor, setting drawing parameters, dialogue boxes, and some drafting command tools, and will learn how to get help when you need it. The single-view drawing that you create in this chapter should look like figure 3.1.

Figure 3.1:
The completed PART1 drawing, which you will create in this chapter.

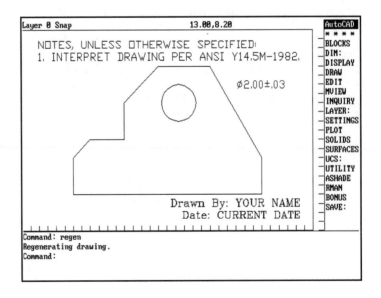

Establishing Parameters and Values for PART1

The PART1 drawing uses the parameters shown in table 3.1. All the parameters except Limits are defaults, so you do not need to set them. AutoCAD's automatic setup routine prepares the drawing sheet. In Release 10, the root menu contains the Setup routine.

Table 3.1
Parameters for the PART1 Drawing

Parameter	Setting
Axis	.5
Grid	1
Snap	.2
Units	Decimal 0.00
Limits	0,0 to 17,11
Layer Name	0
State	Current
Color	7 (White)
Linetype	Continuous

Entering the Drawing Editor

Enter the drawing editor by beginning a new drawing. Starting at the main menu, type **1** at the `Enter Selection:` prompt. AutoCAD then displays the `Enter NAME of drawing:` prompt. At this prompt, type **PART1** and press Enter. The main menu disappears and is replaced by the drawing editor screen. You are now ready to start the PART1 drawing.

 Remember to press Enter after typing any information for which you are prompted.

AutoCAD's Automatic Drawing Setup

The automatic sheet setup routine is invoked by selecting the Bonus option from the root menu. Click on Bonus with your pointing device. (Press Ins to activate the screen menu if you want to use the arrow keys instead of the mouse.) Click on next to move to the second page of options, and then select Mvsetup. AutoCAD now prompts you at the command line: Paperspace/modelspace is disabled. The old setup will be invoked unless it is enabled. Type **N** or **No** to the Enable Paper/Modelspace? <Y>: prompt so that we use the non-paperspace/model space setup routine. You will use the new paperspace/model space setup routine in later chapters. Select decimal from the Unit Type menu. Select FULL from the Decimal Scale menu. Select B- 11x17 from the Sheet Size menu.

You can progressively select any of the units, scales, and sheet sizes presented in the screen menu and shown in figures 3.2, 3.3, and 3.4. You also may select other sheet sizes. If you need to set up a drawing sheet size that is not listed on the screen menu, simply click on OTHER... and enter the new drawing parameters. You are prompted to provide the coordinate position of the lower left corner and the upper right corner of the drawing sheet. You must specify these positions in the current unit values, such as decimal (2.5) or architectural (2'6") values.

Figure 3.2:
AutoCAD's unit types.

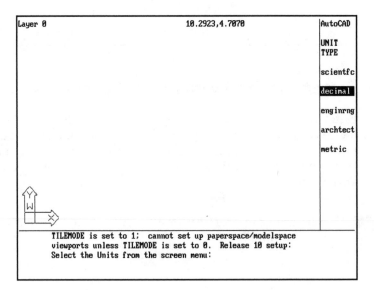

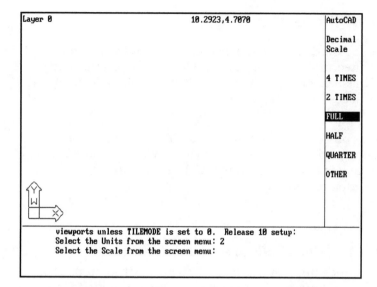

Figure 3.3:
AutoCAD's decimal scales.

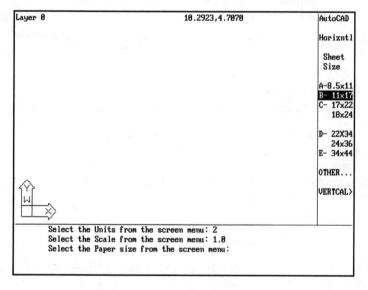

Figure 3.4:
AutoCAD's sheet sizes.

After you select 11x17 as a sheet size, AutoCAD generates the drawing area to the limits of 0,0 as the lower left corner and 11,17 as the upper right corner. The Mvsetup option then generates a sheet size border at the drawing limits and returns you to the root menu. This setup procedure uses an AutoLISP routine to get input from you and to execute several AutoCAD commands. It uses the Units and Limits commands to set up the drawing, then uses the Insert command to insert the border. The border is stored in another drawing file named BORDER.DWG.

Selecting a Unit of Measure

Drafters and designers use AutoCAD in many disciplines for scientific, mechanical, engineering, and architectural drawing. AutoCAD provides several unit choices because each of these disciplines may use different units to describe a drawing. The choices are accessed by the Units command.

 The *Units* command controls the format and display for inputting coordinates, distances, and angles. You specify the system of units, the precision, the system of angle measurement, the precision of angle display, and the direction of angles.

The types of units available in AutoCAD include:

- **Scientific (1.55E+01)**. Defines units in scientific notation.
- **Decimal (15.50)**. Defines units in decimals. You specify the number of digits to the right of the decimal. These units may be interpreted for any decimal unit, including metric units.
- **Engineering (1'-3.50")**. Defines units in feet and inches. Inches are displayed in decimal inches.
- **Architectural (1'-3 1/2")**. Defines units in feet and inches. Fractions of inches are displayed as real fractions.
- **Fractional (15 1/2)**. Defines units in inches and fractional parts of inches.

As AutoCAD points out in the text screen for the Units command, these systems can be used with any basic unit of measurement, except for the engineering and architectural modes. Decimal mode, for example, is perfect for metric units as well as for decimal English units. AutoCAD's default is decimal notation with four digits to the right of the decimal point.

The following exercise shows you how to set decimal units to two digits to the right of the decimal with the Units command:

At the Command: prompt, type **Units** to start the Units command. The drawing editor screen disappears as AutoCAD switches to text mode. In text mode, the Units command displays a series of prompts and messages that show you the five types of units you can use in your drawing. The first prompt appears as follows:

```
Systems of units:      (Examples)
     1. Scientific     1.55E+01
     2. Decimal        15.50
     3. Engineering    1'-3.50"
     4. Architectural  1'-3 1/2"
     5. Fractional     15 1/2
Enter choice, 1 to 5 <2>:
```

Press Enter at the `Enter choice, 1 to 5 <2>:` prompt. This selects the default response of 2, which tells AutoCAD that you want the drawing to be measured in decimal units. AutoCAD then needs to know how many digits you want to appear to the right of the decimal point when the program displays a measurement. The following prompt appears:

```
Number of digits to right of decimal point (0 to 8) <4>:
```

Press 2 in response to this prompt, to set the decimal units to two digits to the right of the decimal.

The Units command continues by enabling you to set the system for measuring angles. This can be set for various disciplines such as machine, architectural, and civil (surveying) drafting. The following prompt appears:

```
Systems of angle measure:           (Examples)

    1. Decimal degrees              45.0000
    2. Degrees/minutes/seconds      45d0'0"
    3. Grads                        50.0000g
    4. Radians                      0.7854r
    5. Surveyor's units             N 45d0'0" E

Enter choice, 1 to 5 <1>:
```

Press Enter at the `Enter choice, 1 to 5 <1>:` prompt, to accept the default selection 1. This choice tells AutoCAD to measure degrees in decimal units. AutoCAD then needs to know how many digits to display to the right of the decimal point when displaying an angle measurement. The following prompt appears:

```
Number of fractional places for display of angles (0 to 8) <0>
```

Press Enter at this prompt to accept the default response of 0 decimal places. This tells AutoCAD that you want angle measurements to appear only as whole numbers, and not as fractions.

AutoCAD then needs to know the direction of angle 0. The following prompt appears:

```
Direction for angle 0:

    East   3 o'clock  =  0
    North 12 o'clock  =  90
    West   9 o'clock  =  180
    South  6 o'clock  =  270

Enter direction for angle 0 <0>:
```

At the `Enter direction for angle 0 <0>:` prompt, press Enter to accept the default position of 0 degrees. By default, AutoCAD measures all angles in a counterclockwise direction, starting from angle 0. You can change this so that the angle is measured in the clockwise direction. AutoCAD displays the following prompt so that you can change the direction of angle measurement: `Do you want angles measured clockwise? <N>`. Press Enter at this prompt to accept the default response of N (for no). This tells AutoCAD that you want to measure angles counterclockwise.

Some drafters choose not to accept AutoCAD's default position (direction) for angle 0. You can change the angle direction with the Units command by entering new values instead of accepting the defaults shown here.

 No matter what units you set, you can always enter your input in decimal form.

The Units command controls the display, input, and dimensioning formats, but not the accuracy of your data. You can enter input with greater accuracy than the units you have selected can show, but the display will be rounded off. Using the previous settings, for example, 0.3125 would be accepted at its absolute accuracy, but the coordinates display and prompts would round it off to 0.31. Do not let this rounding off process cause you to make mistakes. When you do dimensioning in a later chapter, you will learn techniques for adjusting units.

A number of other accuracy or positioning tools also are available for drawing.

Now the Units command is finished and the `Command:` prompt reappears. You are still in text mode, however, and need to return to the drawing editor. To switch from text mode to graphics mode, press F1. You also can press F1 to switch from graphics mode to text mode. You can use F1 to switch between modes any time.

Setting the Drawing Aids

AutoCAD's drawing aids are positioning tools that are used for locating specific points on a drafting sheet or part. Drafters always have been concerned with accuracy in developing graphic representations, but AutoCAD gives accuracy a new meaning. The geometry that makes up a part now can be drawn to the accuracy of fourteen decimal positions (.00000000000001, for example). To maintain such accuracy, AutoCAD offers very precise positioning tools.

Ortho, Grid, Snap, and Axis are four positioning tools that you should learn to set and use immediately. The state of the grid and axis appears on the drawing screen. The status line above the drawing area displays the status of Snap and

Ortho, and shows you which drawing layer is current. Use either the screen menu or the dialogue boxes to set them.

Some commands can be used transparently; that is, they can be executed while you are in the middle of another command. To do this from the keyboard, an apostrophe must precede the command name, like 'Example. Some of the toggle functions such as Ortho, Snap, and Coords are transparent commands as well.

Setting Drawing Tools Using the Screen Menus

If your system does not support pull-down menus, you can set the drawing tools using the screen menus or by typing the individual commands. Even if you set your drawing tools with the dialogue box, read on for more information on each setting.

Although you do not need to set it now, you probably have noticed the Ortho toggle.

The *Ortho* command restricts your drawing lines, polylines, and traces to horizontal and vertical lines. Ortho controls the angle at which you pick the second point in many drawing and editing commands. Ortho is a toggle, and the default setting is off.

Ortho also may be toggled transparently by using the dialogue box, or by pressing Ctrl-O or F8 on the IBM-style keyboard.

The *Grid* command is a drawing aid that displays a series of dots on the current viewport at any user-defined increment. It helps you keep the space in which you are working and the size of your drawing entities in perspective. Grid toggles off and on and accepts numeric values. The default settings are 0.0000 and off.

Grid assists you with locating positions or distances on the drawing screen. The grid can be set at equal XY spacing, on or off, and at an aspect ratio (differing XY spacing). Avoid spacing grid dots too closely together; otherwise, your screen display will be slow or impossibly dense. A Snap option setting of 0 makes the grid equal to the Snap value and adjusts it each time Snap is changed. For the best use of Grid and Snap, set them to different values. It is common to set the Grid to larger increments (.5, 1, 1.5, and so on) and the snap to smaller increments (.1, .2, .3, and so on). If you enter a number and an X, such as 4X, then the grid is set to that number times the snap setting. Grid may be toggled transparently within the dialogue box or by pressing Ctrl-G or F7.

To set a one-inch grid spacing, for example, type **Grid** at the `Command:` prompt, and then type **1** at the prompt that follows.

Axis is another excellent drafting alignment tool. It works similarly to Grid. The *Axis* command creates ruler marks, or ticks, on the bottom and right side of your screen. These marks are a visual drawing aid. The default setting is off and the default value is 0.0000.

To set a .5-inch axis, for example, type **Axis** at the `Command:` prompt, and then type **.5** at the prompt that follows.

Axis and Grid are only visual aids and do not affect accuracy. Snap enables you to snap to the grid dots or increments of the grid to help you position your cursor.

The *Snap* command enables you to move the crosshairs at any defined increment. You can constantly modify the increment value and turn the setting on and off. The default setting is 1.0000 and off.

With Snap toggled on and equal to your grid spacing, your cursor will move only from one grid dot to another. This helps you locate a position on the drawing quickly and accurately. You can set Snap to any spacing, aspect ratio, rotation, or style (isometric or normal), as well as to on or off. Snap can be toggled transparently by using the Ddrmodes dialogue box or by pressing Ctrl-D or F9.

To set a .20-inch snap spacing, for example, type **Snap** at the command prompt, then type **.2** at the prompt that follows.

If you pick a point with Snap off, AutoCAD takes the coordinates of the pointer's pixel position and does not round the point input to match the displayed value. Although it appears as 0.25,0.25, a point actually might be 0.2487123,0.2512345 in the drawing data base. Using Snap when picking points shows the coordinates in the exact increment values. One of the benefits of AutoCAD is that it improves accuracy, so use Snap or another form of precise point entry.

Setting Drawing Tools with a Dialogue Box

The drawing aids dialogue box is a quick and convenient way to select drawing aid commands and change their status.

The *Ddrmodes* (Dynamic dialogue DRawing MODES) command controls the settings of drawing aids such as Snap, Grid, and Axis with a dialogue box.

If your system supports the Advanced User Interface (AUI) feature, you also can use Ddrmodes to set Snap, Grid, and Axis. They also may be set by their individual command names or by selecting them from the screen menu. One advantage of using Ddrmodes instead of individual commands is that it can be used transparently, although some settings may not take effect in the middle of some commands.

To view a dialogue box, type **Ddrmodes** at the Command: prompt. Your screen should resemble figure 3.5.

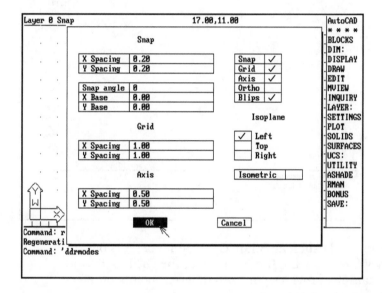

Figure 3.5:
Setting exercise drawing tools using dialogue box.

The box at the upper right, with Snap, Grid, Axis, Ortho, and Blips, shows a group of toggles. A check mark indicates that an item is toggled on. To change a toggle, move your pointer to highlight the check box next to the setting label and click on it. Specific values for Snap, Grid, and Axis may be set by highlighting the input boxes next to their key labels, such as the 1.00 next to X Spacing under Grid. You then type in the desired input value. When you type or click on the input box, the Cancel and OK boxes appear. To accept the input, press Enter or click on OK. Click on Cancel to abort the setting. The permanent Cancel and OK buttons at the bottom of the dialogue box accept or cancel all of the settings which were made during the last time the Ddrmodes (drawing tools) dialogue box was invoked.

To set Snap, Grid, and Axis, use your pointing device to click on the input value box to the right of the X and Y spacing boxes. Change the setting to 1, and then press Enter. (The Y spacing changes to match the new setting.) Then click on Grid in the check box so that a check mark appears. Next, click on the X spacing box under Snap, type **.2**, and press Enter. Then click on Snap in the check box. Finally, click on the input value box at the right of Axis X and Y spacing, type **.5**, and press Enter. Then click on Axis in the check box. You accept the changes by clicking on the OK box at the bottom of the screen. Your PART1 drawing should now resemble the illustration in figure 3.6.

Figure 3.6:
Snap, Grid, and Axis set.

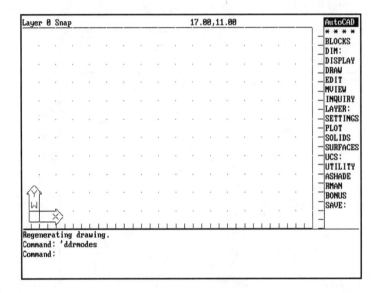

When setting drawing tools such as Snap, Grid, and Axis, it is best to set complimentary values. Setting the Snap to .2, the Grid to .5, and the Axis to 1., for example, provides you with different points of reference to assist you in your drawing tasks.

Snap, Grid, and Axis may be changed at any time to assist you in the current display. Various Snap, Grid, and Axis settings may be set and saved, with views and in different viewports. This is discussed later in the chapter.

Use Snap, Grid, and Axis to assist you in "lining up" orthographic views.

Navigating Using AutoCAD's Coordinate System

The coordinate point is the key element of the AutoCAD drawing database. AutoCAD stores points in the Cartesian coordinate system with coordinate values such as 1,2.5,0. In the default orientation of the 2D Cartesian coordinate system, positive X axis values are to the right of the 0,0 base, and negative X values are to the left of the base. Positive Y axis values are above the 0,0 base, and negative Y values are below it. If you use 3D, positive Z values are toward the viewer, and negative Z values are away from the viewer, "into" the screen. This default orientation can be changed, but the three axes always maintain the same orientations to each other.

The Axis, Grid, and Coords displays on the status line give you an indication of where the 0,0 base is located and what portion of the coordinate system is being displayed.

The User Coordinate System Icon

The *User Coordinate System* (UCS) icon or symbol is shown at the lower left of the screen when you first enter the drawing editor. This indicates the orientation of the current coordinate display. You can either set this icon to position itself at 0,0,0 or suppress its display altogether with the Ucsicon command.

 The *Ucsicon* command graphically displays the origin and viewing plane of the current UCS. Type **Ucsicon** at the Command: prompt, and you see that the default settings for the icon are on and Noorigin (displayed at the lower left corner). Noorigin tells AutoCAD to display the icon (when enabled) at the lower left corner of the viewport, regardless of the location of the UCS origin. The Origin option displays the icon (when enabled) to be displayed at 0,0,0, of the current coordinate system. When the origin is off screen or if the icon cannot be positioned at the origin without being clipped (masked) at the viewport edges, the icon is displayed at the lower left corner of the current viewport.

The World Coordinate System (WCS) is AutoCAD's default coordinate system. As figure 3.7 illustrates, WCS is designated by a W near the center of the icon. AutoCAD also enables you to define any number of user coordinate systems. A user coordinate system (UCS) is a local system that is offset in any or all axes from the 0,0,0 WCS base. It also can be rotated to any angle in 3D space. You will learn the techniques for this procedure in Chapters 15, 16 and 17.

In any coordinate system, you may specify points with Cartesian coordinates (XYZ axis distance from the 0,0,0 base) such as 1,2,3 or with polar coordinates (distance and angle from 0,0 in the XY plane only) such as 2<45 for 2 units at 45 degrees. The Z value can be omitted in 2D drawings. Cartesian coordinates may be *absolute* offsets from the 0,0,0 base, or *relative* to a previous point. Polar coordinates are always relative to the previous point.

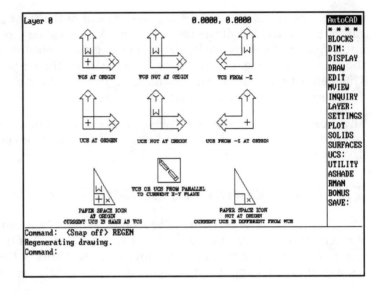

Figure 3.7:
UCS icon displays.

Absolute Coordinates

You may specify absolute coordinate values in the XY (or XYZ) axis directions. For the starting point of a line, for example, enter the distance in the X axis direction from the 0,0 position, and the distance from 0,0 in the Y axis direction. The values for XY are separated by a comma. AutoCAD automatically will designate the Z as zero if no Z value is entered. You may designate coordinate values in positive or negative axis directions (XY or -X-Y). The default is positive, so you must precede a negative direction with a minus sign. The positive and negative absolute coordinate directions are illustrated in figure 3.8.

Relative Coordinates

Relative Cartesian coordinates were established in figure 3.9 by typing @ (the "at" symbol) before the coordinate value. This causes AutoCAD to interpret the value as an offset relative to the last point entered, not relative to 0,0. Once you establish a line's starting point, for example, you locate the endpoint relative to the starting point, such as @1.5,0. This would draw a 1.5-unit-long line in the X direction with no Y offset. You may specify relative Cartesian coordinates with either a default positive or negative direction for any axis.

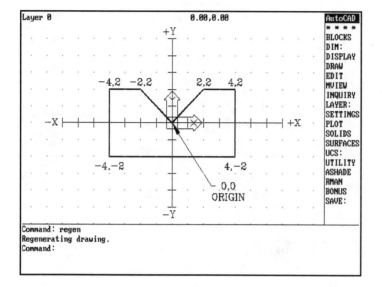

Figure 3.8:
Absolute coordinates.

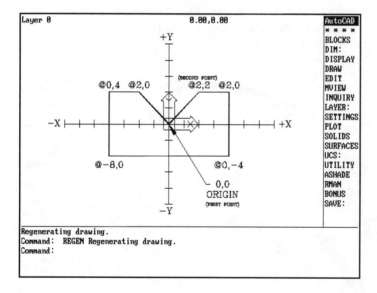

Figure 3.9:
Relative coordinates.

Polar Coordinates

As figure 3.10 shows, polar coordinates are specified relative to the last point by their distance and angle. Type @ before the polar coordinate, followed by the linear distance value, the angle symbol (<), and an angle value.

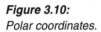

Figure 3.10:
Polar coordinates.

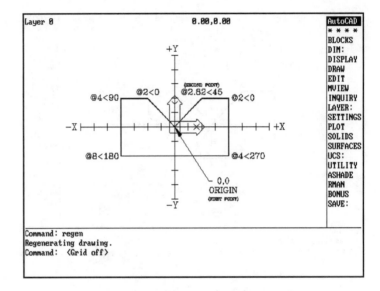

Polar coordinates can be entered with either a positive or negative distance or angle, although negative distances may be confusing. Figure 3.11 illustrates both the positive and negative polar angles.

Figure 3.11:
Positive and negative polar angles.

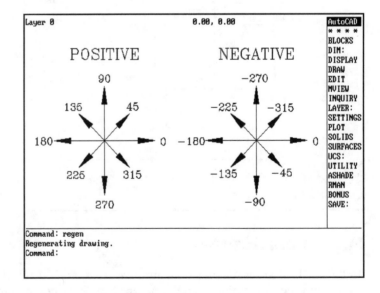

Integrating Absolute, Relative, and Polar Coordinates

You can develop drawings using one type of coordinate entry or, as figure 3.12 shows, any combination of all three types of coordinate display.

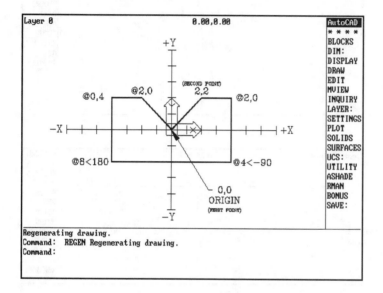

Figure 3.12:
Combination of several coordinate types.

You will find that each of the coordinate entry methods is most useful in specific situations, so it is important to know all three.

 Release 11 has introduced two methods of entering 3D coordinates: *Spherical Point Format* and *Cylindrical Point Format.*

The Coordinate Readout

The Coords read-out on the status line shows the cursor location. Its default shows the last point picked in XY coordinates, such as 2.0000,3.0000. When you toggle Coords by pressing Ctrl-D or F6, the read-out continually updates to display the current location of the cursor.

When toggled at the Command: prompt, Coords updates the XY coordinates. Coords displays polar coordinates when appropriate and XY coordinates otherwise, when toggled once in most commands. If you toggle it a second time during a command, it will display, as figure 3.13 illustrates, absolute XY coordinates. Toggle it again and the readout returns to its original status (see fig. 3.14).

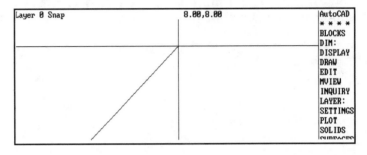

Figure 3.13:
Absolute coordinate readout.

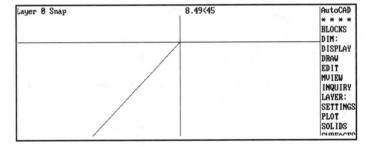

Figure 3.14:
Polar coordinate read-out.

As you draw, toggle Coords as needed and watch the read-out. This is an efficient way to locate and pick points, if your Snap is set appropriately.

Drafting a Part

The following exercise shows you how to use the Line command to draw the part outline. You can draw a continuous series of lines by picking a starting point with your pointing device, and then selecting any number of sequential end-points. As you draw each line, it *rubber-bands* from the previous point selected. The exercise shows you the absolute, relative, and polar coordinate inputs you need to draw the part. For variety in point input, the PART1 drawing (see fig. 3.1) provides dimensions if you want to pick points, with Snap and Coordinate displays to guide you.

Drawing an Object with Lines and Circle

The *Line* command enables you to draw straight line segments. You can enter 2D or 3D points by entering a number at the `From point:` prompt and a series of numbers at the `To point:` prompts. Type **C** to close a series, **U** to undo the previous segment, and press Enter at the `From point:` prompt to continue the previous line or arc.

If you enter a wrong value, simply press Backspace to fix it. If you have already pressed Enter or have picked the wrong point, you can type **U** or select `Undo`, and the last line drawn will be undone. You may erase all lines back to the original starting point. Once a command has been completed, you can type **U** or select `Undo` to cancel the entire previous command.

Now you will draw the first few lines. When you select either the screen or pull-down menu Line items, the screen menu pages to a set of tools for drawing lines. You will draw some lines with the pointing device and other lines from the keyboard, with Snap on. You also will draw with Ortho on and off.

Continuing the previous PART1 drawing, select the Draw and Line commands from either the pull-down or screen menu, or type **Line** at the keyboard, and follow these steps:

Drawing the Object	
`Command:` **Line**	Starts the Line command
`From point:` *Press F8 and F9 to toggle Ortho and Snap on, and then type* **14,2**	Selects first point
`To point:` *Press F6 to toggle Coords on, and then type polar point* **@11<180**	Selects second point
`To point:` *Type polar point* **@2<90**	Selects third point
`To point:` *Press F8 to toggle Ortho off, and then type polar point* **@1.41<45**	Selects fourth point
`To point:` **@2,0**	Selects fifth point
`To point:` **@0,2**	Selects sixth point
`To point:` **@2,2**	Selects seventh point
`To point:` *Press F6 to toggle Coords off. Then type absolute point* **11,9**	Selects eighth point
`To point:` **@3,-5**	Selects ninth point
`To point:` **C**	Closes drawing

Except for the circle and dimensions, our screen should resemble the PART1 drawing shown in figure 3.1. Now you are ready to add the circle.

The *Circle* command enables you to draw circles. The default method uses a <Center point> and <Radius>. If the Dragmode command is set to on or auto (the default), you can determine the size of the circle by dragging it on the screen.

If you select Circle from the Draw pull-down menu, AutoCAD presents a menu page—illustrated by figure 3.15—with five options for creating circles. These options are: Cen, Dia (center, diameter); Cen, Rad (center, radius); 2-Point; 3-Point; and TTR (tangent-tangent-radius). If you select Circle from the Draw side menu, these five options will appear in similar fashion.

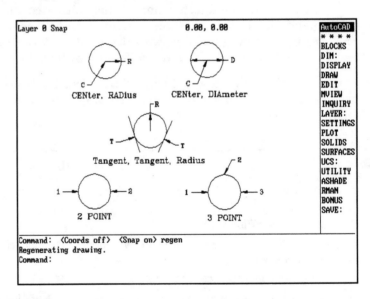

Figure 3.15:
AutoCAD's Circle options.

When you select one of these menu options, it executes the Circle command and provides the input parameters to prompt you for the type of circle you selected. After accessing the Circle command, you can enter the desired parameters manually in the command area. After you establish the first point of the circle, move the cursor in any direction and you will see a varying circle attached to it. This action is called *dragging*. With Snap on, you can drag the circle to the desired size and accurately pick the radius.

Drawing the Circle

Command: **Circle**	Starts the Circle command
3P/2P/TTR/<Center point>: **9.2,7**	Selects center point of circle
Diameter/<Radius>: **1**	Selects radius of 1

Remember, you can either type specific radii or diameter values, or you can show values by picking points on the screen to designate the size of the circles. Your drawing should now resemble figure 3.16.

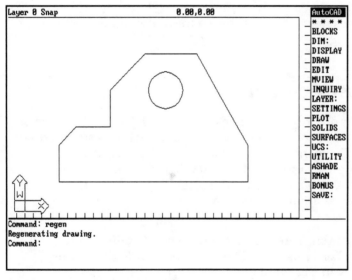

Figure 3.16:
PART1 drawing with the circle added.

Using Text Tools

Now you can add some annotations. Drafting projects commonly require text for title block information and drawing notes.

 The *Text* command enables you to enter text in your drawing. It is an older command than Dtext, and does not show your text characters on the screen as you enter them. It places the text string when you end the text input.

 The *Dtext* (Dynamic Text) command prompts for the same text parameters as the Text command, but draws the text characters on the screen as you type them. The Dtext command displays a rectangular character box to show where the next character will be placed.

Dtext is the preferred text entry command because it displays characters as they are entered and enables you to enter multiple lines of text in one command by pressing Enter after each line. Move the Dtext box and pick a point if you want to start a new line at a new location.

The *Qtext* (Quick Text) command draws boxes in place of text strings and attributes. This saves time when redrawing or regenerating the screen. The box or rectangle is the height and approximate length of the text string. The default setting is off.

Text characters can be slow to redraw and regenerate because they consist of vectors. Use Qtext when you have large amounts of text to enter and when plotting.

Applying Text Justification

When you execute the Text or Dtext commands (see fig. 3.17 and 3.18) from one of the AutoCAD menu choices, you get a menu page that includes several different justification formats. These include: Left <default>, Align, Fit, Center, Middle, Right, Top Left, Top Center, Top Right, Middle Left, Middle Center, Middle Right, Bottom Left, Bottom Center, and Bottom Right. You also can designate the size (height) and rotation angle you want.

The Top Left, Top Center, Top Right, Middle Left, Middle Center, Middle Right, Bottom Left, Bottom Center, and Bottom Right justification options are new in Release 11.

If you select the Dtext command from the Draw pull-down menu, be aware that it maintains pre-set options. To use the pull-down for the following exercise, select the Options menu. Then click on DTEXT OPTIONS   > for the appropriate parameters. See Chapter 2 for more information on setting Options.

The following exercise displays the use of the Dtext command, using default (left) justification and a larger text height. Place the text anywhere you like.

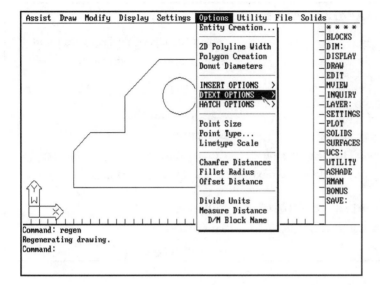

Figure 3.17:
The Options pull-down menu with Dtext options selected.

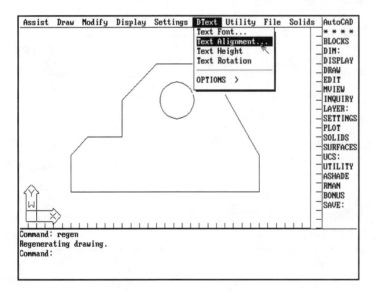

Figure 3.18:
The Text Alignment option.

Adding Text to the Drawing

Command: **Dtext**	Starts the Dynamic Text command
Justify/Style/<Start point>: *Click on any point in the circle*	Selects starting point for text
Height <0.20>: **.4**	Sets larger text height
Rotation angle <0>: *Press Enter*	Accepts default
Text: **Just Testing**	Enters text
Text: *Press Backspace until all the text is gone*	Erases text

Move the cursor and pick point 1,10 for the next text entry. Press F6 to toggle Coords on to verify selection.

Text: **Notes, unless otherwise specified:**	Enters text
Text: **1. Interpret per ANSI Y14.5M-1982.**	Enters text
Text: *Press Enter*	Ends text entry

Your screen should resemble figure 3.19.

Figure 3.19:
Text added to the PART1 drawing.

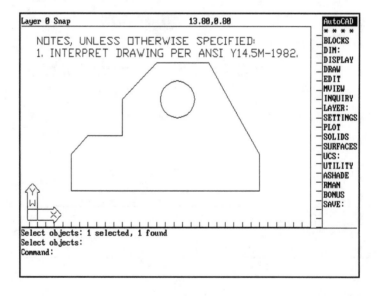

Editing Text Using a Dialogue Box

AutoCAD enables you to edit text within dialogue boxes. This simplifies the task of changing or editing text within an AutoCAD drawing.

Once the dialogue box is displayed, you may position the text cursor by moving the arrow to the desired location and pressing the pick button on your pointing device. The editing cursor will then appear in reverse video at the designated location. You then enter or delete characters as needed. If the line of text is longer than the dialogue box, the left angle bracket (<) and the right angle bracket (>) appear at each end of the line. This informs you of the presence of hidden characters without scrolling. You can scroll to the beginning or the end of the hidden text by picking a directional angle bracket.

AutoCAD provides the following editing options:

- **Typing Text.** Inserts a text character at the cursor, shifting the text string to the right.
- **< or Ctrl-B.** Moves the text cursor to the left.
- **> or Ctrl-F.** Moves the text cursor to the right.
- **Del or Ctrl-D**. Deletes the character at the text cursor.
- **Backspace**. Deletes the character to the left of the text cursor.
- **Ctrl-X.** Deletes all characters from the text cursor to the end of the text string. If the text cursor is positioned over the first character of a line, the entire line is deleted.

Text editing using dialogue boxes is not available on versions prior to Release 11.

If you are using Release 11, type **Ddedit** at the Command: prompt to see how it works. Click on note No. 1 (INTERPRET PER ANSI...) with your mouse to activate the dialogue box, and then, as shown in figure 3.20, click on the text string in the dialogue box. You can edit the text from the keyboard if you wish. As figure 3.21 illustrates, click on the OK box to the right of the text string when you have finished editing, and then click again on the OK box at the bottom of the dialogue box to accept the changes.

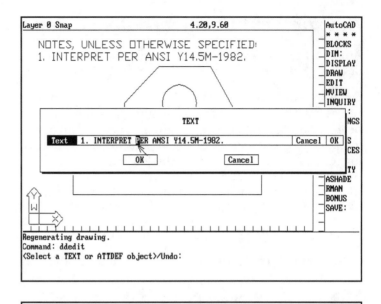

Figure 3.20:
Position the text cursor here and enter text.

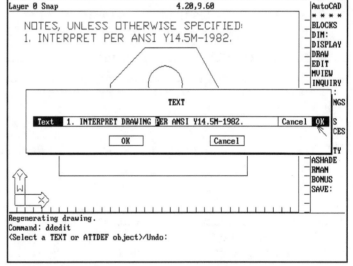

Figure 3.21:
The edited text line.

Inserting Text Control Codes

Some characters or symbols are not available on the standard keyboard. You can enter them with control codes by typing two percent symbols and a specified code letter at the insertion point in the text. The following control codes are available in AutoCAD:

%%O Draws overscore line

%%U Draws underscore line

%%D Draws degrees symbol

%%P Draws plus/minus symbol

%%C Draws diameter symbol

%%% Draws percent sign

%%nnn Draws ASCII character with decimal code *nnn*

The following exercise shows how to enter the diameter and the plus or minus symbols in your text:

Entering Special Characters with Control Codes

Command: **Dtext**	Starts the Dynamic Text command
Justify/Style/<Start point>: *Pick a point on the screen and click with mouse*	Specifies the text insertion point
Height <0.40>: *Press Enter*	Accepts default
Rotation angle <0>: *Press Enter*	Accepts default
Text: **%%C2.00%%P.03** *(see fig. 3.22)*	Enters the diameter and plus/minus symbols
Text: *Press Enter*	Ends text entry

The default text style that you have been using, called Standard, is efficient but crude. You have many other choices.

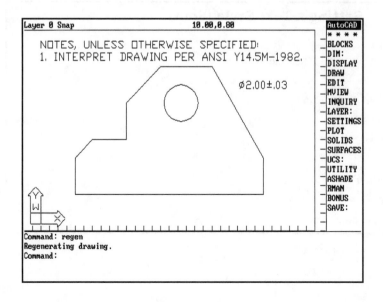

Figure 3.22:
The codes generate the diameter and plus/minus symbols.

Using Various Text Styles

The appearance of text in AutoCAD is determined by the style setting. A style is defined by a text *font* (a set of character definitions) and modified by a number of style parameters that are set with the Style command.

The *Style* command enables you to create new text styles, modify existing styles, and view a list of defined styles. The style name is arbitrary; you can use up to 31 characters. A style is named by assigning it a text font. Font files have the SHX extension.

AutoCAD provides many fonts to choose from, and you can define an infinite number of style variations from them. Fancy or elaborate fonts take longer for AutoCAD to regenerate than simple fonts.

You can view the available fonts from the Options pull-down menu. Click on DTEXT OPTIONS, and then on Text Font ... to enter AutoCAD's three-page icon menu. Click on Next to view other fonts, and then on Exit to return to the drawing screen. You can select a font by clicking on the box next to the icon. AutoCAD loads the new font and prompts you to change its settings or to accept the defaults. Most of the fonts are shown in figures 3.23 and 3.24.

You also can change a font from the keyboard, as shown in the following exercise:

Setting a Text Style (Font)

Command: **Style**

Text style name (or ?)<STANDARD>: **Romanc**

New style. **Romanc**

New style. Height <0.00>: *Press Enter*

Width factor <1.00>: *Press Enter*

Obliquing angle <0>: *Press Enter*

Backwards? <N> *Press Enter*

Upside-down? <N> *Press Enter*

Vertical? <N> *Press Enter*

Romanc is now the current text style.

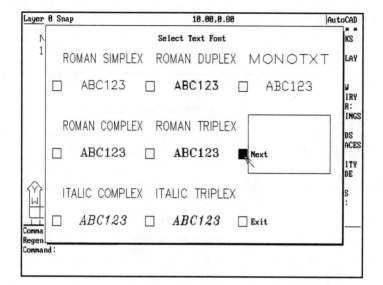

Figure 3.23:
Some available text fonts.

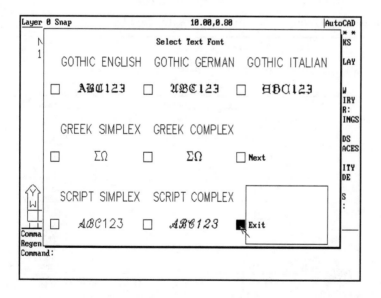

Figure 3.24:
More text fonts.

You can set any of the options to change the style, of course. The height option is noteworthy. If set to zero, the Text commands prompt for and control height. If set to any other value, the height style is fixed and the Text commands do not prompt for it.

The following exercise shows you how to create fancy text for the PART1 drawing, using the Text command:

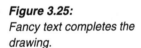

Generating ROMANC Text

Command: **Text**	Starts the Text command
Justify/Style/<Start point>: **J**	Selects justification mode
Align/Fit/Center/Middle/Right/ TL/TC/TR/ML/ MC/MR/BL/BC/BR: **BR**	Selects lower right corner for justification
Bottom/right point: *Click at a point at lower right of screen*	Specifies position for justification
Height <0.40>: *Press Enter*	Accepts default
Rotation angle <0>: *Press Enter*	Accepts default
Text: **Drawn By: (Your Name)** *Type your name*	Enters justified text
Command: *Press Enter*	Repeats the Text command
TEXT Justify/Style/<Start point>: *Press Enter*	Accepts the default
Text: **Date: (Today's date)** *Type today's date*	Enters justified text

Your completed PART1 drawing should resemble figure 3.25.

Figure 3.25:
Fancy text completes the drawing.

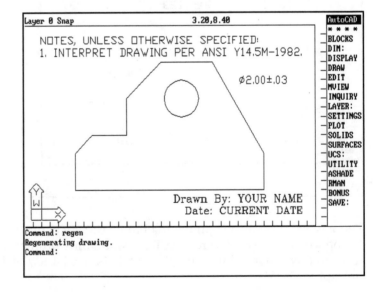

When you execute the Text command, the previous text (if any) is highlighted. By pressing Enter at the <Start point>: prompt, you accept by default the previous style, justification, height, and rotation angle without being prompted for each one, and the new line is positioned under the previous one.

Many styles can be defined, but only one style can be current. To change the style, use the Style option of the Text command or use the Style command and accept its default options.

Saving and Quitting

The *Save* command, as the name implies, saves your drawing to the disk. It updates the drawing file and leaves you in the drawing editor for further editing. It also creates a backup (.BAK) file. After typing or selecting Save, a file dialogue box (as fig. 3.26 illustrates) appears on the screen. The *Quit* command exits the drawing editor without updating the drawing file. Any data entered since the file was previously saved will not be saved.

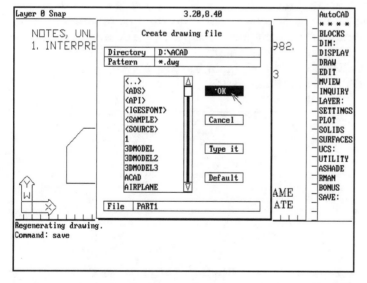

Figure 3.26:
The file dialogue box.

You can save the drawing under the default directory and file name, in this case PART1 in the AutoCAD directory. You also can direct the file to be saved under any other existing directory and file name (such as \ACAD-DWG\PARTY) by pointing the arrow at the directory listing or the directory button and picking it. The directory button will be highlighted when you pick it, and you may enter the new directory/subdirectory and file name from the keyboard.

You can save your drawing from the File pull-down menu by clicking on Save and then clicking on the OK button in the file dialogue box (see fig. 3.26). To save your drawing from the keyboard, type **Save** at the Command: prompt and press Enter twice.

You should save your drawing file periodically to avoid disasters. A day's worth of drawing can be completely wiped out by a split-second power outage if you have not saved your file.

If you want to take a break, you can quit the drawing editor. Be sure to save your drawing first so you do not lose your work. Type **Quit** at the Command: prompt, and then type **Y** at the prompt that follows. You also can select the File pull-down menu, click on Quit, and then click on Yes.

The End command will be explained later in this chapter.

Getting Help When You Need It

As you progress in AutoCAD, you may become confused on occasion. Help is available almost anytime you need it. The *Help* command provides information about the operation of individual commands. Type **Help** or a question mark at the Command: prompt. You are then prompted for a command name. Press Enter to view a list of available topics. You can press Enter again and again to view more topics, as shown in figures 3.27, 3.28, 3.29, and 3.30.

Figure 3.27:
Commands.

```
     AutoCAD Command List   (' - Transparent command)

     APERTURE    CHANGE      DIVIDE      EXTEND      ISOPLANE
     ARC         CHPROP      DONUT       FILES       LAYER
     AREA        CIRCLE      DOUGHNUT    FILL        LIMITS
     ARRAY       COLOR       DRAGMODE    FILLET      LINE
     ATTDEF      COPY        DTEXT       FILMROLL    LINETYPE
     ATTDISP     DBLIST      DVIEW       ' GRAPHSCR  LIST
     ATTEDIT     DDATTE      DXBIN       GRID        LOAD
     ATTEXT      DDEDIT      DXFIN       HANDLES     LTSCALE
     AUDIT       ' DIMODES   DXFOUT      HATCH       MEASURE
     AXIS        ' DDLMODES  EDGESURF    ' HELP / '? MENU
     BASE        ' DDRMODES  ELEV        HIDE        MINSERT
     BITMODE     DDUCS       ELLIPSE     ID          MIRROR
     BLOCK       DELAY       END         IGESIN      MOVE
     BREAK       DIM/DIM1    ERASE       IGESOUT     MSLIDE
     CHAMFER     DIST        EXPLODE     INSERT      MSPACE

     Press RETURN for further help.




                            Commands.
```

```
AutoCAD Command List  (' = transparent command)

MULTIPLE     PSPACE        RSCRIPT       STYLE        VIEWPORTS
MVIEW        PURGE         RULESURF      TABLET       VIEWRES
OFFSET       QTEXT         SAVE          TABSURF      VPLAYER
OOPS         QUIT          SCALE         TEXT         VPOINT
ORTHO        REDEFINE      SCRIPT        'TEXTSCR     VPORTS
OSNAP        REDO          SELECT        TIME         VSLIDE
'PAN         'REDRAW       'SETVAR       TRACE        WBLOCK
PEDIT        'REDRAWALL    SHADE         TRIM         XBIND
PFACE        REGEN         SHAPE         U            XREF
PLAN         REGENALL      SHELL/SH      UCS          'ZOOM
PLINE        REGENAUTO     SKETCH        UCSICON      3DFACE
PLOT         RENAME        SNAP          UNDEFINE     3DMESH
POINT        'RESUME       SOLID         UNDO         3DPOLY
POLYGON      REVSURF       STATUS        UNITS
PRPLOT       ROTATE        STRETCH       'VIEW

At the "Command:" prompt, you can enter RETURN to repeat the last command.

Press RETURN for further help.




                       More commands.
```

Figure 3.28:
More commands.

```
          AutoCAD System Variable List

ACADPREFIX    CELTYPE       DIMCLRD       DIMTAD       DWGPREFIX
ACADVER       CHAMFERA      DIMCLRE       DIMFAC       ELEVATION
AFLAGS        CHAMFERB      DIMCLRT       DIMTIH       EXPERT
ANGBASE       CLAYER        DIMDLE        DIMTIX       EXTMAX
ANGDIR        CMDECHO       DIMDLI        DIMTM        EXTMIN
APERTURE      COORDS        DIMEXE        DIMTP        FILEDIA
AREA          CVPORT        DIMEXO        DIMTOFL      FILLETRAD
ATTDIA        DATE          DIMGAP        DIMTOH       FILLMODE
ATTMODE       DIMALT        DIMTFAC       DIMTOL       FRONTZ
ATTREQ        DIMALTD       DIMLIM        DIMTSZ       GRIDMODE
AUNITS        DIMALTF       DIMPOST       DIMTVP       GRIDUNIT
AUPREC        DIMAPOST      DIMRND        DIMTXT       HANDLES
AXISMODE      DIMASO        DIMSAH        DIMZIN       HIGHLIGHT
AXISUNIT      DIMASZ        DIMSCALE      DISTANCE     INSBASE
BACKZ         DIMBLK        DIMSE1        DRAGMODE     LASTANGLE
BLIPMODE      DIMBLK1       DIMSE2        DRAGP1       LASTPOINT
CDATE         DIMBLK2       DIMSHO        DRAGP2       LASTPT3D
CECOLOR       DIMCEN        DIMSOXD       DWGNAME      LENSLENGTH

Press RETURN for further help




              AutoCAD system variables list.
```

Figure 3.29:
AutoCAD system
variables list.

When you continue by pressing Enter for further help, AutoCAD will display the AME command list, the AME system variable list, point entry help, and object selection help.

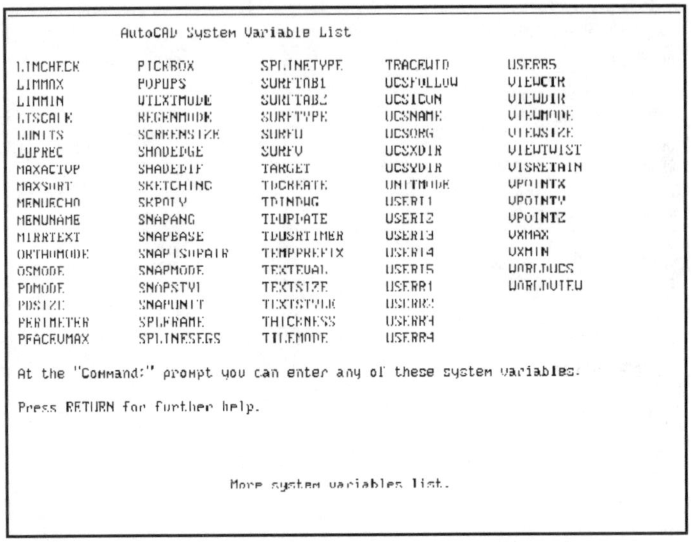

Figure 3.30:
More system variables list.

```
                 AutoCAD System Variable List

   LTMCHECK      PICKBOX        SPLINETYPE     TRACEWID      USERR5
   LIMMAX        POPUPS         SURFTAB1       UCSFOLLOW     VIEWCTR
   LIMMIN        UTEXTMODE      SURFTAB2       UCSICON       VIEWDIR
   LTSCALE       REGENMODE      SURFTYPE       UCSNAME       VIEWMODE
   LUNITS        SCREENSIZE     SURFU          UCSORG        VIEWSIZE
   LUPREC        SHADEDGE       SURFV          UCSXDIR       VIEWTWIST
   MAXACTVP      SHADEDIF       TARGET         UCSYDIR       VISRETAIN
   MAXSORT       SKETCHINC      TDCREATE       UNITMODE      VPOINTX
   MENUECHO      SKPOLY         TDINDWG        USERI1        VPOINTY
   MENUNAME      SNAPANG        TDUPDATE       USERI2        VPOINTZ
   MIRRTEXT      SNAPBASE       TDUSRTIMER     USERI3        VXMAX
   ORTHOMODE     SNAPISOPAIR    TEMPPREFIX     USERI4        VXMIN
   OSMODE        SNAPMODE       TEXTEVAL       USERI5        WORLDUCS
   PDMODE        SNAPSTYL       TEXTSIZE       USERR1        WORLDVIEW
   PDSIZE        SNAPUNIT       TEXTSTYLE      USERR2
   PERIMETER     SPLFRAME       THICKNESS      USERR3
   PFACEVMAX     SPLINESEGS     TILEMODE       USERR4

At the "Command:" prompt you can enter any of these system variables.

Press RETURN for further help.



                     More system variables list.
```

Asking for Assistance about Specific Commands

To learn more about individual commands, enter the command's name at the Help Command: prompt, or use 'Help or '? transparently in the middle of other commands. The following exercise shows you how to get information about the Circle and Line commands.

Getting Help with the Circle Command

Command: **Help** or **?**	Starts the Help command
Command name (RETURN for list): **Circle**	Displays information about Circle command (see fig. 3.31)
Command: **Line**	Starts the Line command
From point: **'?** or **'Help**	Displays information about Line command
>>Do you want more help for the LINE command? <N> *Press Enter*	Declines more help
Resuming LINE command. From point: **Ctrl-C**	Cancels Line command
Command: **F1**	Toggles to the graphics screen

You can customize your Help file by adding drafting standards or other information to it. *Maximizing AutoCAD, Volume I* (New Riders Publishing) explains how to do this.

The CIRCLE command is used to draw a circle. You can specify the circle
in several ways. The simplest method is by center point and radius.

Format: CIRCLE 3P/2P/TTR/<Center point>: <point>
           Diameter/<Radius>: <radius value>

To specify the radius, you can designate a point on the circumference of
the circle or enter a radius value. If it is more convenient to enter the
diameter than the radius, reply to the "Diameter/<Radius>" prompt with "d".

The circle can also be specified using three points on the circumference
(reply "3p" when prompted for the center point), or by designating two
endpoints of its diameter (reply "2p"). For these methods, you can "drag"
the last point or specify object snap "Tangent" points.

In addition, you can draw a circle by specifying two lines (and/or other
circles) to which the circle should be tangent, and a radius. Enter "TTR"
for this option.

See also: "Circle Command" in chapter 4 of the AutoCAD Reference Manual.

Command:

Displaying help for the Circle command.

Figure 3.31:
Displaying help for the Circle command.

Using Drafting Inspection Tools

Most drafting projects conform to rigorous standards of accuracy. Use the following options to inspect a drawing for correct parameters and geometry or to get information about existing objects.

- **Area.** Calculates an area and perimeter
- **Dblist.** Lists data base information (see List)
- **Dist.** Measures the distance between two points
- **Id.** Identifies XYZ values of a pick point
- **List.** Lists drawing information on selected entities
- **Status.** Provides screen and parameter status
- **Time.** Provides information on drawing time

The inquiry tools are particularly useful for specific design tasks, such as checking the tolerances of mating parts. They display their results in whatever units format you have set up. The following exercise will provide a closer look at a few of AutoCAD's inquiry (or inspection) tools.

The *Area* command enables you to calculate the area by picking a series of points or by selecting an entity (such as a circle or polyline). AutoCAD not only calculates the area but also informs you of the perimeter and the line length or circumference. You can keep a running total by adding and subtracting areas. The default picks points to define the area.

You can add or subtract areas to determine an area of unusual shape. The following exercise shows you how AutoCAD calculates the area of your circle and the area of your entire part. You may continue the previous drawing or edit the drawing named PART1.

Calculating Area and Perimeter

Command: **Area**

<First point>/Entity/Add/Subtract: **A**

<First point>/Entity/Subtract: *Pick a point on the polygon's perimeter with the mouse*

(ADD mode) Next point: *Pick another perimeter point*

(ADD mode) Next point: *Pick another perimeter point*

(ADD mode) Next point: *Press Enter*

<First point>/Entity/Subtract: **S**

<First point>/Entity/Add: **E**

(SUBTRACT mode) Select circle or polyline: *Click on the circle's perimeter with mouse*

(SUBTRACT mode) Select circle or polyline: *Press Enter*

<First point>/Entity/Add: *Press Enter*

You can continue to add or subtract any number of entities or sets of points within a single Area command.

The *Dist* (distance) command determines the length of an imaginary 2D or 3D line, its angle in the XY plane, its angle from the XY plane if 3D, and the delta XY (or XYZ) between two points. To measure the distance between two points, for example, type **Dist** at the Command: prompt. At the First point: prompt, pick any point on the drawing screen and click with your pointer. Do the same at the Second point: prompt, and the distance calculations appear.

The *ID* command identifies the absolute XYZ coordinates of any selected point. To check the position of a point, type **ID** at the Command: prompt, then click on a point on the drawing screen with your pointer and the coordinates are displayed.

The *List* command provides information on selected entities within a drawing. The *Dblist* (database) command provides information on all entities within a drawing. These commands list layer assignment, XYZ position relative to the current UCS, and color and linetype (if not the default Bylayer).

When you enter the List command, you are prompted to select an entity. You can select an individual entity or you can select multiple entities. AutoCAD then returns a text screen of information that includes linetypes, layers, locations, lengths, angles, and perimeters.

The following exercise shows you how to list information for a line, circle, and text:

Listing Information about Entities

Command: **List**

Select objects: *Pick the bottom line of the part with mouse*

1 selected, 1 found.

Select objects: *Pick the circle*

1 selected, 1 found

Select objects: *Pick the upper text string*

1 selected, 1 found.

Select objects: *Press Enter*

If the listing scrolls off the screen, you can press Ctrl-S to halt the scroll and can continue to scroll by pressing any key. If you have a printer, you can press Ctrl-Q before executing the command to echo the data to the printer. Pressing Ctrl-Q again turns off the printer echo. Press F1 at the Command: prompt to return to the graphics screen.

The *Status* command gives you current information on drawing limits, extents, the drawing aids settings, and some system information. The status report is a text screen.

To view this information, type **Status** at the Command: prompt. All entities created are counted, even if they have been erased. Press F1 at the Command: prompt at the bottom of the screen to toggle back to the graphics screen.

Take time to look over your drawing's status. This information can answer many questions you may have later.

The *Time* command is useful for checking the progress of drawings. It displays the current date and time; date and time the drawing was created; date and time the drawing was last updated; and the current amount of time in the drawing editor. You also can set an elapsed timer, which is on in the default setting.

To view the time information in your PART1 drawing, type **Time** at the Command: prompt. If you wish to change the default setting for the elapsed timer, type **Off** at the Display/ON/OFF/Reset: prompt. Press F1 at the same prompt to toggle back to the graphics menu.

Using AutoCAD's Built-in Calculator

AutoCAD provides the *Calc* command—a built-in calculator for performing mathematical functions while working in the AutoCAD drawing editor. You can find it within the Bonus screen menu under CALC.

The following exercise demonstrates how to use the Calc feature. Select Bonus from the screen menu. Then select Calc (calculator). At the First number: prompt, type **144**. If you type **S** at the Calc: Clear/Exit/Mem/Sq-rt/Trig/Y^x or + - * / <Clear>: prompt, the program calculates square root and displays The square root of 144.00 is 12. In order to exit the Calc command, type **E** at the Calc: Clear/Exit/Mem/Sq-rt/Trig/Y^x or + - * / <Clear>: prompt.

Saving and Exiting the Drawing Editor

The *End* command updates (saves) the drawing file and exits to AutoCAD's main menu. It combines the Save and Quit commands into one step. The old drawing file becomes the new BAK file. To use it, simply type **End** at the Command: prompt or select End from the File pull-down menu.

Your drawing should now be saved to the AutoCAD or D3D-ACAD directory of your hard disk. You should back up your work on floppy disks for security, however.

The following exercise uses the DOS Copy command to copy the PART1.DWG file from the subdirectory to a formatted floppy disk in drive A. You also might want to erase the drawing file(s) on the hard disk with a Delete command.

Backing Up Using the DOS Copy Command

Enter selection: **0**   Exits to DOS from main AutoCAD
                                                            menu

C:\ACAD> *Place a formatted disk in drive A and*   Copies file from ACAD subdirectory
type: **COPY ACAD\PART1.DWG A:**   to drive A

If you configured AutoCAD to run the ACAD Y14.5 Program, the ACAD.BAT batch file
resets the AutoCAD variables and returns you to the root directory.

C:**D3D-ACAD>SET ACAD=**

C:**D3D-ACAD>SET ACADCFG=**

C:**D3D-ACAD>CD **

Put a formatted disk in drive A

C:\> **COPY ACAD\PART1.DWG A:**   Copies it from ACAD subdirectory to
                                                            drive A.

Or

C:\> **COPY D3D-ACAD\PART1.DWG A:**   Copies it from D3D-ACAD
                                                            subdirectory to drive A.

C:\> **DIR A:**   Displays the file(s) on drive A

Volume in drive A has no label
Directory of A:\

PART1   DWG   4704   1-30-92   5:18p   (Your data will vary)

C:\> **COMP ACAD\PART1.DWG A:**

Or

C:\> **COMP D3D-ACAD\PART1.DWG A:**   Verifies the copy

C:ACAD\PART1.DWG and A:PART1.DWG   Declines further comparisons
Eof mark not found
Files compare ok
Compare more files (Y/N)? **N**

As you proceed through this book, back up the drawings you want to save. You
should have at least two current copies at all times. If you want to delete some
drawings so that your hard disk does not become cluttered, type **DEL** and the
file name (such as ACAD\PART1.DWG) at the C:\> prompt.

Summary

This has been a brief tour of AutoCAD's menu options, electronic drawing sheet, positioning tools, inquiry commands, and file handling procedures. As you progress through this textbook, your ability to use AutoCAD for technical drafting and design will continue to expand.

4

AUTOCAD'S LINE CONVENTIONS

In this chapter:

- Understanding polylines
- Drawing the PART2 profile
- Assigning linetypes and colors
- Changing a drawing's linetypes and colors

Overview

In order to ensure uniformity in drafting, many practices have been standardized. One such standard is the types of lines which are used in drawings to specify various features. Like other processes in drafting, line types have been standardized by the American National Standards Institutes and may be referenced by ANSI Y14.2.

Drafting line types vary in two different ways. First, lines may be either thick or thin. The actual thickness depends on the size of the drawing (the hard copy size to be produced) and the type of line being drawn. For example, an object line type (object profile) should be drawn thick, and hidden line type should be drawn thin.

AutoCAD maintains certain linetypes as a part of its program. Some of these line types have been named according to the ANSI Y14.2 standard and what has been termed the "alphabet of lines" in most traditional drafting programs. AutoCAD also maintains the ability to develop thick and thin line type variations. These two line types are: trace lines and polylines. The polyline is AutoCAD's most versatile line since it may be drawn and edited in many different ways.

In this exercise you will use some of AutoCAD's line type conventions to develop a single view drawing, named PART2 and illustrated in figure 4.1. You will develop a wide polyline, draft lines, and then change their linetype properties to develop hidden and center lines.

Figure 4.1:
The completed PART2 drawing, which you will create in this chapter.

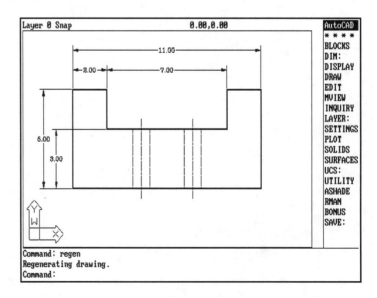

Establishing Parameters and Values for PART2

Remember that throughout the exercises in this textbook you are to press Enter after responding to a prompt. At the AutoCAD main menu, enter the drawing editor by doing the following steps:

```
Enter Selection: 1
Enter NAME of drawing: PART2
```

The AutoCAD drawing screen appears, and you can begin a new drawing.

The PART2 drawing uses the parameters shown in table 4.1. AutoCAD's automatic setup routine prepares the drawing sheet, but it will be necessary that you set some of the drawing parameters shown in table 4.1. In Release 10, the root menu contains the Setup routine.

Table 4.1
Parameters for the PART2 Drawing

Parameter	Setting
Axis	.5
Grid	1
Snap	.5
Units	Decimal 0.0000.
Limits	0,0 to 17,11.
Layer Name	0
State	Current
Color	7 (white)
	3 (green)
	1 (red)
Linetype	Continuous Hidden Center

The automatic sheet setup routine is invoked by selecting the Bonus option from the root menu. Click on Bonus with your mouse. (Press Ins to activate the screen menu if you want to use the arrow keys instead of the mouse.) Click on next to page to the second page of options, and then select Mvsetup. Type **No** at the Enable Paper/Modelspace?<Y>: prompt. Select decimal from the Unit Type menu. Select FULL from the Decimal Scale menu. Select B- 11x17 from the Sheet Size menu.

Now, at the `Command:` prompt, set the drawing tool parameters of Snap, Grid and Axis. Set Snap to .5, Grid to 1.0, and Axis to .5.

As described in Chapter 3, you can select any of the units, scales, and sheet sizes presented in the menu. You may also choose other sheet sizes. If you need to set up a drawing sheet size which is not listed on the screen menu, simply select from the Sheet Size menu `OTHER...` and enter the new drawing parameters. You are prompted to provide the coordinate position of the lower left corner and the upper right corner of the drawing sheet. You must specify these positions in the current unit values.

Understanding Polylines

Polylines are different from ordinary lines in several ways. You can draw 2D or 3D polylines. 3D polylines and the 3DPOLY command are covered later in the textbook, but for now you will concentrate on 2D polylines.

A *polyline* is a series of line and arc segments that are interconnected because they share the same vertices and are processed as a single entity. Figure 4.2 illustrates several examples of polylines.

Command

The *Pline* command draws 2D polylines. Pline starts with a `From point:` prompt. After entering the first point, you can continue in Line mode or Arc mode. Each mode has its own set of prompts. To edit polylines, you can use Pedit as well as most of the regular edit commands. Polyline options provide many useful tools for the drafter. One of these tools is to create wide lines. It is often necessary for a drafter to use various line thicknesses to develop a drawing. In this exercise we will use a wide 2D polyline to draw PART2's profile object lines.

A single polyline can have any combination of straight or arc line segments. The joints between segments are called vertices. Arcs are circular, but other curves can be approximated by combinations of straight and arc segments. The Pedit command offers automatic curve fitting, splines, and other ways to modify existing polylines. You also can modify polylines by inserting, moving, or deleting vertices, or by joining several lines, arcs, and polylines into one polyline. A segment can have any width and can even be tapered. The default width is 0. Because a polyline is a connected sequence of line and arc segments, the entire polyline may be treated as one object.

Entities created by the Donut, Ellipse, and Polygon commands are polylines. The Area command finds the enclosed area of a polyline. The Fillet and Chamfer commands globally modify all the vertices of a polyline.

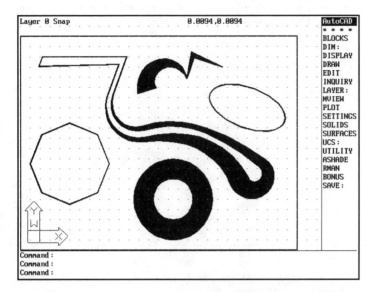

Figure 4.2:
Example polylines.

Drawing the PART2 Profile

Although you may use the pull-down menu by selecting Draw and then selecting Pline or you may select the same choices from the screen menu, we recommend that you do the following exercise from the keyboard. If you make an error
in coordinate entry before pressing the Enter key, use the Backspace to edit. If
an incorrect coordinate point has been entered, select the Undo function by
typing **U** and the last polyline segment will be removed. You may then continue
from the previous point. You will use wide lines in this drawing. Complete the
following steps to draw the PART2 profile:

Drawing the Profile

Command: **Pline**	Starts the Pline command
From point: **3,3**	Establishes a starting point with a line-width of 0.00
Arc/Close/Halfwidth/Length/Undo/Width/ <Endpoint of line>: **W**	Accesses Width option
Starting width <0.0000>: **.03**	
Ending width <<0.0300>>: *Press Enter*	Defaults to starting width
Arc/Close/Halfwidth/Length/Undo/Width/ <Endpoint of line>: **@0,5**	Relative point
Arc/Close/Halfwidth/Length/Undo/Width/ <Endpoint of line>: **@2,0**	

Drawing the Profile—continued

```
Arc/Close/Halfwidth/Length/Undo/Width/
<Endpoint of line>: @0,-2

Arc/Close/Halfwidth/Length/Undo/Width/
<Endpoint of line>: @7,0

Arc/Close/Halfwidth/Length/Undo/Width/
<Endpoint of line>: @0,2

Arc/Close/Halfwidth/Length/Undo/Width/
<Endpoint of line>: @2,0

Arc/Close/Halfwidth/Length/Undo/Width/
<Endpoint of line>: @0,-5

Arc/Close/Halfwidth/Length/Undo/Width/          Closes and exits
<Endpoint of line>: C
```

Your drawing should look like the polygon shown in figure 4.3.

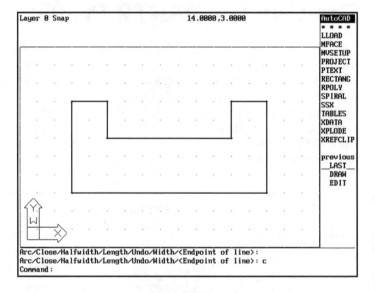

Figure 4.3:
*PART2 profile drawn
with wide polylines.*

You also can draw thick lines with the *Trace* command. Although Trace is not used often by most production drafters, it may prove to be handy on occasion. A *Trace line* is a line with width. Traces are drawn like lines, by selecting the points where the lines begin and end. Traces can be as wide as you want. They are solid unless Fill mode is off; then only the outlines are drawn. *Fill* controls the visibility of solid fill in polylines, traces, and solids.

Trace and polylines are filled to make them appear solid. You may decide to display trace and polylines as two parallel line segments (closed at the ends) or you can fill them in solid.

Just to be safe, save the PART2 drawing now by selecting the File and Save commands from either the screen or the pull-down menu, or by typing Save at the Command: prompt. AutoCAD now displays the Save dialogue box. Press the Enter key or select OK and AutoCAD saves the drawing as PART2.

Assigning Linetypes and Colors

Every AutoCAD entity has layer, thickness, linetype, and color properties. When you need the flexibility of individual linetypes or colors assigned to an entity, you have that option through the Linetype and Color commands or through the Ddemodes Entity Creation Modes dialogue box.

As figures 4.4 and 4.5 show, the *Ddemodes* (Dynamic Dialogue Entity Creation Modes) *dialogue box* shows the current settings for layer, color, linetype, elevation, and thickness. You can change any of these variables. Layer, color, and linetype present another dialogue box when selected.

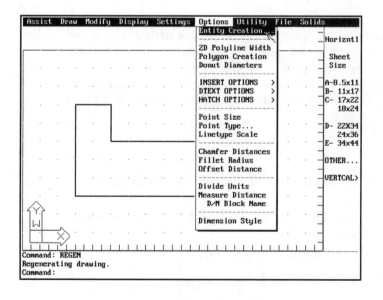

Figure 4.4:
Entity Creation pull-down menu.

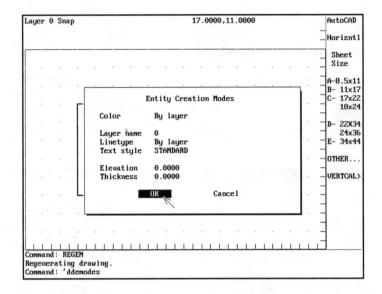

Figure 4.5:
*Ddemodes Entity
Creation Modes dialogue
box.*

Choosing Entity Linetypes

Line colors and types may be controlled in two ways: by using the Layer command (covered in later chapters) and by using the Linetype command to assign a default linetype.

Linetype assigns linetypes to entities, loads linetype definitions stored in library files, and creates new linetype definitions. Linetypes are based on dash-dot line segments. You can control the linetypes of new entities explicitly or by their layer assignment. You also can set linetype with the Ddemodes dialogue box. The default setting is Bylayer.

Linetype's options are:

■ **?** Lists all linetypes in a linetype definition file (not those in the drawing)

■ **Load** Loads one or more linetypes (? and * wildcards load several or all linetypes at once)

■ **Set** Sets the linetype for all new entities, regardless of layer

Figures 4.6 and 4.7 show AutoCAD's predefined linetypes.

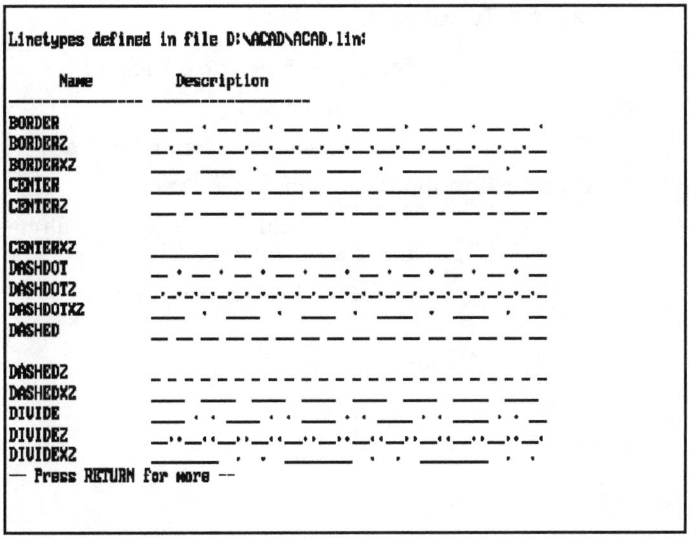

Figure 4.6:
AutoCAD's predefined
linetypes (Page 1)

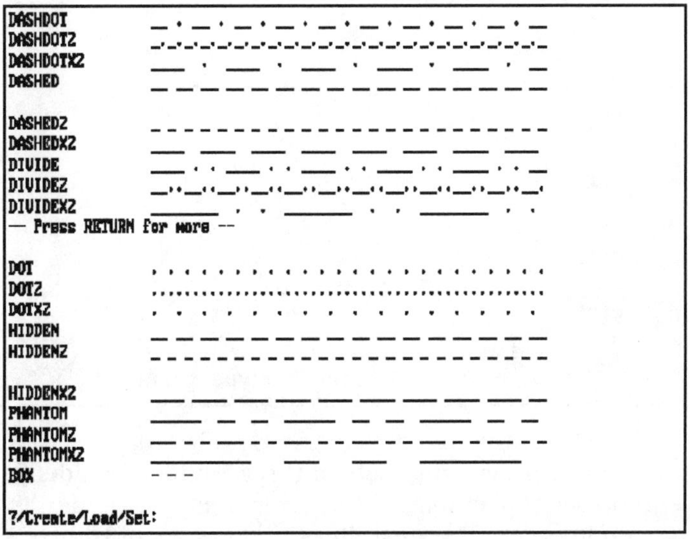

Figure 4.7:
Linetypes (Page 2)

You can load Linetypes from the pull-down menu by accessing the Utility command and then selecting LTypes. You also can load linetypes from the screen menu by selecting `Settings` and then `Linetyp:`, or you can type in the following at the command area:

Loading Linetypes

Command: **Linetype**	Starts the Linetype command
?/Create/Load/Set: **L**	Loads linetypes
Linetype(s) to load: *****	Asterisk wildcard for all linetypes

If your system supports AUI, the file dialogue box appears; if not, press Enter.

Select **OK**	AutoCAD searches the default directory for the linetype files
Linetype BORDER2 loaded. Linetype BORDERX2 loaded. Linetype CENTER loaded. Linetype CENTER2 loaded. Linetype CENTERX2 loaded. Linetype DASHDOT loaded. Linetype DASHDOT2 loaded. Linetype DASHDOTX2 loaded. Linetype DASHED loaded. Linetype DASHED2 loaded. Linetype DASHEDX2 loaded. Linetype DIVIDE loaded. Linetype DIVIDE2 loaded. Linetype DIVIDEX2 loaded. Linetype DOT loaded. Linetype DOT2 loaded. Linetype DOTX2 loaded. Linetype HIDDEN loaded. Linetype HIDDEN2 loaded. Linetype HIDDENX2 loaded. Linetype PHANTOM loaded. Linetype PHANTOM2 loaded. Linetype PHANTOMX2 loaded.	AutoCAD loads these linetypes
?/Create/Load/Set: *Press Enter*	Exits the Linetype command

Each linetype, except Continuous, is provided in sets of three. Hidden, Hidden2, and Hiddenx2, for example, represent variations of the same linetype. Hidden is the standard dash-space hidden linetype. The dash lines and spaces of Hidden2 are one-half as long as Hidden, and the dash lines and spaces of Hiddenx2 are two-times as long as Hidden. By using various combinations of linetypes and linetype scale (Ltscale), you can plot sheets which have multiple drawings in different scales and still maintain appropriate line standards.

If you need additional linetypes, you can create them through customization. For more information on this process, refer to the *AutoCAD Reference Manual* or to *Inside AutoCAD* and *Customizing AutoCAD* (New Riders Publishing).

Changing the Linetype To Draw Hidden Lines

From the pull-down menu, select Options, Entity Creation..., and Linetype. Then scroll down the menu and select Hidden. Next select OK to designate proper selection and exit the Linetype dialogue box. Finally, select OK from the Change Properties dialogue box. You also can select from the screen menu Settings, Linetyp:, Set, and hidden.

Doing this exercise at the command area, you type the following:

Setting Hidden Linetype

Command: **Linetype**	Starts the Linetype command
?/Create/Load/Set: **S**	Sets linetype
New entity linetype (or ?) <BYLAYER>: **Hidden**	Sets hidden
?/Create/Load/Set: *Press Enter*	Exits to Command

Using Linetype Scale

Linetype patterns may appear to be continuous if the line segment is very short, so polyline curves and short segment series do not work well with broken linetypes. A scale that is too large or too small for the display or plot also may make a broken linetype appear continuous.

To insure that the linetype you are drafting looks and plots to ANSI Y14.2 standards, the scale factor of all non-continuous lines may be controlled by the LTSCALE system variable and command. You can vary the plotted and displayed scale by changing this linetype scale factor, which applies to all non-continuous linetypes contained within the current drawing.

LTSCALE (LineType SCALE) determines the dash and space settings for linetypes. The LTSCALE is a global value. All linetypes (except for continuous) are multiplied by the LTSCALE. The default setting is 1.0000. An LTSCALE of 0.375 works well for full-scale drawings. Drawings which will be plotted to other scales should be set to 0.375 times their plot scale. The LTSCALE should be set for plotting, not screen display. You sometimes need to adjust it temporarily to differentiate lines on screen. If you do, remember to reset it before plotting. The following instructions set LTSCALE to an acceptable value for full-scale output.

To set the Linetype scale factor, type the following:

```
Command: LTSCALE
New scale factor <1.0000>: .375
```

The View Resolution command works together with LTSCALE to make linetypes display properly on the screen.

You can control the screen resolution of curved entities by using the Viewres command. *Viewres* controls fast zooms and the display resolution of arcs, circles, and linetypes. The default setting is for fast zooms with a resolution factor of 100 percent. Fast zoom allows most zooms and pans at redraw, not regeneration, speed.

AutoCAD's default setting is designed to save drawing time by simplifying the display of curves. Since curves are made up of a series of straight lines called *vectors* (or chords), the more vectors that are used to make a curve the more that object looks like a smooth curve. Therefore, the higher the Viewres setting, the smoother your curves are on the screen. But there is a price to pay for good looking curves. The higher the Viewres setting, the slower your machine draws.

In order to set Viewres to get fast zooms, but smoother curves, try typing in the following:

Setting the View Resolution

```
Command: Viewres

Do you want fast zooms?<Y> Y

Enter circle zoom percent (1-20000)<100>: 1000
```

When your drawing contains a large number of arcs or circles, set the Viewres to 100. This increases your drawing speed. Also, it is not necessary to increase the viewres value before printing or plotting. The zoom percentage affects only the graphics display. During printing or plotting, the zoom percentage is ignored and curves are plotted with the optimal number of vectors.

Establishing Entity Colors

Color adds more than aesthetic appeal to your work. As your drawings become more complex, different colors increase entity recognition and expand drafting productivity. Individual color assignments are called entity colors. AutoCAD uses seven standard named colors. Other colors may be made available by specifying their numbers if your graphics card and monitor support additional colors.

Standard Color Designations

1 Red	5 Blue
2 Yellow	6 Magenta
3 Green	7 White
4 Cyan	

These colors may be assigned by the Color command. The *Color command* controls the color of new entities, overriding the default layer color. To change the color of existing entities, use the Chprop command. To control layer colors, use the Layer command. Use a color number or name to set a new color. You can also set the current entity color with the 'Ddemodes dialogue box. The default setting is Bylayer.

If you set the new entity color to 3 (green), then all new entities will be drawn in green, regardless of layer, until you change the color setting again. Linetype is similarly controlled.

To set the color property to green, select the following from the pull-down menu: Options, Entity Creation..., Color, Green, OK, and OK. You also can set the color property to green by selecting the following from the screen menu: Settings, Color, and green. Or you can type in the following at the command area:

```
Command: COLOR
New entity color <BYLAYER>: G
```

With the linetypes loaded, Linetype Hidden set, Linetype Scale set and Color set, we are ready to continue drafting PART2

Changing a Drawing's Linetypes and Colors

With the current properties set to Linetype Hidden and Color green, entities will be drawn using these parameters until properties (or other parameters such as layers) are again changed.

You may follow the coordinate input provided below or use the dimensioned drawing at the start of the chapter to pick the starting and ending locations of the four hidden lines.

Using the current properties settings, by selecting Draw and then Line, you can use the pull-down menu or the screen menu to draw the hidden lines of the PART2 drawing. Or you can type in the following at the command area:

Adding Hidden Lines

Command: **Line**

From point: **6.5,3**   Establishes absolute coordinate

To point: **@3<90**   Establishes polar coordinate

To point: *Press Enter*   Ends the Line command

Command: *Press Enter*   Repeats the Line command

Line From point: **7.5,3**

To point: **@3<90**

To point: *Press Enter*

Command: *Press Enter*

Line From point: **9.5,6**

To point: **@3<270**

To point: *Press Enter*

Command: *Press Enter*

Line From point: **10.5,6**

To point: **@3<270**

To point: *Press Enter*

Your drawing should now have the four hidden lines shown in figure 4.8.

Changing properties after you have drawn entities provides an efficient technique for production drafting. Instead of continuously setting the properties or layers before drawing different linetypes or colors, it is often more efficient to draw entities which make up a part and then change their properties later.

Chprop redefines the layer, color, linetype, and 3D thickness properties of existing entities. Use Chprop instead of Change to change entity properties.

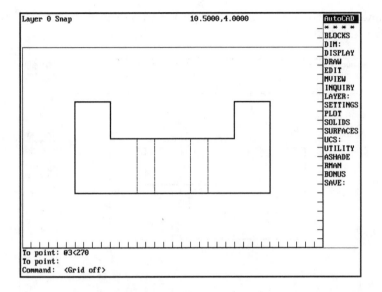

Figure 4.8:
PART2 with hidden lines added.

The *Change* command is also capable of being used to modify properties like color and linetype, but Chprop is specifically designed for this operation. The Change command is designed to be used for modifying existing geometry and is covered in Chapter 11.

You will now draw the centerlines for the hidden line holes with the current property settings (linetype hidden and color green). You may follow the coordinate input provided in the following exercise or use the dimensioned drawing at the start of the chapter (see fig. 4.1) to pick the starting and ending locations of the two lines. Using the pull-down or screen menu, select Draw and Line. Or you can type in the following at the command area:

Drawing the Centerlines

Command: **Line**	Starts the Line command
From point: **7,2.5**	
To point: **@4<90**	
To point: *Press Enter*	Ends the Line command
Command: *Press Enter*	Repeats the line command
Line From point: **10,2.5**	
To point: **@4<90**	
To point: *Press Enter*	

Your drawing should now show the two lines drawn in Linetype Hidden and color green as illustrated in figure 4.9.

Figure 4.9:
The two lines in Linetype Hidden.

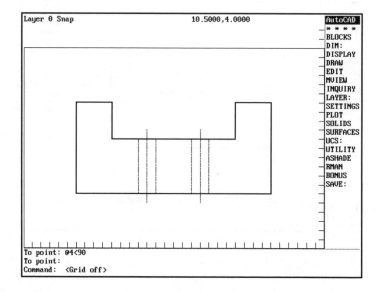

To change the properties of the two lines to make the appropriate centerlines, complete the following steps at the keyboard:

Changing the Two Lines to Red Centerlines

```
Command: Chprop
Select objects: 1 selected, 1 found Pick line 1 (see fig. 4.10)
Select objects: 1 selected, 1 found Pick line 2 (see fig. 4.10)
Select objects: Press Enter
Change what property (Color/LAyer/LType/Thickness)? C
New color <BYLAYER>: R
Change what property (Color/LAyer/LType/Thickness)? LT
New linetype <BYLAYER>: Center
Change what property (Color/LAyer/LType/Thickness)? Press Enter
```

As figure 4.11 illustrates, your drawing should now show the linetypes in center. Also, notice on your screen that their color is now red.

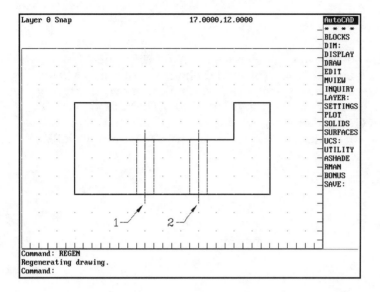

Figure 4.10:
Pick these two lines.

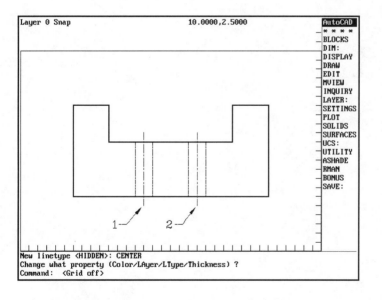

Figure 4.11:
The properties are changed.

To finish this lesson, type **End** at the following Command: prompt.

Your drawing is saved as PART2, and you exit the drawing editor.

Summary

This chapter has shown you how to use polylines to create wide lines, how to load and use various linetypes, and how to set and change entity properties. Polylines and polyline editing (Pedit) provide you with a wide range of drawing tools and will, therefore, be used often throughout *AutoCAD: Drafting and 3D Design*. You also set and changed entity properties. You should find that controlling entity properties will certainly enhance your AutoCAD drafting skills.

5

Drawing and Erasing Simple Entities

In this chapter:

- Establishing parameters and values for PART3
- Drawing the PART3 profile
- Drawing the circles
- Redrawing the screen
- Drawing arcs
- Using object selection and erasing techniques

Overview

When drafting, mistakes are commonly made. In traditional drafting, correcting mistakes required time-consuming, and often messy, processes to erase or clean up unwanted geometry. This could involve erasing entire lines, or small overlaps of lines, by using special tools such as erasing shields. AutoCAD's semi-automatic editing tools eliminate the need for erasers and all the other tools which were used for traditional drafting to trim and break lines.

AutoCAD has a very complete set of editing tools, but regardless of which tool is used, AutoCAD requires you to specify which entity or entities are to be edited by indicating a *selection set*. A selection set may be designated as a single entity, or as many entities as you wish. This process saves you a great deal of time by not having to erase entities one at a time. To assist you even more with the selection process, AutoCAD provides a wide range of techniques for choosing a selection set.

By becoming familiar with the selection set options, you will greatly enhance your drafting and designing efficiency. Chapter 5 guides you through the methods for selecting objects, as well as shows you how to easily undo a mistake, or any number of mistakes, you may have made. This chapter will show you how to use these powerful editing tools, as you create a single view drawing named PART3 and illustrated in figure 5.1.

Figure 5.1:
The completed PART3 drawing, which you will create in this chapter.

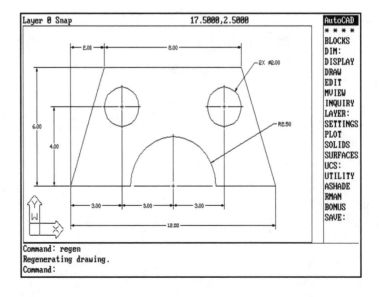

Establishing Parameters and Values for PART3

Remember that throughout the exercises in this textbook you are to press Enter after responding to a prompt. At the AutoCAD main menu, enter the drawing editor by doing the following steps:

```
Enter Selection: 1
Enter NAME of drawing: PART3
```

The AutoCAD drawing screen appears, and you can begin a new drawing.

The PART3 drawing uses the parameters shown in table 5.1. Although AutoCAD's automatic setup routine prepares the drawing sheet for you, it will be necessary that you set some of these parameters before starting the PART3 drawing.

Table 5.1
Parameters for the PART3 Drawing

Parameter	Setting
Axis	.5
Grid	1
Snap	.5
Units	Decimal 0.0000
Limits	0,0 to 17,11
Layer Name	0
State	Current
Color	7 (White)
Linetype	Continuous

To set up the drawing sheet, select BONUS from the screen menu and then select Mvsetup (you need to page to the Mvsetup option). Type **No** at the Enable Paper/Modelspace? <y> prompt. Now, select decimal from the Unit Type menu. Next, select FULL from the Decimal Scale menu and select B- 11x17 from the Sheet Size menu.

Now set the positioning tools: Snap, Grid, and Axis. At the Command: prompt, type **Snap** and then type **.5**. Type **Grid** and then type **1**. Finally, type **Axis** and type **.5**.

Drawing the PART3 Profile

You may follow the coordinate input provided in the next section or use the dimensioned drawing illustrated by figure 5.1 to pick the starting and ending locations for the lines that make up the drawing's profile.

Although you may use the pull-down menu by selecting Draw and then selecting Line or you may select the same choices from the screen menu, you are encouraged to do the following exercise from the keyboard. Complete the following steps to draw the polygon profile:

 If you enter a wrong value, simply press Backspace to fix it. If you have already pressed Enter or picked the wrong point, you can type **U** followed by pressing Enter or select Undo. In the Line command, U or Undo will remove the last line developed so you can simply continue from the previous point. You may undo all lines back to the original starting point.

Drawing the Profile

Command: **Line**	Starts the Line command
From point: **2.5,2.5**	Establishes absolute coordinate
To point: **@2,6**	Establishes relative coordinate
To point: **@8<0**	Establishes polar coordinate
To point: **@2,-6**	
To point: **@3.5<180**	
To point: **@2.5<90**	
To point: **@5<180**	
To point: **@2.5<-90**	
To point: **C**	Closes the polygon and ends the line command

Your drawing should now look like the object shown in figure 5.2.

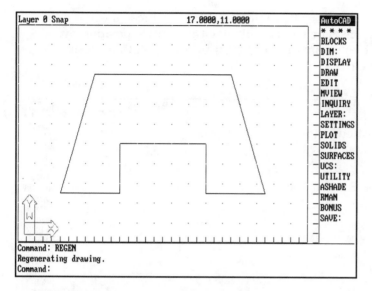

Figure 5.2:
PART3 profile.

Drawing the Circles

To add two circles to the drawing, either select the Draw and Circle commands from the pull-down or screen menus and then select Center and diameter, or follow these steps:

Drawing Circles

Command: *Type* **Circle**	Starts the Circle command
3P/2P/TTR/<Center point>: *Type* **5.5,6.5**	Specifies the circle's center point
Diameter/<Radius>: **D**	Selects Diameter option
Diameter: **2**	Establishes diameter of two

If you used the pull-down menu, the Circle command automatically repeats. If you selected the Circle command from the screen menu, or typed the Circle command, you can repeat the command by pressing either Enter or the Space bar.

Drawing the Second Circle

Command: *Press Enter or the Space bar*	Repeats the Circle command
3P/2P/TTR/<Center point>: *Type* **@6,0**	
Diameter/<Radius>: **D**	Selects the Diameter option
Diameter: **2**	Establishes a diameter of two

Note Remember, you can type specific radii or diameter values as you did in the preceding exercise, or you can display the relative position by toggling coords on by pressing F6 and then picking points to designate the size of the circles.

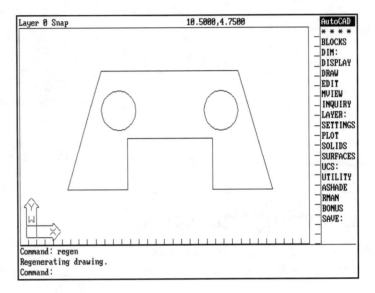

Figure 5.3:
PART3 drawing with the circles added.

Just to be safe, save the PART3 drawing now by typing the following at the Command: prompt.

    Command: **Save**

AutoCAD will now display the Save dialogue box. Press Enter or select OK and PART3 will be saved.

Redrawing the Screen

After you have developed or edited geometry, AutoCAD leaves small crosses called *blips* at each point of reference. Also, when you erase entities, AutoCAD temporarily removes grid dots and other entities that lie within the erasure zone. You can restore the drawing by using one of the following commands:

Redraw cleans up the current *viewport* (the screen's graphics area). *Redrawall* cleans up all viewports. Blips are removed and any entities or parts of entities that seem to have disappeared during editing are redrawn. Grid dots are redrawn if the Grid is on. These are transparent commands. (If the Grid is on, you can get the same effect by toggling the Grid by pressing F7 twice or by pressing Ctrl-G twice.)

Regen causes the current viewport to be regenerated (recalculated and redrawn); *Regenall* regenerates all viewports. When a drawing is regenerated, the data and geometry associated with all entities is recalculated. Regen and Regenall are not transparent commands. You can cancel a regeneration by typing Ctrl-C.

Regenauto enables you to control some (not all) regenerations. Some changes, such as block redefinitions, linetype scale changes, or redefined text styles, require a regeneration before they are made visible. Sometimes, particularly when making multiple changes, you do not want to wait for these regenerations. You can turn Regenauto off and use the Regen command to regenerate the screen when you are ready to look at the results.

To get rid of the blips left over from creating lines and circles, type the following command:

```
Command: Redraw
```

That's all there is to it. Remember that you could accomplish the same thing by toggling Grid off by pressing the F7 key twice. From this point on, you should redraw the screen whenever you feel it is necessary.

Drawing Arcs

The *Arc* command draws a circle segment in nearly any possible way. This command draws any segment of a circle greater than one degree and less than 360 degrees. Except for the Three-point option, arcs are constructed in a counterclockwise direction. An arc or line can be drawn immediately tangent to the last arc or line by defaulting its Start point: or From point: prompts. The default is three-point arc construction in which you pick three points that don't lie on a straight line, but you can use several other methods.

The order in which you pick the starting and ending point of an arc determines in which direction the arc is generated. You may, however, override this default by designating an arc's starting direction.

AutoCAD provides eleven different *methods* or techniques for drawing arcs. Some of these methods are illustrated in figure 5.4.

Pick points. Three points on the arc

SCE. Start point, Center, Endpoint

SCA. Start point, Center, included Angle

SCL. Start point, Center, Length of chord

SEA. Start point, Endpoint, included Angle

SER. Start point, Endpoint, Radius

SED. Start point, Endpoint, starting Direction

CSE. Center point, Start point, Endpoint

CSA. Center point, Start point, Angle

CSL. Center point, Start point, Length of chord

Enter. Continuation of previous line or arc

Arc options may be invoked by entering the following letters. Prompts indicate which options are available at each sequence of the Arc command.

A. Included Angle

C. Center

D. Starting Direction

E. Ending point

L. Length of chord

R. Radius

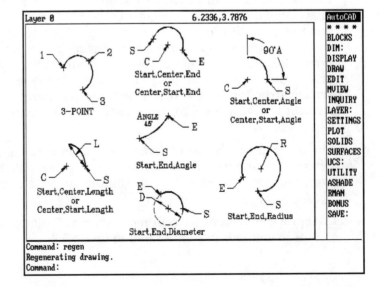

Figure 5.4:

Techniques for drawing arcs.

Make sure Snap is on. Then use the Center-Start-End method to draw the arc for this exercise. After invoking the Arc command, respond to the first prompt by establishing the center point and then entering the center coordinates. Next, you enter the starting point and then the ending point of the arc. Because arcs are drawn in AutoCAD counterclockwise, the arc's location is determined by the order of the starting point and ending point selections.

Drawing the Arc

Command: **ARC**   Begins the Arc command

Center/<Start point>: **C**   Activates center point

Center: **8.5,2.5**   Establishes center point of arc

Start point: *Pick at point 1 (see fig. 5.5) with your mouse*

Angle/Length of chord/<End point>: *Pick opposite side at point 2 (see fig. 5.5) with your mouse*

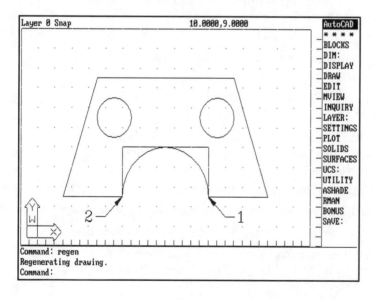

Figure 5.5:
PART3 drawing with the arc established.

Using Object Selection and Erasing Techniques

AutoCAD's editing commands correct mistakes. You can use the Erase command to remove incorrectly drawn or unwanted entities. Your drafting production will be greatly enhanced by understanding AutoCAD's Erase, Oops and other editing commands, as well as AutoCAD's entity selection options. AutoCAD's editing commands are located on the screen submenu named Edit and on the pull-down menu named Modify. By selecting either of these options, AutoCAD automatically pages to the available edit commands.

The simplest editing command is the Erase command. Erase deletes entities from the drawing. The only trick when using Erase is selecting the entities you want to erase. At the `Select Objects:` prompt, you decide which objects to select for editing. This editing procedure is common to most editing commands.

Applying AutoCAD's Object Selection

The basic concept of AutoCAD's object selection is the *selection set*, which consists of the group of objects that you select. After making your selections, press Enter to exit object selection and execute the editing command at hand.

There are several methods for selecting objects:

- **Pick Point.** Selects a single object (must be within the pickbox range, or pixel size, of the pick point)
- **Last.** Selects the last object created
- **Previous.** Selects all objects in the previously completed selection set
- **Window.** Selects all objects that are visibly contained within a window indicated by two opposite corner points
- **Crossing.** Selects all objects either within or crossing the window
- **Multiple.** Enables multiple selections by any method before adding them to the selection set
- **Add.** Adds the selections that follow to the selection set
- **Remove.** Removes the selections that follow from the selection set
- **Undo.** Undoes the previous selection operation (add or remove)
- **BOX.** Combines Window and Crossing for one selection (If you pick points left to right it works like Window, but if you pick right to left it works like Crossing.)
- **Single.** Exits Object Selection automatically after successful selection by any one of the above methods, eliminating the need to press Enter
- **Auto.** Combines Box and Pick Point for the selections that follow

You may use any combination of these modes when building a selection set. You need only enter the uppercase portion of the names. Most monitors distinguish between Window and Crossing by showing the crossing box with a dashed line and the window box with a solid line.

Each object selection returns a message like *n* found or *n* selected, *n* found as it adds entities to the selection set. When an entity has been selected, most monitors highlight it; however, the highlighting method varies. The highlighting can be a color change, or blinking lines, or dashed lines. Highlighting adds to the selection time, but you can turn it off when selecting complex objects. Use Setvar to set Highlight to 1 for on or 0 (zero) for off.

Although you can use Box, Single, and Auto manually, there is no real advantage to doing this. If you know what and how you want to select, you can enter W or C manually, as easily as Box or AU, and you can press Enter as easily as entering SI. Box, Single, and Auto are intended to be built into menu items to make object selection more automatic. For example, most pull-down Modify menu items use Single and Auto modes combined.

Combining Single and Auto modes works like this: if you pick a point that is on an entity, the entity is selected and object selection is completed without pressing Enter. But if you pick a point which is not on an entity, the program goes into Box mode, allowing either a Window or Crossing selection. The choice is determined by where you pick the second opposite corner point. If the second corner is to the right, AutoCAD attempts to select a Window. If the second corner is to the left, Autocad attempts a Crossing window. If the program fails to find an object, it repeats. As soon as any object is selected, the program completes and exits object selection.

 Sometimes Snap gets in the way of object selection, preventing you from getting the cursor right on or adjacent to the point or window you want to select. Toggle Snap off when needed but be sure to toggle it back on when drawing, or you may draw inaccurately.

Selecting Objects for Erasing

Try using Erase with several of the object selection modes in the PART3 drawing. Before you start, press F9 to turn off Snap.

Selecting and Erasing Entities

Command: **Erase**	Starts the Erase mode
Select objects: *Pick line 1 (see fig. 5.6)*	Selects first line for erasing
1 selected, 1 found	Indicates first line is highlighted
Select objects: *Pick line 2 (see fig. 5.6)*	Selects second line for erasing
1 selected, 1 found	Indicates second line is highlighted
Select objects: *Pick line 3 (see fig. 5.6)*	Selects third line for erasing
1 selected, 1 found	Indicates third line is highlighted
Select objects: *Press Enter*	Completes object selection and executes Erase command

---

Figure 5.6:
Erasing, the Pick Point technique.

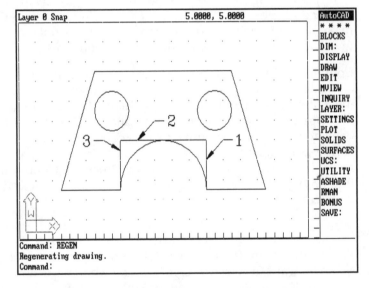

If the lines disappear, you have performed this exercise correctly.

Using Oops To Replace Mistaken Erasures

The three erased lines will be used again to demonstrate erasing with a Crossing selection set. Use the Oops command to bring these entities back. Oops restores the last entity, or group of entities, deleted by the most recent Erase command.

    Command: **Oops**

Notice that the notch lines are back in figure 5.7.

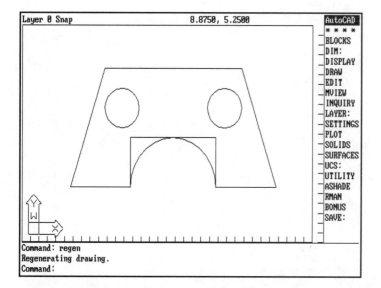

Figure 5.7:
Oops undoes the last command.

Using the Window and Crossing Options To Erase

When you erase using the Window option, only entities which are entirely within the window are erased. If an entity is only partially inside, it is not erased. When the Crossing option is used, all entities which intersect within the crossing window are erased whether or not they extend outside the crossing window.

To erase the two circles with the Window option, complete the following steps:

Using the Window Option To Erase Entities	
Command: **Erase**	Starts the Erase command
Select objects: **W**	Begins Window option
First corner: *Pick left point 1 (see fig. 5.8)*	
Other corner: *Drag and pick point 2 (see fig. 5.8)*	
2 found	Highlights the circles
Select objects: *Press Enter*	Ends selection set and circles disappear

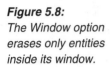

Figure 5.8:
The Window option erases only entities inside its window.

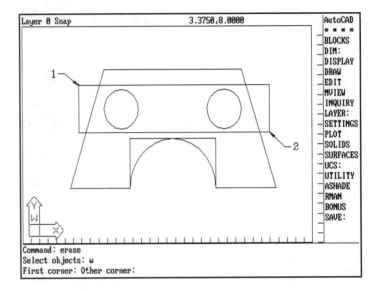

To select the three lines with the Crossing option, complete the following steps:

Using the Crossing Option To Erase Entities

Command: **Erase**	Starts Erase command
Select objects: **C**	Selects the lines with Crossing
First corner: *Pick right point 3 (see fig. 5.9)*	
Other corner: *Drag and pick point 4 (see fig. 5.9)*	
4 found	Highlights all three lines and the arc

Now, remove Arc from the selection set.

```
Select Objects: R
Click the pickbox on any part of the arc
Remove objects: Press Enter completes the object selection
and executes the Erase command.
```

Using the U, Undo, and Redo Commands

Although the selected circles and lines are gone, they can be brought back again. If Oops only steps back one Erase command, how do you get the previously erased lines and circles back? Use the U or Undo commands, which offer more flexibility and control in reversing commands. If you perform another command operation after incorrectly erasing entities, use the U and Undo commands.

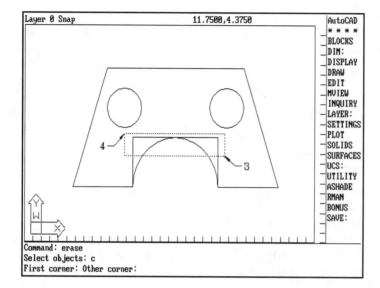

Figure 5.9:
The Crossing option erases entities that it contains or touches.

The *U* and *Undo* commands enable you to step back through your drawing, reversing previous commands or groups of commands. Undo keeps track of the previous commands in a temporary file. This file is cleared at the end of each drawing editor session or when you plot. U undoes a single command or group per execution. Undo offers additional controls.

The U command can undo one command at a time until your drawing is back to the state at which you started the current working session (or just after the last plot). Use this command to restore the notch lines by typing the following:

```
Command: U
ERASE Indicates that the erased notch lines are now restored (see fig. 5.10)
```

Repeat the U command to restore the two circles.

When U or Undo undoes a command (or group), the name of the command (or the word GROUP) being undone is displayed at the command prompt. A *group* can be a group of commands executed by a menu item, or it can be a group you create with the Undo options shown next. If you undo too much, you can use the Redo command.

The Undo command enables you to undo several commands at one time, and provides special functions such as:

- **Auto-Undo.** Used to group commands in menus
- **Back.** Undoes back to the last marked place in the drawing

- **Control.** Controls the range of the Undo and U commands: One only allows one command to be undone; All is the normal default; and None disables U and Undo
- **End.** Ends a grouping of commands
- **Group.** Starts grouping a series of commands
- **Mark.** Establishes a marked position in the drawing for the Back option to find
- **<Number>.** Specifies the number of preceding operations to be undone as one step

An outstanding drafting feature of the Undo command is the Mark option. If you have completed one phase of a drafting project and are about to begin a new one, you can set a mark. Then if the next phase is experimental, or does not work out, you can use the Back option to go back to the place in your drawing where you set the mark. Be careful though; without the mark, you may go back to the beginning of the current drawing session.

Redo simply reverses the last U or Undo command. A group, the Undo Back, or <Number> options are treated as a single Redo operation.

Undo and Redo are helpful editing tools to have in your AutoCAD tool kit. Apply them as needed in your drafting projects. There will be many occasions when you try a command or a series of commands that do not turn out the way you would like. This is when the U, Undo, and Redo commands prove invaluable.

Erase one last time the three notch lines to complete the drawing. Use any of the erase options which have been discussed in this chapter. When finished, your drawing should look like figure 5.10. To end this lesson do the following steps:

    Command: **End**

Your drawing is saved as PART3, and you exit the drawing editor.

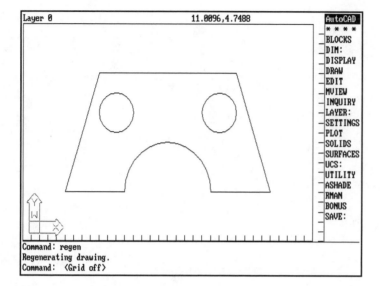

Figure 5.10:
*The edited PART3
drawing.*

Summary

This chapter showed you how to use the Arc command and how to perform various erasing options. As with all drafting, erasing must be done at one time or another. You are now prepared to use the Erase, Oops, (U)ndo, and Redo commands when necessary.

Chapter 6 introduces you to some more drafting commands and explains how to control the way drawings are displayed on the screen in TILEMODE model space.

6

Drafting In TILEMODE Model Space

In this chapter:

- Setting up multiple viewports in TILEMODE model space
- Controlling the screen display with Pan and Zoom
- Drawing the PART4 profile
- Drawing polygons
- Saving and restoring views
- Saving and restoring viewport configurations

119

Overview

As you have discovered when using AutoCAD, it is sometimes difficult to distinguish details of drawings displayed on a monitor. To overcome this problem, AutoCAD can magnify (zoom) and displace (pan) images. When objects are too large to display in their entirety at high magnification, AutoCAD enables you to set up multiple viewports (windows) in the drawing editor. Viewports may be either TILEMODE model space viewports or non-tilemode paper space viewports. TILEMODE viewports are one or more drawing editor windows which are joined along common edges and always fill the drawing editor portion of the display.

The benefits of using multiple viewports include the ability to set parameters differently in each viewport. For example, you could be working on a long drawing such as a jet aircraft. If you magnified (zoomed) it, you could only display a small portion of the craft at one time. Using viewports, you could set up multiple viewing areas, each displaying a different portion of the craft. Additionally, you may set the parameters, such as the grid spacing and snap spacing, differently for each viewport. To make moving around on your drawing even easier, AutoCAD lets you save and restore viewport configurations and specific views within a single viewport. You can save any number of viewports and single views; this technique makes your drafting and designing time more productive.

In Chapter 6, you will use these screen control tools, and a few new drawing commands, to create a new part, PART4, as illustrated in figure 6.1. You will work with polygons and various options for displaying your drawings in TILEMODE model space.

Figure 6.1:
The PART4 drawing.

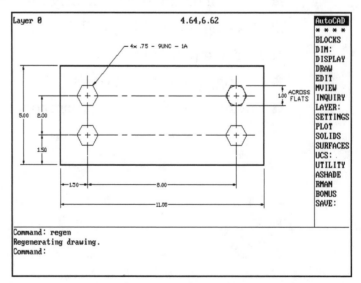

AutoCAD enables you to work in two different drawing spaces, model space and paper space. Model space is a 2D or 3D environment in which TILEMODE is on. You have done all your drawing so far in model space. All of AutoCAD's drawing, editing, and annotation commands are active within TILEMODE model space. Paper space is a 2D-only display format in which you can arrange, annotate, and plot multiple views of your drawings. Paper space and model space with TILEMODE off will be discussed in Chapter 7.

Beginning the Drawing

 Note Remember to press Enter after typing any information for which you are prompted.

Enter the drawing editor by beginning a new drawing at the main menu. Type **1** at the `Enter Selection:` prompt, and then type **PART4** at the prompt asking for the name of the drawing.

The PART4 drawing uses the parameters shown in table 6.1. Most of the parameters except Limits, Grid, and Snap are defaults, so you do not need to set them. AutoCAD's automatic setup routine prepares the drawing sheet. In Release 10, the root menu contains the Setup routine.

Table 6.1
Parameters for the PART4 Drawing

Parameter	Setting
Grid	.5
Snap	.25
Units	Decimal 0.0000
Limits	0,0 to 17,11
Layer Name	0
State	Current
Color	7 (White)
Linetype	Continuous
TILEMODE	1 - Model Space

Use AutoCAD's automatic setup routine in TILEMODE on (model space) to prepare the drawing sheet. Set up an 11x17 B-size drawing sheet, with decimal units, in full scale. If you need assistance with this procedure, refer to Chapter 3.

The Mvsetup option works differently with TILEMODE off. TILEMODE off and its counterparts, paper space and model space, are covered in Chapter 7. Using Mvsetup with TILEMODE off will be discussed in Chapter 15.

Setting Up Multiple Viewports in TILEMODE Model Space

You need to set up multiple viewports in TILEMODE model space to develop your PART4 drawing. A *viewport* is the active portion of the drawing screen. So far you have been using the default single viewport.

The *Vports* command enables you to divide your screen into several viewing areas. Each viewport can display a different view of your drawing. Each viewport contains its own drawing display area and can have independent magnification, viewpoint, snap, grid, viewres, ucsicon, dview, and isometric settings. You can independently execute the Zoom, Regen, and Redraw commands in each viewport. You may define up to four viewports on the 640K version and 16 viewports on the 386 version at any one time.

You can create TILEMODE model space viewports using the following Vports options:

- **Save.** Assigns a name to the current viewport configuration and preserves all associated information. You may use names with up to 31 characters. The name may contain letters, digits, and the dollar sign ($), hyphen (-), and underscore (_).
- **Restore.** Redisplays a previously saved viewport configuration.
- **Delete.** Deletes a named viewport configuration.
- **Join.** Merges to adjacent viewports.
- **SIngle.** Returns you to a single viewport. The single viewport will display the last current viewport.
- **?.** Displays the identification numbers of the active viewport configuration. You also may list all saved viewport configurations.

To divide the screen into two viewports, as shown in figure 6.2, either access the Settings and Vports commands from the screen menu or type in the following at the command area:

Setting Multiple Viewports

Command: **Vports**

Save/Restore/Delete/Join/SIngle/?/2/<3>/4: **2**

Horizontal/<Vertical>: *Press Enter*

You will develop the polygon bolt heads in the close-up (zoomed) viewport while you view the entire drawing in the other.

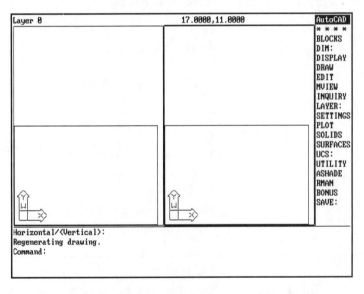

Figure 6.2:
Two viewports, with a border in each.

When you first set multiple viewports, they all display the current drawing—in this case, your B-size border. Only one viewport is active, however. To activate a viewport, click on it with your mouse; AutoCAD displays a bold border around it. The active viewport displays the cursor, and the nonactive viewport(s) displays an arrow.

Many of AutoCAD's commands may be started in one viewport and continued in a different one. You can select the Line command and attach a line's starting point to an entity in the active viewport for example, and then activate a viewport with a higher magnification (zoom) and attach the endpoint of the line to an easily-recognized position. This is a useful technique in 2D and 3D computer drafting.

While the Vports command subdivides the current viewport, the Join command merges two viewports into one rectangular viewport. You can combine these two commands to create non-standard viewport configurations. Viewport settings also can be named, saved, and restored so you do not have to rebuild a particular viewport configuration.

Positioning tools may be set to different parameters in each viewport. This enables you to set the appropriate positioning tools regardless of the various zoom specifications.

Now that you have created two viewports, you can set different positioning tools in each. Make sure the left viewport is current by moving the arrow to the left viewport and clicking the mouse. Then follow these steps:

Setting Snap and Grid in Two Viewports

Command: **Snap**	Starts the Snap command
Snap spacing or ON/OFF/Aspect/Rotate/Style <0.2500>: **.5**	Sets left viewport snap
Command: **Grid**	Starts the Grid command
Grid spacing (x) or ON/OFF/Snap/Aspect <0.5000>: **1**	Sets left viewport grid
Now, move arrow to right viewport and click to make it current	
Command: **Snap**	Starts the Snap command
Snap spacing or ON/OFF/Aspect/Rotate/Style <0.5000>: **.25**	Sets right viewport snap
Command: **Grid**	Starts the Grid command
Grid spacing (x) or ON/OFF/Snap/Aspect <0.5000>: **.5**	Sets right viewport grid

Your drawing should display a different grid spacing in the two viewports as illustrated in figure 6.3.

Controlling the Screen Display with Pan and Zoom

As your drawings become larger and more detailed, you will need to manipulate the magnification and locations of drawings on the screen. Two commands that perform these operations are Pan and Zoom.

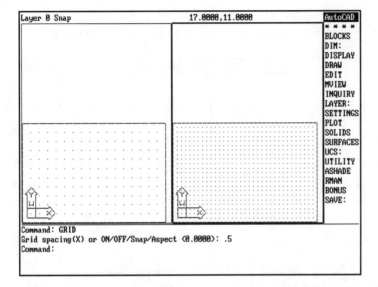

Figure 6.3:
Two viewports with
different parameters.

Displacing the Drawing Using Pan

If you think of the viewport as a window to your drawing, think of the Pan command as moving the drawing around behind that window. The *Pan* command enables you to scroll around the screen without altering the current zoom ratio. It is similar to repositioning paper on a drafting board to access a different drawing part. You do not physically move entities or change your drawing limits; you move your display window across your drawing. The default setting provides a displacement in relative coordinates.

The Pan command uses the displacement value between two points. You can enter the points from the keyboard or select them with your mouse. The first point of displacement is where you move the drawing from and the second point of displacement is where you move the drawing to. The cursor trails a line from the first point, showing the pan path as you move to the second point.

The following exercise shows you how to use the Pan command to reposition the border drawing in the center of the left viewport:

Panning the Drawing Up

Command: **Pan**

Displacement: *Click at the center of the border area*

Second point: *Click at the center of the left viewport*

Regenerating drawing.

The border drawing should be centered in the *left* viewport as illustrated in figure 6.4. Now use Zoom to move in for some close work in the right viewport.

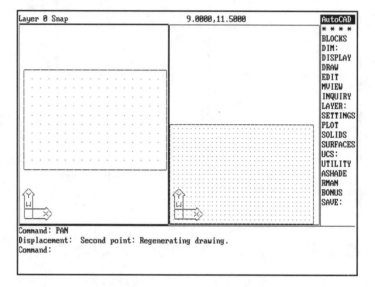

Figure 6.4:
Pan repositions the border.

Taking a Closer Look Using Zoom

The *Zoom* command magnifies or reduces any part of an active viewport. It is generally used to increase the viewing resolution of drawings. You will find it is easier to draw or edit specific entities when a part of the drawing is magnified, especially if your mouse is sensitive and you find it difficult to control the pointer when doing work in small, localized areas of a drawing. You can use the Zoom command in the following ways:

■ **Number.** Magnifies to a specified scale, relative to the Zoom All view.

■ **NumberX.** Magnifies to a specified scale, relative to the current viewport. (3X is three times as large as the previous display, for example.)

■ **NumberXP.** Magnifies a current TILEMODE off model space view relative to the paper space scale. (2XP is two times paperspace scale.)

■ **Zoom All.** Displays the entire drawing or limits, whichever is larger.

■ **Zoom Extents.** Displays the entire drawing as large as possible, ignoring limits.

■ **Zoom Window.** Displays the rectangular area defined by two diagonally opposite corner points. Once you pick the first corner of the window, you find a box attached to the cursor. Drag the box to enclose the portion of the drawing to be magnified, and then pick the second corner.

■ **Zoom Center.** Magnifies relative to a center point and view height.

- **Zoom Left.** Magnifies relative to a user-selected left corner point and view height.
- **Zoom Previous.** Restores the previous zoom. It can be repeated up to 10 views back.
- **Zoom Dynamic.** Interactively displays the entire drawing as you choose a window to use the Zoom command.
- **Zoom Vmax.** Backs out as far as possible on the current viewport without forcing a complete regeneration of your drawing.

The Zoom Center and Zoom Left commands enable you to default to the current center or left corner point by pressing Enter. They then present the current view height as a default. Activate the *right* viewport, and then use the Zoom Center command as follows:

Using Zoom Center

```
Command: Zoom
All/Center/Dynamic/Extents/Left/Previous/Vmax/Window/<Scale(X/XP)>: C
Center point: 4,5.5
Magnification or Height <21.2500>: 12
```

Your screen should resemble figure 6.5.

The right viewport is the primary working viewport. This places the magnified image of PART4 close to the screen menu where selections are easy to make. You can watch the entire drawing update in the left viewport after each operation.

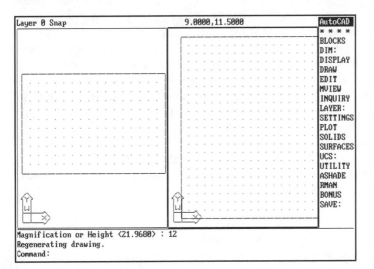

Figure 6.5:
Right viewport zoomed.

Drawing the PART4 Profile

Now draw the object profile in the *left* viewport and watch what happens in the right viewport. Use the Polyline command to make a wide object line.

You may follow the coordinate input provided in the following exercise or use the dimensioned drawing shown in figure 6.1 to pick the starting and ending locations for the lines which make up the drawing's profile.

Entering Coordinates for the PART4 Profile

```
Command: Pline

From point: 3,3

Current line-width is 0.00

Arc/Close/Halfwidth/Length/Undo/Width/<Endpoint of line>: W

Starting width <0.0000>: .0325

Ending width <0.0325>: Press Enter

Arc/Close/Halfwidth/Length/Undo/Width/<Endpoint of line>: @5<90

Arc/Close/Halfwidth/Length/Undo/Width/<Endpoint of line>: @11<0

Arc/Close/Halfwidth/Length/Undo/Width/<Endpoint of line>: @5<270

Arc/Close/Halfwidth/Length/Undo/Width/<Endpoint of line>: C
```

Your drawing should now be displayed in the two viewports as shown in figure 6.6.

Next, use the Zoom Dynamic command to magnify the object profile in the left viewport. *Zoom Dynamic* interactively magnifies or reduces any part of the drawing, using three boxes and an hourglass to cue you for input. The viewport temporarily redraws to show the extents of the entire drawing. The four corner markers—illustrated in figure 6.7—indicate the currently generated area within which you can pan and zoom without a regeneration. The hourglass comes on to tell you when a regeneration is required. The fixed solid box is the current view box. Use the moveable solid new view box to show where you want to go. It is initially sized and located to duplicate the current view box. When the X displays at the center of the new view box, you can drag its position. When an arrow displays at the side of the new view box, you can drag its size. It always resizes in proportion to the viewport. You can switch between the X to move and the arrow to resize by clicking your mouse. You exit the command and execute the zoom by pressing Enter or the Spacebar.

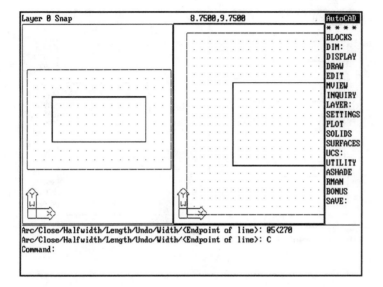

Figure 6.6:
PART4 profile.

This dynamic operation is an excellent tool for simultaneous zoom and pan operations. Activate the left viewport, and then follow these steps to fill the left viewport with the object profile. Issue the Zoom command. Select the Dynamic option from the `All/Center/Dynamic/Extents/Left/Previous/Vmax/Window/<Scale(X/XP)>:` prompt. Then click to get the resizing arrow (see fig. 6.8). Drag to just larger than the width of the object profile (see fig. 6.9) and click to get the X to move. Move side to side and watch the hourglass. Repeat the resizing if needed to fill the box with the object profile. Center the box on the profile and press Enter to execute the zoom (see fig. 6.10).

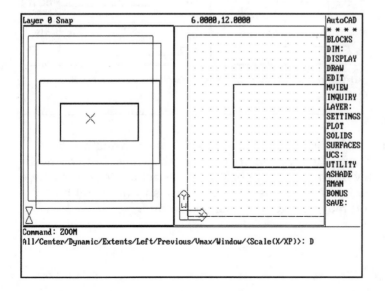

Figure 6.7:
The Zoom dynamic screen.

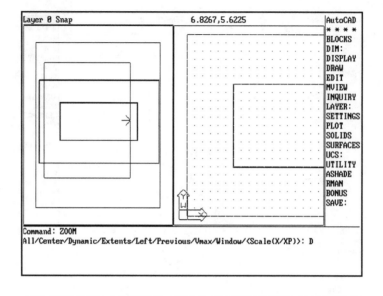

Figure 6.8:
Changing the new view box size.

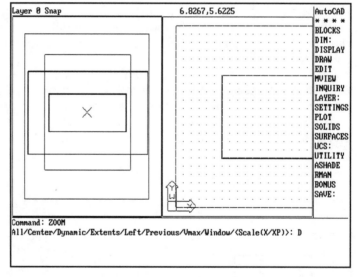

Figure 6.9:
Locating the new view box.

While the Zoom Dynamic selection screen is displayed, your drawing will be redrawing. This may take some time with more complex drawings, but you need not wait for the entire drawing to regenerate before you select a Zoom Dynamic new view box size and position. As soon as you can establish where and how large you wish to zoom, you may execute the Zoom command.

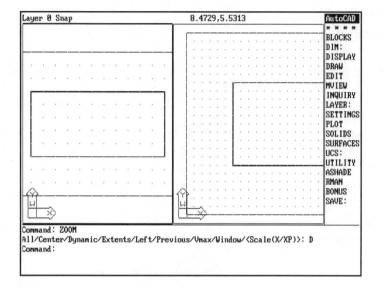

Figure 6.10:
The resulting display.

Drawing Polygons

Now you will add four hexagon bolt heads to the drawing using variations of the Polygon command.

Regular polygons are geometric figures which have three or more sides of equal length and equal interior angles. Polygons actually are a zero-width closed polyline. As such, a polygon may be edited using the Pedit options which are covered more thoroughly in Chapter 15.

The *Polygon* command draws 2D regular (all sides equal) polygons from 3 to 1,024 sides. The size of the polygon is determined by specifying the radius of a circle in which the polygon is inscribed (inside), or circumscribed (outside), or by specifying the length of one of the polygon's sides. Polygons are closed polylines.

It is most common for polygons, such as bolts and nuts, to be called out by the diameter dimension across their flats. If this is the dimensioning information you are provided, then select the circumscribed method of construction. If you are provided with the dimension across the corners, then select the inscribed method.

You can set the pull-down menu to develop polygons using preset parameters. You will use this technique later; for now, select `Polygon` from either the Draw pull-down or screen menu or enter the Polygon command at the keyboard.

Now construct the first hexagonal polygon using the circumscribed method (across the flats). Make the *right* viewport active and follow these steps:

Constructing a Polygon

Command: **Polygon**	Starts the Polygon command
Number of sides: **6**	Selects six sides
Edge/<Center of Polygon>: *Type* **4.5,4.5** *or pick equivalent point with mouse*	Selects starting point
Inscribed in circle/Circumscribed about circle (I/C): **C**	Selects circumscribed method
Radius of circle: **.5**	Establishes radius

Now press Enter to return to the Command: prompt and try the inscribed method (across the corners).

Command: **Polygon**	Repeats the polygon command
Number of sides: **6**	Selects six sides
Edge/<Center of Polygon>: *Type* **4.5,6.5** *or pick equivalent point with mouse*	Selects starting point
Inscribed in circle/Circumscribed about circle (I/C): **I**	Selects inscribed method
Radius of circle: **.5774**	Establishes radius

Your drawing should now resemble that in figure 6.11.

Save the right viewport as a view so that you can easily recall it.

Saving and Restoring Views

As the drawing becomes complex, you want to eliminate unnecessary regenerations. You can substitute the Pan and Zoom commands you just performed with a single View command.

 The *View* command enables you to save, name, and restore the current display or a windowed area in either TILEMODE model space or paperspace. The view name can be up to 31 characters.

Save the left part of your display as a view named Left. Then, after you pan to the right side of the part, you can restore your Left view, eliminating the need for the Pan command.

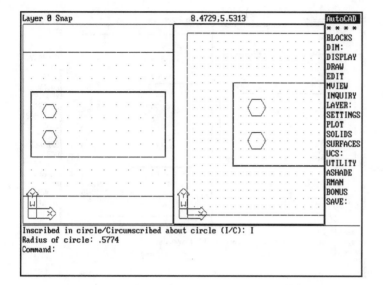

Figure 6.11:
Two hexagonal polygons
are drawn.

Make sure your *right* viewport is current and follow these steps at the keyboard:

▶ ## Saving the Left View

Command: **View**

?/Delete/Restore/Save/Window: **S**

View name to save: **Left**

With the Left view saved, pan across to the right side of the profile and draw the other two hexagonal polygons, as shown by figure 6.12, by completing the following steps:

▶ ## Panning to the Right

Command: **Pan**

Displacement: *Pick a point at the right side of the viewport*

Second point: *Pick a point at the left side of the viewport*

Regenerating drawing.

Figure 6.12:
The panned right viewport.

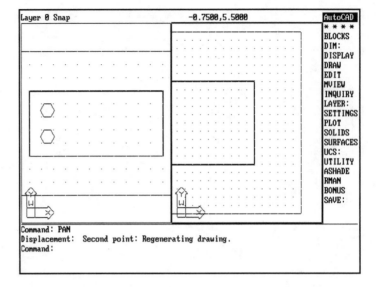

Now generate the two remaining hexagonal polygons using either the pull-down or screen menu. If your system does not support AUI, refer to the earlier sequence for developing polygons and use the keyboard.

The AutoCAD pull-down menu was developed recognizing that many drafting operations are performed repeatedly. With polygons, for example, you can set the parameters for a running polygon. AutoCAD sets these parameters through a series of prompts. Select `Polygon Creation` from the Options pull-down menu and follow these steps:

Setting the Polygon Creation Options

Enter default number of polygon sides: **6**

6

Command:

Inscribe or Circumscribe polygons (I/C): **C**

"C"

Select Draw from the pull-down menu and then click on Polygon. Do the following steps:

Polygon Number of sides: 6

Edge/<Center of polygon>: **12.5,4.5**

Inscribed in circle/Circumscribed about circle (I/C):

C

Radius of circle: **.5**

> ### Setting the Polygon Creation Options—continued
>
> The command repeats until another selection or cancelled.
>
> Edge/<Center of polygon>: **12.5,6.5**
>
> Inscribed in circle/Circumscribed about circle (I/C):
>
> C
>
> Radius of circle: **.5**
>
> Edge/<Center of polygon>: *Press Ctrl-C to cancel*

Your drawing should now resemble figure 6.13.

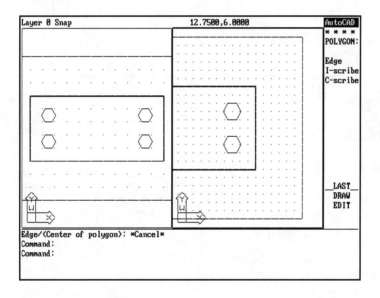

Figure 6.13:
All four polygons are now developed.

Once AutoCAD has regenerated a view of the drawing, you can zoom to smaller views and pan (move the view from side to side) within that regenerated area without having to regenerate the drawing again. Panning and zooming then occur at redraw (redisplay without recalculation) speed, which is much faster than regeneration.

Now restore the left half view which you saved earlier by typing **View** at the Command: prompt. Type **R** for Restore and type **Left** at the View name to restore: prompt.

Your screen should resemble figure 6.14.

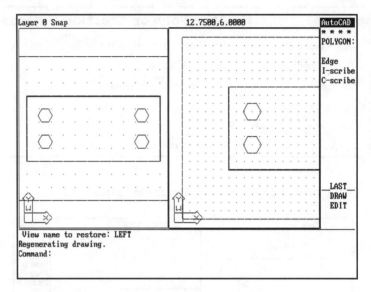

Figure 6.14:
The left view is restored.

Saving and Restoring Viewport Configurations

It is time-consuming to set up viewport configurations. In many cases, each viewport will have different positioning parameters, zooms, layers displayed, and display various parts of your drawing. Each of these steps is intricate, and to redo them would waste your time. Therefore, before leaving TILEMODE model space, you should save this viewport configuration.

Viewport configurations may be saved and restored at any time. To save the current configuration, follow these steps at the keyboard:

Saving and Returning Viewport Configurations

Command: **Vports**

Save/Restore/Delete/Join/SIngle/?/2/<3>/4: **S**

Name of viewport to save: **2View**

Now return to a single viewport configuration. Make sure your *left* viewport is current and follow these steps:

Command: **Vports**

Save/Restore/Delete/Join/SIngle/?/2/<3>/4: **SI**

Your drawing screen should resemble figure 6.15.

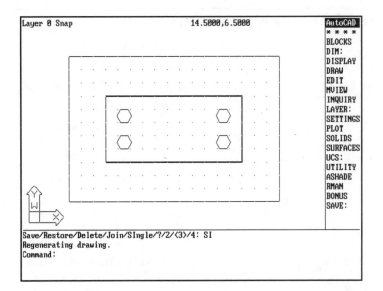

Figure 6.15:
Back to a single viewport.

Now restore your 2View viewport configuration, by typing in the following:

Restoring a Viewport Configuration

Command: **Vports**

Save/Restore/Delete/Join/SIngle/?/2/<3>/4: **R**

Name of viewport to restore: **2View**

Your screen should display the 2View viewport configuration again.

By using a combination of saved viewports and views, you can efficiently, with few screen regenerations, name your viewport configurations and views so that they will be easily remembered and recognized. As the number of saved viewports and views increases, however, remember that you can type **?** to see the list. The view list also designates whether a view is saved in (M)odel space or (P)aperspace.

Viewport and view parameters are saved with the drawing file. They will be maintained if it becomes necessary to edit your existing drawing. You can display this information by completing the following steps:

Displaying the Viewport and View Lists

Command: **View**	Starts the View command
?/Delete/Restore/Save/Window: **?**	Asks to see list
View(s) to list <*>: *Press Enter*	Displays a list (see fig. 6.16)
Command: *Press F1*	Returns to graphics screen
Command: **Vports**	Starts the Viewports command
Save/Restore/Delete/Join/SIngle/?/2/<3>/4: **?**	Asks to see list
Viewport configuration(s) to list <*>: *Press Enter*	Displays entire list (see fig. 6.16)
Command: *Press F1*	Returns to graphics screen

Now save your PART4 drawing and exit the drawing editor by typing **End** at the Command: prompt.

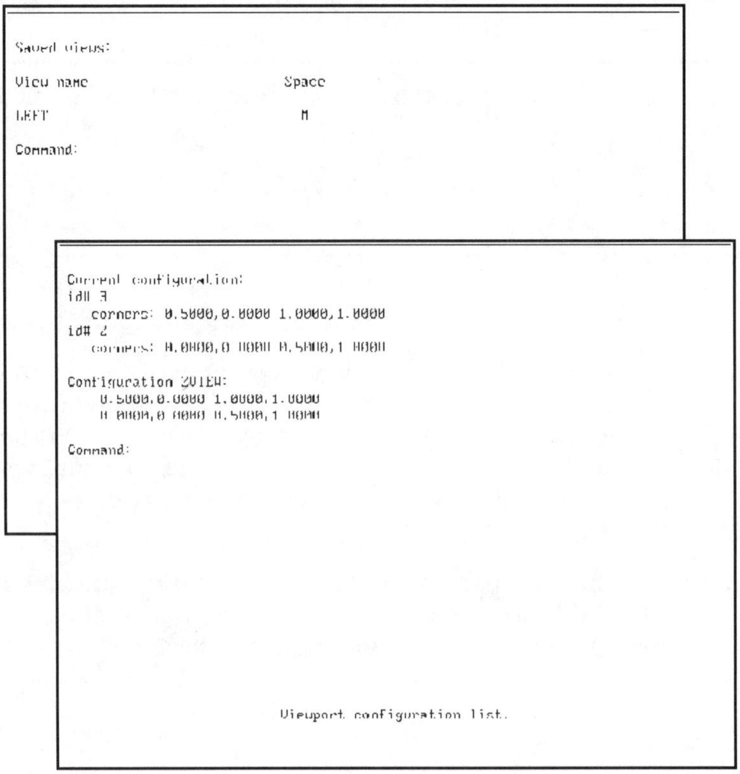

Figure 6.16:
View list and Viewport configuration list.

```
Saved views:

View name              Space
LEFT                    M

Command:
```

```
Current configuration:
id# 3
    corners: 0.5000,0.0000 1.0000,1.0000
id# 2
    corners: 0.0000,0.0000 0.5000,1.0000

Configuration 201EW:
    0.5000,0.0000 1.0000,1.0000
    0.0000,0.0000 0.5000,1.0000

Command:
```

Viewport configuration list.

Summary

This chapter showed you how to control your screen display and drawing views in TILEMODE model space. You also learned the use of the Polygon command for developing any regular polygon which has from 3 to 1,024 sides. You should find the Polygon command a very useful tool when developing bolts, nuts, and other polygon-shaped objects.

In Chapter 7 you will learn to control your display in paper space. You will also learn how to prepare the paper space for display for scaling your drawings and plotting multiple views.

7

DRAFTING IN PAPER SPACE

In this chapter:

- Adding ellipses
- Using paper space tools for drafting
- Magnifying objects relative to the paper space scale
- Stretching and moving entities
- Using paper space viewports to create drawings
- Plotting your drawings

Overview

AutoCAD's Release 11 introduced paper space, a new drawing environment designed to assist you in organizing your drawing or "drawing sheets" for output to hard copy. Paper space is also termed non-tilemode when TILEMODE is off. In Chapter 6, you created multiple viewports in TILEMODE, but these viewports had to have common edges and always filled the drawing editor. Paper space viewports, on the other hand, can be positioned virtually any where on the drawing editor of the screen. Paper space viewports can be any size, they can overlap, and they may even be edited in different ways.

When you originally create paper space viewports, they are created in an environment or drawing world which is separate from AutoCAD's "common" drawing environment. Most drawings are created in AutoCAD's model space. In fact, when you first enter AutoCAD, you enter TILEMODE model space. When you switch to paper space, you are no longer in model space, although model space is also available in paper space. There are many benefits of working with TILEMODE off, some of which include the capability of creating drawing sheets with multi-detail views in user desired locations and scales.

This chapter's exercises show you how to create a single new drawing and display it in multiple paper space viewports. You will learn how to edit geometry efficiently, how to switch back and forth between tilemode and non-tilemode as easily as one-two-three, and how to use paper space as a tool to create plot-ready drawings.

Establishing Parameters and Values for PART5

The following exercises step you through the use of AutoCAD commands to create a single view drawing—named PART5 and illustrated in figure 7.1.

Remember that throughout the textbook exercises you are to press Enter after responding to a prompt. At the AutoCAD main menu, enter the drawing editor by doing the following steps:

Beginning the PART5 Drawing

```
Enter Selection: 1
Enter NAME of drawing: PART5
```

The AutoCAD drawing screen appears, and you can begin a new drawing.

The PART5 drawing uses the parameters shown in table 7.1. The units are default settings, so you do not need to set them. AutoCAD's automatic setup routine prepares the drawing sheet. If you think that you need to prepare the drawing sheet anyway, refer to Chapter 3.

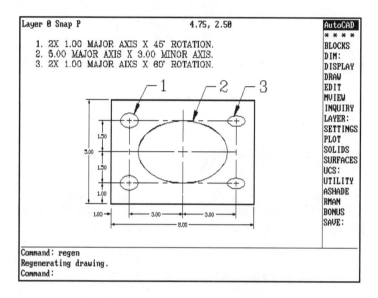

Figure 7.1:
The completed PART5 drawing, which you will create in this chapter.

Table 7.1
Parameters for the PART5 Drawing

Parameter	Setting
Grid	.5
Snap	.25
Units	Decimal 0.0000
Limits	0,0 to 12,9
Layer Name	0
State	Current
Color	7 (White)
Linetype	Continuous

At this point you are in AutoCAD's TILEMODE model space. While you are here, set up a few parameters and develop a portion of your PART5 drawing. Then you will switch to paper space and continue the exercise.

Set the positioning tools in the single viewport, as follows:

Setting Snap and Grid

Command: **Snap**

Snap spacing or ON/OFF/Aspect/Rotate/Style <1.0000>: **.25**

Command: **Grid**

Grid spacing (X) or ON/OFF/Snap/Aspect <0.0000>: **.5**

Now you will draw the object profile, using the Polyline command to make a wide object line.

Drawing the Object Profile

You can follow the coordinate input provided in the exercise that follows, or re-fer to the dimensioned drawing at the start of this chapter and pick the starting and ending locations for the lines that make up the drawing's profile:

Coordinates for the PART5 Profile

Command: **Pline**

From point: **2,2**

Current line-width is 0.00

Arc/Close/Halfwidth/Length/Undo/Width/<Endpoint of line>: **W**

Starting width <0.0000>: **.0325**

Ending width <0.0325>: *Press Enter*

Arc/Close/Halfwidth/Length/Undo/Width/<Endpoint of line>: **@5<90**

Arc/Close/Halfwidth/Length/Undo/Width/<Endpoint of line>: **@8<0**

Arc/Close/Halfwidth/Length/Undo/Width/<Endpoint of line>: **@5<270**

Arc/Close/Halfwidth/Length/Undo/Width/<Endpoint of line>: **C**

Your drawing now should resemble figure 7.2.

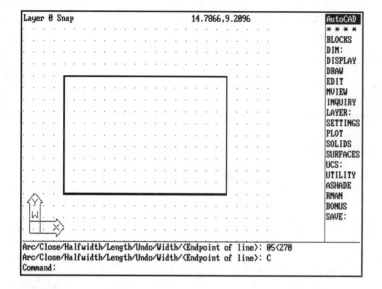

Figure 7.2:
The PART5 profile.

Adding Ellipses

Next you will add an elliptical hole in the center of PART5. If you view a circle from any angle, other than perpendicular to its axes, the viewed shape is called an ellipse. AutoCAD provides several ways to specify the dimensions of an ellipse. Ellipses are commonly defined by their distance across the major axis and its amount of rotation. AutoCAD also enables you to define ellipses by their axis and eccentricity, and center and two axes methods.

The *Ellipse* command provides several methods for constructing ellipses. The default setting assumes a first axis defined by `Axis endpoint 1` and an `Axis endpoint 2`; the other axis distance is defined as half the length of the other axis.

Use AutoCAD's default settings for generating the large elliptical hole in the part, as follows:

Drafting an Ellipse

Command: **Ellipse**

<Axis endpoint 1>/Center: **3.5,4.5**

Axis endpoint 2: **@5<0**

<Other axis distance>/Rotation: **@1.5<0**

Your drawing should display the ellipse, as shown in figure 7.3.

Figure 7.3:
PART5 with an elliptical hole.

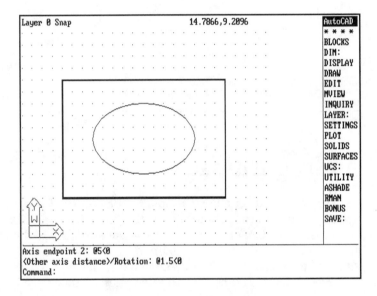

```
Layer 0 Snap                      14.7866,9.2096        AutoCAD
                                                        * * * *
                                                        BLOCKS
                                                        DIM:
                                                        DISPLAY
                                                        DRAW
                                                        EDIT
                                                        MVIEW
                                                        INQUIRY
                                                        LAYER:
                                                        SETTINGS
                                                        PLOT
                                                        SOLIDS
                                                        SURFACES
                                                        UCS:
                                                        UTILITY
                                                        ASHADE
                                                        RMAN
                                                        BONUS
                                                        SAVE:

Axis endpoint 2: @5<0
<Other axis distance>/Rotation: @1.5<0
Command:
```

Note The Ellipse command approximates an ellipse by drawing a polyline composed of short arc segments. You thus can edit an ellipse using the Pedit command.

Using Paper Space Tools for Drafting

Paper space provides tools for arranging, annotating, and plotting various views of your drawings. Paper space also provides a means for developing virtually any custom viewport configuration for model space drafting that you might need.

Setting TILEMODE for Paper Space

Command: **TILEMODE**

New value for Tilemode <1>: **0**

Entering Paper space.

Use Mview to insert Model space viewports.

Regenerating drawing.

Notice the new paper space icon in the lower left corner of figure 7.4.

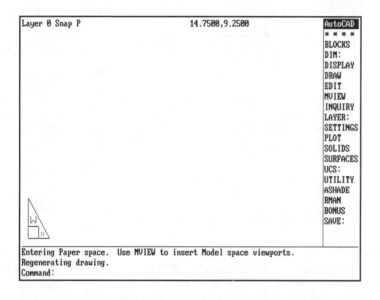

Figure 7.4:
Your drawing disappears and the paper space icon is displayed.

Creating Viewports in Paper Space

After you entered paper space, your drawing should have disappeared from the paper space screen. Remember that your drawing was created in TILEMODE model space. To redisplay it in paper space, you need to create a MetaView (Mview) of the most recent TILEMODE model space viewport(s).

The *Mview* command operates in paper space when TILEMODE is off and provides several methods for creating and controlling new viewports. If you invoke the Mview command in model space, AutoCAD automatically switches to paper space until the command sequence is completed. Metaviews can be created and controlled by using various options.

Create a Metaview to fit into the displayed paper space area, as follows:

Creating a Mview

Command: **Mview**

ON/OFF/Hideplot/Fit/2/3/4/Restore/<First Point>: **F**

Regenerating drawing.

Your PART5 drawing is redisplayed in paper space. Notice the paper space icon in the lower left corner of the display. Your drawing should resemble figure 7.5.

Figure 7.5:
Your drawing reappears in paper space.

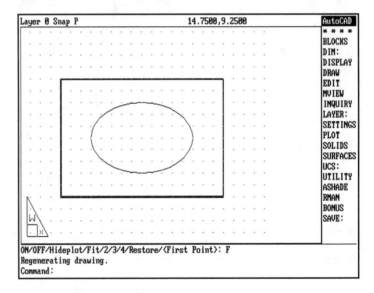

Paper space has been designed as an infinitely large sheet of electronic paper. Think of paper space as enabling you to draw on top of your current drawing, as if you placed a sheet of glass over your drawing and drew on the sheet of glass. A paper space viewport is an entity unto itself, much the same as a line or a circle.

Metaview Options

You can make Metaviews using the following options:

- **ON/OFF.** Controls the display status of the model space viewport. If the viewport is off, AutoCAD does not regenerate it. This greatly enhances the speed of the system if you are working with complex viewport configurations.

- **Hideplot.** Performs hidden line removal on the contents of a designated viewport when plotting the viewport in paper space.

- **Fit.** Creates a viewport the size of your current display area.

- **2,3,4.** Creates 2, 3, or 4 viewports to your specifications.

- **Restore.** Translates saved viewport configurations (Vports) into paper space viewports. When prompted, you may restore the default or existing model space configuration or enter the name of any saved viewport configuration.

- **<First Point>.** Prompts you to select the first point of a new viewport window. After selecting the first point, you will be prompted for the second point. Any two diagonal points may be entered or picked.

Note

As you create new viewports, the default setting is on. Your system dictates how many active viewports you may have. The 640K DOS version may have up to four, while the 386 and UNIX versions may have up to 16. If you are using the 386 version, for example, and already have 16 viewports on the display and decide you need another one, AutoCAD enables you to insert this new viewport but will not regenerate one of the original 16. AutoCAD always will regenerate as many of the selected viewports as possible under your system. If you are not sure how many viewports your system supports, you can check the MAXACTVP system variable.

Now back out with the Zoom command to take a look at this electronic sheet, as follows:

Zoom Out in Paper Space

Command: **Zoom**

All/Center/Dynamic/Extents/Left/Previous/Vmax/Window/<Scale (X/XP)>: **C**

Center point: **6,4.5**

Magnification or Height <9.0000>: **16**

Regenerating drawing.

Your paper space viewport should now resemble figure 7.6. Notice that the viewport is framed with a border.

Figure 7.6:
Your drawing zoomed center in paper space.

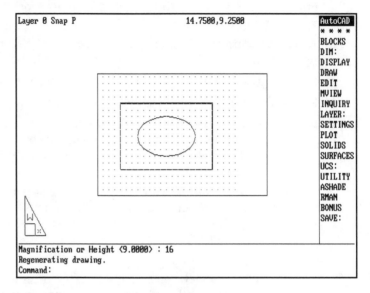

Using Model Space with TILEMODE Off

Remember, you cannot directly edit your model space drawing in paper space. To edit it you can go to model space with TILEMODE off.

The *Mspace* command switches you from paper space (TILEMODE off) to model space. At least one viewport must be active for AutoCAD to switch from paper space to model space.

To see how the Mspace command works, type **Mspace** at the `Command:` prompt. You also can enter paper space or model space by typing the shortcut commands, **PS** and **MS**.

As shown in figure 7.7, your viewport now displays the UCS icon. The UCS icon indicates that you are in model space (Mspace) and can now directly edit your drawing. Also, the current Mspace viewport is outlined with a heavy border.

You can do everything in this viewport that you could do previously on a TILEMODE model space viewport and more.

Continue drawing PART5 by drafting and editing four more ellipses in Mspace.

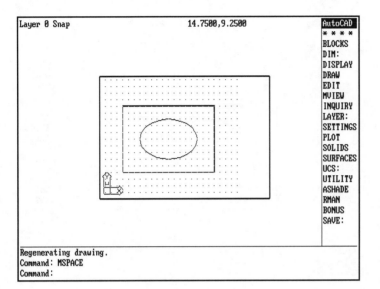

Figure 7.7:
*The UCS icon is
displayed in Mspace.*

Drafting in Mspace

Command: **Ellipse**

<Axis endpoint 1>/Center: **2.5,3**

Axis endpoint 2: **@1<0**

<Other axis distance>/Rotation: **R**

Rotation around major axis: **45**

Now try another variation of ellipse by completing the following steps:

Command: *Press Enter*

<Axis endpoint 1>/Center: **C**

Center of ellipse: **3,6**

Axis endpoint: **@.5<0**

<Other axis distance>/Rotation: **R**

Rotation around major axis: **45**

Your drawing now should display the ellipses as shown in figure 7.8:

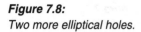

Figure 7.8:
Two more elliptical holes.

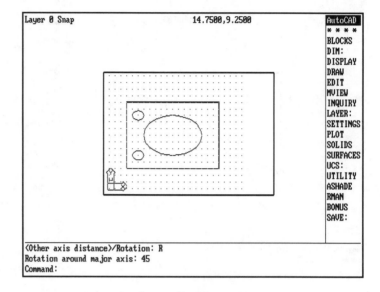

Using Multiple Viewports in Paper Space

AutoCAD enables you to have up to 16 paper space viewports at any time. You can, therefore, set up paper space viewports much the same as you set up TILEMODE model space viewports in Chapter 6, but with a few differences. Paper space viewports can be any size, scale, and located anywhere in paper space. Paper space viewports can be adjacent to each other, separated from each other, or overlapping. You decide how to position and size your paper space viewports.

Change the display magnification to make room for additional viewports, as follows:

Changing the Magnification and Center

Command: **PS**

Command: **Zoom**

All/Center/Dynamic/Extents/Left/Previous/Vmax/Window/<Scale (X/XP)>: **C**

Center point: *Pick the midpoint of the right-hand viewport frame.*

Magnification or Height <16.0000>: **20**

Regenerating drawing.

The regenerated drawing shows you that you are working on an infinitely large sheet of electronic paper. If you toggle Coords by pressing F6 to update the Cartesian readout and move your cursor around, you see that 0,0 is still in the lower left of the viewport. If you move the cursor outside the viewport (to any side), you see the coordinate readout display coordinate positions. You could zoom out again, and more coordinate space would appear around the viewport.

Now invoke the Mview command to insert another viewport into your paper space, as follows:

Creating the Second Viewport

Command: **Mview**

ON/OFF/Hideplot/Fit/2/3/4/Restore/<First Point>: **16,7**

Other corner: **24,14**

Regenerating drawing.

Your screen now shows a second viewport (see fig. 7.9). This new paper space viewport displays the current model space along with its drawing.

Now, make one more metaview below the one you just developed, as follows:

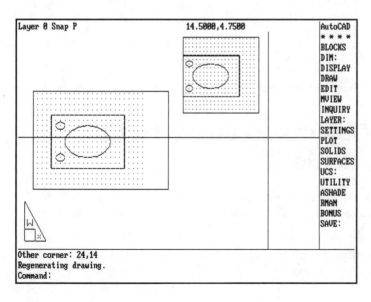

Figure 7.9:
The second viewport is created.

Creating the Third Paper Space Viewport

Command: **Mview**

ON/OFF/Hideplot/Fit/2/3/4/Restore/<First Point>: **16,6**

Other corner: **24,-5**

Regenerating drawing.

Command: **Mspace**

Your drawing should now resemble figure 7.10.

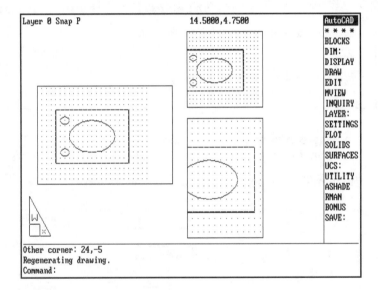

Figure 7.10:
Paper space with three viewports.

Magnifying Objects Relative to the Paper Space Scale

You usually use the Zoom options to temporarily increase the magnification of an object, thus improving accuracy. You then may zoom back out to view the entire object.

AutoCAD offers another important Zoom option: Zoom XP, which magnifies the entity or selection set within a selected viewport relative to the existing paper space scale.

This option provides an important tool for setting up electronic sheets for output. Remember that you can organize viewports and views anywhere you like on the electronic paper space sheet. Zoom XP enables you to easily add detail drawings to your sheet in a specified scale (2"=1", for example).

Type **MS** at the Command: prompt to enter model space, make the upper right viewport current, then follow these steps:

Zooming the Viewport Relative to the Paper Space Scale

Command: **Zoom**

All/Center/Dynamic/Extents/Left/Previous/Vmax/Window/<Scale (X/XP)>: **C**

Center point: **9,6**

Magnification or Height <10.1023>: **2XP**

Regenerating drawing.

The part is now zoomed in the upper right viewport two times the paper space scale (which is full). Your screen should resemble figure 7.11.

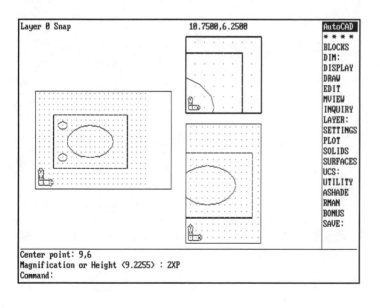

Figure 7.11:
The part is zoomed 2X
the paper space scale.

Now make the lower right viewport current and zoom the drawing there, as follows:

Zooming the Lower Right Viewport

Command: *Press Enter*

All/Center/Dynamic/Extents/Left/Previous/Vmax/Window/<Scale (X/XP)>: **C**

Center point: **8.5,4.5**

Magnification or Height <14.1432>: **1XP**

Regenerating drawing.

The part is zoomed in the lower right viewport equal to the paper space scale (1=1). Your screen should resemble figure 7.12.

Figure 7.12:
The part is zoomed equal to the paper space scale.

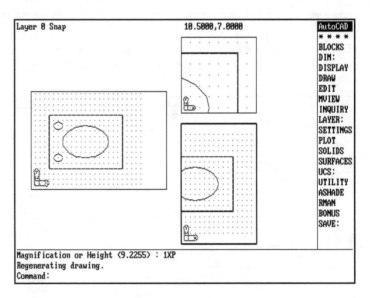

You now are ready to finish drafting the part. You need to add two more ellipses to the drawing, first in the lower right viewport, as follows:

Drawing an Ellipse

Command: **Ellipse**

\<Axis endpoint 1>/Center: **C**

Center of ellipse: **9,3**

Axis endpoint: **@.5<0**

\<Other axis distance>/Rotation: **R**

Rotation around major axis: **60**

Now make the upper right viewport current and follow these steps:

Command: *Press Enter*

\<Axis endpoint 1>/Center: **C**

Center of ellipse: **9,6**

Axis endpoint: **@.5<180**

\<Other axis distance>/Rotation: **R**

Rotation around major axis: **60**

Your drawing should resemble figure 7.13.

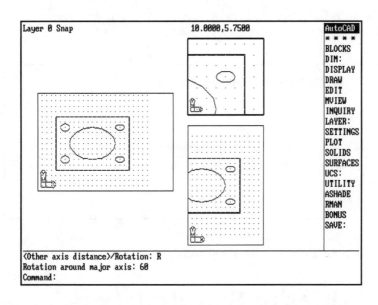

Figure 7.13:
The two ellipses are added to the drawing.

Saving a Viewport as a View

You can save a current viewport display as a view. Views may be saved and re-stored in any active viewport.

Make sure that the upper right viewport is current, and follow these steps:

Saving the View in the Upper Right Viewport

```
Command: View
?/Delete/Restore/Save/Window: S
View name to save: 2XTOPR
```

The name of this view is an acronym, of sorts, representing the scale (2X) and the center location of the zoom on the part (upper right). This is just one of many ways to develop names for views; use any view-naming convention that works for you. You will restore this view when you get your paper space sheet ready for plotting.

Now that you have finished drafting the part, erase the upper right and lower right viewports and prepare your drawing to plot in paper space, as follows:

Erasing the Viewports

```
Command: PS
Command: Erase
Select objects: 1 selected, 1 found   Pick the upper right viewport frame
Select objects: 1 selected, 1 found   Pick the lower right viewport frame
Select objects: Press Enter
Command: Regen
```

Your screen should display a single viewport, as shown in figure 7.14.

Stretching Entities or Selection Sets

Entities and selection sets may be stretched or shortened using the Stretch command.

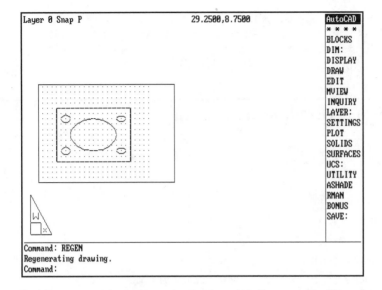

Figure 7.14:
*The two small viewports
are erased.*

The *Stretch* command enables you to extend (or shrink) certain entities by selecting them with a crossing window and picking a base and
new point of displacement. You can stretch lines, arcs, traces, solids,
polylines, and 3D faces. Entity endpoints inside the crossing window
are moved, those outside the crossing window remain fixed, and the
lines or arcs crossing the window are stretched. Entities which are
defined entirely within the crossing window (all endpoints, vertices,
and definition points) are simply moved. The definition point for a
block or shape is its insertion base point; for a circle, the center point;
for text, the lower left corner.

The Stretch command enables you to change the shape of geometry while still
preserving connections. When associatively dimensioned geometry is stretched
with the DIMASO system variable on, dimensions will be updated to reflect the
size change.

When stretching arcs, the arc's center point and its starting and ending angles
are adjusted so that the distance from the midpoint of the chord to the arc is
held constant. Traces and solids are handled as lines, whereas polylines are
handled segment-by-segment. Polyline width, tangent, and curve fitting information is not modified by the Stretch command.

Viewports, like entities, may be modified after their creation. Paper space
viewports may be erased, as shown earlier in this chapter, and they may be
moved, scaled, copied, and stretched.

Use the Stretch command to change the shape of your viewport from the existing 12"x9" sheet to a 17"x11" sheet. Make sure you are in paper space, then complete the following steps to stretch the viewport 5" in the positive X axis direction:

Stretching the Viewport along the X Axis

Command: **Stretch**

Select objects to stretch by window...

Select objects: **C**

First corner: *Pick first point (see fig. 7.15)*

Other corner: *Pick second point (see fig. 7.15)*

Select objects: *Press Enter*

Base point: *Pick the lower right corner of the viewport*

New point: *Type* **@5<0** *or pick point 5" to the right of the viewport corner*

Your viewport should be stretched to the right as figures 7.15 and 7.16 illustrate.

Figure 7.15:
Pick points for stretching.

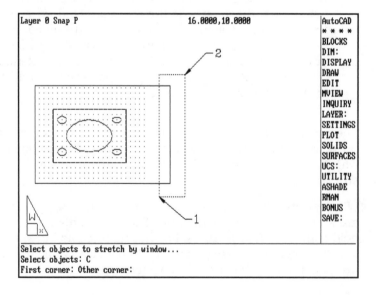

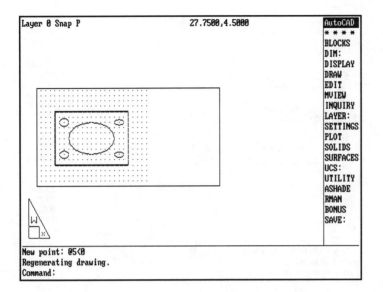

Figure 7.16:
The paper space viewport is stretched.

Now stretch the viewport 2" in the positive Y Axis direction, as follows:

Stretching the Viewport along the Y Axis

Command: **Stretch**

Select objects to stretch by window...

Select objects: **C**

First corner: *Pick first point (see fig. 7.17)*

Other corner: *Pick second point (see fig. 7.17)*

Select objects: *Press Enter*

Base point: *Pick the upper left or right corner of the viewport*

New point: *Type* **@2<90** *or pick point 2" up from upper corner of the viewport*

Your viewport should be stretched upward as shown in figure 7.17.

You now have changed your electronic paper space sheet to 17x11. Return to model space and reposition the part in the viewport using the Move command. Move the part 1" upward. This centers the part vertically in this larger viewport. Then create two new viewports to the right of the part drawing. These new viewports will be used to create scaled detail drawings of your part.

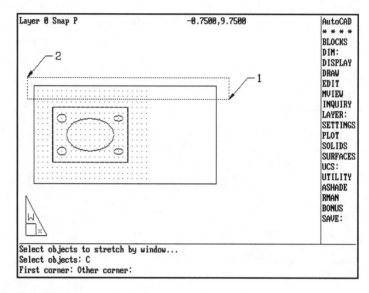

Figure 7.17:
Pick points for stretching.

Moving Entities

The *Move* command enables you to reposition entities or selection sets anywhere in 2D or 3D space. You move entities by first clicking on them and then entering, or clicking on, their base point of displacement (from where the entity will be moved) and their second point of displacement (to where the entity will be moved). The command uses standard object selection. The original entity or selection set remains unchanged. You can show and drag displacement by picking two points or by using an absolute XY displacement value.

Be careful that you do not press Enter accidentally at the second point prompt. If you do, your first point will be erroneously interpreted as a displacement, sending the move out of the current view where you cannot see it.

Now move the part drawing up 1" to center it vertically. Make sure you are in model space and follow these steps:

Moving Entities

```
Command: Move
Select objects: W
First corner: Pick first point
Other corner: Pick second point
6 selected, 6 found
Select objects: Press Enter if the part is dotted
Base point of displacement: Type 2,2 or pick the point
Second point of displacement: Type @1<90 or pick a point 1" up from base point
```

The part should move 1" upward, as figures 7.18 and 7.19 illustrate.

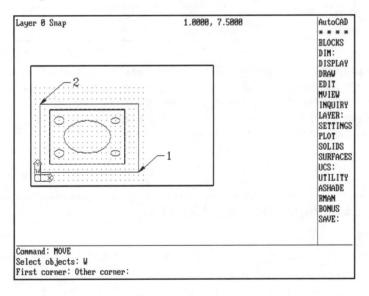

Figure 7.18:
Before the part is moved.

Using Paper Space Viewports To Create Drawings

By creating, saving, and restoring various views, you can build drawings. If you establish a primary paper space view of a border and title block, for example, you can add multiple Metaviews onto this drawing sheet to create your multi-detail drawings. This procedure will be covered more thoroughly in later chapters.

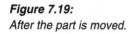

Figure 7.19:
After the part is moved.

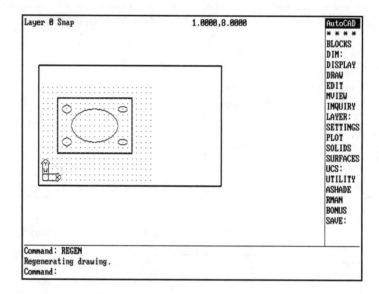

For now, you will use paper space viewports to build a simple drawing. Get the paper space sheet ready for plotting. Use the Restore command to retrieve your saved view of the upper right 60 degree ellipse in one new viewport, and set one other viewport with the lower left 45 degree ellipse. Thus, you can see how to plot details (or entire part drawings) at preferred scales to build a drawing.

Follow these steps:

Restoring the Saved View

Command: **Mview**

ON/OFF/Hideplot/Fit/2/3/4/Restore/<First Point>: *Type* **12,6** *or pick equivalent point*

Other corner: *Type* **16,10** *or pick on equivalent point*

Regenerating drawing.

Make sure this new viewport is current, and follow these steps:

Command: **View**

?/Delete/Restore/Save/Window: **R**

View name to restore: **2XTOPR**

Your drawing now should display the restored view in this new viewport, as shown in figure 7.20.

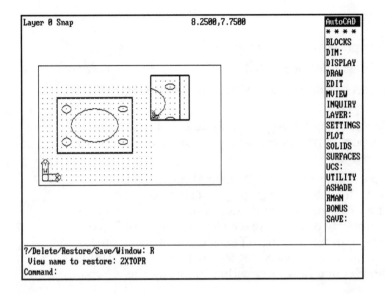

Remember, this view was scaled at two times the paper space scale (1"=1") using the Zoom XP option before it was saved. This viewport now provides you with a 2"=1" scaled detail of your part.

Now create one more viewport and locate a 45-degree ellipse detail within it, as follows:

Creating Your Own Detail Drawings

Command: **Mview**

ON/OFF/Hideplot/Fit/2/3/4/Restore/<First Point>: *Type* **12,5** *or pick equivalent point*

Other corner: *Type* **16,1** *or pick equivalent point*

Regenerating drawing.

Make sure the new viewport is current. Then zoom into the lower left ellipse. The new viewport shows the lower left ellipse zoomed two times the paper space scale.

Plotting Your Drawings

When you plot in paper space, the plot is specified by how much of your drawing (including viewports) falls within the plot options you select during the plot operation.

These rules apply:

- Partially visible viewports will not be plotted.

- Inactivate viewports will not be plotted.

- An activated viewport within the plottable paper space view will be plotted.

- The remove hidden lines option applies only to paper space entities, and each viewport is processed for hidden lines according to its own Hideplot settings.

- Paper space viewports maintain properties just as other entities do. You can change the color or linetype property of the viewport frame by using the Chprop command. More importantly, you can change the layer property of paper space viewport frames. This provides the mechanism for turning off selected viewport frames when plotting. This is how you can plot a drawing which contains superimposed paper space viewports without plotting the viewport frame.

- Paper space viewport layers also can be controlled individually (on a per-viewport basis) by using the Vplayer command. The Vplayer command enables you to control the visibility of layers per viewport. This command operates only when TILEMODE is off.

If you are using a plotter or printer plotter, step through the following exercise. If you are unable to plot your drawing at this time, read through the following sequence and then end your drawing session.

The *Plot* and *Prplot* (Printer plot) commands are the two methods for getting hard copies from your drawing file. The Plot command directs your drawing to a plotter or to a plot file. The Prplot command directs your drawing to a printer plotter (such as a dot matrix or laser printer). If you plot from the main menu, by selecting either the third or fourth menu options, you will be asked which drawing file you want to plot. If you plot from within the drawing, by typing **Plot** or **Prplot** at the Command: prompt, it is assumed you want to plot the current drawing. Only layers that are on and thawed will be plotted.

For a test plot, scale is not critical and either plotting or printer plotting is all right (both will be referred to generically as plotting). If your plotter cannot handle up to 17x11 in full size, plot it to fit the paper instead of 1:1 scale by typing **F** at the Command: prompt.

For both plotters and printers, you can write the plot to a file. This writes a file of your current drawing in the output format of your plotter (or printer) configuration. It prompts for file name and adds the extension PLT for plotter file or LST for printer plot file. The file contains data that would have been sent directly to the plotter. Because all circles, curves, and text are converted to many little vectors, a PLT or LST file may be up to five times larger than a DWG file.

Plotting to files is useful with RAM-resident plot spooling programs that can plot or print in the background as you draw. Plotting to file also may be necessary for plotting in a network environment or plotting to a port that AutoCAD's configuration does not support. If your plotter configures only as a serial device in AutoCAD but as a network device or parallel port in your system, for example, you can plot to file and then send it to the device or port using network commands, the DOS Print command, or the DOS Copy/B command and option.

The following plotter parameters are for a HP DraftPro plotter. Your plotter might be different, so the values may differ. If you are configured for and connected to a plotter (or printer plotter), follow these steps:

Plotting the PART5 Drawing with Multiple Views

Command: **PS**

Command: **Plot** or **Prplot**

What to plot — Display, Extents, Limits, View or Window <D>: **E**

Plot will NOT be written to a selected file
Sizes are in Inches
Plot origin is at (0.00,0.00)
Plotting area is 32.00 wide by 20.00 high (MAX size)
Plot is NOT rotated 90 degrees
Pen width is 0.010
Area fill will NOT be adjusted for pen width
Hidden lines will NOT be removed
Plot will be scaled to fit available area

Do you want to change anything? <N> **Y**

Plotting the PART5 Drawing with Multiple Views—continued

Entity Color	Pen No.	Line Type	Pen Speed	Entity Color	Pen No.	Line Type	Pen Speed
1 (red)	1	0	16	9	1	0	16
2 (yellow)	1	0	16	10	1	0	16
3 (green)	1	0	16	11	1	0	16
4 (cyan)	1	0	16	12	1	0	16
5 (blue)	1	0	16	13	1	0	16
6 (magenta)	1	0	16	14	1	0	16
7 (white)	1	0	16	15	1	0	16
8	1	0	16				

```
Line types:  0 = continuous line     Pen speed codes:
             1 = ..................
             2 = . . . . . . . . . .  Inches/Second:
             3 = -------------------  1, 2,  4,  8, 16
             4 = - - - - - - - - - -
             5 = -- -- -- -- -- -- -  Cm/Second:
             6 = --- --- --- --- ---  3, 5, 10, 20, 40
             7 = -- - -- - -- - -- -
             8 = __--__--__--__--__-
```

Enter line types, pen speed codes
blank=go to next, Cn=go to Color n,
S=Show current choices, X=Exit

Do you want to change any of the above parameters? <N> *Press Enter*

You are now prompted for plotting to file, units, and several other factors. The plot origin is the lower left extreme of the available plot area. The plotting size is the available plot area for the currently set sheet size. You can enter a standard size, such as A or D, or you can enter X,Y width and height to specify other sizes. Plots can be rotated for landscape or portrait orientation. The plotter pen width should be set to the smallest pen width; it controls the line spacing for area fills and wide polylines. You can adjust area fill boundaries to compensate for pen width or have the pen center line scribe the boundary. Hidden line removal applies to 3D. The plotting scale is 1:1 in this case, but if your plotter doesn't handle 17x11 size, use a smaller scale or type **F** for fit, and then follow these steps:

Units, Origin, and Scale

```
Write the plot to a file? <N> N
Size units (Inches or Millimeters) <I>: Press Enter
Plot origin in Inches <0.00,0.00>: Press Enter

Standard values for plotting size

Size   Width  Height
A      10.50  8.00
B      16.00  10.00
C      21.00  16.00
MAX    32.00  20.00

Enter the Size or Width,Height (in Inches) <MAX>: Type B or press Enter for MAX

Rotate 2D plots 90 degrees clockwise? <N> Press Enter
Pen width <0.010>: Press Enter
Adjust area fill boundaries for pen width? <N> Press Enter
Remove hidden lines? <N> Press Enter
Specify scale by entering:
Plotted Inches=Drawing Units or Fit or ? <F>: 1=1
Effective plotting area: 21.00 wide by 16.00 high

Position paper in plotter.
```

After you step through all the settings and the plotter and paper are properly set up and positioned, press Enter to start the plot.

Ending Your Drawing

```
Press RETURN to continue or S to Stop

for hardware setup Press Enter

Processing vector: 160

Plot complete.

Press RETURN to continue: Press Enter

Command: End
```

Summary

This chapter explained how to control your screen display and views in the TILEMODE off paper space mode, and how to use the Ellipse command for developing any elliptical shape and at any rotation angle.

In Chapter 8 you will develop a generic drafting prototype drawing for efficient drawing and plotting. You will see how to save valuable time by developing, and re-using, prototype drawings with preset drafting parameters and annotations.

8

PROTOTYPE DRAWINGS

In this chapter:

- Setting and changing system variables
- Saving a dimensioning style
- Creating a border and title block
- Setting a user coordinate system
- Organizing layers with linetypes and colors
- Establishing standards for general notes
- Creating a paper space bordered sheet and title block

Overview

Information is often repeated from drawing to drawing. This standard information can include pre-printed borders and title blocks for various sheet sizes, pre-printed or sticky-back legends, general notes, and BOMs (bills of materials).

AutoCAD's prototype drawings enable you to automate routine elements in your CAD drawings. A *prototype drawing* is simply an existing drawing that is used as the starting point for a new drawing. You can have any number of prototypes, and one particular prototype can be preset in the configuration menu as the default prototype. Others can be called from the main menu when you start a new drawing.

Prototype drawings can provide more than just pre-drawn borders and title blocks, however. AutoCAD has many settings, drawing layers, dimensioning settings, viewport configurations, and other system variables. If one of your objectives for using AutoCAD is to reduce drafting time, it is not efficient for you to set up drawing parameters each time you begin a new project. By creating a series of prototype drawings, you will have a system already geared to fit your 2D or 3D drafting and design needs every time you start a drawing.

The main aspects of drawing setup are system settings such as drawing size, snap, grid, coords, ortho, text styles, and dimensioning setup, and standard graphic elements such as title blocks and borders. These components can be controlled by several methods, including prototype drawings, startup menus, and automatic AutoLISP routines that set up your drawing. The best system is a combination of all three methods, which can automate the handling of multiple sheet sizes and plot scales. For simplicity, however, you will create a single multi-purpose prototype drawing as illustrated by figure 8.1 which incorporates both system settings and graphic elements.

This will be a generic 2D prototype, not specific to any particular industrial discipline. The sheet size, border, drawing arrangement, title block format, supplemental data block format, standard tolerance block, treatment block, finish block, parts list, and revision block are all defined according to ANSI Y14.1 standards to maintain consistency.

Note The exercises in this chapter shows you how to develop a prototype in decimal inch measurements. If you need to draft in ISO-SI metric, you will find that with a few size and variable modifications this exercise provides an excellent guide to the creation of metric prototypes.

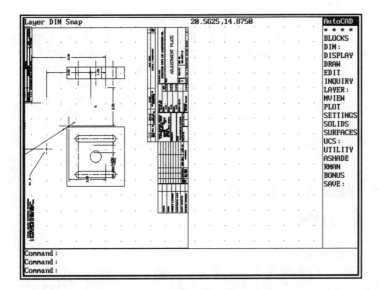

Figure 8.1:
Prototype title block with PLATE drawing.

Creating a Generic Drafting Prototype

This chapter shows you how to create a C-size (22x17) prototype drawing, which you should name PROTO-C. This prototype is designed for use in this book's exercises. It is an example of a typical startup prototype, which you can copy and modify to suit the needs of your particular application. The most straightforward part is making the drawing settings.

Settings commonly made in most drawings include snap, grid, units, text height, and style, all of which were used in the previous chapter. You also will set the drawing size, zoom the screen, and make the other settings shown in table 8.1 This table is typical of how groups of settings are displayed as a guide to drawing setup.

Table 8.1
Prototype Drawing Settings

COORDS	GRID	LTSCALE	SNAP
Dist<Angle	1.0/On	0.375	0.0625/ON

TEXT HEIGHT	APERTURE	PICKBOX
0.1255	5	2

UNITS	Decimal, all defaults.
STYLE	Romans
LIMITS	0,0 to 22,17
ZOOM	0.8
VIEW	All

The AutoCAD: Drafting and 3D Design Disk includes a ready-to-use prototype drawing named PROTO-C. Unless you are familiar with all of the above settings, as well as dimension variables, layers, and UCSs, perform the following exercises for practice. Do not save the results, however. You can skip the repetitive parts. If you are familiar with this material, read along to see if you can learn anything new.

If you do not have the AutoCAD: Drafting and 3D Design Disk, create the PROTO-C prototype drawing before proceeding to the next chapter.

Starting the Drawing and Setting the Limits

The first step is to use the Limits command to make a C-size drawing sheet. You want to set up your drawing area as 22x17, the dimensions of a C-size sheet. This will work fine for full scale. Other scales are discussed at the end of this chapter.

The *Limits* command determines your drawing area or boundaries, defined by the absolute coordinates of the lower left and upper right corners. You can modify these values or turn limits checking on and off by means of the Limits command. The default settings are from 0,0 to 12,9 with limits checking off.

The limits checking feature is enabled by turning limits on. When limits checking is on, you cannot enter points outside the drawing limits. This avoids the problem of accidentally drafting entities outside the drawing sheet. Do not turn limits checking on yet because later you will set up a scratch area for temporary drawing and parts development that is deliberately outside the drawing sheet.

Some versions of AutoCAD Release 10 become slow in object snapping and entity selection if you draw outside the limits. This was fixed in the AutoCAD Release 10 c7 and later versions. Updates are available from your dealer. Your version is shown in the header of the main menu.

Begin a new drawing named TEMP=, or just read along.

Begin a new drawing named PROTO-C=.

This method of naming a drawing (name=) tells AutoCAD not to use any proto-type drawing. When you use this naming convention upon entering the drawing editor, AutoCAD sets all environment parameters to default values.

To set the limits, type **Limits** at the Command: prompt and press Enter at the ON/OFF/<Lower left corner> <0.0000,0.0000>: prompt. Establish a new sheet size of 22,17.

The corner values for the Limits command can be any value. Instead, using 0,0 for the lower left corner, for example, you can use a negative coordinate.

You are using the default settings, so you do not need to set units. The unit display precision option (number of digits to the right of the decimal point in the Units command) controls how many digits the coordinate readout displays and dimensions. If you set it to three digits, the readout will look like this: X.XXX. Although only three digits display, you can enter more precise values. If you enter .0625, for example, AutoCAD records the exact value in the drawing data-base even though the displayed value is rounded off to .063 units.

The default is four places (0.0000). You can easily control precision as needed by setting the LUPREC (Linear Units of PRECision) and DIMRND (DIMension ROUNDing) system variables. It is generally recommended that you leave preci-sion set to a large number, such as four. The extra places will not hurt anything and can help avoid errors that can occur when the coords display roundoff mis-leads you into thinking an inaccurate but rounded-off number is accurate. The DIMRND system variable can control the precision of dimensioning indepen-dently of display units precision.

Setting and Changing System Variables

When you use commands such as Snap, Grid, and Limits, AutoCAD stores the settings as system variables. A system variable is a stored setting with a name by which it can be accessed and changed. AutoCAD has over 130 system vari-ables. Grid, for example, affects two variables: GRIDMODE and GRIDUNIT. GRIDMODE is a grid on or off setting represented by 1 for on and 0 for off. (All system variables use 1 for on and 0 for off.) GRIDUNIT is a point or coordinate value, such as 1.0000,1.0000 for a one-unit square grid. The values always are shown in current units, although you can enter them in decimal form with any precision, regardless of current units.

System variables can be set by one of two ways: using the Setvar or transparent 'Setvar command, or directly from the Command: prompt. Each method has its advantages.

First, 'Setvar can be invoked while you are using a different command. You can be in the Line command, for example, and decide that you need to reset your SNAPUNIT system variable. The transparent 'Setvar command enables you to do this.

If you are at the Command: prompt and wish to set a system variable, however, it is unnecessary to use the Setvar command to invoke the system variable. All system variables can be called by typing their name at the Command: prompt.

 The *Setvar* command retrieves and modifies system variables. Most system variables also are modified through AutoCAD commands. A few system variables are of the read-only variety. Type **?** to see a listing of all variables.

Follow these steps to change a system variable while using the Line command:

Calling Up a System Variable

Command: **Line**

To point: **'Setvar**

>>Variable name or ?: **Snapunit**

>>New value for SNAPUNIT

<0.1250,0.1250>: **.1,.1**

Now, when you resume the Line command at the To point: prompt, the program uses the new 0.1 unit snap.

When used in the middle of another command, 'Setvar suspends that command temporarily. 'Setvar's double angle bracket prompt (>>) indicates suspension.

You also should set system variables individually for the sake of simplicity. The Units command, for example, steps through a long series of options, but each has its own system variable. You can use Setvar or type the system variable name at the Command: prompt to change one variable without having to deal with related settings. You can change the precision of linear units to three by selecting Setvar from the Settings screen or pull-down menu and then typing **LUPREC**, or you simply can type **LUPREC** at the Command: prompt.

You can set LUPREC to 3, for example, by typing **Luprec** at the Command: prompt and then typing **3** at the New value for Luprec <4>: prompt.

The similar AUPREC variable sets the precision of angular units. Try it on your own.

You can set snap, grid, and similar settings with their commands or through menu and dialogue boxes, but you will find it easier to access the system variables from the `Command:` prompt instead. The following is a list of the variables you need to set for this chapter's prototype. The use of some of these settings will become clearer in later exercises or chapters.

- **APERTURE.** Sets the object snap "target" size in pixel units. See the Osnap command definition for details.

- **COORDS.** Has three settings. 0 for off (updates only when a point is picked), 1 for continuous XY update, and 2 for continuous dist<angle display update.

- **GRIDMODE.** Turns the grid on (1) and off (0).

- **GRIDUNIT.** Shows a coordinate value representing the XY grid spacing.

- **PICKBOX.** Sets the object selection box size in pixel units. When selecting objects, the pickbox, not the cursor, is displayed on the screen to aid in picking objects or entities. The pickbox must touch the entity you want to pick. Using too large a size, however, might touch entities you do not want.

- **SNAPMODE.** Turns the snap on (1) and off (0).

- **SNAPUNIT.** Shows a coordinate value representing the XY snap spacing.

- **TEXTSIZE.** Sets the current text height.

- **TEXTSTYLE.** Sets the current text style.

- **UCSICON.** Turns the USC icon display on and off, and enables you to make it display at the 0,0,0 origin point.

Snap has several other variables which control rotation, style, and base point. You can offset the snap grid to any increment base point, rotate it to any angle, and set it to isometric style. The grid and axis follow snap's style, angle, and base point.

The aperture and pickbox are sized in pixels above and below the cursor crosshairs, so a setting of 5 yields a total height of 10 (5 above and 5 below). You might like your aperture and pickbox larger or smaller than the settings used in this chapter, depending on your video resolution. The greater your resolution, the larger your preference probably will be.

Continuing in the PROTO-C drawing, set the system variables by completing the following steps:

```
                    Setting the System Variables
Command: Aperture
New value for APERTURE <10>: 5
Command: Coords
New value for COORDS <0>: 2
Command: Gridmode
New value for GRIDMODE <0>: 1
Command: Gridunit
New value for GRIDUNIT <0.0000,0.0000>: 1,1
Command: Pickbox
New value for PICKBOX <3>: 2
Command: Snapmode
New value for SNAPMODE <0>: 1
Command: Snapunit
New value for SNAPUNIT <1.0000,1.0000>: .0625,.0625
Command: Textsize
New value for TEXTSIZE <0.2000>: .125
Command: Ucsicon
ON/OFF/All/Noorigin/ORigin <On>: OR
Command: Textstyle
TEXTSTYLE = "Standard" (read only)
Command: Regen
```

You probably noticed some inconsistency in the execution of these settings. If used transparently with 'Setvar or at the Command: prompt, some settings take effect immediately, some after the next bit of input, and some do not take effect until after the current command is ended. Some settings do not display until you *regenerate* (recalculate and redisplay) the screen, even if they take effect immediately. That is the purpose of the final command entry in the preceding set of steps.

Some variables, such as TEXTSTYLE, cannot be changed by Setvar or at the Command: prompt. These read-only variables can be changed only by the commands that control them. Use the Style command to set TEXTSTYLE, as follows:

◀

Setting TEXTSTYLE

Command: **Style**

Text style name (or ?) <STANDARD>: **Romans**

New style.

Now scroll down to Romans in the font file dialogue box that appears on the screen, pick it, and select the OK box. Accept AutoCAD's default settings by pressing Enter at the following prompts:

```
Font file <txt>: Romans
Height <0.00>: Press Enter
Width factor <1.00>: Press Enter
Obliquing angle <0>: Press Enter
Backwards? <N> Press Enter
Upside-down? <N> Press Enter
Vertical? <N> Press Enter
Romans is now the current text style.
```

Unless you have the AutoCAD: Drafting and 3D Design Disk, save the PROTO-C drawing so you do not have to establish the settings again. Type **Save** at the Command: prompt and then press Enter at the File name <PROTO-C> prompt.

Getting the Prototype Ready for Dimensioning

AutoCAD uses over 40 variables to control dimensioning. You will explore dimensioning with AutoCAD in detail later, but while creating the prototype drawing, you need to preset some dimensioning variables. Dimensioning variables consist of three primary types: those that control dimensioning scale of components, those that control dimensioning style such as tolerancing, and those that toggle dimensioning options on and off.

You can set dimensioning variables with the Setvar command, the AutoCAD Dim command mode, or directly from the Command: prompt.

To set up the prototype drawing to control dimensioning variables according to ANSI Y14.5, the following dimension variables should be reset. For a complete listing and description of all dimensioning variables, refer to the system variables table in Appendix A of the *AutoCAD Reference Manual*.

- **DIMASZ.** Controls arrow size from base to point. (It also controls text fit.)
- **DIMCEN.** Controls circle/arc center tick marks and center extension lines. The positive default of 0.09 causes AutoCAD to generate only a .09-long tick mark at the center of the circle/arc. A zero value causes no marks or lines to be drawn. A negative value defines the length of the tick mark and the distance which the extension lines project past the circle/arc perimeter.
- **DIMDLI.** Controls the dimension line increment (spacing between dimension lines) for continuous and base line dimensions.
- **DIMEXE.** Specifies how far the extension line extends beyond the dimension line.
- **DIMEXO.** Specifies the extension line offset from the dimension origin points.
- **DIMTXT.** Controls height of dimensioning text.
- **DIMZIN.** Controls whether or not leading and trailing zeros will be generated. See your *AutoCAD Reference Manual* for complete details.

Figure 8.2 illustrates the use of these variables.

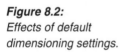

Figure 8.2:
Effects of default dimensioning settings.

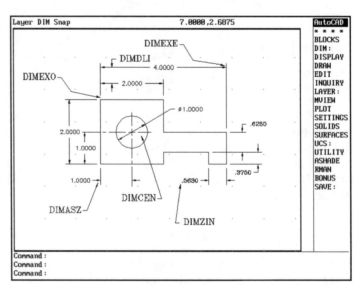

Use the following instructions to set each of the dimension variables described previously:

Setting Dimension Variables

```
Command: Dimasz
Current value <0.1800>
New value: .125
Command: Dimcen
Current value <0.0900>
New value: -.1
Command: Dimdli
Current value <0.3800>
New value: .5
Command: Dimexe
Current value <0.1800>
New value: .125
Command: Dimexo
Current value <0.0625>
New value: .125
Command: Dimrnd
Current value <0.0000>
New value: .001
Command: Dimtxt
Current value <0.1800>
New value: .125
Command: Dimzin
Current value <0>
New value: 4
Command: Save (unless you have the AutoCAD: Drafting and 3D Design Disk)
```

An overall size variable named DIMSCALE controls all of these size-related dimensioning variables. For a full size plot scale, leave DIMSCALE set to 1. Scaling is explained at the end of this chapter.

The preceding settings are your defaults. You will adjust DIMCEN, DIMDLI, and others which have been left at AutoCAD's standard defaults as you need them.

Saving a Dimensioning Style

AutoCAD enables you to set a series of dimensioning variables, just as you have done, and then save this configuration as a dimensioning style. Setting dimensioning variables for various drafting tasks can be time consuming. Dimensioning styles enables you to set and save any combination of dimensioning variables under a name of your choice. Dimensioning styles then can be restored at any time using the Dim and Restore commands.

It would be simple to set one dimensioning style for tolerance dimensioning, for example, diameter dimensions with leaders only, dimension line increment spacing (DIMDLI) to 1", and if you want to be fancy, extension lines in red, dimension lines in yellow, and dimension text in green. You could then name and save this dimensioning style as TOL1 for tolerance dimensioning style 1. You then could make a style for limit dimensioning, and so on.

Name and save your current dimensioning style. Make sure that you have the Dim: prompt before you save a dimensioning style. If you use the Save command at the Command: prompt, it will be interpreted as though you want to save your drawing file, as follows:

Saving a Dimensioning Style

```
Command: Dim

DIM: Save

?/Name for new dimension style: ANSI1

DIM: Press Ctrl-C
```

 As you begin to use additional dimensioning techniques, set and save them as a dimensioning style and then add them to your prototype drawing.

You also can include graphic elements, such as a border and title block, in your prototype.

Creating a Border and Title Block

To plan your title block, you need to consider the border that your plotter can accommodate. Most plotters cannot (and you normally would want them to) plot all the way to the edges of the paper. You need to allow room for a border that fits within the available plot area of your particular plotter (or printer). The AutoCAD Plot and Prplot commands display what this available area is. To do this check, your AutoCAD must be configured for a plotter or printer-plotter.

▶ **Checking the Area of Your Plotter**

Command: *Type* **Plot** *or* **PRPLOT**

What to plot — Display, Extents, Limits, View, or Window: *Press Enter*

Your plotter or printer-plotter's current plotting parameters should be displayed. Then, if you type **Y** at the Do you want to change anything? <N>: prompt, you see the plotting entity color, pen number, linetype, and pen speed information.

Press Enter several times and you see the following information on the screen. The information might differ depending on the type of plotter connected to your workstation.

```
Standard values for plotting size
Size    Width    Height
A       10.50     8.00
B       16.00    10.00
C       21.00    16.00
D       33.00    21.00
MAX     44.72    23.30
```

To complete your check, press Ctrl-C at the Enter the Size or Width, Height (in Inches) <MAX>: prompt, and then press Enter. The preceding information shows the typical maximum areas available for various size plot sheets, in this case an HP DraftPro plotter.

The C-size area shown in the preceding example is 21 inches wide by 16 inches high. This is the maximum effective plotting area that you can plot without clipping any portion of the drawing. In other words, the largest full-scale object that this plotter can plot on a C-size sheet is 21x16. You need to design the border to fit within that area, therefore. If your plotter has a smaller maximum effective plotting area, you will have to adjust the border dimensions in the following exercises. If larger, you can expand them, but it might be simpler to just leave them at 21x16. In the example, the ANSI standard C-size sheet had to be changed to account for the C-size effective plotting area of the HP DraftPro plotter.

Drafting a Polyline Border

The border, title block, weight block, application block, parts list, and revision list are drawn using AutoCAD's Pline command. After it is completed, the prototype should match figure 8.3. First, draw the simple outer border with a polyline.

Figure 8.3:
The completed sheet.

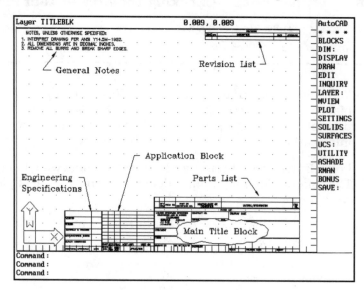

Use the following coordinates to draw the border centered on the sheet (limits), with a 0.02 width polyline on layer 0. You will draw using the default starting width of .02 and using relative coordinates. Do not worry if you cannot see the points as you draw. You can type your coordinates outside the current view, then zoom out to see your work when finished.

Drafting the Border

```
Command: Pline
From point: .53125,.53125
Current line-width is 0.00
Arc/Close/Halfwidth/Length/Undo/Width/<Endpoint of line>: W
Starting width <0.0000>: .02
Ending width <0.0200>: Press Enter
Arc/Close/Halfwidth/Length/Undo/Width/<Endpoint of line>: @0,15.9375
Arc/Close/Halfwidth/Length/Undo/Width/<Endpoint of line>: @20.9375,0
Arc/Close/Halfwidth/Length/Undo/Width/<Endpoint of line>: @0,-15.9375
Arc/Close/Halfwidth/Length/Undo/Width/<Endpoint of line>: C
```

You might wonder why you did not just draw from 0,0 to 21,16, or from .5,.5 to 21.5,16.5. The exercise had you start at approximately .5,.5 to center the border in the 22x17 limits. It was necessary to offset the center a bit more, to .53125,.53125. If you had drawn a full 21x16 border, its center line would be right on the plot extents, and the outer half of the polyline width would be outside the maximum plotting area. The outer half of the width would get clipped, not plotted. So in the exercise, you shrank the border by 1/16 inch and offset it by 1/32 inch to fit within the limits. This makes the border size 20-15/16 inches, which is convenient for later snapping.

If you use the Zoom All command, you can view the drawing from a distance. Complete the following steps to do this:

Viewing the Drawing Using Zoom

```
Command: Zoom
All/Center/Dynamic/Extents/Left/Previous/Vmax/Window/<Scale(X/XP)>: A
Regenerating drawing.
```

AutoCAD then displays the entire drawing.

Setting a User Coordinate System

To make drawing easier, use the UCS command to align the border with the snap and coordinate system. You placed the 0,0 point of the limits at the corner of the electronic 22x17 drawing sheet and sized the border in 0.0625 (1/16) increments. The rest of the title block is also in 0.0625 increments. It would be great if the border and title block aligned with the 0.0625 SNAPUNIT setting, or if 0,0 were at the corner of the border instead of the sheet. The border is offset to 0.53125,0.53125, however. You can compensate for this with the UCS command.

The *UCS* (User Coordinate System) command enables you to redefine the location of 0,0 and the direction of X,Y. The default UCS is the WCS (World Coordinate System). You can set your user coordinate system with the UCS command or with the Dducs dialogue box.

Although the UCS is intended primarily for 3D work, it also is valuable in 2D to align the coordinate system with drawing points. With it set to the corner of your border, all drawing points can be entered relative to the new 0,0 corner instead of to the limits corner (which currently is -.53125,-.53125).

You will examine the UCS command and the Dducs dialogue box in detail in the textbook's 3D chapters. For now, just offset the UCS's 0,0 origin and save the new UCS with the name BDR by completing the following steps:

Setting and Saving a UCS

```
Command: UCS
Origin/ZAxis/3point/Entity/View/X/Y/Z/Prev/Restore/Save/Del/?/<World>: O
Origin point <0,0,0>: .53125,.53125
Command: Press Enter
UCS
Origin/ZAxis/3point/Entity/View/X/Y/Z/Prev/Restore/Save/Del/?/<World>: S
?/Name of UCS: BDR
```

Until the UCS is changed again, 0,0 is at the corner of the border and the lines you draw are on the snap increment.

Organizing Layers with Linetypes and Colors

You drew the border on the default layer, layer 0. Other parts of the title block will be drawn on other layers. If you are familiar with overlay drafting, AutoCAD's layers will seem familiar. AutoCAD enables you to organize your drawing into any number of layers. You are always drawing on a layer, whether it is the default layer 0 or a layer that you have created with the Layer command.

The Layer command controls layers that act like transparent drawing overlays. You can create (with the Make or New options) an unlimited number of layers and give them names up to 31 characters long. You can set any layer active (current), turn layers on (visible) or off (invisible), freeze or thaw layers, and control their colors and linetypes. When a layer is frozen, it is disregarded by AutoCAD and will not be plotted, calculated, or displayed. You draw on the current layer. The default settings for new layers are white with continuous linetype. You also can control layers with the Ddlmodes dialogue box.

Most drawings, including the drafting exercises in this textbook, require multiple drawing layers. The following exercises show you how to create drawing layers with specific names, linetypes, and colors. These exercises also show you how to change the current layer, turn layers on and off, and freeze and thaw them. You will need the layers in table 8.2 for the title block and for other drawing purposes.

Table 8.2
The Prototype's Layers

Purpose	Layer Name	State	Color	Linetype	Pen
Floating	0	ON	7 (White)	CONTINUOUS	Med
Main title block	TITL-CX	ON	7 (White)	CONTINUOUS	Med
Border, title outline	TITL-OT	ON	7 (White)	CONTINUOUS	Med
Engineering spec. block	SPEC-CX	ON	7 (White)	CONTINUOUS	Med
Outline engr. spec.	SPEC-OT	ON	7 (White)	CONTINUOUS	Med
Part application	APPL-CX	ON	7 (White)	CONTINUOUS	Med
Outline part usage	APPL-OT	ON	7 (White)	CONTINUOUS	Med
Part inventory	PART-CX	ON	7 (White)	CONTINUOUS	Med
Outline part inventory	PART-OT	ON	7 (White)	CONTINUOUS	Med
General notes	NOTES	ON	3 (Green)	CONTINUOUS	Med
Other text	TEXT	ON	3 (Green)	CONTINUOUS	Med
Construction lines	CONST	ON	6 (Magenta)	CONTINUOUS	None
Object lines	OBJECT	ON	2 (Yellow)	CONTINUOUS	Bold
Center lines	CL	ON	1 (Red)	CENTER	Thin
Hidden lines	HL	ON	3 (Green)	HIDDEN	Med
Hatches & fills	HATCH	ON	4 (Cyan)	CONTINUOUS	Thin
Phantom lines	PL	ON	4 (Cyan)	PHANTOM	Thin
Dimension lines	DIM	ON	1 (Red)	CONTINUOUS	Thin
Dashed lines	DL	ON	1 (Red)	DASHED	Thin

The four center columns (Layer Name, State, Color, and Linetype) are AutoCAD's layer data. The information in the Purpose and Pen columns was added to help you understand layer usage. AutoCAD supports a number of linetypes which can be assigned to layers for screen display and plotting. If you have a color display, layers will display in the colors assigned to them. Normally, you do not plot in colors, but AutoCAD makes plotter pen assignments by color. Three pen line weights have been established and assigned to the seven colors shown in the preceding table's Color and Pen columns. Yellow is bold; red and cyan are thin; green and white plot medium; magenta is not plotted; and blue is not used because it is hard to see on many displays.

Five layers have similar pairs of names. The extension -CX (for CompleX) indicates that the major complexity of an item's entities go on that layer. The outline of the item goes on the corresponding -OT (OuTline) layer. The border you just drew, for example, will be changed to the TITL-OT layer, and you will add to it a simple outline of the main title block's perimeter. The text and interior lines of the title block, however, will be placed on the TITL-CX layer. This enables you to freeze the TITL-CX layer so that AutoCAD does not waste time calculating and displaying it while you pan and zoom your drawing. The TITL-OT layer provides an outline to help you keep track of the area available for drawing objects.

This is only one of many ways to organize layers. For more information along these lines, consult *Maximizing AutoCAD Volume I* (New Riders Publishing).

Using the Modify Layer Dialogue Box

You can invoke the Layer command at the keyboard through the screen, tablet, or pull-down menus, or you can use the Ddlmodes dialogue box, using the settings shown in table 8.2 and in figures 8.4, 8.5, 8.6, and 8.7.

Figure 8.4:
Modify layer dialogue box.

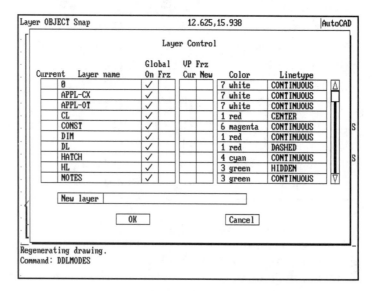

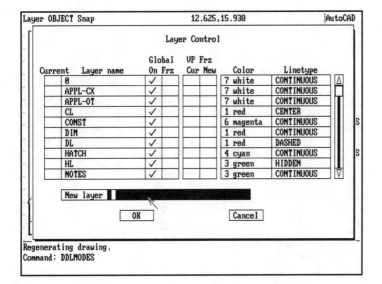

Figure 8.5:
Enter the layer name.

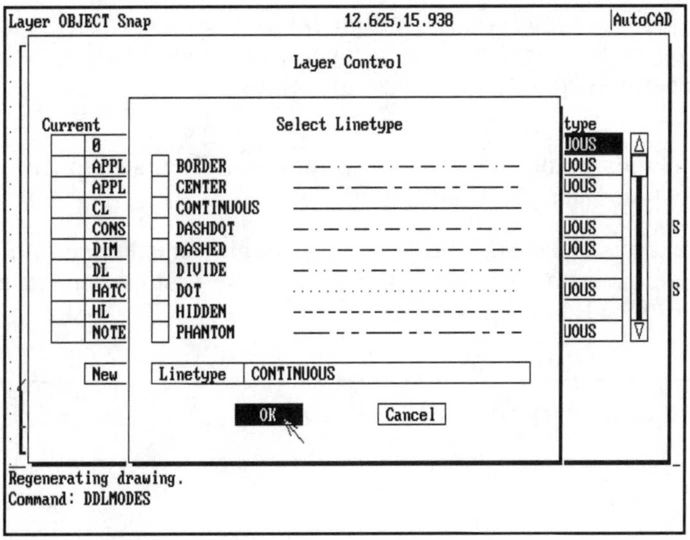

Figure 8.6:
Selecting layer linetypes.

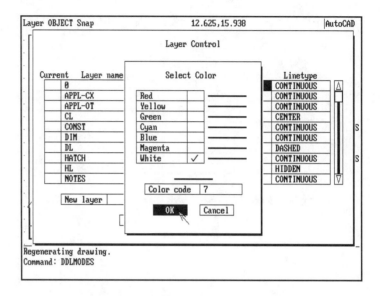

Figure 8.7:
Selecting layer colors

The *Ddlmodes* (Dynamic Dialogue Layer Modes) command presents a dialogue box to control layer options. The options include setting the current layer, creating new layers, renaming layers, and modifying layer properties (color, linetype, on/off, freeze, and thaw).

You need to load more linetypes using the Linetype command. Then set up the layers and take a closer look at their colors and linetypes.

Use either the Ddlmodes exercise that follows, or read through the exercise and use the Layer command exercise that comes next. Notice in the first exercise the use of the asterisk wildcard for all linetypes

---

Creating Layers with Ddlmodes

Command: **Linetype**

?/Create/Load/Set: **L**

Linetype(s) to load: *****

File to search acad: *Press Enter or select OK for the standard linetype file*

?/Create/Load/Set: *Press Enter to exit*

To use the Modify Layer dialogue box, type **Ddlmodes** at the Command: prompt. Or, click on Layer Control... in the Settings pull-down menu and then highlight the box next to New layer. Either type **CL** or select OK to accept the layer name. Then select 7 White, the default color box in the new layer's row. Next select Red and OK to accept it. Then select Continuous, the default linetype box in the new layer's row. Next select Center and OK to accept it. Now highlight New layer and start the process over for the next layer.

Set up layers as shown in table 8.2. Scroll back to the TITL-OT layer and select Current, which sets layer TITL-OT to be current. Now select OK to exit the Modify Layer dialogue box.

To change a layer's name, highlight the old name and enter the new name and press Enter, or type **OK** to accept it.

After all layers are set up and the modify layer dialogue box displays the layer status correctly, click on OK to exit the dialogue box. The name of the new current layer, TITL-CX, should appear at the upper left of the screen on the status line.

Using the Layer Command

The Layer command can do anything Ddlmodes can do. Using Layer is often more efficient for one or two quick settings. This command also has the advantage of being able to apply settings to multiple layers, with wildcard name entry. Layer's options include the following:

- **?.** Lists all existing layers
- **Make.** Makes a new layer and sets it current
- **Set.** Sets an existing layer current
- **New.** Creates one or more new layers, but does not set them current
- **ON** and **OFF.** Turns one or more existing layers on or off (invisible)
- **Color** and **Ltype.** Assigns a new color or linetype to one or more existing layers
- **Freeze** and **Thaw.** Freezes and thaws one or more existing layers

All the Layer options except Make and Set accept multiple layer names. You can enter all the layer names you want, separating each name by a comma; for example: OBJECT,HL,CL. You also can use wildcards when naming layers for the on, off, color, linetype, freeze, and thaw options. A name such as PART??? would apply to both PART-CX and PART-OT.

If you did not use the Ddlmodes command to set up the prototype drawing's layers, use the following exercise to create layers with the Layer command. You can use tablet and screen menus or just type the command, options, and layer names.

Creating Layers with the Layer Command

```
Command: Layer
?/Make/Set/New/ON/OFF/Color/Ltype/Freeze/Thaw: M
New current layer <0>: TITL-OT
?/Make/Set/New/ON/OFF/Color/Ltype/Freeze/Thaw: N
New layer name(s): TITL-OT,SPEC-CX,SPEC-OT,APPL-CX,APPL-OT,PART-CX,PART
OT,NOTES,TEXT,CONST,OBJECT,CL,HL,HATCH,PL,DIM
?/Make/Set/New/ON/OFF/Color/Ltype/Freeze/Thaw: L
Linetype (or ?) <CONTINUOUS>: Center
Layer name(s) for linetype CENTER <TITL-OT>: CL
?/Make/Set/New/ON/OFF/Color/Ltype/Freeze/Thaw: C
Color: R
Layer name(s) for color 1 (red) <TITL-OT>: CL,DL,DIM
```

Continue assigning the rest of the colors and linetypes illustrated in figure 8.8. Pressing Enter at the ?/Make/Set/New/ON/OFF/Color/Ltype/Freeze/Thaw: prompt exits the Layer command.

You did not have to preload the linetypes that you used. Unlike Ddlmodes's Modify Layer dialogue box, the Layer command automatically attempts to load linetypes as needed.

The AutoCAD: Drafting and 3D Design disk's Y14.5 Menu System includes a menu section for turning the prototype layers on or off, and invoking their other options.

Listing Layers

You should list the layers to be sure they are right. To do this, check the status of your layers with the ? layer option. The listing order of the layers depends on the order in which they were created. Figure 8.8 displays the first page of a typical listing.

Complete the following steps (except the last step if you have the AutoCAD: Drafting and 3D Design disk) to list the layers:

```
   Layer nam╜      State      Color        Linetype
-----------------  ------    --------      ---------
0                   On       7 (white)     CONTINUOUS
APPL-CX             On       7 (white)     CONTINUOUS
APPL-OT             On       7 (white)     CONTINUOUS
CL                  On       1 (red)       CENTER
CONST               On       7 (white)     CONTINUOUS

DIM                 On       1 (red)       CONTINUOUS
DL                  On       7 (white)     DASHED
HATCH               On       7 (white)     CONTINUOUS
HL                  Off      7 (white)     HIDDEN
NOTES               On       7 (white)     CONTINUOUS

OBJECT              On       7 (white)     CONTINUOUS
PART-CX             On       7 (white)     CONTINUOUS
PART-OT             On       7 (white)     CONTINUOUS
PL                  On       7 (white)     PHANTOM
SPEC-CXSPEC-OT      On       7 (white)     CONTINUOUS

-- Press RETURN for more --_
```

Figure 8.8:
Listing the layers.

Listing Layers

Command: **Layer**

?/Make/Set/New/ON/OFF/Color/Ltype/Freeze/Thaw: **?**

Layer name(s) for listing <*>: *Press Enter*

?/Make/Set/New/ON/OFF/Color/Ltype/Freeze/Thaw: *Press Enter*

Command: **Save**

If any of your names, colors, or linetypes are wrong, correct them now and then save your drawing.

Changing the Current Layer

Although you set the TITL-OT layer current with the Make option, you also can set a new layer current (active) with the Set option, like this:

Setting the Current Drawing Layer—Example

?/Make/Set/New/ON/OFF/Color/Ltype/Freeze/Thaw: **S**

New current layer <0>: **TITL-OT**

?/Make/Set/New/ON/OFF/Color/Ltype/Freeze/Thaw: *Press Enter*

Command: **Save**

Set Ltscale to an acceptable value for full-scale output and invoke the Viewres command for better screen resolution of curved entities, as follows:

Setting the Linetype Scale Factor and View Resolution

Command: **Ltscale**

New scale factor <1.0000>: **.375**

Command: **Viewres**

Do you want fast zooms?<Y> *Press Enter*

Enter circle zoom percent (1-20000)<100>: **1000**

Using a Title Block Format

With the layers, colors, and linetypes set, you now are ready to complete the prototype drawing's title block. You can avoid the necessity and expense of purchasing pre-printed title blocked sheets by developing your own title blocks on your prototypes. The title block presented in this exercise contains the following parts:

Contract Number Block	Treatment Block
Drawn Block	Finish Block
Approval Blocks	Similar To Block
Design Activity Name and Address Block	Weight Blocks
Drawing Title Block	Application Block
Size Block	Part Dash Number
Quantity Required Per Assembly	Drawing Number Block
Next Assembly and Used On	Scale Block
Additional Approvals Block	Release Date Block
Sheet Block	Parts List
Standard Tolerance Block	

All of these parts are shown on the title block illustrations and are sized and located according to ANSI Y14.1 standards. If you have the AutoCAD: Drafting and 3D Design Disk, your PROTO-C file includes all of these blocks, with most on frozen layers. If you do not have the AutoCAD: Drafting and 3D Design Disk, you can draw the entire title block, or you can skip part of it. Only the main title block, the parts list, and the revision list are necessary for later exercises, although all parts are shown in the textbook illustrations.

The major parts of the title block are created on different pairs of layers so that layers can be turned off or frozen. Draw the outline of each area on the ????-OT layers, and the complex portions (internal lines and text) on the ????-CX layers. This enables you to turn complex lines and text off by freezing their layers, which will speed up your drawing regenerations and redraws. If you want to freeze or turn off both parts of a pair, use a wildcard, such as TITL??? for TITL-CX and TITL-OT.

Drawing the Main Title Block

Draw the main title block as shown in figure 8.9. Set the corresponding layer current as you draw each part of the title block. The bold lines are controlled by polyline width instead of the layer's color/pen setting, so medium lines, bold lines, and text can be on the same layer. Medium lines can be zero-width polylines, or you can use the Line command for them.

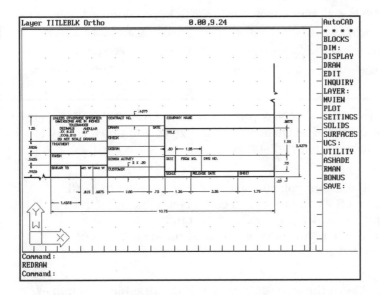

Figure 8.9:
Main title block.

All lines are on the 0.0625 snap of the UCS that you saved under the name BDR, but you might have to adjust the snap increment to 0.3125 to enter some of the text. You might find a 0.5-unit grid easier to work with. Use Snap and Grid to adjust them. Snap and Grid should be dynamic. Modify them as needed. You will find it easier to draw if coords are toggled (Ctrl-D or F6) to show DIST<ANGLE. You can type the coordinates or just pick the DIST<ANGLE shown on the coords line with your cursor. All of the lines are at right angles, so toggling ortho on (Ctrl-O or F8) also will make drawing easier.

First, zoom in to the area you want to draw in. Use a Zoom Window option, which enables you to specify the area by its corners. Then draw the title block outline (the bold top and left lines) on layer TITL-OT. Make sure layer TITL-OT shows current on the status line before you begin this part of the exercise.

Continue in the PROTO-C Drawing

```
Command: Zoom
All/Center/Dynamic/Extents/Left/Previous/Window/Scale(X): W
First corner: 10,-.5
Other corner: 22,8
Command: Pline
From point: 20.9375,2.9375
Current line-width is 0.0200
```
Toggle F8 coords. The width is .02, coords show DIST<<ANGLE, and ortho is toggled on.
```
Arc/Close/Halfwidth/Length/Undo/Width/<Endpoint of line>: @10.75<180
Arc/Close/Halfwidth/Length/Undo/Width/<Endpoint of line>: @2.9375<270
Arc/Close/Halfwidth/Length/Undo/Width/<Endpoint of line>: Press Enter to exit
```

The outline now is on layer TITL-OT. Now put the rest on layer TITL-CX. Several parallel lines need to be drawn. The Offset command gives you an easy way to draw one line and copy it by an offset distance.

 The *Offset* command enables you to copy an entity parallel to itself, once you establish an offset distance. You can offset a line arc, circle, or polyline by giving an offset distance or a through point. Offset is particularly powerful when you have a series of parallel, but otherwise identical, lines to draw.

Temporarily reset your UCS to the lower left corner of the title block to make point entry easier. You can use an @ (the shorthand character for last point) to enter the point because it is the end of the last polyline drawn.

Drawing the Complex Main Title Block

```
Command: UCS
Origin/ZAxis/3point/Entity/View/X/Y/Z/Prev/Restore/Save/Del/?/<World>: O
Origin point <0,0,0>: @
Command: Layer
```

Drawing the Complex Main Title Block—continued

Set layer TITL-CX current

Command: **Pline**

Draw the line between the UNLESS OTHERWISE SPECIFIED *and the* CONTRACT NO. *boxes*

From point: **2.75,0**

Current line-width is 0.0200

Arc/Close/Halfwidth/Length/Undo/Width/<Endpoint of line>: **@2.9375<90**

Arc/Close/Halfwidth/Length/Undo/Width/<Endpoint of line>: *Press Enter*

Command: **Offset**

Copy the line to the right

Offset distance or Through <Through>: **2.75**

Select object to offset: *Pick the last polyline*

Side to offset? *Pick point to the right, and it copies it*

Select object to offset: *Press Enter to exit*

Command: **Pline**

Draw the rest of the bold lines. Use OFFSET where efficient

Command: **Line**

Draw and offset the thin lines

You need text to complete the title block. Most text is 0.1 high, but you will have to temporarily set text height to 0.08 for the ACT. WT and CALC WT boxes. Most text is left justified, but use C (for Center) justification for the UNLESS OTHER-WISE SPECIFIED, DATE, and FSCH NO. boxes. Do not draw the dimensions; they are just there to guide you. Temporarily set snap to .03125 when needed. Zoom in on the parts if it makes entering the text easier. The Zoom command's P (for Previous) option will return you to the current view.

Complete the following steps to add the title block text to your drawing:

Adding the Title Block Text

Command: **Dtext**

Start point or Align/Center/Fit/Middle/Right/Style: **C**

Center point: **1.375,2.75**

Height <0.1250>: **.1**

Rotation angle <0>: *Press Enter*

Text: **UNLESS OTHERWISE SPECIFIED**

Text: **DIMENSIONS ARE IN INCHES**

Adding the Title Block Text—continued

Text: **TOLERANCES**

Text: **DECIMALS   ANGULAR**

Text: *Press Enter*

Command: *Press Enter*

Type in the tolerances with left justified text

DTEXT Start point or Align/Center/Fit/Middle/Right/Style: *Pick a spot under* DECI-MALS

Height <0.1000>: *Press Enter*

Rotation angle <0>: *Press Enter*

Text: **.XX %%p.03 %%p1%%d**

Text: **.XXX%%p.010**

Text: **DO NOT SCALE DRAWING**

Text: **TREATMENT**

Pick another point to enter more text

Text: *Press Enter*

Enter the rest of the text. Watch the .1 and .08 heights!

That completes the main title block. Now use the same techniques to draw the parts list illustrated by figure 8.10.

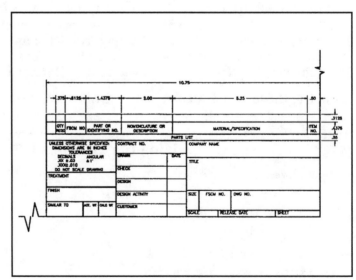

Figure 8.10:
The parts list.

> ### Drawing the Parts List
>
> Command: **Layer**
>
> *Set layer PART-OT current*
>
> Command: **Zoom**
>
> *Use Previous if needed to get the whole title block*
>
> Command: **Pline**
>
> *Draw the bold lines*
>
> Command: **Line**
>
> *Draw the other lines*
>
> Command: **Layer**
>
> *Set layer PART-CX current*
>
> Command: **Dtext**
>
> *Add the text*

The revision list should always be visible on all drawings, so put it on layer
TITL-OT along with the main title block outline. Now use the Zoom command to
move to the upper right corner of the drawing and create a revision block as
shown in figure 8.11.

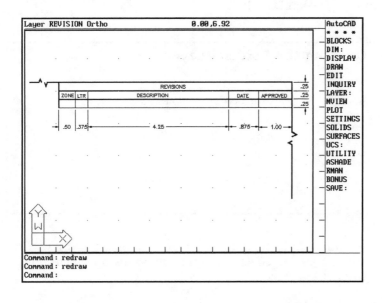

Figure 8.11:
Revision list.

Creating the Current Revision List

Command: **Layer**

Set layer TITL-OT current

Command: **Zoom**

Use Zoom A for All to the entire sheet

Command: *Press Enter*

Command: **Zoom**

Zoom W for Window, to the upper right corner

Command: **Pline**

Draw the bold lines

Command: **Line**

Draw the other vertical lines

Command: **Dtext**

Add the text, 0.1 high, M for middle justification

The border, too, will always be visible. You drew it on layer 0, but it would make more sense if it were on the TITL-OT layer. Change the border's layer by completing all of the following steps (Do not execute the Save command if you have the AutoCAD: Drafting and 3D Design Disk.):

Creating the Border's Layer

Command: Chprop

Select objects: 1 selected, 1 found. *Pick the border polyline*

Select objects *Press Enter*

Change what property (Color/LAyer/LType/Thickness) ? **LA**

New layer <0>: **TITL-OT**

Change what property (Color/LAyer/LType/Thickness) ? *Press Enter to exit*

Command: **Save**

The rest of the title block is optional. If you want to create a complete ANSI Y14.1 sheet, you can add an application block and an engineering specifications block, as illustrated in figure 8.12.

Complete the following steps to do the application block:

Set layer APPL-OT current. Draw the top and left line with Pline. Set layer APPL-CX current. Use Line and Offset to create the rest of the lines. Finally, use Dtext, 0.1 high and middle justified, to add the text.

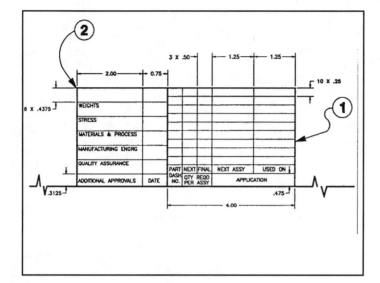

Figure 8.12:
Optional application and engineering specifications blocks.

Complete the following steps to do the engineering specifications block:

Set layer SPEC-OT current. Draw the top and left line with Pline. Set layer SPEC-CX current. Use Line and Offset to create the rest of the lines. Use Dtext, 0.1 high and middle justified to add the text. Finally, save, unless you have the AutoCAD: Drafting and 3D Design Disk.

Establishing Standards for General Notes

General notes can apply to a specific part being drawn, or they can be standardized to apply to all of your drawings. If you have standard general notes, you can make them a part of your prototype drawing. In any case, general notes should conform to the following standards:

- Notes should be clear, concise, and imperative.
- Notes should be parallel to the lower edge of the border.
- Notes should be in standard upper case text and not underlined.
- Locate general notes in upper left of B,C,D,E,F sheets, and do not exceed an 8-inch width.
- Punctuate according to rules of English grammar and avoid non-standard abbreviations.
- Sequence notes by fabricating or manufacturing process.

Use the following instructions to add general notes to the PROTO-C drawing. When applying this to your own work, both parts lists and general notes begin on Page 1 and continue as necessary. When the parts list is so long that it extends into the general notes, start the general notes on Page 1 and continue them on subsequent pages. Complete the following steps to add the example notes as illustrated in figure 8.13.

Figure 8.13:
Optional prototype general notes.

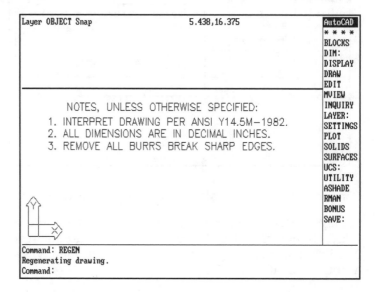

Set layer NOTES current. Zoom to the upper left corner of the drawing. Use 0.125-high, centered text for the NOTES, UNLESS OTHERWISE SPECIFIED heading. Use 0.125 Dtext with the default left justification for the rest of the notes. Finally, save, unless you have the AutoCAD: Drafting and 3D Design Disk.

Controlling Layer Status

You can control which layers will be off (calculated but not displayed), frozen (not calculated or displayed), or thawed and on (displayed normally). If you want to display only the object lines of a drawing, turn off or freeze layers such as CONST, HL, CL, TEXT, and DIM. You can enter multiple layer names with wildcards or on one line with names separated by commas. Turning off or freezing unneeded layers increases your drafting speed and efficiency because unnecessary information is not displayed or plotted. You can control the status of layers by using either the screen menu, tablet menu, or the layer dialogue box.

If you try to draw on a layer that is off, your lines will disappear. AutoCAD protects you from accidentally turning the current layer off by giving a `Really` want layer 0 (the current layer) off? <N> prompt. Simply respond by typing **Yes** if you want it off.

During normal drawing, you do not need to see the interior lines and text of the title block, application block, parts list, and engineering specifications block. Turn these layers off or, better still, freeze them by freezing ????-CX. Their -OT outline layers still display so you can see what space the blocks occupy. If, when starting a new drawing, you want to freeze both layers for the application block, parts list, and engineering specifications block, you can do so by specifying APPL-??,PART-??,SPEC-??. Then, to later call up different parts of the title format, simply thaw or turn on its layer.

Paper Space Viewport Layer Control

The Layer command controls and affects layers globally. The Vplayer command enables you to control the status of layers individually, in each paper space viewport. You can make a layer visible (ON or Thawed) in one paper space viewport, for example, while it is investable (OFF or Frozen) in another paper space viewport. You can have any combination of layers displayed or investable in one, or all, of the TILEMODE off (paper space) viewports.

The following options control Vplayer:

- **Freeze.** Enables you to specify one or more layers to freeze in one or more viewports.

- **Thaw.** Enables you to thaw layers that were frozen in selected viewports.

- **Reset.** Restores the default visibility setting for a layer in a selected viewport.

- **Newfrz.** Creates new layers that are frozen in all viewports. This enables you to create a new layer but have it displayed only in a single working viewport.

- **Vpvisdflt.** Enables you to set a default visibility per viewport for any layer. This default decides the status of layers in all new viewports.

All of these options require you to select the viewports in which the settings will be made. You are prompted in one of the following ways:

- **All.** Applies changes to all viewports, including those that are OFF or Frozen

- **Select.** Waits for you to make a selection or selection set

- **<Current>.** Applies changes to the current viewport only

Dialogue Paper Space Viewport Layer Control

You also can use the layer dialogue box, the Ddlmodes command shown in figure 8.14, to control the status of layers in paper space viewports.

Figure 8.14:
*Layer dialogue box
Viewport options.*

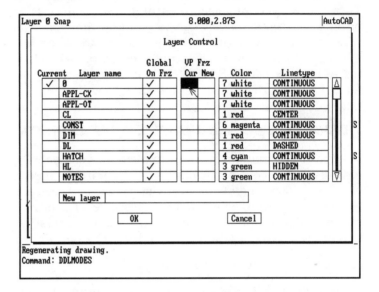

Paper space layers can be controlled from the dialogue box by using the following Viewport Freeze options:

- **Cur.** Heads the Viewport Freeze Current column. This column controls the freeze/thaw status of the layers in the current paper space viewport. A check designates the layer is frozen.

- **New.** Heads the ViewPort Freeze New column. This column controls how layers will be displayed in new paper space viewports. A check designates that the layer(s) will be frozen in any subsequently created viewport.

Startup Layer Status for the Prototype

Set the status of layers on your prototype drawing so that the drawing is ready for drafting upon initial startup. The following exercise shows how to set up the drafting prototype. Freeze layers that are commonly unused during initial drawing tasks. You can turn them off instead, or you can set OBJECT as your default current layer. Complete the following steps to set the prototype layers. (If you have the AutoCAD: Drafting and 3D Design Disk, skip the Save command at the end of the exercise.):

Setting the Prototype Layers

Command: **Layer**

?/Make/Set/New/ON/OFF/Color/Ltype/Freeze/Thaw: **S**

New current layer <>: **OBJECT**

Command: **Layer**

?/Make/Set/New/ON/OFF/Color/Ltype/Freeze/Thaw: **F**

Layer name(s) to Freeze: **????-OT,SPEC-??,APPL-??,PART-??,NOTES**

Layer ?/Make/Set/New/ON/OFF/Color/Ltype/Freeze/Thaw: *Press Enter*

Command: **Save**

The OBJECT layer is now current. When you begin a new drawing from PROTO-C, OBJECT will be the active drawing layer. Only the border, revision block, and main title block outline will be visible; the rest of the title layers are frozen to speed up display and regeneration time. Put important text, such as the drawing name and number, on the TITL-OT layer to keep it visible.

Saving a View ALL

Finally, you need to add a scratch USC and a couple of views to the prototype drawing to make drawing easier. After AutoCAD has regenerated a view of the drawing, you can zoom to smaller views and pan (move the view from side to side) within that regenerated area without another regeneration. Panning and zooming then occur at redraw (redisplay without recalculation) speed, which is much faster than regeneration. A Zoom All always regenerates (often twice, to find the drawing extents). You can eliminate many of these regenerations by saving a view ALL. You will make view ALL about 20 percent bigger than the border to allow a little buffer. This buffer eliminates accidental regenerations caused by a pan or zoom extending slightly beyond the edge of the border.

Use the Zoom command to move out to a view that is slightly bigger than the entire drawing, and save it as ALL. Use a zoom scale factor of 0.8, so the drawing extents fill 80 percent of the screen. (By contrast, a scale of 0.8X would fill 80 percent of the screen with the current view.) You also will have to restore BDR, the prototype's default UCS, and use Plan to orient the UCS view. Start by making a BDR view, as follows:

▶

Creating View ALL

```
Command: UCS
Origin/ZAxis/3point/Entity/View/X/Y/Z/Prev/Restore/Save/Del/?/<World>: R
?/Name of UCS to restore: BDR
Command: Plan
<Current UCS>/Ucs/World: Press Enter
Command: Zoom
All/Center/Dynamic/Extents/Left/Previous/Vmax/Window/Scale(X/XP): .8
Regenerating drawing.
Command: View
?/Delete/Restore/Save/Window: S
View name to save: ALL
```

Creating a Paper Space Bordered Sheet and Title Block

Now you need to create a paper space view of our prototype drawing border. You have already created the bordered and title block sheet; therefore, it is a simple matter to insert it into a paper space viewport. Once this drawing sheet is in paper space, you will be able to work in TILEMODE model space and transfer your completed drawings to the paper space sheet or work directly in TILEMODE OFF Mspace/Pspace. This choice will be yours. Either technique can be used to accomplish the exercises contained in this book.

▶

Creating a Paper Space Drawing Sheet

```
Command: TILEMODE
New value for TILEMODE <1>: 0
Entering Paper space. Use MVIEW to insert Modelspace viewports.
Regenerating drawings.
Command: Mview
ON/OFF/Hideplot/Fit/2/3/4/Restore/<First Point>: F
Regenerating drawing.
```

Your prototype drawing sheet should now be displayed in paper space, as shown in figure 8.15

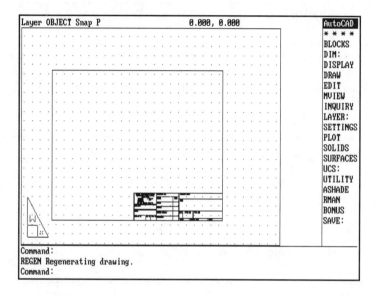

Figure 8.15:
The prototype drawing sheet in paper space.

Checking and Ending the Prototype

Before ending this session, switch TILEMODE on again and check some of your settings.

Switching Back to TILEMODE Model Space

Command: **TILEMODE**

New value for TILEMODE <0>: **1**

Regenerating drawing.

As you worked, you changed snap, ortho, layers, and other settings. Check your settings against table 8.3, which follows, and table 8.2. Change any settings if you need to. Then end your drawing. If you have the AutoCAD: Drafting and 3D Design Disk, you do not need to end because you already have a final PROTO-C drawing.

Table 8.3
Prototype Drawing Settings

GRID	SNAP	COORDS	TEXT HEIGHT	ORTHO
1.0/ON	0.0625/ON	DIST<ANGLE	0.125	Off

Complete the following steps to check the PROTO-C drawing and end this session, as follows:

Checking and Ending PROTO-C

Command: **Layer**

Check the layers, colors, and linetypes. Check the frozen layers. Make sure OBJECT is current.

Command: **Setvar**

Set TEXTSIZE back to 0.125. Check and adjust the other settings in table 8.2.

Command: **End**

You have a finished C-size prototype. To use it in new drawing startups, simply enter the new drawing name equal to it, such as newname=PROTO-C, or configure it as the default.

That completes the required prototype setup, although a modified version of this prototype will be used for 3D drafting and design later in the book. The following optional section is intended specifically for 3D work. You can skip this section until you edit this prototype for 3D in a later chapter, or if time permits, complete it now.

Setting Up a Scratch View and UCS

It would be convenient if you could draw in a scratch area on any layer, without interfering with your drawing. Then you could experiment or develop parts in clear space, and move them into your main drawing when done. You can do this with the help of the UCS command. You have already offset the UCS origin and saved a UCS. To make a scratch area, you will create a SCRATCH UCS as illustrated in figure 8.16.

The SCRATCH UCS has its origin at the WCS (World Coordinate System) coordinates of -.53125,-.53125, exactly the opposite offset of your BDR UCS origin. Scratch has its XY axes rotated 180 degrees from the WCS, so they also are exactly opposed to BDR's XY axes. When you draw in the SCRATCH UCS, it appears just as normal as the BDR UCS, with its own local axes. After you draw a part there, you can move it into the real drawing by simply rotating it 180 degrees about the WCS 0,0 origin. Because the positive coordinates of SCRATCH extend in the opposite directions of the positive coordinates of BDR, they will not get in each other's way during normal drawing.

After creating the UCS, you can orient the display view to it with the Plan command, which will be fully explained in the 3D chapters. For now, you just need Plan to do its default, which is like a Zoom All oriented to the current UCS.

Although you still are in the temporary offset UCS, you can specify WCS coordinates by prefacing them with an asterisk, such as *0,0 for the WCS origin.

To create a Scratch UCS, complete the following steps:

Creating a SCRATCH UCS

Command: **UCS**

Origin,ZAxis/3point/Entity/View/X/Y/Z/Prev/Restore/Save/Del/?/<World>: **3**

Origin point <0,0,0>: ***0,0**

Point on positive portion of the X-axis <-9.7188,-0.5313,0.0000>: ***-1,0,0**

Point on positive-Y portion of the UCS X-Y plane <-10.7188,-1.5313,0.0000>: ***0,-1,0**

Command: *Press Enter*

UCS Origin/ZAxis/3point/Entity/View/X/Y/Z/Prev/Restore/Save/Del/?/<World>: **O**

Origin point <0,0,0>: ***-.53125,-.53125**

Command: **UCS**

Origin/ZAxis/3point/Entity/View/X/Y/Z/Prev/Restore/Save/Del/?/<World>: **Save**

?/Name of UCS: **SCRATCH**

Command: **Plan**

<Current UCS>/Ucs/World: *Press Enter*

Regenerating drawing.

Command: **Zoom**

All/Center/Dynamic/Extents/Left/Previous/Window/<Scale(X)>: **C**

Center point: ***0,0**

Magnification or Height <4.2500> : **34**

Regenerating drawing.

Figure 8.16:
SCRATCH, WORLD,
and BDR UCSs.

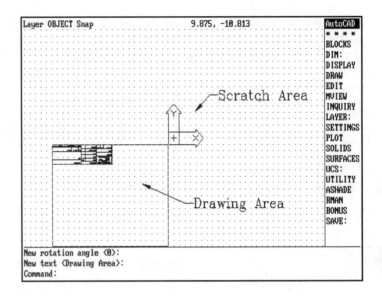

Your drawing should match figure 8.16, without the annotations.

In the preceding exercise, the Plan and Zoom commands each caused the drawing to regenerate. You can eliminate the need for one of these commands by saving a view. Save the upper right part of the display as the view SCRATCH. Then, when you go to the Scratch UCS, you also can restore the SCRATCH view, eliminating the Plan and Zoom steps.

Complete the following steps to save the SCRATCH view:

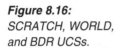

Saving the SCRATCH View

```
Command: View
?/Delete/Restore/Save/Window: W
View name to save: SCRATCH
First corner: -1,-1
Other corner: 22,17
Command: Press Enter
VIEW
?/Delete/Restore/Save/Window: R
View name to restore: SCRATCH
```

The saved and restored SCRATCH view should match figure 8.17.

Now restore the View ALL, to prepare the prototype for drafting, as follows:

Restoring View ALL

Command: **UCS**

Origin/ZAxis/3point/Entity/View/X/Y/Z/Prev/Restore/Save/Del/?/<World>: **R**

?/Name of UCS to restore: **BDR**

Command: **View**

?/Delete/Restore/Save/Window: **R**

View name to restore: **ALL**

Regenerating drawing.

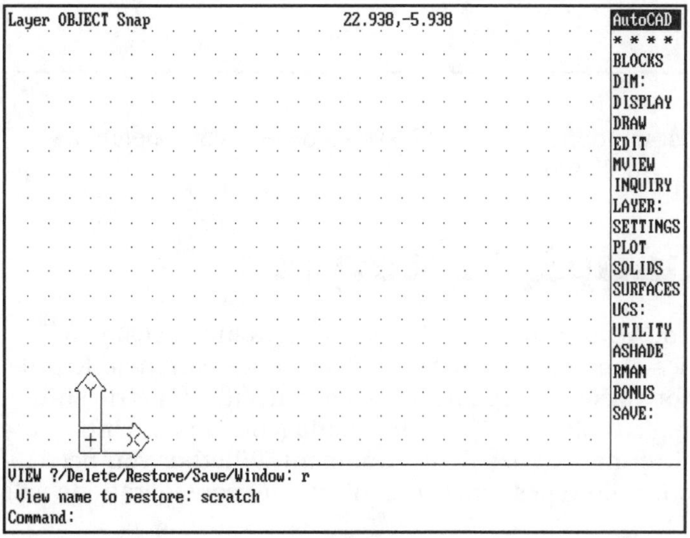

Figure 8.17:
The SCRATCH view.

Your AutoCAD setup probably uses the default name ACAD.DWG as its automatic prototype drawing. New drawings will start up using this default prototype drawing unless you instruct AutoCAD to use a different default. Because most of the textbook exercises use the PROTO-C prototype drawing, make it the default.

Use the following instructions to set up a separate configuration in the SI-ACAD directory for AutoCAD: Drafting and 3D Design's exercises. This way, you can change the default without affecting your normal AutoCAD setup. Do this whether or not you have the AutoCAD: Drafting and 3D Design Disk. Start from the main menu.

You can configure PROTO-C as the default drawing by completing the following steps:

Configuring PROTO-C as the Default Drawing

```
Enter selection: 5

Press RETURN to continue: Press Enter

Enter selection <0>: 8

Enter selection <0>: 2

Enter name of default prototype file for new drawings or . for none <ACAD>:
PROTO-C

Enter selection <0>: Press Enter three times

Enter selection <0>: 1

Command: Quit
```

Now all new drawings will start identically to PROTO-C unless you specify a different prototype with an equal sign.

Organizing Multiple Prototypes

As the number of your AutoCAD drafting and design projects increases, you might need to create a series of prototype drawings. This series can include prototypes that are designed for various sizes and scales of output, SI metric standards, and possibly first-angle projection. Good file management is essential to maintaining a productive drafting and design environment. Whether you need one or one hundred different prototypes, a few organizational considerations will help keep them straight.

- Name your prototypes informatively. The name is only a handle for recalling the prototype, but it also can provide information about the prototype. The drawing in this exercise, for example, is a prototype, C-size, thus the name PROTO-C. The nomenclature or code you use to name and keep track of your prototype drawings is strictly up to you.

- Group prototypes along with other support files in an AutoCAD support directory. You can use the SET ACAD=directory environment setting to tell AutoCAD to look in that directory for support files.

- AutoCAD can automatically load your default prototype drawing. The factory default is ACAD.DWG, but you can assign any name. In the configuration menu, choose 2. Initial drawing setup under the 8. Configure operating parameters submenu.

- Having a different prototype for each sheet size is all right. A different prototype for each combination of sheet size, title block design, and plot scale is simple and reasonable if you only have a few combinations, as has been done in the textbook exercises. This simple approach gets unwieldy, however, if you have several combinations. If you used four different sheet sizes, each with three different title blocks, and you plotted to five different scales, you would need 60 prototypes. That would be a management and maintenance nightmare.

A simple, combined sheet size, scale, title block prototype is fine for these exercises, but you should set up an automated system for real work. Many of the settings mentioned in the textbook for prototyping are scale-dependent — snap, grid, and text height, for example. The simple approach of one prototype for each combination of sheet size and plot scale yields an unwieldy number of combinations.

If you have the Autocad: Drafting and 3D Design Disk's ANSI Y14.5 Menu System, the use of prototypes is greatly simplified. The Y14.5 Menu System contains routines for setting up both decimal inch and SI metric production drafting prototype drawings. The Y14.5 Menu System uses just one prototype for each sheet size and automatically adjusts the scale-related settings for the desired plot scale. You included the title blocks in the prototypes, but they could be kept in separate files and inserted at the appropriate scale by the menu if your application requires various title blocks.

Scaling for Plotting

Many prototype settings are scale-dependent, so you need to understand how scaling is done in CAD drawings to deal with them. In manual drafting, you draw most representations of objects smaller than their real world size so that you can fit them on a sheet of paper (or other media). In CAD, you draw within an unlimited world, set by your drawing limits. This makes drawing much easier because you do not have to scale objects down to draw them. You simply draw in real-world units.

You need to consider the final product, however. In most cases, the final product is the drawing, which must fit on a real sheet of paper. So at plot time, you have to scale the drawing by the same scale factor that you would have used to draw it if you had drawn it manually. You need to draw text and symbols at a size that will look right in the plot when scaled by this plot scale factor.

Scale Factor Settings

When you set the scale factor of an AutoCAD drawing, it affects several drawing parameters. These include sheet size, line width, text size, dimensioning, symbol size, and linetype scale.

Of the drawing parameters presented in the preceding exercises, sheet size is the most important. AutoCAD calls the sheet size setting *limits*. To determine your limits for a particular sheet size, you need to know what scale it is intended for. Consider a C-sized, 22x17 sheet, for example:

Table 8.4
C-Size Scales and Sizes

SIZE	SCALE	LIMITS	DRAWING AREA	PLOT SCALE
C-22x17	FULL	0,0 to 22,17	15x8	1
C-22x17	0.5=1	0,0 to 44,34	30x16	2
C-22x17	0.25=1	0,0 to 88,68	60x32	4
C-22x17	0.125=1	0,0 to 176,136	120x64	8

The important thing to consider when determining limits is the drawing area needed to represent the object. The DRAWING AREA column in table 8.4 is approximate, based on your PROTO-C and allowing for title block, dimensions, and notes. You back into this table when drawing. You know about how big the object to be drawn is, and you know what scale or sheet size you would like to fit it onto. The table tells you if it fits or if you have to try a different sheet size or scale.

Now determine the sheet size, scale, and limits of a 40-inch diameter flange drawn real-world size. The drawing's two orthographic views take up about 60 by 40 inches. According to the drawing size column in the table, it requires a scale of 0.125=1 to fit on a C-size sheet with its available drawing size of 120x64. It is a simple matter of calculation and title block design to extend the above table to other sheet sizes and scales.

Adjusting Settings and Graphics for Scale

After you determine drawing scale, adjust your scale-dependent drawing settings. If you want text to be 0.125 on the plot at a scale of 0.125=1 (1:8), for example, multiply 0.125 text height by 8, and draw it one unit high.

All scalar dimension variables must be similarly adjusted. The DIMSCALE system variable makes this easy. Just reset DIMSCALE to the plot scale factor shown in the preceding table, and AutoCAD multiplies it against the other dimensioning variables when you draw dimensions. Other settings such as grid and snap, and graphics such as polyline thicknesses, also are multiplied by this same factor. In fact, the Y14.5 Menu System uses DIMSCALE as a global scale factor for all settings and symbols. Symbols, such as bubbles, are scaled proportionately to text, so a 0.25-inch bubble should be drawn 2 inches (0.25x8) to plot at 0.25 inches. Graphics such as title blocks also should be inserted or rescaled by the same plot scale factor.

When you use PROTO-C to start a new drawing at other than full scale, you need to adjust these settings. The AutoCAD: Drafting and 3D Design Y14.5 Menu System automates this for you. See Chapter 12 for more information on the use of the Y14.5 Menu System. You also can develop your own custom startup routines. See the books *Maximizing AutoCAD, Volumes I* and *II* (New Riders Publishing) for these techniques.

Summary

This chapter showed you how to develop a generic prototype drawing that you can adapt to your own drafting application(s) or use as a springboard for additional prototypes that fit your specific needs.

Chapter 9 uses your new prototype drawing as a starting point for its exercises. You will be introduced to some new commands and techniques that are used for precision drafting and editing and shown how to dimension engineering drawings to industrial standards.

9

2D Orthographic Drafting and Advanced Editing

In this chapter:

- Using multiple viewports
- Working in temporary UCS
- Editing the BRACKET drawing
- Picking precise geometric positions using Object Snaps
- Extending lines
- Mirroring the BRACKET drawing

217

Overview

Although AutoCAD's 3D drafting capabilities are impressive, many parts and objects can be adequately drafted in 2D. In fact, most shop drawings require only fully dimensioned two-dimensional drawings to produce a part in a non-automated manufacturing facility. If 2D drafting supplies the necessary information, 2D is the right tool for the job.

This chapter explains how to draft a dimensioned 2D orthographic drawing of the mounting bracket shown in figure 9.1. You also will learn how editing commands which break, trim, and mirror entities complement the entity creation commands. You will set up multiple viewports and use the Zoom command to manipulate the drawing screen. You also will work with the settings, linetypes, and layers from the previous chapter's prototype drawing.

Figure 9.1:
The completed BRACKET drawing, which you will create in this chapter.

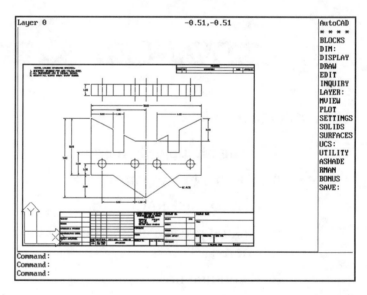

AutoCAD has a number of geometric positioning tools such as the object snap override that enable you to develop very precise geometry. Object snap or Osnaps provide a modifier for picking precise geometric positions. As you will see in the following exercise, object snaps enable you to instruct the computer to find the `endpoint` of a selected line or the `center` of a selected circle. You let the computer do the work for you.

Using a prototype drawing saves time. The PROTO-C prototype developed in Chapter 8 has all the necessary parameters for this exercise. If you do not have the AutoCAD: Drafting and 3D Design Disk, (which contains the PROTO-C drawing) or have not completed Chapter 8, do so before continuing.

Using Multiple Viewports

The following exercise uses two vertical viewports to display different views of the BRACKET drawing. You will edit the drawing close-up in a zoomed viewport while you view the entire drawing in the other.

 Note You will be instructed how to set up your viewports in both TILEMODE model space and paper space. Later exercises will use only one of the techniques, but you can use either one.

Begin a new drawing named BRACKET=PROTO-C. Layer OBJECT should be current. Remember that throughout the exercises in this textbook you are to press Enter after responding to a prompt.

To set up a TILEMODE model space viewport, follow these steps:

Setting Multiple Views

 Begin a new drawing named TEMP=PROTO-C

 Begin a new drawing named BRACKET=PROTO-C

Command: **Vports**

Save/Restore/Delete/Join/Off/?/2/<3>/4: **2**

Horizontal/<Vertical>: *Press Enter and activate the left viewport by clicking on it with your mouse*

You have now divided your screen into two viewports, as illustrated in figure 9.2. To set up a paper space viewport, complete the following steps:

Command: **Tilemode**

New value for TILEMODE <1>: **0**

Entering Paper space. Use MVIEW to insert Model space viewports.

Regenerating drawing.

Use the Erase command and erase the paper space viewport with the bordered sheet already on it.

Command: **Erase**

Command: **Mview**

ON/OFF/Hideplot/Fit/2/3/4/Restore/<First Point>: **2**

Horizontal/<Vertical>: *Press Enter*

Fit/<first point>: **F**

Command: *Type* **Mspace** *and click your mouse on the left viewport to make it active.*

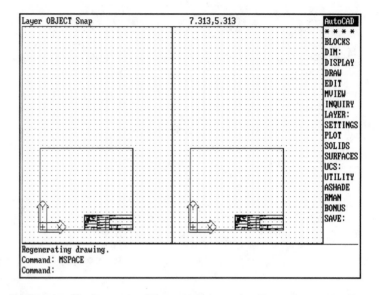

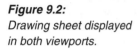

Figure 9.2:
Drawing sheet displayed in both viewports.

You now can work in TILEMODE off model space if you want. If you would rather work in TILEMODE model space, do the following to return to TILEMODE. Type **Tilemode** at the Command: prompt and type **1** at the New value for TILEMODE <0>: prompt.

Multiple viewports display the current drawing when first set. Only one viewport can be active, however. To make a viewport current, move your cursor to that viewport and click with your mouse. AutoCAD displays a bold border around the current viewport. The cursor displays in the active viewport and an arrow displays in the nonactive viewport(s).

Now use the Pan command to reposition the border drawing in the center of the left viewport as follows:

Panning the Drawing Up

Command: **Pan**

Displacement: *Click on the center of the border area*

Second point: *Click on the center of the left viewport*

Regenerating drawing.

The drawing should be centered in the left viewport. Now activate the right viewport and use the Zoom command to work in the right viewport as follows.

Zooming Center

Command: **Zoom**

All/Center/Dynamic/Extents/Left/Previous/Window/<Scale(X)>: **C**

Center point: **9,8**

Magnification or Height <21.2500>: **11**

Your screen should resemble figure 9.3.

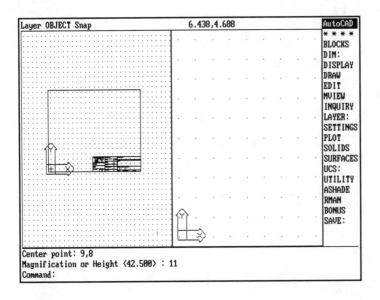

Figure 9.3:
Left viewport panned, and the right viewport zoomed.

Now activate the left viewport and fill it a bit better with the border as follows:

Zooming Dynamically

Command: **Zoom**

All/Center/Dynamic/Extents/Left/Previous/Window/<Scale(X)>: **D**

Your screen should now resemble figure 9.4. Click to get the resizing arrow and drag to about the width of the border and click to get the X to move (see fig. 9.5). Now move the mouse side to side and watch the hourglass (see fig. 9.6). Repeat the resizing if needed to fill the box with the border. Center the box on the border and press Enter to execute the zoom. The resulting display is shown in figure 9.7.

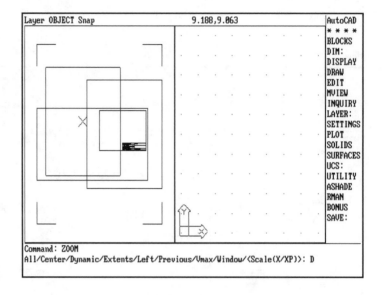

Figure 9.4:
The Zoom dynamic screen.

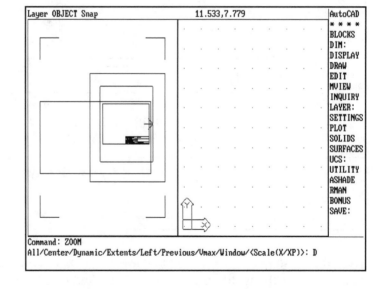

Figure 9.5:
Changing the new view box size.

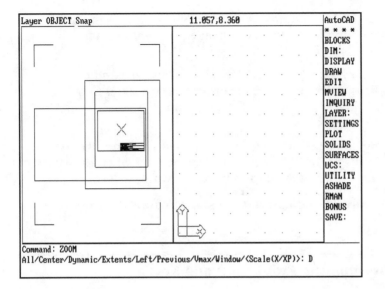

Figure 9.6:
Locating the new view box.

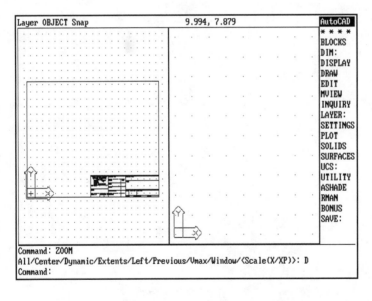

Figure 9.7:
The resulting display.

Drafting the BRACKET Profile

You will develop the BRACKET drawing using a combination of absolute, relative, and polar coordinates in the prototype's BDR UCS and other temporary coordinate systems. Type the coordinates as they are shown, or use Snap, Grid, and your Coords display to guide you in clicking on equivalent points.

 Note Remember that if you make a keyboard mistake, backspace and correct it before you press Enter. If you make other errors, type **U** in the Line command or at the `Command:` prompt to undo it.

Because the bracket is symmetrical, you can draw the left half and use the Mirror command later to copy it to the right half. Toggle Ortho on when drawing vertical and horizontal lines and reset Snap to make drawing easier.

Make the right viewport current and follow these steps to draw the front view and notch:

Drawing the Front View and Notch

```
Command: Snap
Snap spacing or ON/OFF/Aspect/Rotate/Style <1.0000>: 0.125
Command: Line
From point: 12,4
To point: @-3,2
To point: @2<180
To point: @5<90
To point: @4,-2
To point: @1<0
To point: C
Command: Chprop
Select objects: L
1 found.
Select objects: Press Enter
Change what property (Color/LAyer/LType/Thickness) ? LA
New layer <OBJECT>: CL
Change what property (Color/LAyer/LType/Thickness) ? Press Enter
Command: Line
From point: 9,10
To point: @2<-90
To point: @1<0
To point: @2<90
To point: Press Enter
Command: Save
```

Your drawing should resemble figure 9.8. You will trim the notch later.

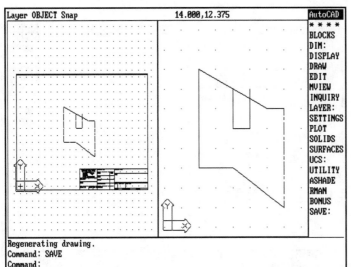

Figure 9.8:
Half bracket with notch.

If your center lines are not showing proper lengths and gaps, change the value of the Ltscale variable. Keep in mind, however, that the on-screen appearance of linetype spacing and the final product, which is the plotted output, may differ. Set the Ltscale factor to achieve the best results in plotted form. The best setting for 1:1 scale is 0.375, so you were asked to pre-set this value on your prototype. You can set it to a different value temporarily to make viewing easier, but remember to reset it before plotting.

Working in a Temporary UCS

Repositioning the coordinate system origin sets a new 0,0 home base, making it simple to position or create entities relative to the new 0,0 origin. This technique is useful for both 2D and 3D drafting.

Because the bracket is symmetrical, position the UCS at its bottom point, as follows:

Changing the Origin of the UCS Icon

```
Command: Ucs
Origin/ZAxis/3point/Entity/View/X/Y/Z/Prev/Restore/Save/Del/?/<World>: O
Origin point <0,0,0>: 12,4
```

Your drawing should display the UCS icon at the new origin, the lower center of the bracket, as shown in figure 9.9.

Figure 9.9:
UCS icon at the new origin.

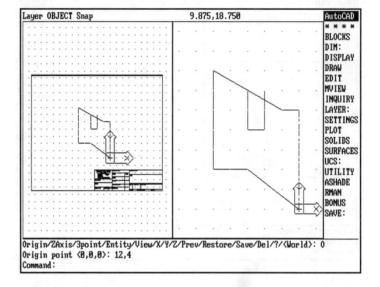

The completed bracket has four holes in it. You will construct two of them now; the other two will be generated later when you mirror the other half of the bracket.

You can draw circles in several ways. Try the default center point and radius, as well as the diameter option. You can drag and click on the radius and diameter with the aid of Snap and Coords, but the following exercise provides the values to type in:

Making the Circles on the Bracket

```
Command: Circle
3P/2P/TTR/<Center point>: -4,3
Diameter/<Radius>: .375
Command: Press Enter
CIRCLE 3P/2P/TTR/<Center point>: -1,3
Diameter/<Radius>: D
Diameter: .75
Command: Save
```

Your drawing should now resemble the one shown in figure 9.10.

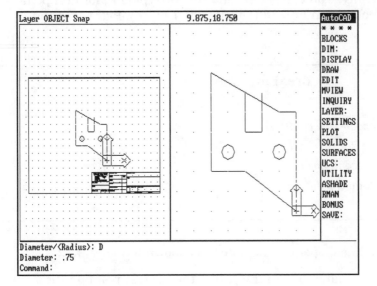

Figure 9.10:
BRACKET with circles.

Editing by Breaking the BRACKET Drawing

AutoCAD's editing commands correct mistakes. They also serve as important drafting tools to modify drawings. Your drafting production will be greatly enhanced by understanding AutoCAD's advanced editing commands.

AutoCAD enables you to break entities into smaller pieces. You can break lines, arcs, or circles by specifying the entity to break, the point to break from, and the point to break to.

The *Break* command enables you to split or erase portions of lines, arcs, circles, 2D polylines, and traces. When you select an object to break, the default assumes your pick point is also your first break point.

When breaking circles, the Break command creates arcs, removing the counter-clockwise portion between the two pick points.

The first pick point is the default first break point, but if it is at an intersection, it may pick the wrong entity. You can get around this by typing **F**, for first point, to reselect your break point. Continue in the BRACKET or TEMP drawing and follow these steps:

Breaking Lines

```
Command: Break
Select object: Pick first point (see fig. 9.11)
Enter second point (or F for first point): F
Enter first point: Pick second point
Enter second point: Pick third point
Command: Save
```

The diagonal is now two lines, opening the notch, as shown in figure 9.12.

If you select a break point that is not on the entity, the nearest point on the entity is used. This will be perpendicular to the break point for lines and at the point of the tangent that would form a perpendicular for arcs and circles. If the break point is off the end of a line or arc, the entire end will be broken off, leaving only one line or arc.

Figure 9.11:
Pick line and points to break.

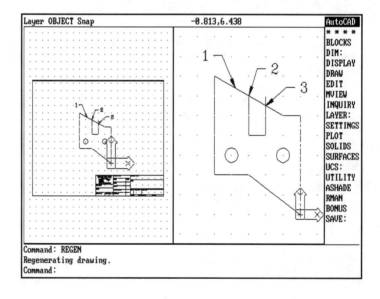

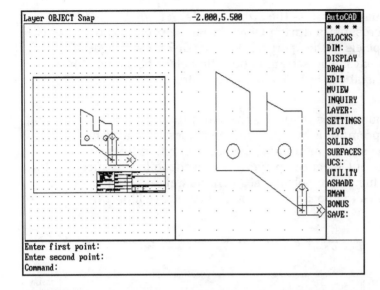

Figure 9.12:
The notch is opened.

You probably had no trouble picking the exact intersections of the lines in your exercise drawing since they were convenient snap points. Realistically, however, pick points often are at an odd geometric spacing, and you cannot snap accurately, or the snap increment required may be so small as to be impractical without zooming way in. AutoCAD's Object Snap modes offer an alternate way to accurately pick points on existing geometry.

Picking Precise Geometric Positions Using Object Snap

Object Snap modes aid point picking by enabling you to specify several modes of geometric points on existing entities. It then filters the pick point and moves it to the nearest point that matches the geometric mode used. You can move to the exact intersection of two lines, circles, or arcs with the Int mode, for example. Think of it as snapping to attachment points on entities.

You can use Object Snap modes amid any point entry by entering the mode(s) desired before picking the point. The Object Snap mode normally searches all objects crossing the aperture and selects the closest potential snap point of the specified type(s). The aperture is a box added to the crosshairs during the Object Snap mode to indicate the range of the Object Snap search area.

The *Aperture* command controls the size of the target box located in the middle of the crosshairs during Object Snap selection. You can change the size in pixels of the aperture box. The default setting is 10 pixels for most displays. The setting is half the height of the box, or the number of pixels above or below the crosshairs.

You enter the Object Snap modes by typing their first three letters and pressing Enter at the `Command:` prompt, or by selecting the modes from a menu. The * * * * option from the screen menu and the `Assist` option from the pull-down menu present lists of Object Snap overrides. In the following mode listing, line and arc apply to a line or arc polyline segment as well as to a line or arc entity. You have 12 modes to choose from, some of these are illustrated in figure 9.13.

Figure 9.13:
Object snap locations.

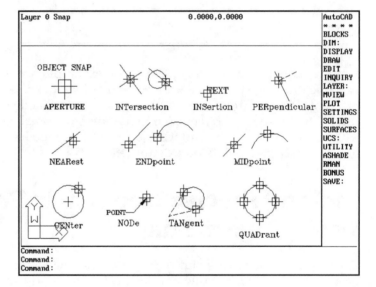

- ■ **CENter.** Snaps to the center point of an arc or circle. Pick it on its circumference or arc.

- ■ **ENDpoint.** Snaps to the closest endpoint of a line or arc. (Type Endp instead of End to avoid having it accidentally interpreted as the End command.)

- ■ **INSert.** Snaps to the insertion point of a shape, text, or block entity.

- ■ **INTersec.** Snaps to the intersection of any combination of two lines, circles, or arcs. Both objects must cross the aperture on the screen.

- ■ **MIDpoint.** Snaps to the midpoint of a line or arc.

- **NEArest.** Snaps to the point on a line, arc, circle, or point entity that is closest to the crosshairs.

- **NODe.** Snaps to a point entity.

- **NONe.** Suppresses or turns off the Object Snap mode.

- **PERpend.** Snaps to the point on a line, circle, or arc that is perpendicular from the previous point or perpendicular to the next point.

- **QUAdrant.** Snaps to the closest quadrant (0, 90, 180, and 270 degree) point of an arc or circle.

- **QUIck.** Overrules the normal Object Snap search of all objects crossing the aperture. When many items are visible on the screen, this search can cause a noticeable delay. If you use QUI mode along with other Object modes, it moves to the first qualified point found instead of searching all possibilities for the nearest. The point found will generally be one of the most recent entities.

- **TANgent.** Snaps to the point on a circle or arc that, when connected to the previous or next point, forms a line tangent to that object.

Continue in the BRACKET or TEMP drawing and try a few of the Object Snap modes while using the Break command, as follows:

Breaking a Line Using Object Snap

Command: *Toggle F9 to turn off Snap*

Command: **U**

Command: **Break**

BREAK Select object: **NEA**

to *Position cursor so aperture corner crosses only the top diagonal, then click (see fig. 9.14)*

Enter second point (or F for first point): **F**

Enter first point: **END**

of *Position cursor so aperture crosses top of left vertical notch line, then click (see fig. 9.15)*

Enter second point: **INT**

of *Position cursor so aperture crosses both diagonal and other vertical notch lines, then click (see fig. 9.16)*

Command: *Toggle F9 to restore snap*

Use the Undo command so you can use the Trim command to open the notch.

Command: **U**

Figures 9.14, 9.15, 9.16, and 9.17 illustrate how your screen should have appeared during this exercise.

You can create accurate drawings in AutoCAD by one of three ways: snapping to a snap increment; entering coordinates (absolute, relative, or polar); and object snapping to existing geometry. Use whichever method best suits the situation.

Figure 9.14:
Pick line to break.

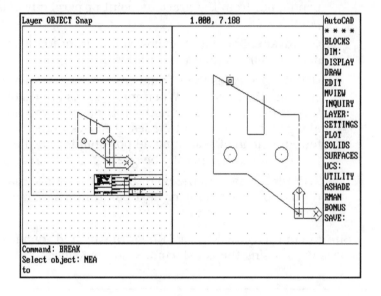

Figure 9.15:
END of first point of break.

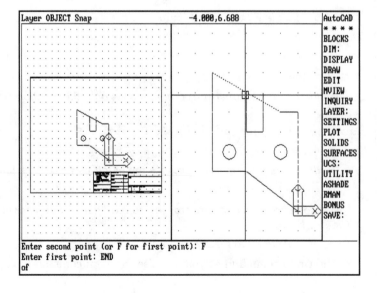

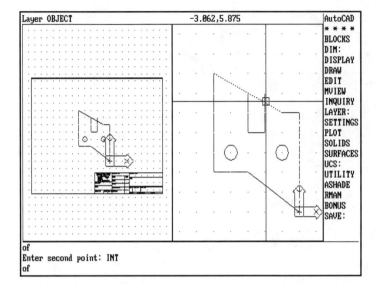

Figure 9.16:
INTersection of second point.

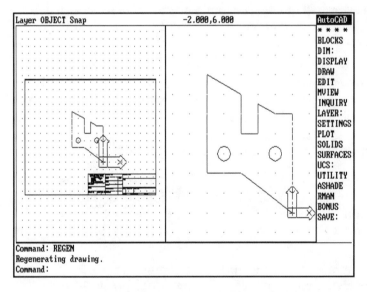

Figure 9.17:
Broken notch.

 These Object Snap modes can be combined. You can choose Int, End, and Mid to find the closest intersection, endpoint, or midpoint, or you can use End and Qui to find the most recent endpoint. Single or multiple Object Snap modes used in this manner are called object snap interrupts or overrides, or transient object snaps. If you need to make a series of picks using the same mode(s), you also can set a running object snap.

Object snaps may be used while you are in paper space mode. You may use the Object Snap mode to pick entities such as the viewport frame along with other entities developed in paper space. If AutoCAD does not find the designated object to snap to in paper space, it automatically switches to model space and searches for that object. AutoCAD automatically switches back to paper space when the search is complete.

The Object Snap Command

The *Object Snap* command sets a running object snap mode or modes. Your specified Object Snap mode remains active, affecting all pick points until you change it.

The default setting is off, or NONe. You can override a running mode by entering a different transient Object Snap mode or modes when a point is requested. The Status command displays the current running Object Snap mode.

The Object Snap mode enables you to make multiple selections without having to select again after every use. You still can use other transient modes or NONe to temporarily suppress the running mode.

Trimming Entities

You could use the Break command to trim off the other vertical notch line, but instead undo the previous break and use the Trim command to do both breaks. The Trim command has a multiple breaking tool that can greatly increase your drawing cleanup speed and accuracy.

The *Trim* command enables you to clip entities that cross a boundary or cutting edge. This command trims off selected entities precisely at user-defined edges, just as a combined Break and Object Snap command would do. You can have more than one cutting edge. Entities such as lines, arcs, circles, and polylines can act both as boundary edges and as objects to trim.

You may use any of the entity selection methods to define the cutting edges. Use the Trim command to precisely trim the unnecessary line segment which crosses the bracket's notch as follows:

Trimming Crossing Lines

Command: **Trim**

Select cutting edge(s)...

Select objects: **C**

First corner: *Pick first point (see fig. 9.18)*

Other corner: *pick second point*

Select objects: *Press Enter*

Select object to trim>Undo: *Pick third point on diagonal line (see fig. 9.18)*

Select object to trim>Undo: *Pick fourth point at end of right vertical (see fig. 9.18)*

Select object to trim>Undo: *Press Enter*

The two verticals trimmed the diagonal and the diagonal trimmed the right vertical. The bracket should now appear as shown in figure 9.19:

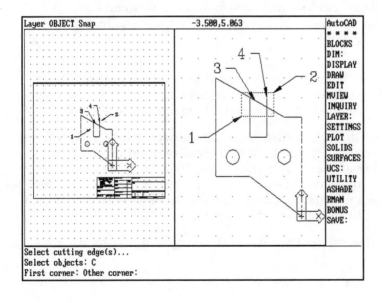

Figure 9.18:
Pick points for trim.

Figure 9.19:
Notch is trimmed.

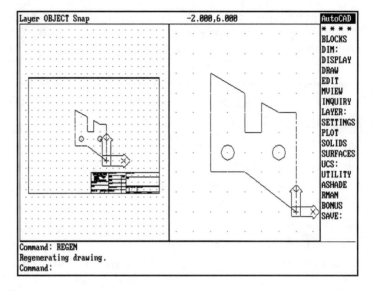

```
Layer OBJECT Snap                    -2.000,6.000                    AutoCAD
                                                                     * * * *
                                                                     BLOCKS
                                                                     DIM:
                                                                     DISPLAY
                                                                     DRAW
                                                                     EDIT
                                                                     MVIEW
                                                                     INQUIRY
                                                                     LAYER:
                                                                     SETTINGS
                                                                     PLOT
                                                                     SOLIDS
                                                                     SURFACES
                                                                     UCS:
                                                                     UTILITY
                                                                     ASHADE
                                                                     RMAN
                                                                     BONUS
                                                                     SAVE:

Command: REGEN
Regenerating drawing.
Command:
```

Extending Lines

Command

Whereas the Trim command trims entities *at* a boundary edge, the *Extend* command extends existing entities *to* a boundary edge. Boundary edges include lines, circles, arcs, and polylines. You can have more than one boundary edge, and an entity can be both a boundary edge and an entity to extend.

To create the top view of the bracket, you only need to draw two horizontal lines, then use the Trim and Extend commands to draw the rest. You also only need to draw its left half; use the Mirror command to create the other half.

Continue in the BRACKET drawing, activate the right viewport, and follow these steps. Type **Pan** at the Command: prompt. Pan the right viewport as shown in figure 9.20. Then type **Line** at the Command: prompt. Then draw the two horizontal lines and draw the top center line as shown in figure 9.21. Refer to figure 9.1 for spacing. Draw the top center line in the current layer (OBJECT) and then use the Chprop command to change it to the layer named CL.

Use the Extend command to extend the three vertical object lines upward.

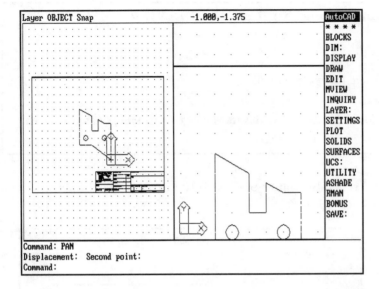

Figure 9.20:
Panned view.

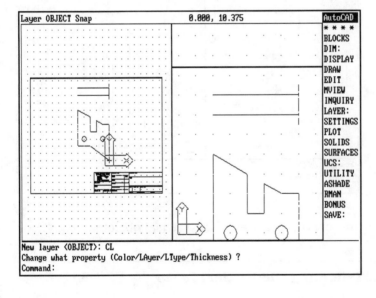

Figure 9.21:
Panned view with top and center lines.

Using Extend To Draw the Top View

```
Command: Extend

Select boundary edge(s)...

Select objects: Pick the new top horizontal line

Select objects: Press Enter

<Select object to extend>/Undo: Select each vertical line to be extended near its top end

<Select object to extend>/Undo: Press Enter
```

Your drawing now should resemble figure 9.22 with the three vertical lines extended to meet the top horizontal line.

Figure 9.22:
The three vertical lines extended.

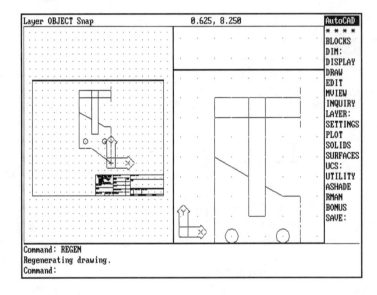

You now need to trim the in-between portions of the vertical object lines.

Trimming the Vertical Lines

```
Command: Trim

Select boundary edge(s)...

Select objects: Pick new bottom horizontal and both top diagonal lines

Select objects: Press Enter

<Select object to trim>/Undo: Pick each vertical in the middle

<Select objects to trim>/Undo: Press Enter
```

Your drawing now should show the vertical lines trimmed (see fig. 9.23).

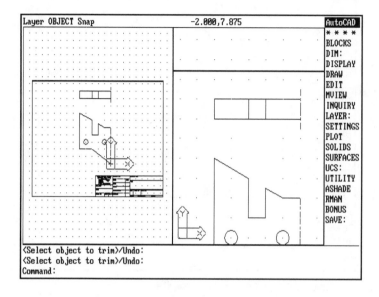

Figure 9.23:
The vertical lines trimmed.

The next step is to create the circle center lines in the upper view.

Creating Two New Center Lines

Command: **Offset**

Offset distance or Through <Through>: **T**

Select object to offset: *Select top center line*

Toggle F8 Ortho ON.

Through point: *Align vertical crosshairs exactly on center of circle and pick*

Select object to offset: *Pick new line at same point*

Through point: *Align on center of other circle and pick*

Select object to offset: *Press Enter*

You drawing now should show the two new center lines (see fig. 9.24).

Repeat this process to offset one of the notch lines in the upper view to create each of the four hidden lines of the circle edges. Then use the Chprop command to change these lines to layer HL. Notice that they become green and hidden linetype.

Figure 9.24:
The two offset center lines.

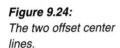
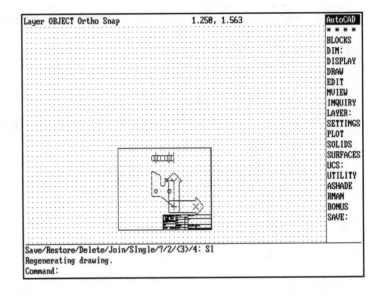

```
Save/Restore/Delete/Join/SIngle/?/2/<3>/4: SI
Regenerating drawing.
Command:
```

▶ Repeating the Process

```
Command: Offset
Command: Chprop
Command: Save
```

The four new hidden lines should make your drawing resemble the one shown in figure 9.25. This completes the left half of the drawing.

Figure 9.25:
The four hidden lines added.

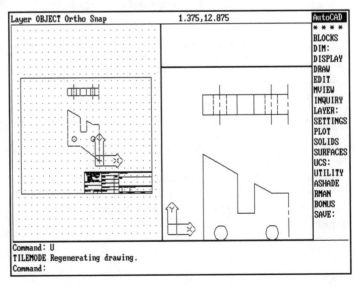

```
Command: U
TILEMODE Regenerating drawing.
Command:
```

You can complete the right half with a single Mirror command. If you have been working in paper space, switch back to TILEMODE. Now, switch back to a single viewport to make it easier to work on the entire object, as follows.

Switching Back to a Single Viewport

Command: **Tilemode**

New value for TILEMODE <0>: **1**

Command: **Vports**

Save/Restore/Delete/Join/SIngle/?/2/<3>/4: **SI**

When you switch back to a single viewport, the image from the previous current viewport fills the screen. Use the Zoom command to resize your drawing as the one shown in figure 9.26. Changing viewports should become as common a drafting process as setting Snap, Grid, or Object Snap. Whenever you find that you need to view your drawing in another format, reset the Vports command.

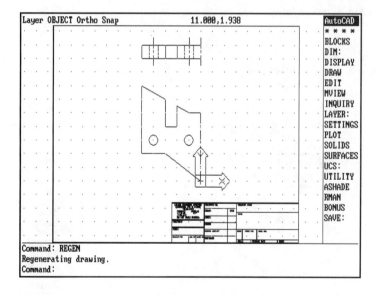

Figure 9.26:
The drawing zoomed in a single viewport.

Mirroring the Bracket

You can use the Mirror command on any entity or group of entities. This is a great time saver for drawing symmetrical objects such as gaskets and brackets.

The *Mirror* command creates identical images of a selected group of entities. You can keep the original group of mirrored entities or you can delete it if you simply want to flip it to another viewport. The default does not delete the originals. The Mirror command also can reflect text or keep it right-reading when mirroring an image, controlled by the MIRRTEXT system variable. The default setting for MIRRTEXT is 1 (on) to mirror (reflect) text.

Retain the old object while you duplicate it to create the right side of the bracket in the following exercise. Make sure Ortho and Snap are toggled on, and follow these steps:

Mirroring the Bracket

Command: **Mirror**

Select objects: **C**

First corner: *Pick first corner point for window (see fig. 9.27)*

Other corner: *Pick second corner point for window*

Select objects: *Press Enter*

First point of mirror line: **0,0**

Second point: **@1<90**, *or pick any point directly above or below the first point with Ortho on*

Delete old objects? <N> *Press Enter*

Command: **End**

Figure 9.27:
Crossing window for mirror.

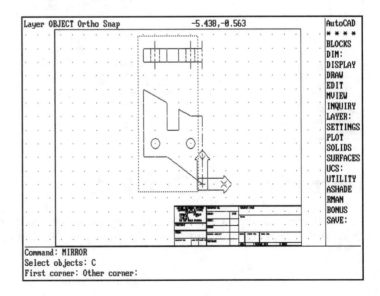

Your completed BRACKET drawing should now look like figure 9.28.

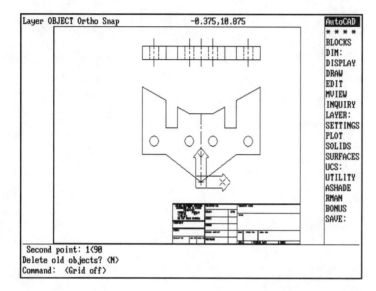

Figure 9.28:
Completed BRACKET views.

Summary

This chapter introduced you to many of the advanced editing techniques used to develop 2D engineering drawings. It should be clear by now that drafting accuracy, efficiency, and productivity increase when editing tools are applied.

Most drafting projects require dimensioning. Chapter 10 will guide you through the use of a few of AutoCAD's dimensioning commands and techniques.

10

DIMENSIONING ENGINEERING DRAWINGS

In this chapter:

- ■ Using AutoCAD'S built-in dimensioning
- ■ Dimensioning in model space and paper space
- ■ Dimensioning the BRACKET
- ■ Drafting with tolerances

Overview

Dimensioning plays an important role in communicating size descriptions and other information. Dimensions should provide a complete and unambiguous description of a part. Manufacturers need to know what materials to use, the size and location of all features, and special instructions or specifications. With the product itself at stake, it is critical that dimensioning conform to an industry-wide standard so that drawings will provide a single interpretation of how a part is to be produced. Wherever possible, drawings in *AutoCAD: Drafting and 3D Design* conform to the Geometric Dimensioning and Tolerancing (GDT) standards of ANSI Y14.5.

Using AutoCAD will not change where dimensions are placed on a drawing. A drafter must still use the traditional rules of dimensioning, but the process of dimensioning changes dramatically. Drafters need only to signal AutoCAD where to start a dimension, where to conclude that dimension, and where to place the dimension text. Using that input, AutoCAD will automatically draw extension lines, dimension lines, arrows, and the dimension text. Dimension text can be displayed in any of the unit values available by AutoCAD, with or without tolerances, and in limit form if you choose.

In this chapter, you will edit the mounting bracket developed in Chapter 9. The bracket drawing is also available on the AutoCAD: Drafting and 3D Design disk. If you do not have the disk or have not completed Chapter 9, you will need to do so before proceeding with this exercise. If you are ready to continue, this chapter introduces many of AutoCAD's basic dimensioning features and some rules to govern their use. After you complete this chapter, your bracket should look like figure 10.1.

Figure 10.1:
The dimensioned figure which you will complete in this chapter.

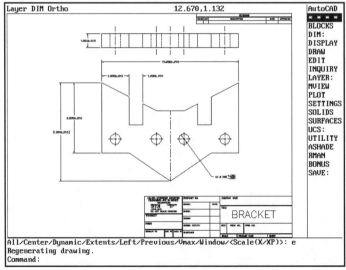

Using AutoCAD'S Built-In Dimensioning

AutoCAD's automatic dimensioning maintains complete integrity with drawing accuracy. Dimensioning is a separate mode within AutoCAD, indicated by a `Dim:` prompt which replaces the `Command:` prompt. Numerous subcommands and system variables are available in dimensioning mode, but AutoCAD's drawing and editing commands are not available.

The *Dim* command activates the dimensioning mode. The `Command:` prompt changes to `Dim:`, and only the subcommands associated with dimensioning are active. The *Dim1* command activates the dimension mode for a single command and then returns to the regular command prompt.

You already should be familiar with dimensioning terms such as dimension lines, extension lines, and leaders. If you are not, refer to *Inside AutoCAD Special Edition* (New Riders Publishing) or the *AutoCAD Reference Manual* for definitions and examples.

When you are in the dimensioning mode, you only need to type the first three letters, such as HOR for horizontal, to execute a command. AutoCAD's dimensioning commands fall into the following categories:

■ Linear Dimensioning Commands

The *ALIgned* command draws the dimension line parallel to the extension line origin points or to a selected entity.

After you create the first linear dimension, the *Baseline* command dimensions the rest of the entities at a set increment from the previous dimension line using the same first point of origin of the extension line. You provide only the second extension point for each.

After you create the first linear dimension, the *Continue* command dimensions the rest of the entities, each chained to the previous entity. If the dimension text does not fit, the dimension line will be incremented from the previous dimension line. All you provide is the second extension point.

The *HORizontal* command draws the dimension line horizontally.

The *ROTated* command draws the dimension line at an angle that you define.

The *VERtical* command draws the dimension line vertically.

- Angular Dimensioning Command

  The *ANGular* command measures the dimension angle between two non-parallel lines.

- Radius Dimensioning Command

  The *RADius* command dimensions circles and arcs by placing a radius line (half a diameter line and containing one arrow head) through the center of the circle or arc.

- Diameter Dimensioning Command

  The *DIAmeter* command dimensions circles and arcs by placing a dimension line through the center of the circle or arc.

- Ordinate Dimensioning Command

  The *ORDinate* command dimensions an X or Y coordinate of a feature. Also called the Datum Dimensioning command, it draws a leader line along with dimensioning text in the direction orthogonal to the coordinate axes.

- Associative Dimensioning Commands

  The *HOMetext* command moves associative dimension text to its default location.

  The *NEWtext* command enables you to revise associative dimension text, adopting the current dimension variable settings.

  The *OBLique* command angles linear associative dimensions.

  The *OVErride* command updates an associative dimension modifying one or more of the dimension variables on a one-time basis.

  The *REStore* command sets current a selected dimensioning style.

  The *SAVe* command creates a new, named dimensioning style based on the current dimensioning variable settings.

  The *TEDit* command edits the position and orientation of the dimension text of a selected dimension.

  The *TROtate* command changes the orientation of a selected dimension text.

  The *UPDate* command modifies associative dimension entities to adopt the current dimension variables.

  The *VARiables* command lists selected dimension style settings.

- Dimensioning Utility Commands

  The *CENter* command constructs a dimensioning center mark or center lines for circles and arcs.

  The *EXIt* command returns you from dimensioning mode to the command prompt. You also can press Ctrl-C to exit.

The *LEAder* command draws a leader, made up of arrow head, lines, and text, from where the arrow head is placed to where you want the dimension text or notes to be placed.

The *REDraw* command refreshes the current viewport display.

The *STAtus* command lists the current settings of the dimension variables.

The *STYle* command enables you to change the text style of your dimensioning text.

The *Undo* command, in the dimensioning mode, voids the latest dimensioning operation. You can undo one step at a time until you reach the beginning of the current dimensioning mode session.

- Dimensioning Variables

  Dimensioning variables are system variables that control the formats for your dimensions, such as arrow head or tick mark size, text location, and size. Some of the variables contain values while others act as on and off switches. These variables are accessed through the Setvar command, as dimensioning subcommands, or accessed at the `Command:` prompt.

Associative Dimensioning

Nonassociative dimensioning generates each dimension as a set of individual line, solid, and text entities. To update, you have to select and erase each entity and redo the dimensioning command.

Associative dimensions are single entities, with control points picked at the dimension points. When you modify an object by stretching or scaling it, the associative dimension automatically updates as if the dimension lines are linked to the object. This allows dimensions to be automatically updated when you edit the geometry of a drawing. Associative dimensioning, which is controlled by the dimension variable DIMASO, is AutoCAD's default. Associative dimensioning is explored further in Chapter 11.

Customizing Dimensioning

Standard automatic dimensioning is easy with AutoCAD. No single style of dimensioning meets everyone's standards, however, so AutoCAD provides numerous system variables with which you can alter dimensioning style. You set the dimension variables required to make AutoCAD conform to ANSI Y14.5 standards in Chapter 14 with the prototype drawing. A brief review of these settings follows:

- **DIMASZ.** 0.125 sets the size of the dimension line arrows and affects the fit of text between extension lines.

- **DIMCEN.** 0.1 draws 0.1-inch circle/arc center tick marks with extension lines projecting 0.1 past the circle/arc perimeter.

- **DIMDLI.** 0.5 sets the spacing between dimension lines for successive continuous and baseline dimensions. (You will adjust this as needed when you dimension.)

- **DIMEXE.** 0.125 sets the extension line to extend 0.125 inches beyond the dimension line.

- **DIMEXO.** 0.125 sets the extension line to begin with a 0.125-inch offset from the dimension origin points.

- **DIMRND.** 0.001 rounds places to the right of the decimal to three.

- **DIMTXT.** 0.125 sets your choice of standard height for dimensioning text.

- **DIMTOFL.** 1 draws a dimension line between the extension lines even when text is placed outside.

- **DIMZIN.** 4 suppresses any leading zero before a decimal point for values of less than one inch.

You also use several other variables to control options such as tolerances.

Setting Dimensioning Variables from the Pull-Down Menu

If your system supports AUI, you can set dimensioning variables from the pull-down menu. When you select Set Dim Vars... from the Settings menu, dimensioning variables are presented in the form of icons. You select the appropriate icon, and then respond to the prompts. Figures 10.2 and 10.3 show two of the dimensioning variables icon pages.

Dimensioning Flexibility Leads to Choices

You often must decide how AutoCAD will place its dimensions. You can set AutoCAD to generate dimensions in various ways by manipulating dimensioning variables. Two such cases are as follows:

- AutoCAD can generate diameter dimensions in one of three ways: (1) with a leader pointing at the perimeter of the circle from the outside and the dimension text outside, (2) with a dimension line extending across the diameter of the circle with a leader line and dimension text outside the circle, and (3) with the dimension text placed inside a dimension line extending across the diameter of the circle.

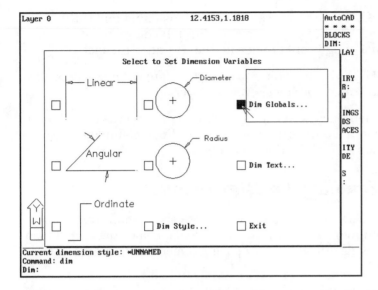

Figure 10.2:
First page of icons for dimension variables.

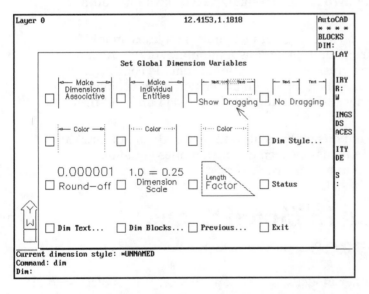

Figure 10.3:
Second page of icons.

■ AutoCAD tends to force limited space dimensions (dimensions in which the text size or text string length does not fit between the extension lines) outside the extension lines. AutoCAD requires 4.3 times the DIMTXT setting plus the text height or string length between extension lines before it places the text between the extension lines. You often will want to force a slightly tighter fit to gain room for additional dimensions. You have three ways to work around this: First, you can use the Move command (if associative dimensioning is off). Second, you can move dimensioning text with the Tedit command. Third, you can use the Stretch command (if associative dimensioning is on) to relocate the text after the fact.

You also can set the DIMTIX dimensioning variable to 1 (on). Dimtix forces all dimension text "between" extension lines, even if it overlaps them.

AutoCAD crosses extension lines occasionally. If it becomes necessary for you to cross an extension line with a dimension line, use the Break command to produce a visible gap on each side of the dimension line.

Recommended Spacing for Dimensions

Dimensioning with AutoCAD sometimes requires more space than traditional drafting, so allow enough room around your views to make your drawing dimensions readable. The following guidelines for spacing dimensions on AutoCAD drawings may be helpful:

- The space between the first dimension line and the part outline should be at least 0.375 inches (10mm), preferably a minimum of 0.5 inches.

- The space between succeeding parallel dimension lines should be at least 0.25 inches (6mm), preferably a minimum of 0.5 inches. The DIMDLI setting presets this to 0.5 for automatic continuing and baseline dimensioning. Space all dimension lines equally and try to match the space between the first dimension line and the part, if possible.

- Try to space your dimension lines at multiples of the snap interval setting. This makes it easy to keep dimension lines equal distances apart and in line with each other.

Dimensioning in Model Space and Paper Space

You can dimension in either model space or paper space. But as discussed in Chapter 7, drawing in paper space is like drawing on a sheet of glass that covers your drawing. In associative dimensioning, it is better to work in TILEMODE model space or TILEMODE OFF model space. AutoCAD then can place the necessary definition points associatively to the part, thus allowing your dimensions to automatically update after using commands such as Trim, Stretch, or Extend.

Dimensioning the Bracket Drawing

In this section, you use a combination of linear, diameter, and dimensioning variables to dimension the bracket. You will concentrate on linear dimensioning for now. Other subcommands and more advanced dimensioning techniques are presented in following chapters.

The first step in dimensioning the bracket is to set the current layer to Dim, which uses red continuous lines. If you are using the Y14.5 Menu System, you can select Dim from the tablet to set the layer. After the Dim layer is set, draw the center lines on the circles in the front view.

 Note Remember that throughout the exercises in this textbook you are to press Enter after responding to a Command: prompt.

You issue dimensioning commands by using the screen or tablet menus or by typing them as shown in the following exercise:

To access the screen menu, select DIM: from the root menu. Then select the type of dimensioning you want, clicking on next to get to the associative options. The linear options and dimensioning variables are also grouped as separate pages, accessed by clicking on LINEAR and Dim Vars. Throughout the following exercises, use the Zoom and Pan commands as needed to better see what you are doing.

If you have the AutoCAD: Drafting and 3D Design Disk, the BRACKET drawing is ready to dimension. If you do not have the disk, use the BRACKET drawing from Chapter 9 and follow these steps:

Generating Circle Center Lines

Command: **Layer**

?/Make/Set/New/ON/OFF/Color/Ltype/Freeze/Thaw: **Set**

New current layer <0>: **Dim**

Command: **Snap**

Snap spacing or ON/OFF/Aspect/Rotate/Style/ <1.0000>: **0.125**

Command: **Dim**

Dim: **Cen**

Select arc or circle: *Pick one of the circles so that center lines appear (see fig. 10.4)*

Dim: *Press Enter*

CEN Select arc or circle: *Pick the second circle, and continue with the other two circles*

The four circles now should have center marks and lines, as shown in figure 10.4.

Figure 10.4:
Pick the circles for center lines.

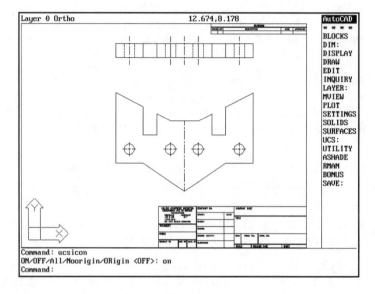

 If you make a mistake, type **U** or click on undo at the screen menu to remove the last dimension and remain in dimensioning mode. When you exit the Dim mode, you can use the Erase command to delete individual dimensions, but typing **U** or clicking on undo after exiting the Dim mode obliterates everything done in the dimensioning mode session. If associative dimensioning is not on, each dimension entity becomes a set of separate lines, solids, and text which must be erased individually.

Linear Dimensioning

Linear dimensions can be HORizontal, VERtical, ALIgned, ROTated, BASeline, and CONtinue (chain). The key to successful dimensioning lies in the order of point selection that controls the direction, orientation, and location of the dimension. If you do not succeed at first, do not be discouraged. Type **U** and try again.

Generally, you first designate the length of the dimension line by picking its start and endpoints. Accuracy is as important here as in drawing, so use the snap or object snap modes as needed. In the exercise that follows, use object snap to locate the two points (for this drawing, snap also works if you zoom in).

Use a snap point to pick the position of the dimension line. The dimension text will be placed at the center of the dimension line.

Start with the top horizontal dimension. Set LUPREC to three places to get the proper dimensioning format.

Horizontal Dimensioning

Dim: **'Setvar**

>>Variable name or ?: **LUPREC**

>>New value for Luprec <4>: **3**

Dim: **Hor**

First extension line origin or RETURN to select: **Endp**

of *Pick first point (see fig. 10.5)*

Second extension line origin: **Endp**

of *Pick second point*

Dimension line location: <Snap On> *Pick third point, 1.5 inches above the object*

Dimension text <10.000>: *Press Enter (see fig. 10.6)*

Your drawing now should resemble figure 10.5

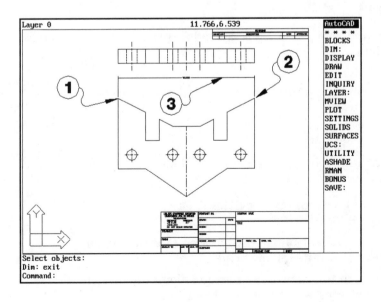

Figure 10.5:
Horizontal dimension.

Figure 10.6:
Detail of dimension text.

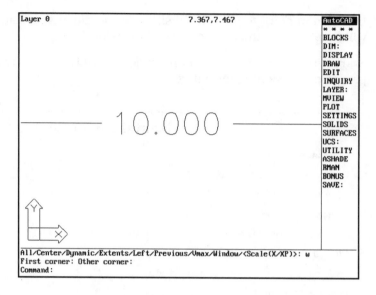

AutoCAD's default dimension is unidirectional and in decimal units representing inches. Dimensions are created with three places to the right of the decimal point because LUPREC set the linear units of precision to 3. If you are using the Y14.5 Menu System, you can easily change the dimensioning precision by selecting .XX, .XXX, or .XXXX from the tablet.

Editing Dimension Text

You can edit the location and rotation of associative dimensioning text by using the Tedit and Trotate commands.

The *Tedit* command edits the position and orientation of a selected associative dimension text.

The Tedit command prompts you to enter the text location. You have five options to reposition the text:

■ **Picking or designating coordinate positions.** Drags the dimension text to the desired location

■ **Left.** Moves the text to the left-most position along the dimension line without interfering with the arrow head

■ **Right.** Moves the text to the right-most position along the dimension line without interfering with the arrow head

- **Home.** Moves the text back to its original default location once it has been repositioned
- **Angle.** Allows text to be placed at any designated angle

The *Trotate* command changes the orientation of a selected associative dimension text.

Edit the position of the 10.000" horizontal dimension text you just completed, as follows:

Editing the 10.000 Dimension Text Position

Dim: **Tedit**

Select dimension: *Pick the 10.000 associative dimension; you can select any point on the associative dimension*

Enter text location (Left/Right/Home/Angle): *Pick a point 1" to the right of original text location*

Your drawing now should resemble figure 10.7.

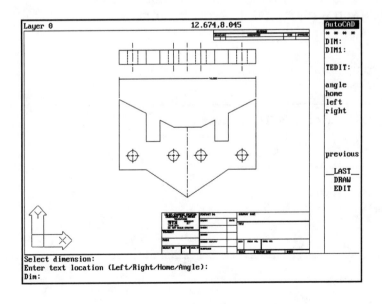

Figure 10.7:
The associative dimension text is moved.

Drafting with Tolerances

To draw dimensions with tolerances or limits, set positive (+) and negative (-) tolerance values and toggle the required tolerance or limits variables on or off. The dimensioning variables for positive and negative limits and tolerancing are as follows:

- **DIMTOL.** On (1) for tolerances appended to dimension, off (0) for none
- **DIMLIM.** On (1) for a pair of limit dimensions instead of single dimension, off (0) for normal
- **DIMTP.** The tolerance (limits) plus value
- **DIMTM.** The tolerance (limits) minus value

You can set these variables from the screen menu dimension variables page by clicking on DIM:, then Dim Vars, then next, and then next, by typing their names at the Dim: prompt or by using the Y14.5 Menu System. With the Y14.5 program, select SET TOLERANCE PLUS, SET TOLERANCE MINUS, and TOLERANCE ON/OFF or LIMITS ON/OFF from the tablet. The menu also provides many of the common tolerance values in easy selections, such as .001, .002, or .003.

 Note The DIMTOL and DIMLIM variables toggle; they cannot be on simultaneously. When you turn one on, the other is turned off.

Set your tolerances by completing the following steps:

Setting Tolerances

Dim: **DIMTOL**

Current value <Off> New value: **On**

Dim: **DIMTP**

Current value <0.000> New value: **.01**

Dim: **DIMTM**

Current value <0.000> New value: **.01**

Updating Dimensions

If associative dimensioning is on, you can use the Update subcommand to update any existing dimension to the current settings. Try it by updating the previous horizontal dimension, as follows:

Updating a Dimension with Tolerances

Dim: **Upd**

Select objects: **L**

Select objects: *Press Enter*

Your drawing now should resemble figures 10.8 and 10.9.

 Note If the DIMTP and DIMTM values are equal, a single ± tolerance is appended. If they differ, separate plus and minus values are appended, one above the other.

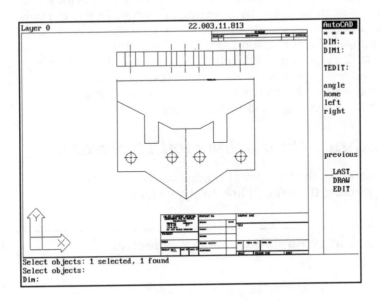

Figure 10.8:
Horizontal dimension with ± tolerance.

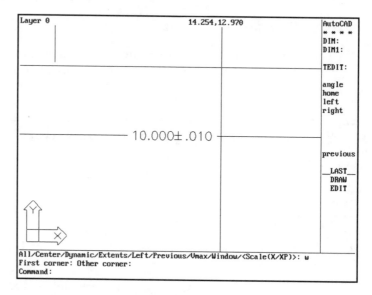

Figure 10.9:
Close-up of ± tolerance.

Selecting Entities To Dimension

Instead of establishing dimensions by picking points, most dimensions (of a line, arc, or circle) also can be determined by selecting an entity. To do so, press Enter when you see the prompt First extension line origin or RETURN to select. Then use normal object selection to select the entity to be dimensioned. AutoCAD extracts the points needed from the entity in AutoCAD's drawing database, and all you need to pick is the dimension text location. The dimension value is then generated based upon the entity's database information. It is much easier than object snap and just as accurate.

Vertical and Continue Dimensions with Tolerances

The Vertical command works as the Horizontal command does. Dimension the bracket's thickness by selecting the left end line entity, as follows:

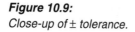

Vertical Dimensioning by Entity Selection

Dim: **Ver**

First extension line origin or RETURN to select: *Press Enter*

Select line, arc, or circle: *Pick line at fourth point (see fig. 10.10)*

Dimension line location: *Pick fifth point*

Dimension text <1.000>: *Press Enter*

The dimension is generated with ± .010 tolerance, as shown in figure 10.10.

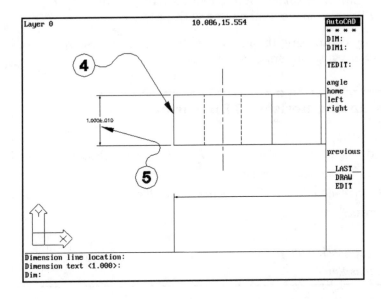

Figure 10.10:
Vertical dimension with ± tolerances.

Continuous (Chain) Dimensions

The Continue command enables you to place dimensions in a continuous chain. You start with a single linear dimension, such as Horizontal. Then, use the Continue command to add a series or chain of subsequent dimensions. For each Continue dimension added to the chain, AutoCAD uses the endpoint of the last dimension as a first point for the next dimension, so you are prompted only for the endpoint of the new extension line. AutoCAD neatly aligns these dimensions into a chain.

 Note The Continue command defaults to continue from the previous dimension created. If you want to continue a previous dimension, you can press Enter at the `Second extension line origin or <Return> to select:` prompt. This enables you to continue from any selected continued dimension.

In the following exercise, you continuously dimension the horizontal location and size of the notch from the left-hand edge of the bracket. Because the one-inch dimension text for the notch will be placed outside the extension lines, you need to dimension from left to right to get the format of the continuous dimensions shown in the following exercise. For limited-space dimensions such as this situation, the location of the dimension text is determined by the direction of your second extension line origin pick. In this example, chain dimensioning from right to left would overlap with unacceptable results. You will be able to avoid problems caused by limited-space dimensions with practice.

Now dimension the notch by completing the following steps. Use the Osnap command or zoom in to where you can snap accurately.

Continuing Horizontal Dimensions

Dim: **Hor**

First extension line origin or RETURN to select: *Pick sixth point (see fig. 10.11)*

Second extension line origin: *Pick seventh point*

Dimension line location: *Pick eighth point, 0.5 inches above the object*

Dimension text <2.000>: *Press Enter*

Dim: **Con**

Second extension line origin: *Pick ninth point*

Dimension text <1.000>: *Press Enter*

Your drawing should resemble figure 10.11.

Figure 10.11:
Horizontal continued dimensions.

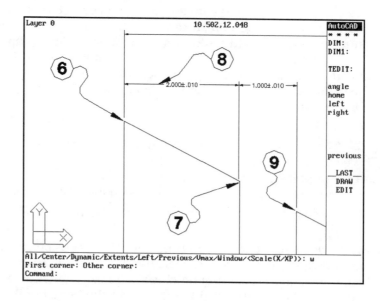

When you use toleranced chain dimensioning to dimension engineering drawings, you may develop an accumulation of tolerance error. The maximum variation between two features is equal to the sum of the tolerances of the intermediate distances. Toleranced chain dimensioning should only be used when accumulation is acceptable to the design intent.

Controlling Dimension Text

Whenever AutoCAD prompts you for dimension text, it presents a default value in angle brackets. You have accepted this default text by pressing Enter thus far, but sometimes you may want to adjust the dimension text. You have the option of entering your own text, which overrides the default as the dimensioning text.

Another, more powerful dimensioning text option is available. You can combine AutoCAD's default dimensioning text with your own text without retyping AutoCAD's default text. To do so, embed a pair of angle brackets in the text. These angle brackets indicate the location for the default text and are replaced by the default text when the dimension is drawn. If the default presented is <.750>, for example, and you want to dimension it as 4x.750, then you would enter **4x< >** as your dimension text, or if <.750> is still the default, you would get (.750) by entering **(< >)** as text.

Baseline Dimensioning

The Baseline command is similar to the Continue command. Baseline dimensioning enables you to dimension multiple locations from one baseline. As with Continue, use any linear dimensioning form to create the base dimension. Its first extension line establishes the starting datum point—the baseline. Subsequent Baseline dimensions use this line as their first extension line, prompting you only for the second extension line origin. AutoCAD automatically draws each baseline dimension line at a spacing from the previous dimension line equal to the value of the DIMDLI (Dimension Line Increment) variable, which was set to 0.5 inch in the prototype drawing. You can change it with Setvar DIMDLI, the DIMDLI dimensioning subcommand, or the Y14.5 Menu System Dim Vars screen or pull-down menus.

Note

The Baseline command defaults to the extension line closest to the selection point as the origin for the first extension line. If you want to continue a previous dimension, you can press Enter at the Second extension line origin or <RETURN> to select: prompt. This enables you to continue from any selected baseline dimension.

Dimension the left side of the front view with the Vertical and Baseline commands. Use dimension text override to make 7.000 the reference dimension. Use Object Snap or zoom in to where you can snap accurately. You will have to temporarily adjust the dimension line increment, DIMDLI, to avoid text overlap.

Follow these steps to create the illustration shown in figure 10.12:

Baseline Dimensions

```
Dim: Ver

First extension line origin or RETURN to select: Pick first point (see fig. 10.12)

Second extension line origin: Pick second point

Dimension line location: Pick a point three inches from object

Dimension text <5.000>: Press Enter

Dim: DIMDLI

Current value <0.500> New value: 1

Dim: Bas

Second extension line origin: Pick third point

Dimension text <7.000>: (<>)

Dim: DIMDLI

Current value <1.000> New value: .5
```

You will need to make frequent adjustments to DIMDLI to get the results you want. Your drawing now should resemble figures 10.12 and 10.13.

Diameter Dimensions with Tolerances

You started with center marks and lines in the circles. The last dimension to be drawn is the diameter dimension for the front view's third circle from the left. Because you are dimensioning a hole, you will generate the dimension with differing upper and lower tolerances. To do so, simply set new values for the DIMTP and DIMTM variables.

Because this circle already has the circle center lines on it, you should temporarily set the value of the DIMCEN dimensioning variable to zero. This prevents the creation of additional circle center lines when you use the Diameter command to dimension the circle. Use Setvar, the DIMCEN dimensioning subcommand, or the Y14.5 Menu System Dim Vars option or pull-down items to set it, and then use the Diameter command to draw the dimension, as shown in the next exercise. (Type **End** at the Command: prompt when finished with the exercise unless you want to do the optional bracket exercise which follows.)

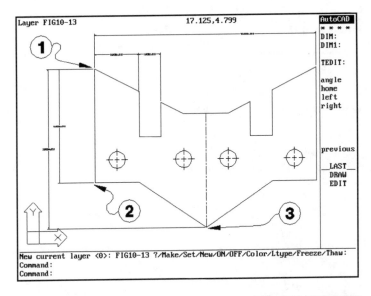

Figure 10.12:
Vertical baseline dimensions.

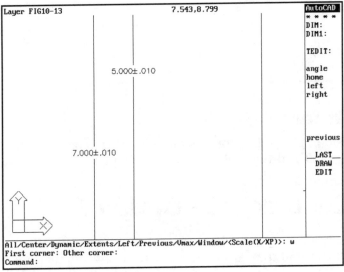

Figure 10.13:
Detail of baseline dimension text.

▶

Diameter Dimensioning Circles

```
Dim: DIMCEN
Current value <-0.100> New value: 0
Dim: DIMTP
Current value <0.060> New value: .06
Dim: DIMTM
Current value <0.060> New value: .002
Dim: Dia
Select arc or circle: Pick leader at fourth point (see fig. 10.14)
Dimension text <.750>: 4X <>
Text does not fit.
Enter leader length for text: Toggle F8 ortho off and pick on fifth point
Dim: DIMCEN
Current value <0.000> New Value: -1
Dim: DIMTP
Current value <0.060> New Value: .010
Dim: DIMTM
Current value <0.002> New Value: .010
Dim: Exit
Command: Zoom
Command: Ucs
Command: Type Save or End
```

Your screen should resemble figure 10.14.

That completes the dimensioning exercises for this chapter. At this point, your drawing should match figure 10.1 at the beginning of this chapter.

Completing the Bracket—Optional

You may complete the dimensioning of the bracket and thaw some of the title block layers, if you want. If you find the datum and feature control symbols a bit tedious, better methods are explained in Chapters 13 and 14. The completed bracket which you will finish in the following optional exercise is shown in figure 10.15.

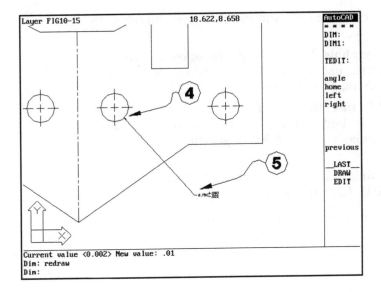

Figure 10.14:
Circle with diameter dimension.

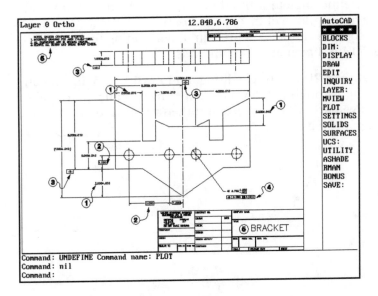

Figure 10.15:
The completed bracket with title text and notes.

Complete the following numbered items as numbered in figure 10.15:

(1) Linear Dimensions. Use the Horizontal and Vertical commands to complete the normal dimensions.

(2) Basic Dimensions. Turn off the DIMLIM variable to generate the dimensions, and then zoom in and add the basic dimension box with a polyline. Create one box, and use the Copy command to replicate it.

(3) Datum Feature Symbols. Draw or copy the boxes like the basic dimensions, and then use the Dtext command to add all of the dashes and identifying letters.

(4) Feature Control Frame. Draw the frame with lines or polylines and add circles. Add the text with the Dtext command, and relocate the cursor as needed. Type **%%c** to get the diameter symbol in the text string.

(5) Title Block. Use the Layer command to thaw layer TITL-CX and NOTES and set TITL-CX current. Add any title text you want.

Finally, invoke the End command and exit AutoCAD.

Summary

Most technical drawings are incomplete without dimensions. AutoCAD provides orderly and accurate size descriptions of mechanical parts. The BRACKET drawing was developed using some of AutoCAD's built-in dimensioning tools while introducing you to ANSI Y14.5 dimensioning standards.

The next chapters expand your 2D drafting, editing, and ANSI Y14.5 dimensioning abilities. They guide you through the development of five detailed parts of a robotic arm. Each of the five parts will be saved and then re-used to develop a final multi-detail working drawing.

11

CREATING A MULTI-DETAIL WORKING DRAWING—PHASE 1

In this chapter:

- Understanding parts and parts libraries
- Drafting the arm
- Drafting the spacing pin
- Drafting the servo motor mount
- Drafting the adjustment plate
- Drafting the pulley

Overview

Your next project is to draft and dimension a robot arm. In this and the next chapter, you will develop the arm, pin, mount, plate, and pulley as individual parts in separate exercises, and save each part as a separate drawing that can be inserted into another drawing, creating a multi-detail drawing as illustrated in figure 11.1. This is called developing a parts library.

Figure 11.1:
The robot arm multi-detail drawing.

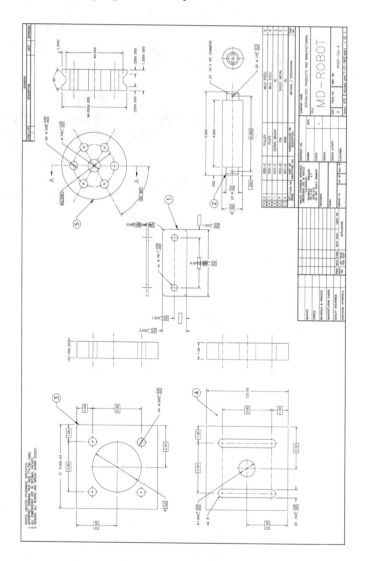

As you draw the parts, you will learn several new drawing and editing commands. These include Array, Base, Block, Chamfer, Copy, Fillet, Insert, Minsert, and Wblock. You also will use several more dimensioning features. Although the dimensioning techniques in this chapter include basic dimensions, the Y14.5 tolerancing required for complete drawings is optional.

This chapter includes three types of exercises: drawing the parts, dimensioning the parts, and saving them for later insertion with the Wblock command. If you have the AutoCAD: Drafting and 3D Design Disk, you can do all three exercises for each part, or you can skip the drawing exercise and go directly to the dimensioning or write blocking exercises. If you do not have the disk, you must do each exercise in sequence. Each part is developed in a new drawing named TEMP. The new TEMP drawing replaces any previous TEMP drawing.

Understanding Parts and Parts Libraries

You can develop a library of the parts commonly used in your industrial or institutional drafting operations. These may include components such as fastening devices, shafts, pulleys, gears, mounting brackets, and springs. The library may be developed in 2D, 3D, or a combination of both, depending upon your requirements.

Parts are groups of entities that can be inserted into any number of drawings, saving you the effort of redrawing them. AutoCAD uses the Block command to group and store entity parts. Blocks can be real-world objects (parts) or symbols such as section markers or bubbles. When you insert a block, you can scale, rotate, or mirror it. You also can insert a block exploded into its constituent entities so that they can be edited.

You can store any number of blocks, visibly or invisibly, in a library drawing or prototype drawing. Then when you start a new drawing with that prototype, or insert that library drawing into the current drawing, all of its blocks will be available for individual insertion and use.

You also can store parts as individual drawing files on disk. This is the approach you will use in Chapter 12. In this case, they are not stored as blocks, but as separate drawings containing the individual entities making up each part or symbol. Keep all three of the parts you create in this chapter in a single temporary file, saving each part as an individual drawing file on disk as you go. Such drawings then can be individually inserted into other drawings as blocks or as their individual constituent entities. In fact, any AutoCAD drawing can be inserted into any other AutoCAD drawing as a block.

The five parts in this library provide you with examples and techniques that can save you valuable drafting time when you need to make changes because of engineering change orders (ECOs) or when you want to use modified parts in other designs. Instead of drafting new parts, you can draft stock parts once, save them as blocks or files, and then modify or reuse the stock part from your library when you need a similar part or when you receive an ECO. Each part drawing, if stored as a separate file, can either be inserted into a new drawing or used as a prototype to be modified.

The exercises in this chapter use the PROTO-C drawing from Chapter 8. Only the prototype's border and main title block are visible initially; the optional title blocks, text, and notes are frozen.

Drafting the Arm

The exercises in this section feature the Fillet command, associative and radius dimensioning, and blocks. You will develop the arm drawing (see fig. 11.2) with two orthographic views, the front and the top.

AutoCAD enables you to do most things in one of several ways. You will use the Pline, Copy, and Stretch commands to draw the arm's profile and top view in the following exercise. After you develop the object lines for the two views, you draw one circle and copy it. You then complete the fillets on each corner of the arm's front view and dimension the arm. The final step is to save the part as a drawing file for later insertion into the multi-detail subassembly drawing.

Figure 11.2:
The arm.

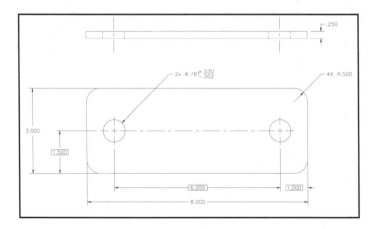

To begin drawing the arm, start a new drawing file named TEMP and follow these steps:

Drawing the Arm's Profile

```
Command: Zoom
All/Center/Dynamic/Extents/Left/Previous/Vmax/Window/<Scale(X/XP)>: C
Center point: 10,9
Magnification or Height <23.1222>: 13
Command: Snap
Snap spacing or ON/OFF/Aspect/Rotate/Style <0.0625>: 0.25
Command: Pline
From point: 6,6
Current line-width is 0.0000
Arc/Close/Halfwidth/Length/Undo/Width/<Endpoint of line>: <Ortho on> Press F8
to toggle ortho on, then use coordinate display to pick at polar point 8.0000<0
Arc/Close/Halfwidth/Length/Undo/Width/<Endpoint of line>: Pick at polar point
3.0000<90
Arc/Close/Halfwidth/Length/Undo/Width/<Endpoint of line>: Pick at polar point
8.0000<180
Arc/Close/Halfwidth/Length/Undo/Width/<Endpoint of line>: C
```

Your drawing should now resemble figure 11.3.

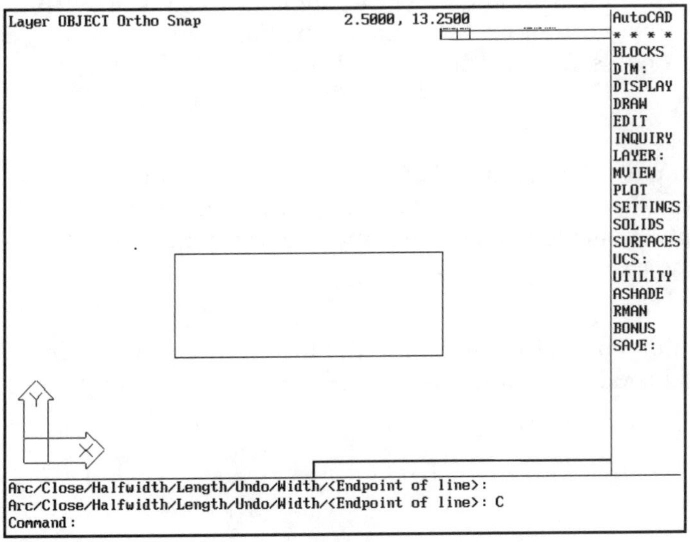

Figure 11.3:
The arm profile.

Copying Entities and Selection Sets

You used the Pline command to draw the front view of the arm profile in the previous exercise. You could do the same to create the top view, or you could use the Copy and Stretch commands.

The *Copy* command creates a replica of an entity or selection set anywhere in 2D or 3D space. The command uses standard object selection. The original entity or selection set remains unchanged. You can show and drag displacement by picking two points or by using an absolute XY displacement value.

When picking points, make your reference (base) point a logical point on the object(s) you are copying.

To do a multiple copy, type **M** at the `Base point:` prompt. The Copy command then reprompts for base point (absolute displacements do not apply here) and repeatedly prompts for second points. You can make as many copies as you want by picking repeated second points. Press Enter to exit the command when you are done.

Another way to enter a displacement is to pick the first point (anywhere will do) and type the second point as a relative or polar point, such as **@2,3** or **@6<90**. To use an absolute displacement, enter an XY value at the base point or displacement prompt and then press Enter at the second point or displacement prompt.

As with the Move command, be careful that you do not press Enter accidentally at the second point prompt. If you do, your first point will be erroneously interpreted as a displacement, often sending the copy out of the current view.

Now use the Copy and Stretch commands to create the top view, and the Circle and Copy commands to add the holes. Continue in the previous TEMP drawing and follow these steps:

Copying and Stretching the Top View

```
Command: Copy
Select objects: L
1 found
Select objects: Press Enter
<Base point or displacement>/Multiple: 6,9
Second point of displacement: Type 6,11 or pick polar point @2<90
Command: Stretch
Select objects to stretch by window...
Select objects: C
First corner: Pick point ① (see fig. 11.4)
Other corner: Pick point ②
Select objects: Press Enter
Base point: Pick any point, such as a corner
New point: Pick point @2.75<90
Command: Circle
3P/2P/TTR/<Center point>: 7,7.5
Diameter/<Radius>: D
Diameter: .781
Command: Copy
Select objects: L
1 found
Select objects: Press Enter
<Base point or displacement>/Multiple: 6,0
Second point of displacement: Press Enter
```

Your drawing should now resemble figure 11.5.

You need to add hidden lines to the top view, but the circle diameters do not fall on snap increments. You could use the Osnap command to snap long lines to the circles' quadrant points, then trim them at the top view polyline. Point filters, however, provide a better way.

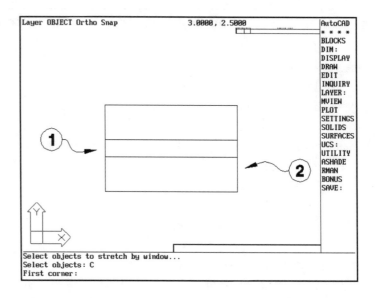

Figure 11.4:
Stretch pick points.

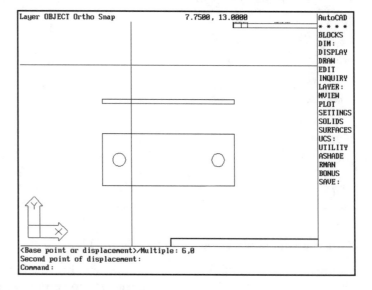

Figure 11.5:
Arm front and top views.

Constructions with Point Filters

Point filters (sometimes called XYZ point filters) were invented for 3D, but they make valuable electronic construction lines in 2D work. Ignore the Z coordinate until you get to the 3D chapters.

In manual drafting, you use construction lines by scribing a temporary line from a known point to the area where you want to establish a new point. Then you establish the new point at some desired distance or aligned to another known point. Point filters work for orthographic points in the same manner. Click on one coordinate of an object, and AutoCAD reprompts for the other(s). To invoke point filters, enter a period and the letter(s) of the coordinate(s) you want to pick first at any prompt that accepts a point. Point filters can be combined with object snaps. After they are combined, you need to re-enter the point filter and object snap modes before repicking if you click on an invalid point.

Use point filters and the Osnap, Line, and Chprop commands to create the top view's hidden lines and center lines. Make sure snap and ortho are on and zoom in if necessary, then follow these steps:

Aligning Using Point Filters

Command: **Line** *(see fig. 11.6)*

From point: **.X**

of **Cen**

of *Pick left circle to set X coordinate*

(need YZ): *Pick Y coordinate at point ①, 0.5 inches above upper view*

To point: *Pick point ②, 0.5 inches below upper view (see fig. 11.6)*

To point: *Press Enter*

Command: **Chprop**

Select objects: **L**

1 found

Select objects: *Press Enter*

Change what property (Color/LAyer/LType/Thickness) ? **LA**

New layer <OBJECT>: **CL**

Change what property (Color/LAyer/LType/Thickness) ? *Press Enter*

Command: **Line**

From point: **.X**

of **Qua**

of *Pick left side of left circle*

(need YZ): *Pick Y coordinate at point ③, on bottom line of upper view (see fig. 11.7)*

To point: *Pick point ④ on top line of upper view*

To point: *Press Enter*

Command: **Chprop**

Select objects: **L**

1 found

Aligning Using Point Filters—continued

Select objects: *Press Enter*

Change what property (Color/LAyer/LType/Thickness) ? **LA**

New layer <OBJECT>: **HL**

Change what property (Color/LAyer/LType/Thickness) ? *Press Enter*

Command: **Copy**

Select objects: **L**

1 found

Select objects: *Press Enter*

<Base point or displacement>/Multiple: **Qua**

of *Pick left side of left circle (see fig. 11.8)*

Second point of displacement: **Qua**

of *Pick right side of left circle*

Command: *Press Enter*

COPY

Select objects: **W**

First corner: *Pick point 6,10*

Other corner: *Pick point 8,12*

3 found

Select objects: *Press Enter*

<Base point or displacement>/Multiple: **Cen**

of *Pick left circle*

Second point of displacement: **Cen**

of *Pick right circle*

Command: **Save**

File name <TEMP>: *Press Enter*

The resulting upper view should resemble figure 11.8.

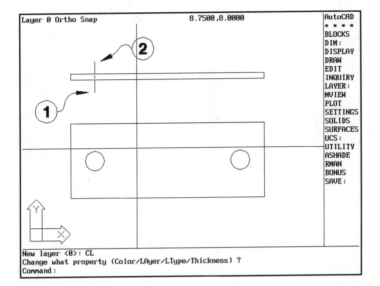

Figure 11.6:
Left hole center line.

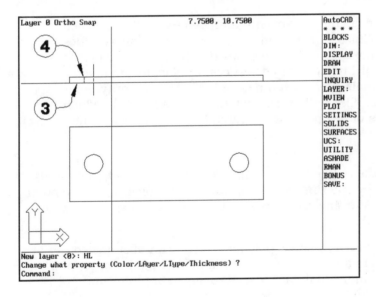

Figure 11.7:
Left hole hidden line.

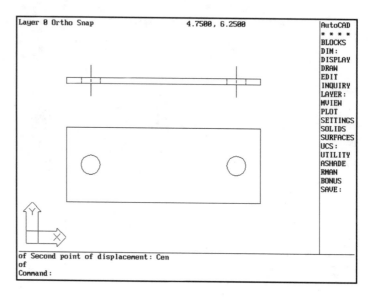

Figure 11.8:
Finished upper view.

Filleting the Arm

Command

The *Fillet* command creates an arc with a predefined radius between any combination of lines, circles, and arcs. It extends or trims entities as needed to draw the specified arc, if geometrically possible. It can be used on a single polyline at selected vertices, or globally at all vertices, but not in combination with other entities. An arc entity is inserted at the preset fillet radius. The default fillet radius is 0, which causes the entities or segments to be extended or trimmed to their intersection point.

You often must define the radius before using the Fillet command. The radius may be specified either by entering the radius value or by clicking on two points on the drawing screen. After the radius is set, it is maintained as the new default value until changed.

The profile you want to fillet is a single polyline, so you can fillet one corner at a time or do all four corners at once. To use the command on one corner at a time treats the entity as four individual lines instead of as a single polyline.

Set the fillet radius to 0.5, then fillet the four corners of the front view. To fillet one corner, pick the two lines close to what will be the fillet corner. To fillet all corners at once, use the Fillet command's Polyline option and select the polyline. Both of these methods are shown in the following exercise:

Filleting the Arm's Corners

```
Command: Fillet
Polyline/Radius/<Select two lines>: R
Enter fillet radius <0.0000>: .5
Command: Press Enter
FILLET Polyline/Radius/<Select two lines>: Pick point ① (see fig. 11.9)
Select second object: Pick point ②
Command: Press Enter
FILLET Polyline/Radius/<Select two lines>: P
Select 2D polyline: Pick the polyline at ②
4 lines were filleted (see fig. 11.10)
Command: Save
File name <TEMP>: Press Enter
```

When you use the Fillet command on circles and arcs, the result may not be what you expect. If so, type **U**, press Enter, and try the command again, picking different endpoints or picking in a different order.

A useful trick with the Fillet command is to connect, extend, or trim two entities to their common geometric intersection by setting the fillet radius to zero. This is a great tool for trimming or extending lines to clean up corners.

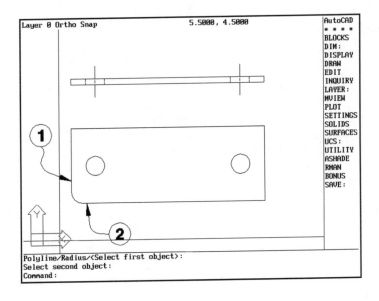

Figure 11.9:
One corner filleted.

Figure 11.10:
Completely filleted arm.

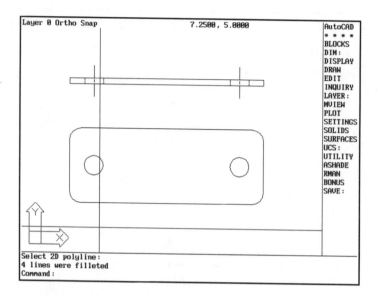

Dimensioning the Arm

The dimensioning exercise that follows features the Radius dimensioning command and AutoCAD's associative dimensioning capability. This exercise assumes that the associative dimension variable, DIMASO, is on (the default).

If you have the AutoCAD: Drafting and 3D Design Disk, you can dimension either the TEMP drawing you just created or the ready-to-dimension ARM-D drawing from the disk. If you do not have the disk, use the TEMP drawing.

Radius Dimensioning

The fillets need a radius dimension, which is done with the dimensioning mode's Radius subcommand. This is virtually identical in operation to the Diameter subcommand. The default radius dimension text begins with the letter R, the standard way of designating a radius dimension, although the prompt does not show the R. To create the 4X R.500 radius dimension, use a text override to preface the radius text with 4X. Also, use the Cen subcommand to add the two hole center marks and lines, and the Hor subcommand to add the two horizontal dimensions shown in figure 11.11. You need them in the following associative dimensioning exercise:

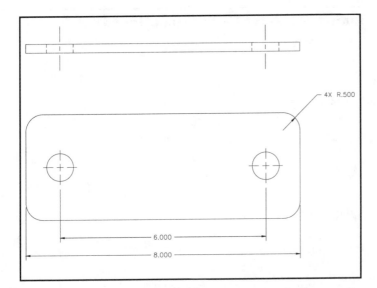

Figure 11.11:
The dimensioned arm.

Dimensioning the Fillet Radius

 Continue in TEMP or begin a new drawing named TEMP=ARM-D.

 Continue in or edit an existing drawing named TEMP.

```
Command: Layer
?/Make/Set/New/ON/OFF/Color/Ltype/Freeze/Thaw: S
New current layer <OBJECT>: DIM
?/Make/Set/New/ON/OFF/Color/Ltype/Freeze/Thaw: Press Enter
Command: Setvar
Variable name or ?: LUPREC
New value for LUPREC <4>: 3
Command: Zoom
All/Center/Dynamic/Extents/Left/Previous/Vmax/Window/<Scale (X/XP)>: C
Center point: 10,7.5
Magnification or Height <8.500> : 8
Command: Dim
Dim: DIMCEN
Current value <-0.100> New value: 0
Dim: DIMTOFL
```

▶ **Dimensioning the Fillet Radius—continued**

```
Current value <Off> New value: ON
Dim: Rad
Select arc or circle: Nea
to Pick arc with point ①, at 45 degrees from center of arc (see fig. 11.12)
Dimension text <0.500>: 4X <>
Text does not fit. Enter leader length for text: Pick point ②
Dim: DIMCEN
Current value <0.000> New value: -.1
Dim: Cen
Select arc or circle: Pick the left circle.
Dim: Cen
Select arc or circle: Pick the right circle.
Dim: Hor
First extension line origin or RETURN to select: Pick point ③
Second extension line origin: Pick point ④
Dimension line location: Pick any point 0.5" below bottom line of arm
Dimension text <6.000>: Press Enter
Dim: Hor
First extension line origin or RETURN to select: Pick point ⑤
Second extension line origin: Pick point ⑥
Dimension line location: Pick any point 1" below bottom line of arm
Dimension text <8.000>: Press Enter
Command: Save
File name <TEMP>: Press Enter
```

You used a little trick with the Osnap command's Nearest option to get the leader line to intersect the arc at exactly 45 degrees. It should resemble figure 11.11. To place a proper gap between the horizontal dimensions and the object, you held the pick points of the extension lines back 0.125 inches from the end/intersection of the line and arc. If you need to move the extension lines to such a point with the Osnap command for accuracy, you can accomplish the same thing by resetting DIMEXO (EXtension line Offset).

Associative Dimensioning

Now watch these associative dimensions adjust along with the geometry when the Stretch and Scale commands are invoked. AutoCAD's default dimensioning, associative dimensioning, automatically updates dimensions when you edit a drawing.

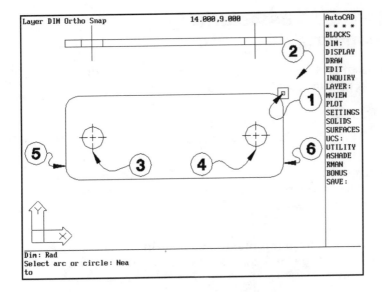

Figure 11.12:
Pick points for radius dimension.

Associative Dimensioning Variables

Two variables control associative dimensioning:

- **DIMASO.** Dimensions that are generated with DIMASO on are associative. DIMASO off causes dimension text, arrows, dimension lines, and extension lines to be generated as separate entities. The default value is on.

- **DIMSHO.** Controls the screen updating of dimensions as they are dragged. If DIMSHO is on, associative dimensions will be constantly recomputed as they are dragged. You should turn DIMSHO off if you are using a computer with a slow processing speed. With DIMSHO off, the original dimension image can be dragged until the final size is determined, then the resulting dimension is calculated and displayed.

Variable settings give associative dimensions much flexibility, but sometimes not enough. If you need to edit them in other ways, such as breaking an extension line, you must first use the Explode command.

Exploding Associative Dimensions

The *Explode* command converts the selected block, polyline, dimension, or hatch into individual entities so that you can selectively edit them.

Stretching and Scaling Associatively Dimensioned Geometry

You now will use the Stretch and Scale commands with associative dimensions. The Stretch command has been introduced. The Scale command is even simpler.

The *Scale* command changes the size of existing entities. The entities are scaled relative to the base point selected. The same scale factor is applied to the XY axes. Enter a numerical scale factor or use the Reference option to pick a reference and new length. A numerical scale factor is the default.

Scale the front view by 1.5, then stretch it one inch longer in the following exercise. This is a good place to use the Undo command to set a mark so you can later undo several steps at once.

Scaling and Stretching the Arms

Command: **Undo**

Auto/Back/Control/End/Group/Mark/<number>: **M**

Command: **Zoom**

All/Center/Dynamic/Extents/Left/Previous/Vmax/Window/<Scale(X/XP)>: **C**

Center point: **13,7**

Magnification or Height <8.000> : **9**

Command: **Scale**

Select objects: **C**

First corner: *Pick corner to select the arm and dimensions with a Crossing window*

Other corner: *Pick second corner of Crossing window*

18 found

Select objects: *Press Enter*

Base point: *Pick the center of right hole*

<Scale factor>/Reference: **1.5**

The object is rescaled and the dimensions are recalculated, as shown in figure 11.13 (You may have to zoom in a bit to read the dimension text)

Command: **Stretch**

Select objects to stretch by window...

Scaling and Stretching the Arms—continued

```
Select objects: C
First corner: Pick corner of Crossing window of right end (see fig. 11.13)
Other corner: Pick other corner of Crossing window
15 found
Select objects: Press Enter
Base point: Pick point ①
New point: <Ortho off> Press F8 to toggle ortho off, then pick point ②
```

The drawing is now altered to reflect the scaling and stretching, as shown in figure 11.14. Note that the updated horizontal and radius dimensions reflect the editing of the object.

Notice that the scale of the dimension entity itself does not change, although the text changes to show the new dimension. If you want larger dimension text, arrows and so on, you need to change the DIMSCALE variable, the overall dimensioning scale factor, and update the dimensions. If you are using Release 10, notice that the radius dimension now sports a center mark because the Stretch command updated all stretched dimensions to the current dimensioning variable settings. To restore it with no center mark, reset the DIMCEN variable and update it.

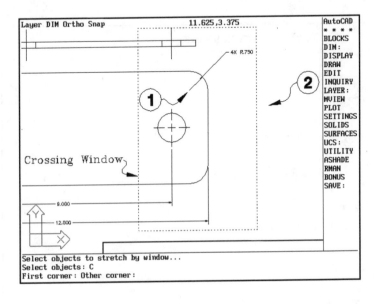

Figure 11.13:
Stretch window.

Figure 11.14:
Results of the Scale and Stretch commands.

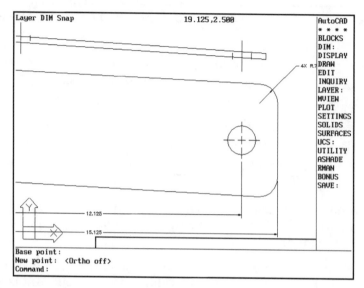

Updating Associative Dimensions

Now adjust the DIMSCALE variable and update the dimensions. If you are using Release 10, also update the DIMCEN variable. Then, use the Undo command to restore the previous drawing conditions. Notice the `Mark encountered` prompt near the end of the exercise. The mark stops Undo.

Updating Dimensions

Command: **Dim**

Dim: **DIMSCALE**

Current value <1.000> New value: **2**

Dim: **Upd**

Select objects: *Select the upper horizontal dimension*

1 selected, 1 found

Select objects: *Select the lower horizontal dimension*

1 selected, 1 found

Select objects: *Press Enter*

(If you are using Release 11, skip to the Undo command.)

Dim: **DIMCEN**

Current value <0.0000> New value: **0**

Dim: **Upd**

Select objects: *Select the radius dimension*

1 selected, 1 found

Updating Dimensions—continued

Select objects: *Press Enter (see fig. 11.15)*

Command: **Undo**

Auto/Back/Control/End/Group/Mark/<number>: **B**

DIM STRETCH SCALE ZOOM

Mark encountered

Command: **Save**

File name <TEMP>: *Press Enter*

After the Undo, your drawing should resemble figure 11.16.

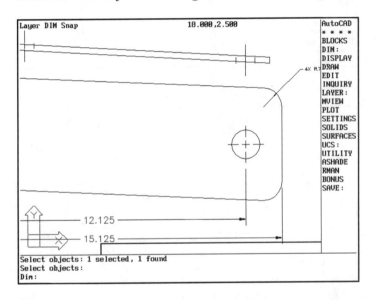

Figure 11.15:
Updated dimensions.

Completing the Arm's Dimensions—Optional

If you want to practice the techniques discussed in Chapters 9 and 10 by completing the arm's dimensions, the following numbered instructions refer to the numbered bubbles in figure 11.17.

(1) **Vertical Dimensions.** Set DIMTOFL off and use the Vertical dimensioning command to complete the normal dimensions, picking the .25 dimension from bottom to top.

(2) **Basic Dimensions.** Set DIMTIX on and DIMGAP to .063, then use the Horizontal and Vertical dimensioning commands to generate the dimensions, Zoom in and add the boxes with polylines.

Figure 11.16:
Restored arm.

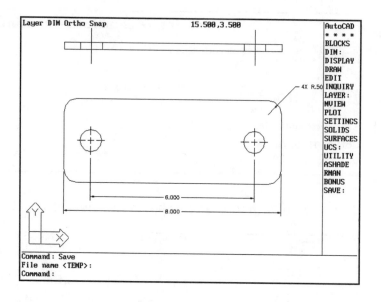

Figure 11.17:
Optional: The completely dimensioned arm.

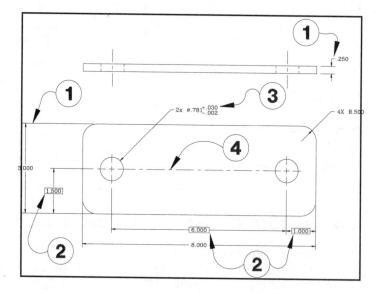

(3) **Diameter with Limits.** Set DIMTOL on, DIMTP to .03, DIMTM to .002, and DIMCEN to 0 (off). Use the Diameter dimensioning command and enter the text as **2X < >**.

(4) **Center line.** Draw the center line on layer CL.

You will insert this completed and dimensioned part into a larger multi-view drawing in Chapter 12, so save it (without title block) as a separate file that can be used as a block. If you want to stop at this point, use the End command to exit your drawing and continue when time permits. You will then edit the existing drawing named TEMP.

Blocking Entities into Groups

You now will block the arm drawing so that it can be inserted into the multi-detail drawing. A block is a set or group of entities which forms a compound object. A block is defined and manipulated by AutoCAD as a single entity. This makes editing (such as moving, copying, rotating, or scaling) blocks very simple. Moving a complex part can be as simple as moving a line, for example.

A block is not an entity; it is a definition in the drawing's database. The block definition contains other entities (even other nested blocks). A block can be defined in a drawing without being in use or visible.

To use a block, you must insert it with the Insert command. An inserted block definition is often casually called a block, but it is more accurately called an *insert* entity. Actually, any drawing file can be inserted into any other by the Insert command. Inserting another file into the current drawing as a block creates a new block definition in the current drawing. The block definition gets the name used in the insertion and contains all of the entities in the inserted drawing file.

The *Block* command defines a group of entities as a block within the current drawing. (Use the Insert command to insert blocks into your drawing.) You define a block by choosing an entity selection set which is deleted from the current drawing and stored as a block definition in the drawing. (The Oops command will restore the entities.) You are prompted for a block name and insertion base point. The base point is a reference point relative to which the block will be inserted and scaled. Such blocks may only be inserted in the drawing within which they are defined.

The *Insert* command inserts an image of a block definition into the current drawing. You pick the insertion point, X,Y,Z scale values, and the rotation angle. The insertion point is relative to the block's base point. The default X scale factor is 1, and the Y scale defaults to equal the X scale. Rotation angle defaults to 0. If you preface the block name with an asterisk, such as *FRONT, then an actual copy of each individual entity in the block's definition is inserted instead of an insert entity image. This is often referred to as *insert** (insert-star) or a **block* (star-block).

The *Wblock* (Write Block) command writes a drawing, a selection set, or a block definition to disk as a new drawing file (not a block definition). A wblock is not an entity; it is a command that creates an ordinary drawing file that can be inserted into other drawings or recalled from the second main menu option: Edit an EXISTING drawing. After you invoke the Wblock command, you are prompted to enter a file name, a block name, an insertion base point, and to select the wblock entities. If you enter an equal sign (=) as a block name, it searches for a block in the drawing that matches the file name. It then writes the block to disk as individual entities in a new drawing file. If you press Enter or Spacebar as a block name, you are required to enter a base point and use normal object selection to select entities which are deleted and written to disk. No new block is created in the current drawing.

The *Minsert* (Multiple Insert) command is a combination of the Insert and (rectangular) Array commands. The Minsert command enables you to insert a multiple copy of a block in a rectangular array pattern. The command has the same prompts as the Insert command for insertion point, XY scaling, and rotation angle, and the same prompts as the Array command for rows and columns.

The *Base* command establishes an alternative insertion base point. Any drawing can be inserted into another drawing. By default, every drawing file has a base point of 0,0,0, relative to which it is inserted into other drawings.

After you create a drawing file using the Wblock command, only layer information, text styles, nested block definitions, and linetypes used by the entities being written to disk are written to the file. UCSs, views, and viewports are never written.

When you need to make repetitive parts, use blocks. Blocks increase efficiency and reduce drawing file size. Each entity adds to a drawing file's byte count. When you create and block an entity once and insert the block definition many times, the entity only exists once in the drawing file, in a block definition. Each time the image is replicated by the Insert command, only one additional entity—an insert entity—is created.

Insert entities are very efficient, only containing X, Y and Z scale values, a rotation, entity properties (layer, color, and linetype), and a reference to the block definition name. Blocks may also contain attributes, which will be covered later. The individual entities of the block definition are not duplicated by the insert entity, so the storage space saved by inserting a block as a single primitive entity is significant. (Inserting a *block duplicates the entities and yields no savings.)

Block definitions may contain other blocks. These are called nested blocks. Nested blocks save space within a drawing file.

Writing the Arm to Disk

You will use the Wblock command later in this chapter to create a drawing file containing only the dimensioned arm, without border, title block, or extraneous information. Block names can be up to 31 characters long, but drawing files are limited to the operating system's capacity—eight characters for DOS. The characters may include letters, numbers, the dollar sign ($), the hyphen (-), and the underline (_). The file name is automatically assigned the extension DWG. It is written to the current directory unless a path is specified.

You can code the file names. Designate a file intended to be inserted as a block, for example, by prefacing the name with a leading letter B, such as B-ARM. Or you can organize them by subdirectory location and have all eight characters available for the name.

After you are prompted for the block name, there are four options you can use:

- **Name** Enters an existing block name to write the entities that comprise its definition.
- **=** Causes the entities that comprise the definition of an existing block name that matches the specified output file name to be written to the file.
- ***** Causes the entire drawing to be written to the file. This is similar to the Save command, except that only pertinent information is written.
- **Press Enter or Spacebar** Prompts you to select objects and the insertion base point.

You will use the Wblock command twice in the following exercise. First, write the entire drawing (including title block) as a file named ARM, separate from your TEMP file. This has the effect of purging all unused data to save disk space. Then invoke Wblock again to write out only the dimensioned arm for later insertion.

Before you begin this exercise, turn the system variable FILEDIA off in order to suppress the dialogue box. Continue in TEMP, or begin a new drawing named TEMP=ARM-W, and follow these steps:

Wblocking the Arm Drawing

 Continue in TEMP, or begin a new drawing named TEMP=ARM-W.

Continue in or edit an existing drawing named TEMP.

Command: **Zoom**

All/Center/Dynamic/Extents/Left/Previous/Vmax/Window/<Scale(X/XP)>: **C**

Center point: **10,8**

Magnification or Height <10.000> : **12**

Command: **Wblock**

File name: **ARM**

Block name: *****

Command: **Wblock**

File name: **B-ARM**

Block name: *Press Enter*

Insertion base point: *Pick point ① (see fig. 11.18)*

Select objects: **W**

First corner: *Pick point ①*

Other corner: *Pick point ②*

34 found

Select objects: *Press Enter*

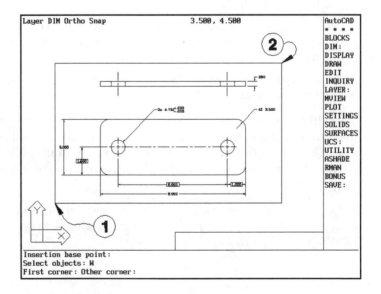

Figure 11.18:
*WBLOCK insertion base
point and window.*

The Wblock command, like the Erase command, deletes the entities. If you need to retain them as individual entities, use the Oops command to restore the drawing after writing the block to disk. If you want the entities in the drawing as a group (a block insert), then continue in the preceding TEMP drawing and use the Insert command as follows:

Reinserting the Arm

```
Command: Insert
Block name (or ?): B-ARM
Insertion point: @
X scale factor <1> / Corner / XYZ: Press Enter
Y scale factor (default=X): Press Enter
Rotation angle <0>: Press Enter
Command: U
INSERT
Command: End
```

The arm came back as a single entity, an insert.

Drafting the Spacing Pin

The exercises in this section feature the Chamfer command and Limit and Leader dimensioning. You will develop the pin drawing with two orthographic views, the front and the right side. You will draw the front view profile, then use the Chamfer command to bevel the corners of one end of the pin. The Mirror command copies it to the other end. After the front view is completed, the Circle and Osnap commands and point filters easily generate the right side view. The finished pin, as illustrated in figure 11.19, will be written to disk for later insertion into the multi-detail subassembly drawing.

To start the pin, draw a 6-inch horizontal center line and change it to layer CL. Use the Pline command to draw the 4x1.25 front view profile and the 0.75x0.5 left end of the shaft, and use the Circle command for the drill hole at the middle of the left end. Either replace the previous TEMP drawing and begin a new drawing named TEMP or edit the existing TEMP drawing and follow these steps:

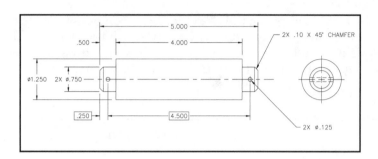

Figure 11.19:
The spacing pin drawing.

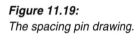

Drawing the Pin's Front View Profile

```
Command: Zoom
All/Center/Dynamic/Extents/Left/Previous/Vmax/Window/<Scale(X/XP)>: C
Center point: 10,9
Magnification or Height <23.1222> : 5
Command: <Ortho on> Press F8 to toggle ortho on
Command: Line
From point:
To point: Pick point 7,9
To point: Pick point 13,9
Command: Chprop
Select objects: L
1 found
Select objects: Press Enter
Change what property (Color/LAyer/LType/Thickness) ? LA
New layer <OBJECT>: CL
Change what property (Color/LAyer/LType/Thickness) ? Press Enter
Command: Pline
From point: 8,9.625
Current line-width is 0.0000
Arc/Close/Halfwidth/Length/Undo/Width/<Endpoint of line>: Pick point @4<0
Arc/Close/Halfwidth/Length/Undo/Width/<Endpoint of line>: Pick point @1.25<270
Arc/Close/Halfwidth/Length/Undo/Width/<Endpoint of line>: Pick point @4<180
Arc/Close/Halfwidth/Length/Undo/Width/<Endpoint of line>: C
Command: Press Enter
PLINE
From point: 8,8.625
Current line-width is 0.0000
```

Drawing the Pin's Front View Profile—continued

Arc/Close/Halfwidth/Length/Undo/Width/<Endpoint of line>: *Pick point @0.5<180*

Arc/Close/Halfwidth/Length/Undo/Width/<Endpoint of line>: *Pick point @0.75<90*

Arc/Close/Halfwidth/Length/Undo/Width/<Endpoint of line>: *Pick point @0.5<0*

Arc/Close/Halfwidth/Length/Undo/Width/<Endpoint of line>: *Press Enter*

Command: **Circle**

3P/2P/TTR/<Center point>: *Pick point 7.75,9*

Diameter/<Radius>: **.0625**

Your drawing should now resemble figure 11.20.

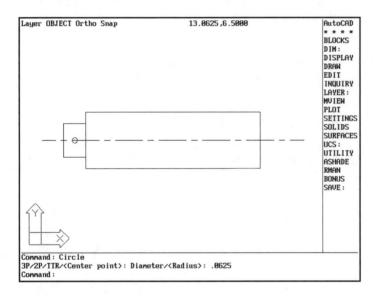

Figure 11.20:
Pin's front view profile.

Chamfering Geometry

The *Chamfer* command is similar to the Fillet command, except it works only on lines and straight polyline segments. The Chamfer command creates a beveled edge for intersecting lines and contiguous segments of a 2D Polyline. It trims or extends two lines or polyline segments at specified distances from their intersection or vertex point and creates a new line to connect the trimmed ends. You can use the command alternatively on an entire polyline at once with the Polyline option. The Chamfer command requires two distance values. The first distance value is applied to the first selected line, the second distance to the second line. The default for distances is 0.

You must specify the first and second chamfer distances before using the Chamfer command to draw a chamfer. You can enter the chamfer distances numerically, or you can designate them by picking two points on the drawing screen. If you need to describe the chamfer in terms of angle and depth (.1 deep x 60 degrees, for example) you will have to use simple trigonometry or geometry to convert the information to two distances (0.1x0.1732, for example).

To chamfer a corner, pick the two lines to be chamfered at their closest ends to the corner. If the chamfer is symmetrical, the picks may be made in any order. If the chamfer is nonsymmetrical, you must pick the lines in order of distance one and distance two.

The Chamfer command trims the existing two lines and generates the new line segment, but this is not a completed chamfer representation. Add the shoulder line to complete it. This is easy to do if you use object snap to locate the starting and ending points.

Now chamfer the pin with a .1x45 degree (0.1x0.1) chamfer, as shown in figure 11.21. Add the shoulder line with Osnap Int, and then use the Mirror command to duplicate it on the right end.

Continue in the previous TEMP drawing and follow these steps:

Figure 11.21:
Chamfered left side of pin.

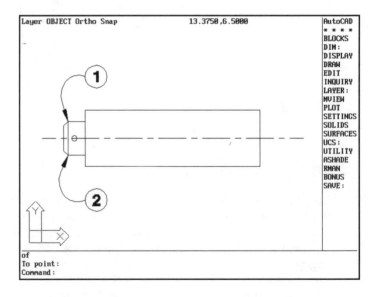

Chamfering and Mirroring the Pin

```
Command: Chamfer
Polyline/Distance/<Select first line>: D
Enter first chamfer distance <0.000>: .1
Enter second chamfer distance <0.100>: Press Enter
Command: Press Enter
CHAMFER Polyline/Distance/<Select first line>: P
Select 2D polyline: Pick polyline at ① (see fig. 11.21)
2 lines were chamfered
Command: Line
From point: Int
of Pick point ①
To point: Int
of Pick point ②
To point: Press Enter
Command: Mirror
Select objects: L
1 selected, 1 found
Select objects: Pick chamfered polyline
1 selected, 1 found
Select objects: Pick circle
1 selected, 1 found
Select objects: Press Enter
First point of mirror line: Mid
of Pick shaft at point ③ (see fig. 11.22)
Second point: Pick any point above, such as point ④, with ortho on
Delete old objects? <N> Press Enter
Command: Save
File name <TEMP>: Press Enter
```

After using the Mirror command, your drawing should resemble figure 11.22.

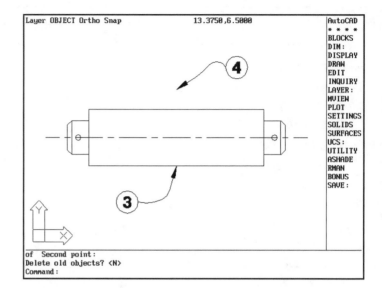

Figure 11.22:
Mirrored right side of pin.

You may complete the pin by drawing the right side view, if you want.

The Pin's Right Side View—Optional

Object snaps and point filters simplify drawing the circles of the right end. Remember that the innermost concentric circle is created by the .1x45 degree chamfer. After you generate the circles, develop the hidden lines which represent the .125 diameter drill holes and the center lines in both the front and side views. The following numbered directions correspond to the numbered bubbles in the completed drawing shown in figure 11.23.

(1) **Zoom.** Zoom to the view shown above.

(2) **Outer Circles.** Draw the .75" and 1.25" outer circles with the Circle command and snap.

(3) **Inner Chamfered Circle.** Use a .Y point filter and Osnap Int for the radius, as follows:

```
Diameter/<Radius>: .Y
of Int
of Pick point ③
(need XZ): Pick any point above the center point
```

(4) **Hidden Drill Hole Lines.** The hidden lines representing the drill holes, which are developed in the right side view, can be drafted in various ways. Here is one way:

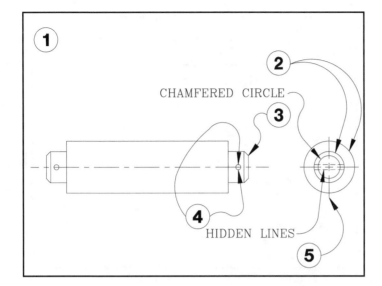

Figure 11.23:
Optional: Completed right side view.

Line. Draw two lines from top and bottom quadrant points of right drill hole (see fig. 11.23, ④), using a QUAdrant object snap with ortho on to start each line. Extend each line through the three circles to right side of drawing.

Trim. Select the second (middle) circle as the cutting edge and trim both ends of both lines.

Chprop. Change both lines to layer HL.

(5) **Center lines.** Set layer to DIM and use the CENter dimensioning command to add center marks to the outer circle, then set layer back to OBJECT.

Finally, save the drawing.

Dimensioning the Pin

The following exercise features Limits dimensioning and the Leader dimensioning subcommand. These dimensions are shown in figure 11.24.

To generate dimensions in limit form, set the DIMTP plus and DIMTM minus tolerance values and toggle the DIMLIM variable on. Also turn DIMTIX (Text Inside eXtension) on to force the text inside the lines. It otherwise would go above or below the extension lines due to limited space.

Set up limits dimensioning and dimension the diameter with vertical dimensions as shown in the following exercise. Continue in TEMP or begin a new drawing named TEMP=PIN-D.

Figure 11.24:
Limits and leader
dimensions.

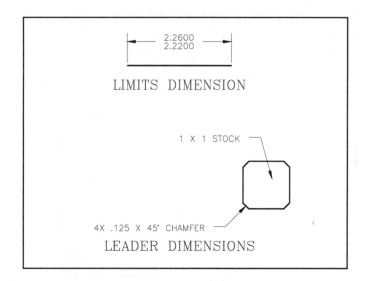

Setting Limits

Continue in TEMP, or begin a new drawing named TEMP=PIN-D.

Continue in or edit an existing drawing named TEMP.

```
Command: Zoom
All/Center/Dynamic/Extents/Left/Previous/Vmax/Window/<Scale(X/XP)>: C
Center point: 8,9
Magnification or Height <6.0000> : 5
Command: Layer
?/Make/Set/New/ON/OFF/Color/Ltype/Freeze/Thaw: S
New current layer <OBJECT>: DIM
?/Make/Set/New/ON/OFF/Color/Ltype/Freeze/Thaw: Press Enter
Command: Setvar
New value for LUPREC <4>: 3
Command: Dim
Dim: DIMTP
Current value <0.000> New value: .003
Dim: DIMLIM
Current value <Off> New value: ON
```

▶ **Setting Limits—continued**

Dim: **DIMTIX**

Current value <Off> New value: **ON**

Dim: **Ver**

First extension line origin or RETURN to select: *Press Enter*

Select line, arc, or circle: *Pick line at ① (see fig. 11.25)*

Dimension line location: *Pick point 6.5,9*

The dimension generated should resemble figure 11.25.

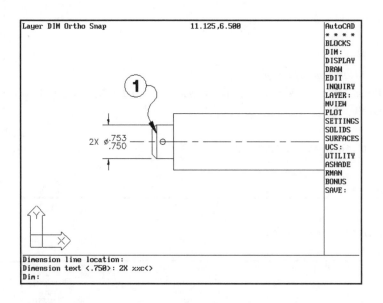

Figure 11.25:
Diameter dimension in limits form.

Pointing to Specific Locations with Leaders

Although the Diameter and Radius dimensioning commands provide automatic leaders when they are developed, you often will want to use the Leader dimensioning command to create leaders that point to specific locations or parts on your drawings.

The Leader command creates both simple (one- or two-segment) and complex (multi-segment) leaders. Complex leaders are developed by picking a leader starting point and then several subsequent endpoints of the leader body. After you complete the leader line(s), pressing Enter generates a horizontal leader shoulder. AutoCAD then prompts you for the dimension text. The text will be justified according to the direction of the shoulder.

The leader shoulder is always horizontal. The default direction is the same direction as the previous segment. You can override that, as shown in the exercise that follows, by making the last segment a short horizontal. When the last segment is horizontal, the shoulder is omitted.

Continue in the dimensioning mode from the previous exercise and draw the leader for the chamfer dimension on the front view, as follows:

Developing a Leader and Text

Dim: **'Pan**

>>Displacement: **-5,0**

>> Second point: *Press Enter*

Dim: **Lea**

Leader start: **Mid**

of *Pick upper chamfer line at right end of shaft*

To point: <Ortho off> *Press F8 to toggle ortho off, then pick point 13,10.375*

To point: *Pick point @.188<0*

To point: *Press Enter*

Dimension text <.750>: **2X .10 X 45%%D CHAMFER**

Dim: **Exit**

Command: **Save**

Your leader should resemble figure 11.26.

Figure 11.26:
Leader with text.

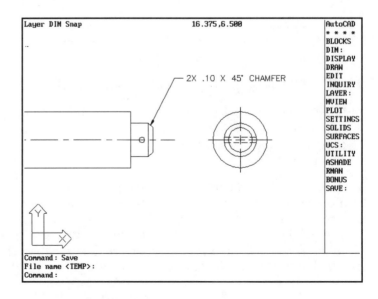

Notice that the previous 0.750 value of the vertical dimension was presented as the default leader text. You can use this as the leader text or embed it with angle brackets < > in the text string. A useful trick is to use another dimension mode to measure something, then cancel or enter a space when prompted for text. The measured dimension will then be the default text for a following leader.

Completing the Pin's Dimensions—Optional

If you want to complete the pin's dimensions, zoom to the view shown in figure 11.27 and complete the following numbered instructions which correspond to the numbered bubbles.

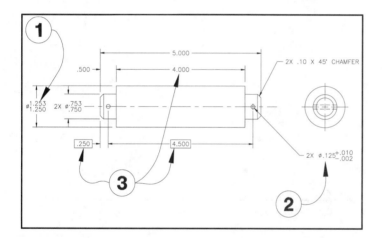

Figure 11.27:
Optional: The completely dimensioned pin.

(1) **Outer Diameter Limits.** Use the Vertical dimensioning command and enter the text as **%%c<>**.

(2) **Hole Diameter with Tolerances.** Set DIMTIX off, DIMTOL on, DIMTP to .01, and DIMTM to .002, and use the Diameter dimensioning command. Pick lower right side of the right hole and enter the text as **2X <>**.

(3) **Horizontal and Basic Dimensions**. Set DIMTOL off and use the Horizontal dimensioning command to generate the dimensions, then add the boxes with polylines.

Write Blocking the Pin to Disk

Use the Wblock command to write block the pin to disk so it can be inserted into the multi-detail drawing. Continue in the previous TEMP drawing and follow these steps:

Wblocking the Pin

Command: **View**

?/Delete/Restore/Save/Window: **R**

View name to restore: **BDR**

Regenerating drawing.

Command: **Wblock**

File name: **B-PIN**

Block name: *Press Enter*

Insertion base point: **5,7**

Select objects: **W**

First corner: **5,7**

Other corner: **16,11**

33 found

Select objects: *Press Enter*

Command: **Quit**

Drafting the Servo Motor Mount

This exercise focuses on the rectangular Array command and on diameter dimensioning large circles to ANSI standards. You will draw the mount in a front and a right side orthographic view. After drawing the front and side profiles, you will draw one circle with center marks and then array it to create four other circles. When the geometry is completed, as illustrated by figure 11.28, you will dimension the mount and write it to disk with the Wblock command for later insertion into the multi-detail subassembly drawing.

To start the mount, use the Pline command to draw the 5x5 front and 1x5 side profiles, and use the Circle command for the 3.0 diameter hole. Begin a new drawing named TEMP and follow these steps:

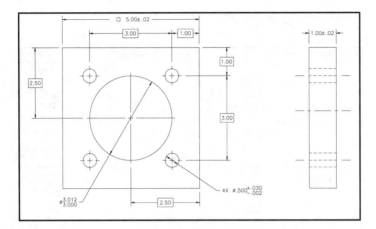

Figure 11.28:
The servo motor mount.

Drawing the Mount's Front and Side Profiles

Command: **Snap**

Snap spacing or ON/OFF/Aspect/Rotate/Style <0.0625>: **0.25**

Command: **Zoom**

All/Center/Dynamic/Extents/Left/Previous/Vmax/Window/<Scale(X/XP)>: **C**

Center point: **10,8**

Magnification or Height <23.1222> : **9**

Command: *Press F8 to toggle Ortho on*

Command: **Pline**

From point: **5,6**

Current line-width is 0.0000

Arc/Close/Halfwidth/Length/Undo/Width/<Endpoint of line>: **@5<0**

Arc/Close/Halfwidth/Length/Undo/Width/<Endpoint of line>: **@5<90**

Arc/Close/Halfwidth/Length/Undo/Width/<Endpoint of line>: **@5<180**

Arc/Close/Halfwidth/Length/Undo/Width/<Endpoint of line>: **C**

Command: **Pline**

From point: **14,6**

Current line-width is 0.0000

Arc/Close/Halfwidth/Length/Undo/Width/<Endpoint of line>: **@1<0**

Arc/Close/Halfwidth/Length/Undo/Width/<Endpoint of line>: **@5<90**

Arc/Close/Halfwidth/Length/Undo/Width/<Endpoint of line>: **@1<180**

Arc/Close/Halfwidth/Length/Undo/Width/<Endpoint of line>: **C**

Command: **Circle**

3P/2P/TTR/<Center point>: **7.5,8.5**

Diameter/<Radius>: **1.5**

Your drawing now should resemble figure 11.29.

Figure 11.29:
Mount's front and side profiles.

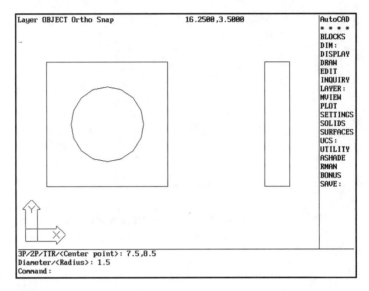

Rectangular Arrays

The *Array* command makes multiple copies of objects in rectangular or polar (circular) patterns. It can be a valuable time-saving drafting tool for spacing entities in patterns. A rectangular array prompts for the number and spacing of rows and columns. A polar array prompts for center point, number of copies to make, the angle to fill with the copies, and whether to rotate each copy.

When you use the Array command, the objects maintain their individual entity properties, such as layer, linetype, and color information.

The following exercise features the rectangular Array command. The polar Array command will be introduced when you draft the pulley later in this chapter.

When you use the rectangular Array command, you are prompted for the number of horizontal rows and vertical columns to be arrayed. You ordinarily set up the array so that the rows and columns are constructed in the positive X and Y directions. This assumes that the lower left object is selected as the object to array and the row and column distances are both positive values. When you enter a negative value for the row or column distance, however, the objects are constructed to the left (negative X for row) or down (negative Y for column).

Continue in the previous TEMP drawing and draw the lower left hole circle and circle center lines shown in figure 11.30. Then use the Array command to duplicate them, as follows:

Using a Rectangular Array

Command: **Circle**

3P/2P/TTR/<Center point>: **6,7**

Diameter/<Radius>: **.25**

Command: Layer

?/Make/Set/New/ON/OFF/Color/Ltype/Freeze/Thaw: **S**

New current layer <OBJECT>: **DIM**

?/Make/Set/New/ON/OFF/Color/Ltype/Freeze/Thaw: *Press Enter*

Command: **Dim1**

Dim: **Cen**

Select arc or circle: *Select the circle*

Command: **Array**

Select objects: **W**

First corner: *Pick first point of window at 5.5,6.5 (see fig. 11.30)*

Other corner: *Pick point 6.5,7.5*

7 found

Select objects: *Press Enter*

Rectangular or Polar array (R/P): **R**

Number of rows (---) <1>: **2**

Number of columns (||||) <1>: **2**

Unit cell or distance between rows (---): **3**

Distance between columns (||||): **3**

Command: **Save**

File name <Temp>: *Press Enter*

If you do not have the AutoCAD: Drafting and 3D Design Disk, you should also save the drawing to file name MENUTEST for use in Chapter 12.

The holes should be arrayed as shown in figure 11.30.

You can designate the distance between rows and columns by defining a unit cell, if you prefer. When you are prompted for the unit cell or distance between rows, click on two points on the drawing screen which represent opposite corners of a rectangle. These picks provide AutoCAD with the row and column spacing. When you enter row and column spacing in this way, the Distance between columns (||||): prompt is ignored.

Figure 11.30:
Entities are rectangularly arrayed.

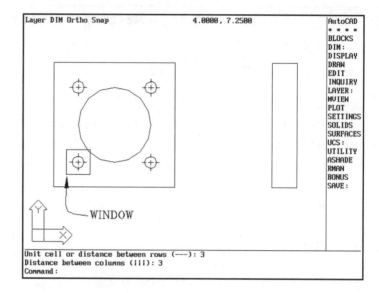

Completing the Two Views—Optional

You may complete the side view of the mount if you want, adding center and hidden lines. Complete the following numbered directions which correspond to the numbered bubbles in figures 11.31 and 11.32. Note that center lines for the small holes and the hidden lines for the large hole are aligned in the right side view. To avoid superimposing linetypes and yet to properly describe the geometry, draw four short lines representative of the ends of the center lines with gaps between them and the object profile.

Figure 11.31:
Optional: Hidden lines and center lines.

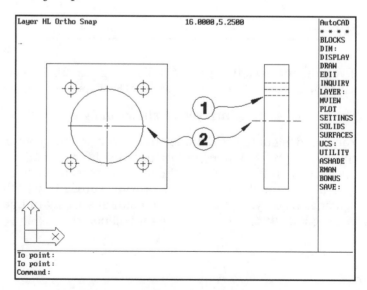

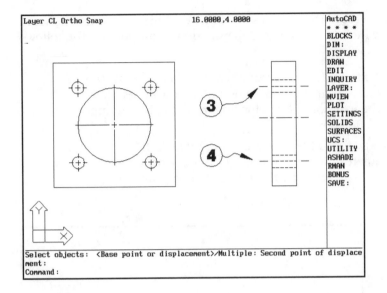

Figure 11.32:
Optional: Copied hidden and center lines.

(1) **Hidden Lines.** Set the layer to HL and draw the top three hidden lines shown in figure 11.31.

(2) **Large Center Lines.** Set the layer to CL and use the Cen dimensioning command to draw the large circle's center line, as shown in figure 11.31. Draw a 2-inch center line for the large hole in the side view.

(3) **Small Center Lines.** Draw two 0.3125-inch line segments aligned with the center top hidden line, but not touching the object profile (see fig. 11.32).

(4) **Bottom Hidden and Center Lines.** Use the Mirror or Copy commands to copy the top hidden and center lines to the bottom.

Save or end the drawing. If you do not have the AutoCAD: Drafting and 3D Design Disk, save the drawing to the file name, MENUTEST. You will use the drawing in Chapter 12 to try out the ANSI Y14.5 Menu System.

Dimensioning Circles to ANSI Standards

The mount demonstrates how to draw diameter dimensions for large circles according to ANSI standards.

Larger circles should be dimensioned with the dimension line extending through the diameter of that circle. The dimension should then have a leader line extending past the perimeter to an open area of the drawing.

AutoCAD enables you to create three styles of diameter dimensions, as shown in figure 11.33. The style which is developed depends upon how you set the following system variables:

- **DIMTIX.** Forces text inside extension lines. If DIMTIX is on, the dimension text is drawn in the middle of a diameter dimension line, or between the extension lines for linear, aligned, and angular dimensions.

- **DIMTOFL.** Places text outside the force line. If DIMTOFL is on and DIMTIX is off, diameter dimension lines with arrowheads are drawn inside a circle or arc, and the text and leader line are drawn outside.

Figure 11.33:
Diameter dimensioning styles.

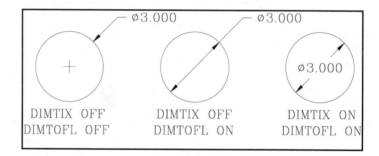

Dimension the 3-inch diameter circle on the mount's front view. Before you dimension, set the Dim layer current, set the limits dimensioning variables, and set the diameter dimension variables.

Continue in TEMP or begin a new drawing named TEMP=MOUNT-D, as follows:

Diameter Dimensioning Large Circles

 Continue in TEMP, or begin a new drawing named TEMP=MOUNT-D.

 Continue in or edit an existing drawing named TEMP.

```
Command: Zoom
All/center/Dynamic/Extents/Left/Previous/Vmax/Window/<Scale (X/XP)>: C
Center point: 6,7
Magnification of Height <9.0000> : 6
Command: Setvar
New value for LUPREC <4>: 3
```

Diameter Dimensioning Large Circles—continued

```
Command: Layer
?/Make/Set/New/ON/OFF/Color/Ltype/Freeze/Thaw: S
New current layer <CL>: DIM
?/Make/Set/New/ON/OFF/Color/Ltype/Freeze/Thaw: Press Enter
Command: Dim
Dim: DIMLIM
Current value <off> New value: On
Dim: DIMTP
Current value <0.000> New value: 0.012
Dim: DIMTOFL
Current value <Off> New value: On
Dim: Dia
Select arc or circle: Pick the 3" circle at ① (This becomes the leader point; see fig.
11.34)
Dimension text <3.000>: Press Enter
Enter leader length for text: Pick at point ②
DIM: Exit
Command: Zoom
All/Center/Dynamic/Extents/Left/Previous/Vmax/Window/<Scale(X/XP)>: P
Command: Save
File name <TEMP>: Press Enter
```

The mount drawing now should contain the diameter dimension inside the circle and the dimension leader and text located outside the circle, as shown before zooming in figure 11.34.

Completing the Mount's Dimensions

If you want to complete the mount's dimensions, use the following numbered instructions which correspond to the numbered bubbles in figure 11.35.

(1) **Hole Diameter with Tolerances.** Set snap to 0.0625, DIMTOFL on, DIMTOL on, DIMTP to 0.03, DIMTM to 0.002, and DIMCEN to 0 (off), then use the Center dimensioning command to dimension the lower right hole. Enter the text as 4X <>.

Figure 11.34:
The leadered diameter dimension.

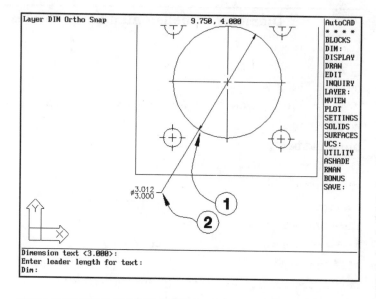

Figure 11.35:
The completely dimensioned mount.

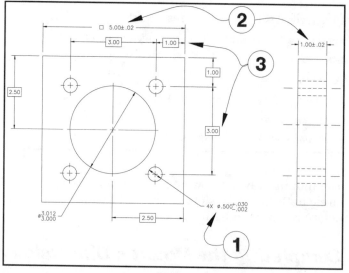

(2) **Horizontal Tolerance Dimensions.** Set DIMTIX on and DIMTOFL off, and reset DIMTP and DIMTM to 0.02. Set LUPREC to 2 with the 'Setvar command. Use the Horizontal dimensioning command for the top side and front view dimensions. For the top front view, enter the text as four leading spaces and <> to make room for the square symbol. Draw the square symbol with lines or a polyline.

(3) **Basic Dimensions.** Set DIMTOL off and use the Horizontal and Vertical dimensioning commands to generate the dimensions. Set snap to 0.03125 and zoom in to add the boxes.

Finally, save or end the drawing.

Writing the Mount to Disk

Write the mount to disk with the Wblock command so it can be inserted into the multi-detail drawing in the next chapter. Use the same procedure you used on the arm and the pin drawings.

Continue in the TEMP drawing and follow these steps:

Wblocking the Mount Drawing

Command: **Wblock**

File name: **B-MOUNT**

Block name: *Press Enter*

Insertion base point: **4,4**

Select objects: **W**

First corner: **3.5,4**

Other corner: **16,13**

65 found

Select objects: *Press Enter*

Command: **Quit**

Drafting the Adjustment Plate

This exercise shows you how to modify an existing block to create similar parts. You will call up the B-MOUNT block and edit its geometry to create the adjustment plate (see fig. 11.36), using the Insert, Change, Stretch, Copy, Move, and Trim commands, and the Arc command's continuation option.

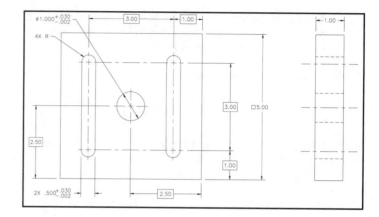

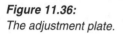

Figure 11.36:
The adjustment plate.

Inserting Pre-Exploded Blocks

You may notice that the plate drawing (fig. 11.36) is similar to the servo motor mount drawing (fig. 11.35) that you wrote to disk in the preceding exercise as B-MOUNT. Now take advantage of that by inserting and editing the previous part.

In the following exercise, you insert B-MOUNT with an asterisk (*) to load its entities individually, not as a block. (This does not create a B-MOUNT block definition in the current drawing.) Then you erase all the extraneous dimensions, hidden lines, and center lines that are not shown in figure 11.37. You also erase the right-hand holes to learn two ways to create the slots: by trimming circles and by stringing lines and arcs together.

Begin a new drawing named TEMP and follow these steps:

Drawing the Plate's Front and Side Profile

```
Command: Snap
Snap spacing or ON/OFF/Aspect/Rotate/Style <0.0625> 0.125
Command: Zoom
All/Center/Dynamic/Extents/Left/Previous/Vmax/Window/<Scale (X/XP)>: C
Center point: 10,9
Magnification of Height <23.1222>: 9
Command: Press F8 to toggle Ortho on
Command: Setvar
Variable name or ?: LUPREC
New value for LUPREC <4>: 2
Command: Insert
```

Drawing the Plate's Front and Side Profile—continued

Block name (or ?): ***B-MOUNT**

Insertion point: **4,4**

Scale factor <1>: *Press Enter*

Rotation angle <0>: *Press Enter*

Command: **Erase**

Select objects: *Pick the top horizontal dimension*

1 selected, 1 found

Select objects: *Pick the square left from the top horizontal dimension*

1 selected, 1 found

Select objects: *Pick the left vertical dimension*

1 selected, 1 found

Select objects: *Pick the box left from the left vertical dimension*

1 selected, 1 found

Select objects: *Pick the lower left diameter dimension*

1 selected, 1 found

Select objects: *Pick the lower right diameter dimension*

1 selected, 1 found

Select objects: *Pick the 1.00 dimension at the upper right of the front view*

1 selected, 1 found

Select objects: *Pick the box left from the 1.00 dimension*

1 selected, 1 found

Select objects: *Pick the third hidden line from the top in the side view*

1 selected, 1 found

Select objects: *Pick the third hidden line from the bottom in the side view*

1 selected, 1 found

Select objects: *Pick the short center line at the upper left of the side view*

1 selected, 1 found

Select objects: *Pick the short center line at the upper right of the side view*

1 selected, 1 found

Select objects: *Pick the short center line at the lower left of the side view*

1 selected, 1 found

Select objects: *Pick the short center line at the lower right of the side view*

1 selected, 1 found

Select objects: **W**

First corner: *Pick point 8.5,6.5*

Other corner: *Pick point 9.5,10.5*

Drawing the Plate's Front and Side Profile—continued

```
14 found
Select objects: C
First corner: Pick point 7,8
Other corner: Pick point 8,9
6 found
Select objects: Press Enter
Command: Dim
Dim: Upd
Select objects: C
First corner: Pick point 4,5
Other corner: Pick point 16,12
37 found
Select objects: Press Enter
Dim: E
Command: Save
File name <TEMP>: Press Enter
```

The mount remnants should now appear as shown in figure 11.37.

Figure 11.37:
Mount remnants for the plate.

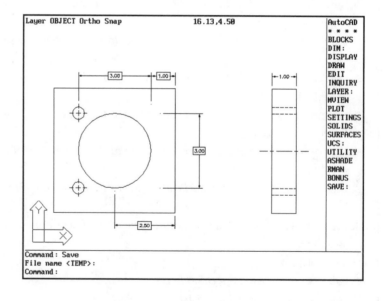

Changing Existing Entities

The *Change* command modifies the geometry or options of existing entities such as lines, circles, text, attribute definitions, and block inserts. You can change the endpoints of lines (the nearest endpoint is pulled to the change point). You can respecify the center and radius of circles. You can enter new text or you can enter new values for any text or Attdef option. You can enter a new origin or rotation angle for a block insert. If you select multiple entities, you will be prompted appropriately for each. After you complete the Change command, you may have to regenerate the screen to see the revisions.

The Change command also is capable of modifying properties such as color and linetype, but use the Chprop command instead.

After changing the radius of the large circle, you will use the Stretch command to adjust the dimension extension lines to the new quadrant points. The instructions tell you to select the node at the end of the dimension line. This node is the associative dimensions definition point (defpoint). These points are visible, but may be difficult to find. They are defined as a node, so you can use the Osnap Node option to snap to it. When these defpoints are stretched, extended, or scaled, the dimension will be recalculated automatically and redisplayed representing these new calculations.

After using the Stretch command, use the Line and Trim commands to make the left-hand slot. You can rework the side view hidden and center lines with the Copy and Move commands. When you use the Multiple option at the Copy base point prompt, it reprompts for the base point. After you pick a base point, you are continuously prompted for the second point of displacement (positions of the multiple copies) until you terminate the command. The pick points for the Stretch, Move, and Copy commands are shown in figure 11.38.

Figure 11.38:
Pick points for the Stretch, Move, and Copy commands.

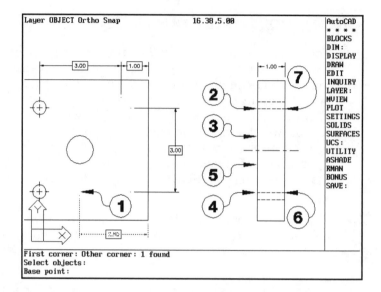

Continue in the previous TEMP drawing and follow these steps:

Editing the Mount To Make a Plate

Command: **Zoom**

All/Center/Dynamic/Extents/Left/Previous/Vmax/Window/<Scale(X/XP)>: **C**

Center point: **11,9**

Magnification or Height <9.00> : **8**

Command: **Change**

Select objects: *Click on the large center circle*

1 selected, 1 found.

Select objects: *Press Enter*

Properties/<Change point>: *Press Enter*

Enter circle radius: **.5**

Command: **Stretch**

Select objects to stretch by window...

Select objects: **C**

First corner: *Pick point 7,6.5*

Other corner: *Pick point 8,7*

1 found

Select objects: *Press Enter*

Base point: *Pick end of dimension line at point ① (7.5,7)*

Editing the Mount To Make a Plate—continued

```
New point: QUA
of Pick bottom of center circle
Command: Layer
?/Make/Set/New/ON/OFF/Color/Ltype/Freeze/Thaw: S
New current layer <OBJECT>: DIM
?/Make/Set/New/ON/OFF/Color/Ltype/Freeze/Thaw: Press Enter
Command: Dim
Dim: Cen
Select arc or circle: Pick the center circle
Dim: E
Command: Layer
?/Make/Set/New/ON/OFF/Color/Ltype/Freeze/Thaw: S
New current layer <DIM>: OBJECT
?/Make/Set/New/ON/OFF/Color/Ltype/Freeze/Thaw: Press Enter
Command: Setvar
Variable name or ?: LUPREC
New value for LUPREC <2>: 4
Command: Line
From point: TAN
to Pick left side of top hole
To point: TAN
to Pick left side of bottom hole
To point: Press Enter
Command: Press Enter
LINE From point: TAN
to Pick right side of bottom hole
To point: TAN
to Pick right side of top hole
To point: Press Enter
Command: Trim
Select cutting edge(s)...
Select objects: L
1 found
Select objects: Pick the other new tangent line
1 found
Select objects: Press Enter
```

> ### Editing the Mount To Make a Plate—continued
>
> ```
> <Select object to trim>/Undo: Pick top circle inside slot
> <Select object to trim>/Undo: Pick bottom circle inside slot
> <Select object to trim>/Undo: Press Enter
> Command: Move
> Select objects: Pick hidden line ②
> 1 selected, 1 found
> Select objects: Press Enter
> Base point or displacement: Pick end of line at ②
> Second point of displacement: Pick point at ③
> Command: Move
> Select objects: Pick hidden line ④
> 1 selected, 1 found
> Select objects: Press Enter
> Base point or displacement: Pick end of line at ④
> Second point of displacement: Pick point at ⑤
> Command: Copy
> Select objects: Pick center line in side view
> <Base point or displacement/Multiple: M
> Base point: Pick intersection of center line and right side of side view
> Second point of displacement: Pick point ⑥
> Second point of displacement: Pick point ⑦
> Second point of displacement: Press Enter
> Command: Save
> File name <TEMP>: Press Enter
> ```

The plate is nearly finished, as shown in figure 11.39. It needs only one more slot.

Developing Line-Arc Continuations

Obviously you could copy the slot you have, but for now it will be demonstrated how lines and arcs can be strung together. An arc or line can be drawn immediately tangent to the last arc or line by defaulting its Start point: or From point: prompts.

Draw the arcs for the following exercise with line-arc continuation. After invoking the Arc command, respond to the first prompt by pressing Enter or Spacebar. The arc's starting point and direction will be assigned from the endpoint and ending direction of the last line or arc. The pick points are shown in figure 11.40.

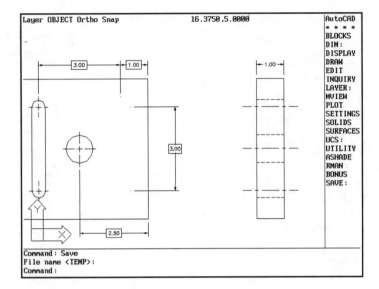

Figure 11.39
Plate with one slot.

Continue in the previous TEMP drawing and follow these steps:

Drawing Lines and Arcs

Command: **Arc**

Center/<Start point>: **C**

Center: *Pick upper center point ① aligned with dimension and center lines*

Start point: *Pick ② .25 to the right of center point*

Angle/Length of chord/<End point>: *Pick ③ .25 to the left of center point*

Command: **Line**

From point: *Press Enter to continue tangent to arc*

Length of line: *Pick ④ aligned with bottom center line*

To point: *Press Enter*

Command: **Arc**

Center/<Start point>: *Press Enter to continue tangent to line*

End point: *Pick point ⑤*

Command: **Line**

LINE from point: *Press Enter*

Length of line: *Pick point ① again*

To point: *Press Enter*

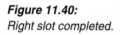

Figure 11.40:
Right slot completed.

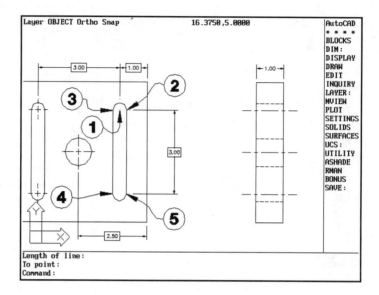

Use the Center dimensioning command to add center lines to both arcs of the right slot. Then set a running Osnap mode of ENDpoint and use the Line command to connect the arc center lines horizontally and vertically. Continue in the TEMP drawing and follow these steps:

▶ Adding Center Lines

```
Command: Layer
?/Make/Set/New/ON/OFF/Color/Ltype/Freeze/Thaw: S
New current layer <OBJECT>: DIM
?/Make/Set/New/ON/OFF/Color/Ltype/Freeze/Thaw:
Command: Dim
Dim: Cen
Select arc or circle: Pick the top arc of the right slot
Dim: Cen
Select arc or circle: Pick the bottom arc of the right slot
Dim: E
Command: Layer
?/Make/Set/New/ON/OFF/Color/Ltype/Freeze/Thaw: S
New current layer <DIM>: CL
?/Make/Set/New/ON/OFF/Color/Ltype/Freeze/Thaw: Press Enter
```

Adding Center Lines—continued

Command: **Osnap**

Object snap modes: **END**

Command: **Line**

From point: *Pick lower end of top center line in left slot*

To point: *Pick upper end of bottom center line in left slot*

To point: *Press Enter*

Command: *Press Enter*

LINE From point: *Pick right end of bottom center line at right of left slot*

To point: *Pick left end of bottom center line of right slot*

To point: *Press Enter*

Command: *Press Enter*

LINE From point: *Pick upper end of bottom center line in right slot*

To point: *Pick lower end of top center line in right slot*

To point: *Press Enter*

Command: *Press Enter*

LINE From point: *Pick left end of top center line at left of right slot*

To point: *Pick right end of top center line of left slot*

To point: *Press Enter*

Command: **Osnap**

Object snap modes: **NON**

Command: **Zoom**

All/Center/Dynamic/Extents/Left/Previous/Vmax/Window/<Scale(X/XP)>: **P**

Command: **Save**

File name <TEMP>: *Press Enter*

The plate is complete, except for optional dimensions. It should resemble figure 11.41.

Completing the Plate's Dimensions—Optional

You may complete the plate's dimensions to match the completely dimensioned plate illustrated by figure 11.42 if you want. You have used the necessary techniques several times in this chapter.

Figure 11.41:
Slot and arc center lines.

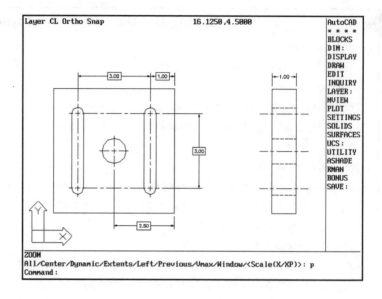

Figure 11.42:
Optional: The completely dimensioned plate.

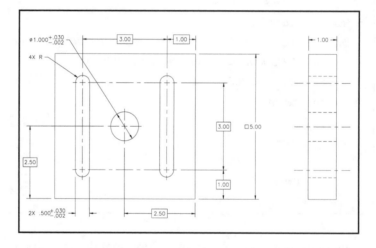

Unless you have the AutoCAD: Drafting and 3D Design Disk, the final step is to write the plate to disk as B-PLATE.DWG for later insertion into the multi-detail working drawing. If you have the optional disk, you already have the B-PLATE.DWG file. If you don't have the disk, continue in the previous TEMP drawing and follow these steps:

Wblocking the Plate Drawing

 You already have the B-PLATE file.

 Wblock both views with dimensions to file name B-PLATE with insertion base point 4,4.

```
Command: View

?/Delete/Restore/Save/Window: R

View name to restore: BDR

Regenerating drawing.

Command: Wblock

File name: B-PLATE

Block name: Press Enter

Insertion base point: 4,4

Select objects: W

First corner: Pick point 3,5

Other corner: Pick point 16,13

79 found

Select objects: Press Enter

Command: Quit
```

Drafting the Pulley

The exercises in this section show how to draft and dimension a two-view orthographic drawing of a pulley as illustrated in figure 11.43. They focus on the polar Array and Hatch commands, on angular dimensioning, and on suppressing dimensioning extension lines.

Develop the front view profile with concentric circles and vertical center line through the circles, and then draw the section view with a polyline by aligning the horizontal crosshair with the front view.

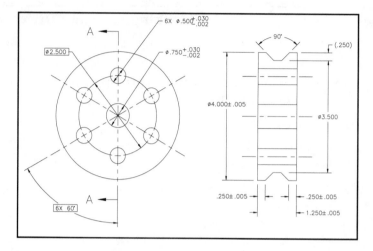

Figure 11.43:
The pulley.

Begin a new drawing named TEMP and follow these steps:

Drawing the Pulley's Front and Section Profiles

Command: **Snap**

Snap spacing or ON/OFF/Aspect/Rotate/Style <0.0625>: **.125**

Command: **Zoom**

All/Center/Dynamic/Extents/Left/Previous/Vmax/Window/<Scale(X/XP)>: **C**

Center point: **10,8**

Magnification or Height <23.1222> : **7**

Command: **Circle**

3P/2P/TTR/<Center point>: **8,8**

Diameter/<Radius>: **2**

Command: *Press Enter*

CIRCLE 3P/2P/TTR/<Center point>: **@**

Diameter/<Radius>: **1.75**

Command: *Press Enter*

CIRCLE 3P/2P/TTR/<Center point>: **@**

Diameter/<Radius>: **1.25**

Command: *Press Enter*

CIRCLE 3P/2P/TTR/<Center point>: **@**

Diameter/<Radius>: **.375**

Command: **Line**

From point: *Pick 8,5.5*

Drawing the Pulley's Front and Section Profiles—continued

```
To point: Pick @5<90
To point: Press Enter
Command: Chprop
Select objects: L
1 found
Select objects: Press Enter
Change what property (Color/LAyer/LType/Thickness) ? LA
New layer <OBJECT>: CL
Change what property (Color/LAyer/LType/Thickness) ? Press Enter
Command: Press Enter
CHPROP
Select objects: Pick the 1.75 radius circle
1 selected, 1 found
Select objects: Press Enter
Change what property (Color/LAyer/LType/Thickness) ? LA
New layer <OBJECT>: H1
Change what property (Color/LAyer/LType/Thickness) ? Press Enter
Command: Line
From point: Pick point 12.5,10
Current line-width is 0.0000
Arc/Close/Halfwidth/Length/Undo/Width/<Endpoint of line>: Pick or enter point
@0.25<0
Arc/Close/Halfwidth/Length/Undo/Width/<Endpoint of line>: @.25,-.25
Arc/Close/Halfwidth/Length/Undo/Width/<Endpoint of line>: Pick or enter point
@.25<0
Arc/Close/Halfwidth/Length/Undo/Width/<Endpoint of line>: @.25,.25
Arc/Close/Halfwidth/Length/Undo/Width/<Endpoint of line>: Pick or enter point
@.25<0
Arc/Close/Halfwidth/Length/Undo/Width/<Endpoint of line>: Pick or enter point
@4<270
Arc/Close/Halfwidth/Length/Undo/Width/<Endpoint of line>: Pick or enter point
@.25<180
Arc/Close/Halfwidth/Length/Undo/Width/<Endpoint of line>: @-.25,.25
Arc/Close/Halfwidth/Length/Undo/Width/<Endpoint of line>: Pick or enter point
@.25<180
Arc/Close/Halfwidth/Length/Undo/Width/<Endpoint of line>: @-.25,-.25
Arc/Close/Halfwidth/Length/Undo/Width/<Endpoint of line>: Pick or enter point
@.25<180
Arc/Close/Halfwidth/Length/Undo/Width/<Endpoint of line>: C
```

The basic layout of the pulley should match figure 11.44.

Figure 11.44:
Basic layout of pulley front.

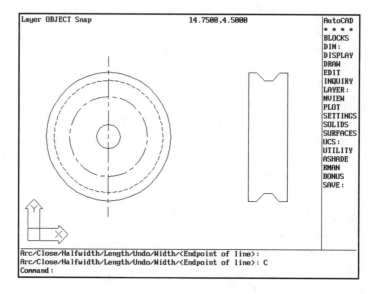

Polar Arrays

You used the Array command earlier in this chapter to copy an object in a rect-angular pattern. It also can be used to copy and space objects in polar, or circu-lar, patterns.

When you select the polar option, you are prompted for the number of items in the array, the angle to fill, and whether or not the objects are to be rotated as they are arrayed. The polar angle between items is the angle to fill divided by the number of items. Include the original object when you count the number of items in the array. The `Angle to fill:` prompt determines the direction around the center point for the array. A positive value indicates a counterclock-wise (CCW) array and a negative value indicates a clockwise (CW) array. For a full circular array, accept the default <360> degrees.

You must use a bit of trickery with temporary circles and the Trim command to get your center lines correct. The dimensioning Center command inserts straight lines, not curved as you need. So temporarily use smaller circles for the holes and trim your vertical and circular center lines (see fig. 11.45). When you select the circles to trim the lines, you can select everything with a window — the extra entities will not be a problem. When you replace the holes with the correct sized circles, the center lines will extend into the circles.

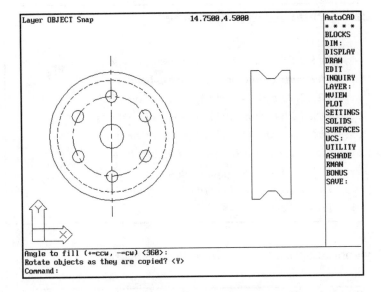

Figure 11.45:
Before trimming with temporary holes.

Continue in the previous TEMP drawing and follow these steps:

Using Polar Array

Command: **Circle**

3P/2P/TTR/<Center point>: *Pick point 8,6.75 at intersection of center lines*

Diameter/<Radius>: *Enter 0.1875 (not 0.25)*

Command: **Array**

Select objects: **L**

1 found

Select objects: *Press Enter*

Rectangular or Polar array (R/P): **P**

Center point of array: *Pick center of pulley at point 8,8*

Number of items: **6**

Angle to fill (+=ccw, -=cw) <360>: *Press Enter*

Rotate objects as they are copied? <Y> *Press Enter*

Command: **Trim**

Select cutting edge(s)...

Select objects: **W**

First corner: **6,6**

Other corner: **10,10**

10 found

Using Polar Array—continued

```
Select objects:
<Select object to trim>/Undo:  Pick 1.25 radius circle at center of top hole
<Select object to trim>/Undo:  Pick vertical line at center of top hole
<Select object to trim>/Undo:  Pick 1.25 radius circle at center of next hole
<Select object to trim>/Undo:  Pick 1.25 radius circle at center of next hole
<Select object to trim>/Undo:  Pick 1.25 radius circle at center of each hole
<Select object to trim>/Undo:  Pick vertical line at center of bottom hole
<Select object to trim>/Undo:  Pick 1.25 radius circle at center of next hole
<Select object to trim>/Undo:  Pick 1.25 radius circle at center of last hole
<Select object to trim>/Undo:  Press Enter
```

After trimming, the pulley should appear as shown in figure 11.46.

Figure 11.46:
After trimming with temporary holes.

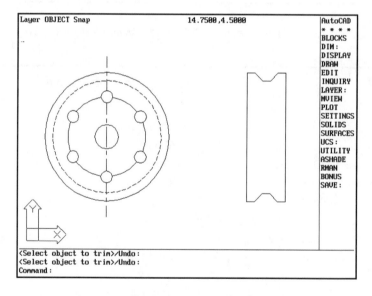

Add center marks to both top and bottom holes on layer DIM, and erase the six temporary holes. Then, draw two real holes at the top and bottom with radii 0.25 (see fig. 11.47). Finally, make a polar array of the vertical lines, center marks, and both holes (see fig. 11.48).

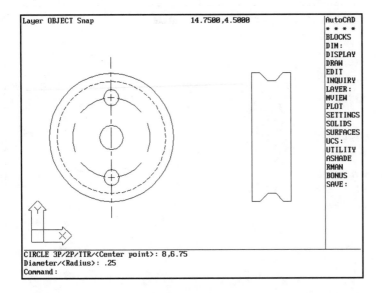

Figure 11.47:
Real holes, lines, center marks before polar array.

Continue in the TEMP drawing and follow these steps:

Completing the Array

Command: **Layer**

?/Make/Set/New/ON/OFF/Color/Ltype/Freeze/Thaw: **S**

New current layer <OBJECT>: **DIM**

?/Make/Set/New/ON/OFF/Color/Ltype/Freeze/Thaw: *Press Enter*

Command: **Dim**

Dim: **Cen**

Select arc or circle: *Pick the top hole*

Dim: Cen

Select arc or circle: *Pick the bottom hole*

Dim: **E**

Command: **Layer**

?/Make/Set/New/ON/OFF/Color/Ltype/Freeze/Thaw: **S**

New current layer <DIM>: **OBJECT**

?/Make/Set/New/ON/OFF/Color/Ltype/Freeze/Thaw: *Press Enter*

Command: **Erase**

Select objects: *Pick the bottom hole*

1 selected, 1 found

Select objects: *Pick the next hole*

► Completing the Array—continued

```
1 selected, 1 found
Select objects: Pick the next hole
1 selected, 1 found
Select objects: Pick the next hole
1 selected, 1 found
Select objects: Pick the next hole
1 selected, 1 found
Select objects: Pick the top hole
1 selected, 1 found
Select objects: Press Enter
Command: Circle
3P/2P/TTR/<Center point>: Pick at 8,9.25
Diameter/<Radius>: .25
Command: Press Enter
CIRCLE 3P/2P/TTR/<Center point>: Pick at 8,6.75
Diameter/<Radius>: .25
Command: Array
Select objects: W
First corner: Pick at 7.75,5
Other corner: Pick at 8.25,11
9 found
Select objects: Press Enter
Rectangular or Polar array (R/P): P
Center point of array: Pick center of pulley at 8,8
Number of items: 3
Angle to fill (+=ccw, -=cw) <360>: Press Enter
Rotate objects as they are copied? <Y> Press Enter
Command: Save
File name <TEMP>: Press Enter
```

Figures 11.48 shows the pulley after executing the Array command.

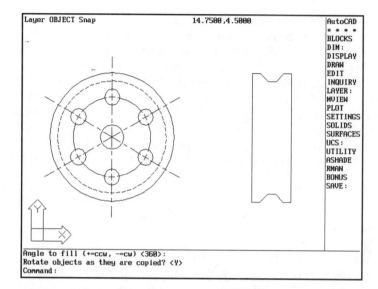

Figure 11.48:
Completed array.

Hatch and Pattern Filling

The right view of the pulley drawing will be a full section view and will therefore have section lines representing a full cutting plane. The hypothetically cut surface is represented by *cross hatching* (parallel lines which run at a 45-degree angle across the part) on the part surfaces where an imaginary cutting plane intersects the object. These section lines, and many other more complex patterns, can be generated with the Hatch command.

Note If you select Hatch from the Draw pull-down menu, be aware that it maintains pre-set options. To use the pull-down for the following exercise, set HATCH OPTIONS > under the Options menu to the appropriate parameters. For more information on setting Options, refer to Chapter 2.

Many drafting disciplines use various hatches and pattern fills. An architectural drafter may use hatch patterns to create different surface textures to designate roofing material, siding, or excavated earth, for example. Many patterns are available in AutoCAD's ACAD.PAT library of standard hatch patterns. You can hatch with any of the available standard patterns, customize your own complex patterns, or define a simple pattern style within the Hatch command.

The *Hatch* command cross-hatches or pattern-fills an area defined by a boundary. The boundary must be continuous and closed, formed by any combination of lines, arcs, circles, polylines, or 3Dfaces. You also can specify the spacing and angle for parallel or cross-hatched continuous lines. The Hatch command's default creates a block with a hidden name and inserts it. If you type an asterisk before the pattern name, such as ***name**, the hatch will be drawn with individual line entities instead. You also can choose one of three styles of hatching for nested boundaries: Normal, Outermost, or Ignore. Hatching is always defined and generated relative to the XY axes and plane of the current UCS.

Hatch Pattern Icon Menus

AutoCAD includes more than 40 different hatch patterns in the ACAD.PAT library. If your system supports the AUI, you may view and select patterns from a three-page hatch pattern icon menu. In Release 10, select Hatch... from the Draw pull-down menu to display these menus. In Release 11, select HATCH OPTIONS > then Hatch Pattern... from the Options pull-down menu to display these menus. The first two pages of the Release 11 pattern icon menus are displayed in figures 11.49 and 11.50.

Many of AutoCAD's pre-defined hatch patterns represent ANSI standard material descriptions. By selecting a specific pattern or naming convention, you will be able to easily represent materials from aluminum to zinc in technically accurate sectional form.

Figure 11.49:
First hatch pattern icon menu.

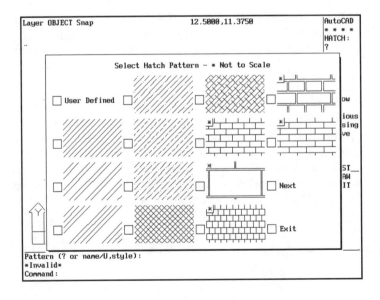

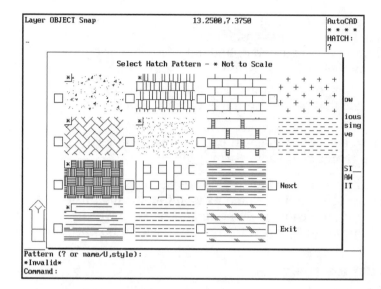

Because the default patterns are internally generated blocks, they may be controlled as single entities. If it is necessary to edit a single line of a pattern, specify it with a leading asterisk or use the Explode command to convert the pattern into individual entities.

Hatch Options

After the Hatch command is invoked, you are presented with four major options for generating or querying patterns. They are:

- **?** Provides a list of pattern names.
- **Name** Inputs the name of the hatch pattern.
- **U (User) Defined Hatching** Presents a series of hatch definition prompts, from which you define a hatch pattern.
- **Style** Provides for the style boundary codes as described below. You specify a style with a comma after the name, such as *name,I.*

Hatch Styles

AutoCAD offers three styles of hatching to accommodate the hatching of nested boundaries, such as several concentric circles. The hatching affects only the boundary objects selected. They are the following:

- ■ **N (Normal).** The default style hatches from the outermost selected boundary inward until it encounters an internal boundary. As each internal boundary is encountered, hatching turns off or on until the next internal boundary is encountered.

- ■ **O (Outermost).** Hatches from the outermost selected boundary inward until it is turned off by an internal boundary. It does not turn back on.

- ■ **I (Ignore Style).** Hatches everything within the outer boundary, ignoring all internal geometry without turning off.

Selected text, attributes, shapes, traces, and solids are treated differently from other entities, except for the Ignore style. Hatching is automatically turned off whenever any of these entities are contacted and turned back on when passed. This procedure avoids the problem of text being obscured within hatched areas.

Hatch and Pattern Boundaries

Hatching boundaries must be carefully defined by separate entities which precisely intersect but do not overlap. Because the sides of the pulley section profile are two continuous lines, you need to break them at each interior line so the individual areas have continuous boundaries. You will use the Break command to divide the lines at each of the areas to be hatched.

Aligning the crosshairs with the top, center, and bottom holes, draw the six visible dividing lines shown in the section view in figure 11.51. Use the Break command to break the polyline profile at its intersections with each line. Because AutoCAD's object selection tends to find the more recent entities first, you cannot select the first line at its intersection with the interior line even if you want it to break there. If you do, AutoCAD tries to select the more recently drawn interior line. You will have to select the outer line in a clear space and then use the F option to reselect the break point at the intersection. The first break will make the polylines the most recent entities, so subsequent breaks can be done without the F option.

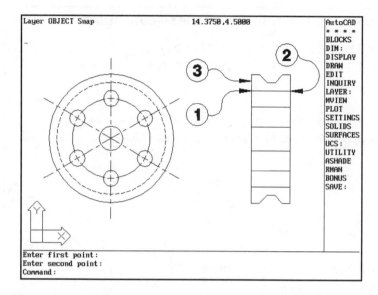

Figure 11.51:
Dividing lines and points of first break.

Continue in the previous TEMP drawing and follow these steps:

Defining Individual Hatch Boundaries

Command: **Line**

From point: *Pick point ① at left side of profile aligned with top of top hole*

To point: *Pick point ② at right side of profile aligned with top of top hole*

To point: *Press Enter*

Command: *Press Enter*

LINE From point: *Pick at left side of profile aligned with bottom of top hole*

To point: *Pick at right side of profile aligned with bottom of top hole*

To point: *Press Enter*

Command: *Press Enter*

LINE From point: *Pick at left side of profile aligned with top of center circle*

To point: *Pick at right side of profile aligned with top of center circle*

To point: *Press Enter*

Command: *Press Enter*

LINE From point: *Pick at left side of profile aligned with bottom of center circle*

To point: *Pick at right side of profile aligned with bottom of center circle*

To point: *Press Enter*

Command: *Press Enter*

Defining Individual Hatch Boundaries—continued

LINE From point: *Pick at left side of profile aligned with top of bottom hole*

To point: *Pick at right side of profile aligned with top of bottom hole*

To point: *Press Enter*

Command: *Press Enter*

LINE From point: *Pick at left side of profile aligned with bottom of bottom hole*

To point: *Pick at right side of profile aligned with bottom of bottom hole*

To point: *Press Enter*

Command: **Osnap**

Object snap modes: **Int**

Command: **Break**

Select object: *Pick polyline profile at point* ①

Enter second point (or F for first point): **F**

Enter first point: *Pick left intersection of top line at point* ②

Enter second point: *Pick same point again*

Command: *Press Enter*

BREAK Select object: *Pick right intersection of top line*

Enter second point (or F for first point): *Pick same point again*

Command: *Press Enter*

BREAK Select object: *Pick left intersection of second line*

Enter second point (or F for first point): *Pick same point again*

Command: *Press Enter*

BREAK Select object: *Pick right intersection of second line*

Enter second point (or F for first point): *Pick same point again*

Command: *Press Enter*

BREAK Select object: *Pick left intersection of third line*

Enter second point (or F for first point): *Pick same point again*

Command: *Press Enter*

BREAK Select object: *Pick right intersection of third line*

Enter second point (or F for first point): *Pick same point again*

Command: *Press Enter*

BREAK Select object: *Pick left intersection of fourth line*

Enter second point (or F for first point): *Pick same point again*

Defining Individual Hatch Boundaries—continued

```
Command: Press Enter
BREAK Select object: Pick right intersection of fourth line
Enter second point (or F for first point): Pick same point again
Command: Press Enter
BREAK Select object: Pick left intersection of fifth line
Enter second point (or F for first point): Pick same point again
Command: Press Enter
BREAK Select object: Pick right intersection of fifth line
Enter second point (or F for first point): Pick same point again
Command: Press Enter
BREAK Select object: Pick left intersection of bottom line
Enter second point (or F for first point): Pick same point again
Command: Press Enter
BREAK Select object: Pick right intersection of bottom line
Enter second point (or F for first point): Pick same point again
Command: Osnap
Object snap modes: NON
Command: Save
File name <TEMP>: Press Enter
```

Each side of the pulley in the section view now consists of separate short lines between each of the six dividing lines.

Use the following instructions to hatch the first area, then use a similar technique to create and hatch the three remaining hatch areas. You can hatch the remaining areas at the same time by selecting the Hatch command and treating all three as one selection set. This procedure provides an efficient means for simultaneously hatching (with the same pattern) various areas on a drawing.

The following exercise shows you how to generate a user-defined 45-degree hatch pattern. This user-defined pattern represents section lines for the full section drawing of the pulley. This technique is usually referred to as creating hatches on the fly. Figure 11.52 shows the window selection for the first hatch.

Figure 11.52:
Window for first hatch.

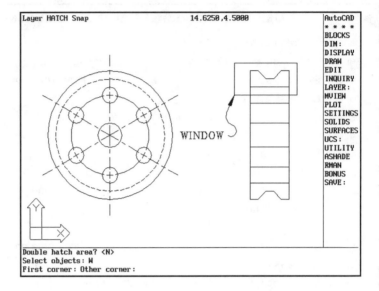

Continue in the previous TEMP drawing and follow these steps:

Creating User-Defined (U) Hatching

Command: **Layer**

?/Make/Set/New/ON/OFF/Color/Ltype/Freeze/Thaw: **S**

New current layer <OBJECT>: **Hatch**

?/Make/Set/New/ON/OFF/Color/Ltype/Freeze/Thaw: *Press Enter*

Command: **Hatch**

Pattern (? or name/U,style): **U**

Angle for crosshatch lines <0>: **45**

Spacing between lines <1.0000>: **.1**

Double hatch area? <N> *Press Enter*

Select objects: **W**

First corner: *Pick point 12,9.25 (see fig. 11.52)*

Other corner: *Pick point 14,10.25*

3 found

Select objects: *Press Enter*

Command: *Press Enter*

HATCH Select objects: **W**

First corner: *Pick point 12,8*

Other corner: *Pick point 14,9.25*

4 found

Creating User-Defined (U) Hatching—continued

Select objects: **W**

First corner: *Pick point 12,6.75*

Other corner: *Pick point 14,8*

4 found

Select objects: **W**

First corner: *Pick point 12,5*

Other corner: *Pick point 14,6.75*

2 found

Select objects: *Press Enter*

Command: **Save**

That completes the two views, without dimensions. Figure 11.53 shows the entities selected for the boundaries of the second Hatch command and the results
of the first Hatch command. Figure 11.54 shows the results of the hatching. A
user-defined pattern was demonstrated, but the ANSI31 hatch pattern at 0.8
scale and 0 degrees creates an identical effect.

Note It is often best to define boundaries with new entities traced over
existing geometry. Put these entities on a unique layer so they can be
easily turned off or erased. This ensures proper boundaries while
leaving the original geometry intact.

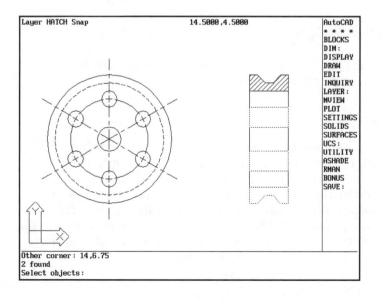

Figure 11.53:
Highlighted entities for
repeated hatch.

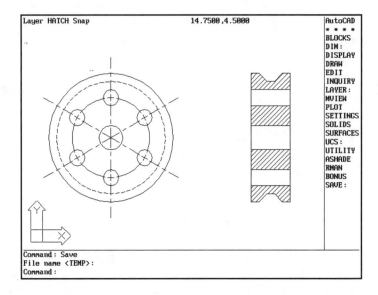

Figure 11.54:
Completed section view hatches.

Tip   Hatches take up disk space. Unlike normal blocks, which can be very efficient due to repetition, each use of the Hatch command creates a unique block that actually takes up slightly more space than if it were individual lines. Closely spaced or broken line patterns can use large amounts of disk space and memory, slowing drawing regeneration to a crawl. Use intricate patterns sparingly, add hatching only before creating the final output, or freeze the hatch pattern's layer to avoid slow regenerations.

Dimensioning the Pulley

This section focuses on developing angular dimensions, as shown in figure 11.55, and on suppressing redundant extension lines.

Angular Dimensioning

The dimension arc created by angular dimensioning spans the angle between two nonparallel straight lines. The lines to be dimensioned do not have to intersect. When you select the Angular variable, you are prompted for the two lines the angular dimension will span. After selecting the two lines, you are prompted for the dimension arc location point. Extension lines generate automatically if the dimension arc does not intersect the line(s) being dimensioned. A prompt for dimension text location also exists. You can either pick a text location or press Enter to default and center the text on the dimension arc.

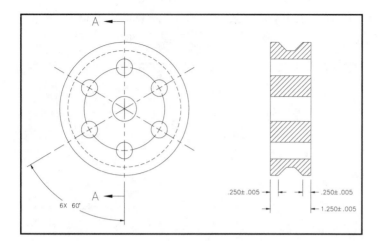

Figure 11.55:
The pulley with
dimensions.

Continue in TEMP or begin a new drawing named TEMP=PULLEY-D and dimension the angle between the polar-arrayed holes, as follows:

Creating Angular Dimensions

 Continue in TEMP, or begin a new drawing named TEMP=PULLEY-D.

 Continue in or edit an existing drawing named TEMP.

```
Command: Zoom
All/Center/Dynamic/Extents/Left/Previous/Vmax/Window/<Scale(X/XP)>: C
Center point: 6.5,5.5
Magnification or Height <7.0000> : 5
Command: Layer
?/Make/Set/New/ON/OFF/Color/Ltype/Freeze/Thaw: S
New current layer <HATCH>: Dim
?/Make/Set/New/ON/OFF/Color/Ltype/Freeze/Thaw: Press Enter
Command: Dim
Dim: Ang
Select arc, circle, line, or RETURN: Pick line at point ① (see fig. 11.56)
Second line: Pick line at point ②
Enter dimension line arc location: Pick point ③
Dimension text <60>: 6X <>
Enter text location: Press Enter
Dim: Exit
```

Extension lines aligning with the two lines selected are now drawn, and the text is placed at the center of the dimension line arc, as shown in figure 11.56.

Figure 11.56:
The angle between holes is dimensioned.

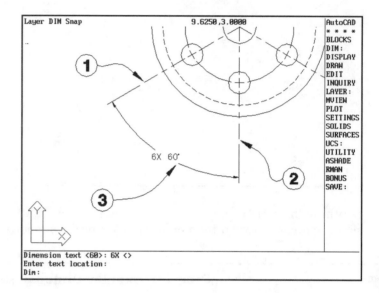

Suppressing Extension Lines

In manual drafting, you draw an extension line only when you need it. You naturally omit an extension line that would overlap or duplicate an existing line. AutoCAD does not always know when to omit an extension line. The next exercise features two techniques for suppressing extension lines: setting the DIMSE1 and DIMSE2 dimension variables, and a trick in which you pick your points.

Extension lines sometimes are superimposed. You can avoid having them overlap by turning one, or both, of the following variables off. You will want to suppress (turn off) extension lines for most Baseline and Continue dimensions (such as those in figure 11.57) and for many other horizontal or vertical dimensions where Baseline or Continue do not work well. You also may want to suppress the first or second extension line of a dimension when the object itself acts as an extension line.

The first technique controls extension lines by setting these dimension variables:

- **DIMSE1.** Suppresses the first extension line. The first extension line is determined by your first extension line location pick.

- **DIMSE2.** Suppresses the second extension line, your second extension line location pick.

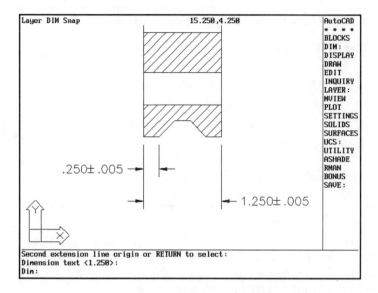

Figure 11.57:
Overlapped extension lines.

Continue in the TEMP drawing and see how the Continue variable works with the default settings as follows:

Overlapped Extension Lines

```
Command: Zoom
All/Center/Dynamic/Extents/Left/Previous/Vmax/Window/<Scale(X/XP)>: C
Center point: 13,6
Magnification or Height <5.0000> : 3.5
Command: Setvar
Variable name or ?: LUPREC
New value for LUPREC <4>: 3
Command: Dim
Dim: DIMTOL
Current value <Off> New value: On
Dim: DIMTP
Current value <0.000> New value: .005
Dim: DIMTM
Current value <0.000> New value: .005
Dim: Hor
First extension line origin or RETURN to select: Pick point 12.75,6
Second extension line origin: Pick point 12.5,6
Dimension line location: Pick point 12.5,5.5
```

Overlapped Extension Lines—continued

Dimension text <.250>: *Press Enter*

Dim: **Con**

Second extension line origin or RETURN to select: *Pick point 13.75,6*

Dimension text <1.250>: *Press Enter*

Dim: **U**

Dim: **Redraw**

Dim: **U**

Dim: **U**

Dim: **E**

When you used the first U to undo the Continue dimension, you could see that the Horizontal and Continue first extension lines were overlapping. Baseline works the same way. That might not seem to be a big problem on the screen, but extensions that overlap may plot poorly on pen plotters.

To overcome this, turn DIMSE1 off for the initial Horizontal dimension, leave it off for all but the last in the series of Baseline or Continue dimensions, and turn it back on for the last Baseline or Continue dimension. Then only the last dimension will draw an extension line, which will serve all the preceding dimensions.

Repeat the previous dimensions with DIMSE1 on to suppress the first extension line, as shown in figure 11.58.

Figure 11.58:
Suppressed second extension line.

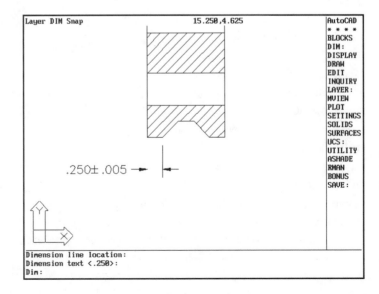

Continue in the previous TEMP drawing and follow these steps:

Controlling DIMSE1 for Baseline Dimensions

```
Command: Dim

Dim: DIMSE2

Current value <Off> New value: ON

Dim: Hor

First extension line origin or RETURN to select: Pick point 12.75,6

Second extension line origin: Pick point 12.5,6

Dimension line location: Pick point 12.5,5.5

Dimension text <.250>: Press Enter

Dim: DIMSE2

Current value <On> New value: OFF

Dim: Con

Second extension line origin or RETURN to select: Pick point 13.75,6

Dimension text <1.250>: Press Enter

Dim: Exit
```

Your drawing might appear the same as before, but this one will plot perfectly.

The second technique for suppressing extension lines uses the extension line pick points to control the extension lines. AutoCAD does not draw an extension line if the point for an extension line origin is aligned with the dimension line location point. You can use this to suppress extension lines simply by where you pick them, without bothering to reset DIMSE1 or DIMSE2. The disadvantage is that your extension line origin points will not necessarily be on the object where they will be sure to be moved, stretched, or scaled with it.

Continue in the TEMP drawing and try this technique for dimensioning the right shoulder as follows:

Controlling Extension Lines by Picking

```
Command: Dim1

Dim: Hor

First extension line origin or RETURN to select: Pick inside of right shoulder at ①

Second extension line origin: Pick on existing right extension line at point ②

Dimension line location: @
```

Controlling Extension Lines by Picking—continued

Dimension text <.250>: *Press Enter*

Command: **U**

Command: **Redo**

Command: **Save**

File name <TEMP>: *Press Enter*

When you used the U command to undo the last dimension, you could see that it did not have a second extension line. Your drawing should resemble figure 11.59.

Figure 11.59:
Dimensions with suppressed extension lines.

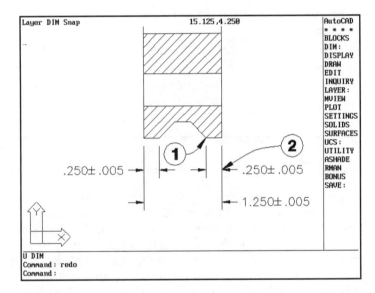

Cutting Planes

Since the right side view is drawn as a sectional view, it needs a cutting plane arrow to show where the section was cut. The cutting plane is shown in figure 11.60 as two large arrows, a bold dash line, and large key letters.

You can get dimensioning's Leader to do most of the work for you, using layer Object for bold lines and an explicit Phantom linetype (overriding the layer linetype default). Then, copy the letter A and the arrow head to the opposite ends of the section line.

Continue in the previous TEMP drawing and follow these steps:

Cutting Plane Lines and Arrows

Command: **Zoom**

All/Center/Dynamic/Extents/Left/Previous/Vmax/Window/<Scale(X/XP)>: **C**

Center point: **10,7.5**

Magnification of Height <3.500> : **8**

Command: **Layer**

?/Make/Set/New/ON/OFF/Color/Ltype/Freeze/Thaw: **S**

New current layer <DIM>: **Object**

?/Make/Set/New/ON/OFF/Color/Ltype/Freeze/Thaw: *Press Enter*

Command: **Erase**

Select objects: *Pick top part of vertical center line through front view*

1 selected, 1 found

Select objects: *Pick middle part of vertical center line*

1 selected, 1 found

Select objects: *Pick bottom part of vertical center line*

1 selected, 1 found

Select objects: *Press Enter*

Command: **Linetype**

?/Create/Load/Set: **S**

New entity linetype (or ?) <BYLAYER>: **Phantom**

?/Create/Load/Set: *Press Enter*

Command: **Dim**

Dim: **DIMSCALE**

Current value <1.000> New value: **2**

Dim: **Lea**

Leader start: *Pick point 7.375,5.375 at ① (see fig. 11.60)*

To point: *Pick point ①*

To point: *Pick point ①*

To point: *Pick point ①*

To point: *Press Enter*

Dimension text <.250>: **A**

Dim: **DIMSCALE**

Current value <2.000> New value: **1**

Dim: **E**

Command: **Copy**

Select objects: **L**

1 found

Select objects: *Press Enter*

<Base point or displacement>/Multiple: *Pick point ④*

Cutting Plane Lines and Arrows—continued

Second point of displacement: *Pick point* ①

Command: *Press Enter*

COPY

Select objects: *Pick arrow head at* ①

1 selected, 1 found

Select objects: *Press Enter*

<Base point or displacement>/Multiple: *Pick point* ①

Second point of displacement: *Pick point* ④

Command: **Linetype**

?/Create/Load/Set: **S**

New entity linetype (or ?) <PHANTOM>: **Bylayer**

?/Create/Load/Set: *Press Enter*

Command: **Save**

File name <TEMP>: *Press Enter*

The resulting section line is shown in figure 11.60.

Figure 11.60:
Section line and arrows.

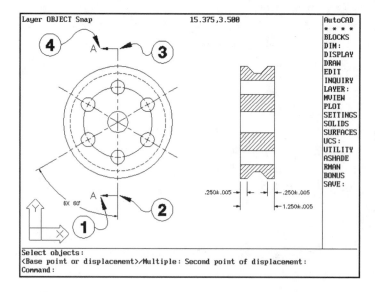

Finishing the Pulley—Optional

If you want to finish the pulley, you need to add more center lines and additional dimensions. Complete the following numbered directions which correspond to the numbered bubbles in figure 11.61.

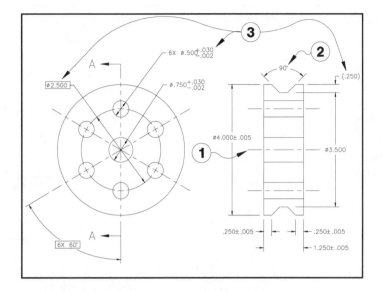

Figure 11.61:
Optional: Completing the
pulley drawing.

(1) **Section View Center Lines.** Set layer CL current and draw center lines through the three holes.

(2) **Angular Dimensioning V-Groove.** Turn layer Hatch off (to avoid object selection interference) and set Dim current. Set DIMTOL off and use the Angular dimensioning command to select the top two sloping lines.

(3) **Remaining Dimensions.** Use the dimensioning techniques you have already learned to create the rest of the dimensions shown in figure 11.61. Save the file.

Writing the Pulley to Disk

Now write the pulley to disk so it can be inserted into the multi-detail drawing in the next section. Continue in the previous TEMP drawing and follow these steps:

Wblocking the Pulley Drawing

 You already have the B-PULLEY file.

 Wblock both views with dimensions to file name B-PULLEY with insertion base point 5,4.

Command: **View**

?/Delete/Restore/Save/Window: **R**

Wblocking the Pulley Drawing—continued

```
View name to restore: BDR
Command: Wblock
File name: B-PULLEY
Block name: Press Enter
Insertion base point: Pick point 5,4
Select objects: W
First corner: Pick point 4,4
Other corner: Pick point 16,12
74 found
Select objects: Press Enter
Command: Quit
```

All of the parts needed for your multi-detail working drawing are now complete.

Summary

This chapter expanded your tool kit of drawing, editing, and dimensioning commands. Its exercises focused on developing parts for a parts library and on calling up and editing a part from your parts library.

The Arm, Pin, Mount, Plate, and Pulley exercises introduced you to many new drafting and editing commands, including the versatile Hatch command and several more of AutoCAD's built-in dimensioning tools.

Although point filters, introduced in the Arm exercise, were created for 3D use, they are among the versatile AutoCAD commands that can be used in a variety of ways.

Associative dimensioning, also displayed in the Arm exercise, automatically updates dimensions to reflect edits made to existing parts. As you continue to use associative dimensioning, you will find that this tool also can work for you in different ways.

To store the exercise drawings in your parts library, you saved them with the Wblock command as individual drawing files. In Chapter 12, these parts will be combined into one multi-detail drawing. As you proceed through *AutoCAD: Drafting and 3D Design*, you will see that blocks are used for many purposes.

Chapter 12 shows you how blocks can be used to build a multi-detail drawing.

12

Creating a Multi-Detail Working Drawing—Phase 2

In this chapter:

- Setting up and drafting the robot arm
- Inserting blocks
- Editing the B-ARM dimensions—optional
- Plotting the multi-detail drawing

355

Setting Up and Drafting the Robot Arm

Working drawings convey the information necessary to manufacture, construct, assemble, or install a mechanical device. They are categorized by drawing types, such as multi-detail, assembly, or exploded assembly, according to their use in manufacturing. The most common multi-view drawings are assembly or exploded assembly drawings. You will use your existing parts, however, to build a multi-detail drawing.

A multi-detail drawing places two or more unique parts on the same drawing sheet(s). Each item is identified by its assigned bubble number. Its relative manufacturing information is provided in a parts listing.

If you have the AutoCAD: Drafting and 3D Design Disk, you can proceed with this exercise. Otherwise, you need each of the robot arm parts that were developed and dimensioned in the previous chapter and moved to separate disk drawing files using the Wblock command.

The following exercise inserts the five parts of the robot arm into the multi-detail drawing. After completing this chapter, your drawing should look like figure 12.1. The exercise focuses on inserting and scaling blocks, and on adjusting associative dimensions.

Figure 12.1:
The robot arm multi-detail working drawing.

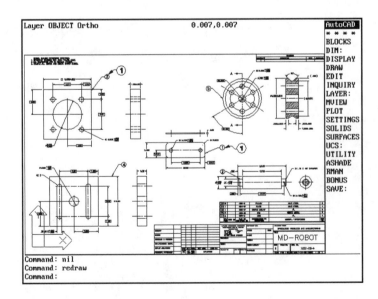

Drawing Setup

These parts will not fit on a C-size prototype drawing, so you need to adapt PROTO-C to make a D-size sheet. Use the Stretch command to adjust its location, UCSs, and limits. The border clearances are generous enough to accommodate any D-size plotter. PROTO-C has a 21x16-inch border centered with 0.5-inch borders in a 22x17-inch sheet. You will stretch the border by 11 and 4 in the X and Y directions, respectively, to make it 32x20 inches with 1-inch borders in a 34x22-inch sheet.

If you have the PROTO-D file, you can ignore the following exercise. Otherwise, begin a new drawing named PROTO-D=PROTO-C and follow these steps: .

Making a D-Size Sheet

 You can skip this. You have the PROTO-D file.

 Begin a new drawing named PROTO-D=PROTO-C.

Command: **Snap**

Set to 0.125

Command: **Layer**

*Thaw and turn on all layers, using the * wildcard*

Command: **Limits**

Set to 0,0 and 34,22

Command: **Zoom**

Set to .8

Command: **Stretch**

Stretch to the right

Select objects to stretch by window...

Select objects: **C**

Enclose all but general notes and left side of border in Crossing window

Base point: *Pick any point*

New point: <Ortho on> *Toggle ortho on and pick point when coordinate readout shows @10<0*

Command: *Press Enter and stretch the top border edge, general notes, and revision block up 4 inches*

STRETCH

Command: **Move**

Making a D-Size Sheet—continued

Select everything and move 0.5,0.5 to recenter in new limits

Command: **UCS**

Origin/ZAxis/3point/Entity/View/X/Y/Z/Prev/Restore/Save/Del/?/<World>: **O**

Origin point <0,0,0>:**Int**

of *Pick lower left corner*

Command: **View**

Save current view to name ALL

Command: **Zoom**

Window 0,0 to 32,20

Command: **View**

Save to name BDR and restore SCRATCH

Now you will create a view that is larger than the drawing, to provide an area for sketches and block construction, like a sketch pad at the side of a drawing table. Follow these steps:

Making a D-Size Sheet (Continued)

Command: **UCS**

Origin/ZAxis/3point/Entity/View/X/Y/Z/Prev/Restore/Save/Del/?/<World>:**O**

Origin point <0,0,0>: **.5,.5**

Command: **UCS**

Origin/ZAxis/3point/Entity,View/X/Y/Z/Prev/Restore/SaveDel/?/<World>: **S**

?/Desired UCS name: **Scratch**

Command: **Zoom**

All/Center/Dynamic/Extents/Left/Previous/Vmax/Window/<Scale (X/XP)>: **W**

First corner: **-1.5,-1.5**

Other corner: **36,24**

Command: **View**

?/Delete/Restore/Save/Window: **S**

View name to save: **Scratch**

▶ **Making a D-Size Sheet (Continued)—continued**

```
Command: View
?/Delete/Restore/Save/Window: R
View name to restore: BDR
Command: UCS
Origin/ZAxis/3point/Entity/View/X/Y/Z/Prev/Restore/Save/Del/?/<World>: R
?/Name of UCS to restore: BDR
Command: Layer
?/Make/Set/New/ON/OFF/Color/Ltype/Freeze/Thaw: F
Layer name(s) to Freeze: Notes,????-??
?/Make/Set/New/ON/OFF/Color/Ltype/Freeze/Thaw: T
Layer name(s) to Thaw: TITLE-OT
Command: End
```

You will use the new prototype to create the MD-ROBOT drawing. The parts list currently has only one line. You need to array it upward to make five lines, then extend the vertical dividing lines to the new top line.

Begin a new drawing from the main menu named MD-ROBOT=PROTO-D, and then follow these steps:

▶ **Starting the MD-ROBOT Drawing**

```
Command: Layer
?/Make/Set/New/ON/OFF/Color/Ltype/Freeze/Thaw: T
Layer name(s) to Thaw: Notes,????-OT
Command: Zoom
All/Center/Dynamic/Extents/Left/Previous/Vmax/Window/<Scale(X/XP)>: W
First corner: 20,0
Other corner: 33,8
Command: Array
Select objects: Pick the top line of parts list
Rectangular or Polar array (R/P): R
Number of rows (---) <1>: 5
```

Starting the MD-ROBOT Drawing—continued

Number of columns (| | | |) <1>: *Press Enter*

Unit cell or distance between rows (---): **Int**

Other corner: **Int**

Command: **Extend**

Select boundary edge(s) ...

Select objects: *Pick new top line*

<Select object to extend>/Undo: *Pick all seven vertical dividing lines*

Command: **View**

?/Delete/Restore/Save/Window: **R**

View name to restore: **BDR**

Command: **Snap**

Snap spacing or ON/OFF/Aspect/Rotate/Style <1.0000>: **0.5**

Now that you are ready to insert parts, your drawing should resemble figure 12.2

Figure 12.2:
Title blocks, expanded parts list, and notes.

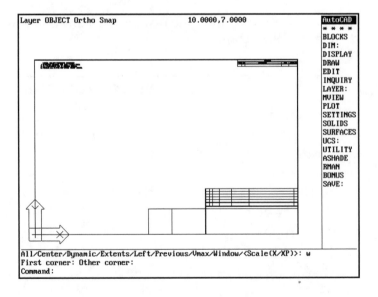

Inserting Blocks

The *Insert* command inserts drawings or blocks into a current drawing. After executing the command, you are prompted for the block name to insert. If the block is already defined in the current drawing, its existing definition is used. If not, AutoCAD searches its library path on disk for a drawing that matches the block name and, if found, inserts it. When inserted, a drawing file creates a block definition (unless inserted with a leading asterisk). You can override and redefine an existing block in the current drawing with a drawing from disk by specifying the name with an equal sign (=) in the same way you start a new drawing from a prototype.

The filename BLOCKNAME=DWGNAME, for example, would redefine the existing block named BLOCKNAME with the contents of the drawing file DWGNAME. The same equal sign technique can be used to insert a new block with a name differing from the drawing file name.

Editable Block Inserts

When a block is inserted, it is treated as a single entity. You can access its individual entities by typing an asterisk (*) before the name of the block, such as *B-ARM, when you insert it. This performs the same function as inserting a block normally and using the Explode command. In either case, the asterisk-inserted or exploded block can be edited.

After the name, the Insert command prompts for the insertion point, which you can specify while dragging the block. Then you set the scale.

When you insert a block file with an *, or explode an existing block reference, you do not have access to the entities that comprise the block. Inserting with an * copies the contents of the block definition into the entities section of the drawing and there is no relation between those entities and the block definition.

Similarly, exploding a block reference replaces an insert entity with a copy of the block definition. Again, no relation exists between the entities just copied and the block definition. The term editable block insert implies that you have some kind of special block reference, and the text even says that you have access to the entities that make up a block—implying that you are editing the block definition. This is not so. The only thing you can do to a block definition is replace it with a new one.

Block Scale and Rotation

After you have provided the block name and insertion point, you are prompted for the scale factors with the X scale factor <1>/Corner/XYZ: prompt. Its default is to prompt for X and Y and to set Z equal to X, but if you type **XYZ**, it also will prompt for the Z scale factor for 3D blocks. AutoCAD multiplies the X and Y dimensions of all entities in the block by the X and Y scale factor you enter. You can even specify negative values so AutoCAD will insert *mirrored* images of the block.

The X and Y scale factors also can be defined by clicking on a corner point on the screen in response to the scale prompt. The X and Y distances from the insertion point to this corner point become the X and Y scales. (This is identical to the Corner option, which makes it somewhat redundant.) If the picked corner point is below or to the left of the insertion point, you get a negative scale. Another convenient way to specify scale with a corner point is to use a point such as @3,7 relative to the insertion point, where 3 becomes the X scale and 7 the Y scale. Using a corner point works best for blocks that are designed to be one unit square, so the lower left corner of the block is at the insertion point and the upper right corner of the block drags to the corner point picked. A simple 1x1 square block, for example, can be inserted with various XY scales to represent any rectangular or square hole.

The final prompt is for the rotation angle relative to the insertion point. The block then can be rotated to any angle. A counterclockwise rotation will be a positive angle and a clockwise rotation will be a negative one.

Continue in the MD-ROBOT drawing and insert the B-PIN, B-PLATE, B-MOUNT, and B-PULLEY blocks, as shown in the following exercise. (After completing the steps for the B-PLATE, repeat the same steps for B-MOUNT at 1,9.5, B-PIN at 20.5,5, and B-PULLEY at 19.5,11.5.) Note in the following exercise that pressing Enter accepts the default settings in angle brackets.

Inserting Blocks into the Current Drawing

```
Command: Insert
Block name (or ?): B-PLATE
Insertion point: 0.5,1.5
X scale factor <1>/corner/XYZ: Press Enter
Y scale factor (default=X): Press Enter
Rotation angle <0>: Press Enter
Command: Press Enter
Command: Save
```

Your drawing should resemble figure 12.3. If you need to adjust the location of these blocks because of conflicts, use the Move command. Remember that AutoCAD recognizes the block as a single entity. Click on any point of the block and AutoCAD selects the entire block. Then drag the block and click on a new point.

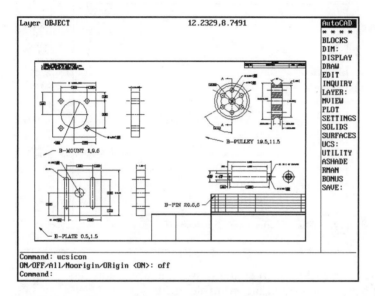

Figure 12.3:
Suggested block insertion points.

The remaining B-ARM block will not fit at full scale. To give you an exercise in block redefinition and dimension updating, it will be inserted at half scale. This makes the dimensions half as big, so you will need to update them and edit the block.

 If you are using Release 11, set DIMLFAC before inserting *B-ARM or exploding the block. AutoCAD resizes the text automatically to match the current dimension style, even *unnamed* blocks.

Editing the B-ARM Dimensions—Optional

Two optional methods are available for inserting and editing these dimensions. Use *-insertion and DIMLFAC updating or use normal insertion and block re-definition in the SCRATCH UCS. Whichever method you choose, be sure LUPREC and all dimension variables are set as they were when the dimension was created before updating each dimension.

Insertion and DIMLFAC

Refer to figure 12.4 as you complete the following optional exercise:

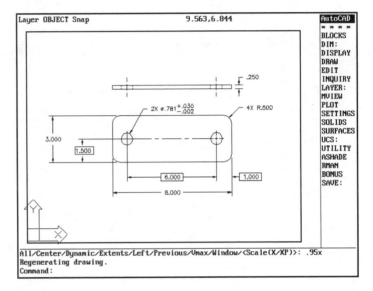

Figure 12.4:
Optional: Editing the B-ARM dimensions.

- ■ **Insert Block.** Insert *B-ARM at 0.5 scale, using a leading asterisk on the name to insert it as individual, editable entities.

- ■ **Edit Dimensions.** Set DIMLFAC (dimension linear factor) to 2. A DIMLFAC of 2 will make the half-size objects measure twice as big to generate the correct dimension text. Use Stretch, Move, Scale, and the dimension Update command to update each dimension. Make sure LUPREC and all dimension variables are set as needed before updating, scaling, or stretching dimensions. Refer to the arm dimensioning exercise in Chapter 11 for the settings. Erase and replace the circle center marks. Use Break to break the top view center lines and hidden lines to create visible gaps, because they are too short for LTSCALE to show gaps. Save the drawing. The other method uses normal insertion and block redefinition.

Insertion and Scratch Block Redefinition

- ■ **Insert Blocks.** Insert B-ARM at 0.5 scale as a normal block insertion into the drawing's BDR view. Change the UCS to Scratch, restore view Scratch, and insert *B-ARM again at full scale to allow editing, taking note of your insertion point for later reference.

- **Edit Dimensions.** Set DIMSCALE to 2 before updating the dimensions, which makes them all twice as big to compensate for the half scale insertion. Use Stretch, Move, Scale, and the dimension Update command to update each dimension. Make sure LUPREC and all dimension variables are set as needed before updating, scaling, or stretching. Refer to the arm dimensioning exercise in Chapter 11 for the settings. Erase and replace the circle center marks. Use the Break command to break the top view center lines and hidden lines to create visible gaps, since they are too short for the Ltscale command to show gaps.

- **Redefine Block.** After all the dimensions are updated, use the Block command to redefine the B-ARM block, employing the previous insertion point as the insertion base point. Restore view BDR and UCS BDR, and you will find the B-ARM block insertion already updated. Now save your drawing.

Numbering and Labeling the Parts and Title Block

Each part in a multi-detail drawing is assigned an identifying part number or letter. In the following example, the parts are identified by bubbles. Each bubble is linked to the part it represents by a leader which points from the bubble to the part. Refer to figure 12.5 for the bubble number/part matchups. You also can enter the part description text in the parts list and any additional title block text you desire before plotting.

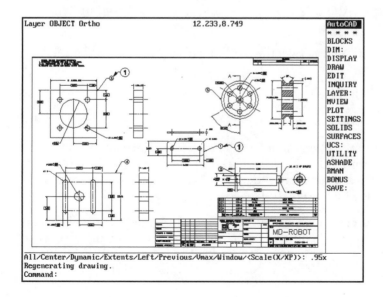

Figure 12.5:
The completed multi-detail working drawing.

Complete the following steps to create the numbered bubbles:

1. Draw the circles first, with 0.25 radius. Use the Style command (or the `Fonts...` selection from the Options pull-down menu) to define the new text style Romand with font file Romand, and default all other settings. Use 0.25-high Dtext with middle justification to enter the key numbers.

2 Set DIMSCALE to 2 and use the Leader dimensioning command to draw the leaders. Use Object Snap's NEArest mode to move from the first `To point:` to the circle, and then cancel the rest of the leader by pressing Ctrl-C.

3. Set DIMSCALE back to 1 and the text style back to Romans.

4. Thaw all layers and set Part-CX current. Set snap to 0.03125 and zoom in to the parts list to add 0.125 text with the Dtext command.

5. Add any other desired title text or notes, adjusting height to 0.1 as needed and setting the appropriate xxxx-CX layer current.

6. End the drawing (to plot it from the main menu) or save it (to plot from the drawing editor).

Plotting the Multi-Detail Drawing

To plot the drawing, thaw all layers (unless you already did in the preceding optional exercise) to display the title block, text, and notes as shown in figure 12.5.

You can plot from the main menu, selecting one of these choices:

```
3. Plot a drawing
4. Printer Plot a drawing
```

Or, you can type **Plot** or **Prplot** at the drawing editor's `Command:` prompt.

The scale is not critical for the check plot that follows, and you may use either the Plot or Printer Plot commands (the generic term plotting will be used for either one). If your plotter cannot handle the D-size drawing sheet, just plot it to FIT (the largest that will fit) instead of 1:1 scale.

For both plotters and printers, you may "write the plot to a file." This will write a file of your current drawing in the output format of your plotter (or printer) configuration. AutoCAD prompts for file name and adds the extension PLT for plotter file or LST for printer plot file. The file contains data that would have been sent directly to the plotter. Because all circles, curves, and text are converted to many little vectors, a .PLT or .LST file may be up to five times larger than a .DWG file.

It is useful to plot to files with RAM-resident plot spooling programs that can plot or print in the background as you draw. It also might be necessary to plot to a file for plotting in a network environment or plotting to a port that AutoCAD's configuration does not support. If your plotter configures only as a serial device in AutoCAD, but configures in your system as a network device or parallel port, you can plot to file and then send it to the device or port using network commands, the DOS Print command, or the DOS Copy/B command and option.

Make sure you are configured for and connected to a plotter (or printer plotter). Select either the Plot or Printer Plot choice from the main menu and begin a drawing named MD-ROBOT, or continue in the previous MD-ROBOT drawing and type **Plot** at the Command: prompt and follow these steps from the plot dialogue:

Plotting the MD-ROBOT Drawing

What to plot — Display, Extents, Limits, View, or Window <D>: **V**

View name: **BDR**

Plot will NOT be written to a selected file

Sizes are in Inches

Plot origin is at (0.00,0.00)

Plotting area is 32.00 wide by 20.00 high (MAX size)

Plot is NOT rotated 90 degrees

Area fill will NOT be adjusted for pen width

Hidden lines will NOT be removed

Plot will be scaled to fit available area

Do you want to change anything? <N> **Y**

You will change pen assignments and scale. Type **Y** again at the bottom of the color assignment menu that appears on your screen, to override the default and change the parameters.

When you set up layers, you designated color 2 (yellow) bold, colors 1 (red) and 4 (cyan) thin, and the rest as a medium pen. You should now set these pen and color relationships. The color assignment menu also enables you to set plotter linetypes. Plotter linetypes can be useful for topographic maps and other applications where individual line or arc segments are too short for AutoCAD's software linetypes. Leave them set to the default 0 (continuous) and rely on software linetypes.

You will learn by trial and error how fast each type and width of pen can go. Set your pen speed in the color setup that follows. You have a limited number of speed increments to choose from (as you saw in the previous exercise) with 1, 2, 4, 8, and 16 denoting inches-per-second, whereas 3, 5, 10, 20, and 40 indicate centimeters-per-second.

The color setup rotates through each color, prompting for pen number, linetype, and pen speed for each. You can shortcut it and jump to any color number at any prompt by entering **Cn** (*n* is the color number). An individual line is shown for each entry in the following exercise, but the screen does not actually scroll during color setup.

Setting Pen/Color and Speed

Enter values, blank=Next value, Cn=Color n, S=Show current values, X=Exit

Layer Color	Pen No.	Line Type	Pen Speed	
1 (red)	1	0	16	Pen number <1>: **C2** Jumps to yellow
2 (yellow)	1	0	16	Pen number <1>: **3** Sets Pen 3 to bold
2 (yellow)	3	0	16	Line type <0>: *Press Enter*
8				
2 (yellow)	3	0	16	Line type <0>: **12** *(or the speed that works for you)*

Continue setting colors 1 (red) and 4 (cyan) to pen 2 (with 8 for speed, perhaps) for thin. The rest of the settings can default to pen 1 for medium, but you may need to set the speed.

| 4 (cyan) | | 2 | 0 | 8 | Pen number <1>: **E**   Exits the menu |

You are now prompted for plotting to file, units, and several other factors. The plot origin is the lower left extreme of the available plot area. The plotting size is the available plot area for the currently set sheet size. You can enter a standard size, such as A or D, or you can enter X,Y width and height to specify other sizes. Plots can be rotated for landscape or portrait orientation. The plotter pen width should be set to the smallest pen width; it controls the line spacing for area fills and wide polylines. You can adjust area fill boundaries to compensate for pen width, or let the pen center line scribe the boundary. Hidden line removal applies to 3D. Your plotting scale will be 1:1 in this case, but if your plotter doesn't handle D-size, use a smaller scale or type **F**, for fit.

After you have stepped through all the settings and the plotter and paper is properly set up and positioned, press Enter to start the plot and follow these steps. You may find that your plotter offers more or fewer sizes as given in the following exercise.

Units, Origin, and Scale

Write the plot to a file? <N> **N**

Size units (Inches or Millimeters) <I>: *Press Enter*

Plot origin in Inches <0.00,0.00>: *Press Enter*

Standard values for plotting size

Size	Width	Height
A	10.50	8.00
B	16.00	10.00
C	21.00	16.00
MAX	32.00	20.00

Enter the Size or Width, Height(in Inches) <MAX>:

Press Enter or type D *(for D-size)*

Rotate 2D plots 90 degrees clockwise? <N> *Press Enter*

Pen width <0.010>: *Press Enter*

Adjust area fill boundaries for pen width? <N> *Press Enter*

Remove hidden lines? <N> *Press Enter*

Specify scale by entering:

Plotted Inches=Drawing Units or Fit or ? <F>: **1=1**

Effective plotting area: 32.00 wide by 20.00 high

Position paper in plotter.

Press RETURN to continue or S to Stop

for hardware setup *Press Enter*

Processing vector: 160

Plot complete.

Press Enter to continue: *Press Enter*

Command: **Quit**

Your robot project is now complete.

Summary

This chapter's exercise used your parts library (developed in a previous chapter) to assist you in creating the D-size multi-detail drawing from five separate drawings.

By using the dimension linear factor (DIMLFAC) and Update commands, you inserted parts from your library at reduced or enlarged scales yet varied the dimension text height and other dimensioning features to reflect the current drawing requirements.

As you proceed through *AutoCAD: Drafting and 3D Design*, you will find that blocks are used for many purposes. In your multi-detail drawing, blocks were inserted in various ways, but they all were inserted and scaled in two dimensions. Future exercises will guide you through the development and manipulation of 3D blocks.

Just about all drawings eventually wind up as hard copy. To ensure that your parts can be plotted at virtually any scale within your plotter's paper size capabilities, it is essential to begin your drawings from prototype drawings. Whether you direct your drawings to a plotter or to a printer plotter, the dialogue is virtually the same. As the multi-detail exercise shows, plotting may be performed in multiple colors, linetypes, speeds, and thicknesses. Although color and linetypes are useful features, assigning varying pen speeds and thicknesses may prove even more useful. Varying a plot's linetype thickness will enhance the hard copy's readability.

Although AutoCAD has extensive plotting features, you should remember that the primary function of hard copies is to convey information to another person. Use the information in this chapter to help you keep your plots as readable as possible.

Chapter 13 will introduce the procedures for creating and storing a symbol library. The library symbols will be used to generate ANSI Y14.5 level dimensioning. To make the ANSI Y14.5 symbols more efficient, you will learn how to attach attribute information to them. Chapter 13 also shows you how attributes can automate the generation of parts lists and the extraction of information for bills of materials.

13

CREATING SYMBOL LIBRARIES AND ATTRIBUTES

In this chapter:

- ■ Building smart symbols with attributes
- ■ Working with the Y14.5—GDT symbol library
- ■ Creating parts and extracting their data
- ■ Extracting attribute information
- ■ Working with template files

371

Overview

AutoCAD's *attributes* are special text values (strings of characters) that are part of an inserted block. Attributes enable you to preset text style, height, layer, color, location, and rotation relative to the block. You could preset all of this with ordinary text entities, but you also would have to preset the text value.

After they are blocked, text entities usually cannot be edited without redefining or exploding the block. Using attributes, you can enter the text value at the time of block insertion and edit the text value or the style, height, layer, color, location, and rotation at any time without exploding or redefining the block. Unlike text, attributes have a prompt to tell the user what sort of value is expected upon insertion.

Attributes were designed for attaching data (such as model numbers, sizes, quantities, and brand names) to blocks. These are called data-laden parts. This data can be accessed or extracted for use in bills of materials or external database programs. Attributes also have a second, equally valuable, use. They can be used to preset, control, and prompt for text such as title block text or symbol identifiers. These are called *smart symbols* or *intelligent text*.

You need numerous standard symbols to do full ANSI Y14.5 drafting and dimensioning. You can avoid drawing these symbols repeatedly by creating a library of symbol blocks. Symbol libraries can include virtually any drafting symbol. If you find yourself repeatedly drafting or copying a geometric object, it probably should be made into a symbol. Making a symbol library, or buying a commercially-developed library, will increase your productivity regardless of your drafting application.

Typical drafting symbol libraries include ANSI Y14.5M GDT (geometric dimensioning and tolerancing) symbols, and welding, fastening, piping, electronic, fluid power, and architectural symbols. Many of these symbols have associated text. The productivity of a GDT symbol library can be greatly enhanced by incorporating text in the form of attributes into the blocks. Such attributes can prompt upon block insertion for values (such as form tolerance) and then automatically insert the values as text with the style, scale, and position controlled.

This chapter shows you how to use attributes to create a library of GDT symbols for dimensioning by ANSI Y14.5 standards, to attach data to parts, and to extract that data for bills of materials. After completing the exercises in this chapter, you will be able to create your own custom symbols and data-laden parts for any drafting application such as the dimensioned MOUNT illustrated in figure 13.1.

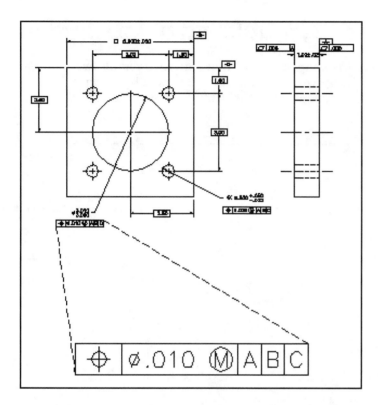

Figure 13.1:
Mount dimensioned with ANSI Y14.5 symbols.

The symbols you create in this chapter will be used in the next chapter for geometric dimensioning and tolerancing. You already have these symbols if you have the AutoCAD: Drafting and 3D Design Disk, so you can pick and choose which chapter exercises you want to do. If you do not thoroughly understand attributes, or if you do not have the AutoCAD: Drafting and 3D Design Disk, you should perform all of the exercises in this chapter.

The exercises in this chapter develop several of the ANSI Y14.5 symbols used in the AutoCAD: Drafting and 3D Design Disk's Y14.5 menu system. This custom menu system with its AutoLISP, macros, and standardized symbols provides a good example of how symbol libraries can make your drafting more productive. If you want to develop a complete ANSI symbol library on your own, the document entitled *American National Standard Engineering Drawings and Related Document Practices, Dimensioning and Tolerancing: ANSI Y14.5M-1982* is recommended.

Building Smart Symbols with Attributes

Symbols can be created in any shape and size that AutoCAD can draw. The first symbol you will create, a feature control frame, is two simple boxes with an attribute for the tolerance as illustrated in figure 13.2. First, you need to plan how it will be scaled and inserted.

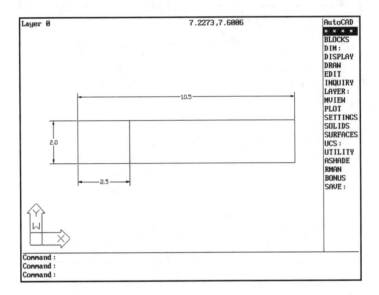

Figure 13.2:
Feature control frame sized for one-inch text.

The scaling method used for your Y14.5 symbols is the same as that used by AutoCAD for dimensioning and dimension text. Set the DIMTXT variable to the height that you want the text to appear in the plotted output, 0.125 in this case. Set the DIMSCALE variable to the inverse of the drawing plot scale, such as 4 for a quarter-scale drawing. When AutoCAD draws a dimension, it scales the text to DIMSCALE x DIMTXT, or 0.125x4=0.5 inch text in this example. Then when the drawing is plotted at quarter scale, the text ends up 0.5 divided by 4, or 0.125 again.

You could make your attribute symbol text 0.125 and scale the rest of the symbol geometry proportionately, but that would lock you into a 0.125 text standard. Instead, make the attribute symbol text one-inch high and insert it at DIMSCALE x DIMTXT. That enables you to change the DIMTXT variable to any standard you want, to change DIMSCALE to any drawing plot scale needed, and to still be sure the symbols are inserted at the correct scale. The Y14.5 Menu System uses this method for scaling dimensions, text, and symbols.

Draw the frame, sized proportionately to one-inch text. Begin a new drawing named TEMP and follow these steps:

Drawing a Feature Control Frame

Command: **Layer**

Freeze TITL-* and set layer DIM current if the prototype drawing is used. Otherwise, create a layer called DIM and set it to current. Also create a layer called TEXT.

Command: **Limits**

<Lower left corner><0.0000,0.0000>: *Press Enter*

<Upper right corner><12.0000,9.0000>: **20,15**

Command: **Zoom**

All/Center/Dynamic/Extents/Left/Previous/Vmex/Window/<Scale (X/XP)>: **All**

Command: **Snap**

Snap spacing or ON/OFF/Aspect/Rotate/Style <1.0000>: **0.25**

Command: **Line**

From point: **1,1**

To point: **@10.5,0**

To point: **@0,2**

To point: **@-10.5,0**

To point: **C**

Command: **Line**

From point: **3.5,1**

To point: **3.5,3**

Attributes: Intelligent Symbol Text

Command

Before you make a block of the feature control frame, use attributes to add the tolerance text. The *Attdef* (ATTribute DEFinition) command defines how attribute text will be prompted for and stored. Attributes are saved in blocks which can contain additional entities.

Three other commands and two entities make up the world of attributes. These commands are defined in more detail when you use them later in the chapter. For now, they are given in abbreviated form:

- **Attdisp.** Controls the display mode of the attribute after the block is inserted

- **Attedit.** Allows editing of the attribute text after it has been inserted into a drawing

- **Attext.** Extracts attribute text and formats it in report form

The Attdef command creates a specification called an *attdef*. An attdef contains all the text style, height, layer, color, location, and rotation information for the attribute, as well as a tag name (used to extract its data), a default text value, and a prompt. To use an attribute, make it part of a block. The block usually contains other entities but can be nothing but an attdef. You can make it a block by using the Block command or by inserting a drawing file that contains attdefs into the current drawing. Such a drawing file can be created by saving the attdefs (and other entities) to disk using the Wblock command. The Change command can be used to change the attribute definition before it is blocked.

When you insert an attribute-laden block, it creates an entity called an *attrib*. Attrib entities are subentities of insert entities (inserted blocks) and are accessible only by AutoLISP, List, Attdisp, Attedit, or Attext. You cannot select them independently of the block insert. If you explode the block insert, it destroys the attribs and reverts them to attdefs.

Defining an Attribute

The following exercise creates an attribute definition which, when inserted in the Y14.5 feature control frame block, prompts the user for a form tolerance value and inserts the value (text) into the frame. An attribute definition has Invisible, Constant, Verify, and Preset modes which are on (Y) or off (N). These will be explained later. For now, use the normal defaults (all off) that make variable attributes visible.

Attach a variable attribute to the feature control frame. Continue in the previous TEMP drawing and follow these steps:

Creating a Tolerance Value Attdef

```
Command: Attdef

Attribute modes—Invisible:N  Constant:N  Verify:N  Preset:N

Enter (ICVP) to change, RETURN when done: Press Enter

Attribute tag: TOLERANCE

Attribute prompt: Enter form tolerance

Default attribute value: Press Enter

Start point or Align/Center/Fit/Middle/Right/Style: Pick a point 0.5 right and up
from corner frame at point 1 (see fig. 13.3)

Height <0.1250>: 1

Rotation angle <0>: Press Enter
```

You now have an attdef entity (see fig. 13.3), that displays its tag name at its start point. To make this usable as an attribute, you must make it a block.

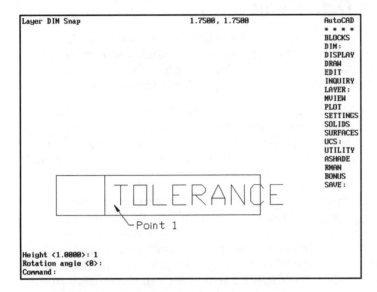

Figure 13.3:
Tolerance attdef.

Including Attributes in Blocks

Attributes may be stored with any block or may even be the only entities in a block. The Block command only defines a block in the current drawing, so use the Wblock command to save a drawing file that can be used as a block in any drawing. Store the form tolerance attribute with the feature control frame as a drawing named S-FRAME, as follows:

Wblocking the Frame and Tolerance Attribute

Command: **Wblock**

File name: **S-FRAME**

Block name (or ?): *Press Enter*

Insertion base point: *Pick the lower left corner of left frame*

Select objects: **W**

Select both frames and the attdef

6 found.

Select objects: *Press Enter*

The frames and attribute disappear and are written to the S-FRAME.DWG file.

Editing Attribute Definitions

If you decide to change some of the data in the attdef entity, and if you have not yet created the block with the Wblock or the Block command, you can use the Change command to edit attdef entities. It works much like the Change command for editing text entities, with additional tag and attribute prompts.

To change the attribute definition after making the block definition, you can either use the Insert command to insert *blockname, or you can use the Explode command to explode a previously inserted attribute-laden block. Either command will separate the block into its individual entities, including the original attdef.

The Explode command destroys any existing attrib entities in the exploded block. In either case, the Change command can modify the attdef and then redefine the block. If you redefine the block in the current drawing with the Block command, it will not be available in other drawings unless saved to disk with the Wblock command. If you use the Wblock command, it is not automatically redefined in the current drawing. To redefine such a block in the current drawing, use the Insert command with an equal sign (=) to reinsert and redefine the block, such as Insert *blockname=filename.*

Be careful when redefining attribute-laden blocks, because all existing insertions of the block will be affected. Existing constant attributes will be lost and replaced by new constant attributes. Existing variable attributes will be retained in previous block insertions, but new variable attributes will not be added. To use new variable attributes, erase the block inserts and reinsert them.

Inserting Attribute-Laden Blocks

Fortunately, you also can edit individual attrib entities (not attdefs) after insertion. You will see how after you insert a couple of blocks. When you insert a block with an attribute, you are prompted for standard block information such as insertion point, scale, and rotation. If it is a normal variable attribute, you are prompted for the value. Insert the feature control frame (S-FRAME) block with its attribute, as follows:

Inserting a Block with Attributes

Command: **Insert**

Block name (or ?): **S-FRAME**

Insertion point: *Pick a point*

X scale factor <1> / Corner / XYZ: **.5**

Scale as a quarter scale drawing with 0.125 text (0.125x4)

Y scale factor (default=X): *Press Enter*

Rotation angle <0>: *Press Enter*

Enter attribute values

Enter form tolerance: **.003**

After the feature control frame block is inserted, you see the Enter form tolerance: prompt. Entering this value automatically inserts it into the feature control frame at the appropriate scale and location, as shown in figure 13.4.

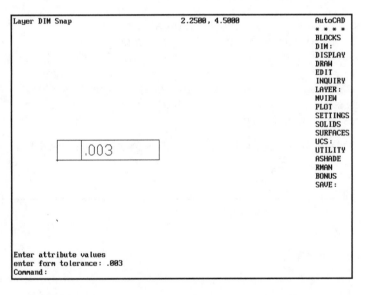

Figure 13.4:
Inserted S-FRAME with tolerance.

You created an insert entity with an attrib subentity attached. Invoking the List command and selecting the block insert will display data for both the insert and attrib entities.

Notice that the block dragged at full scale before insertion. You can, however, drag the block into place at the insert scale rather than the defined scale.

Presetting Block Scale and Rotation

You must give an insertion point first, and then specify scale and angle, so you cannot see the angle or the final size of the block until after it has been placed. This makes it difficult to visually drag blocks into place. You have the option of presetting the scale and rotation, thereby establishing the scale or angle, before the insertion. With presets, you can drag the block at the right scale and angle as you pick the insertion point.

The preset options are not shown in the insert prompt. They are as follows:

- **Scale** and **PScale** will prompt for scale factor which will be preset to X, Y, and Z axes.
- **Xscale** and **PXscale** only preset an X scale factor.
- **Yscale** and **PYscale** only preset a Y scale factor.
- **Zscale** and **PZscale** only preset a Z scale factor.
- **Rotate** and **PRotate** preset rotation angle, which you can enter from the keyboard or by picking two points.

Type the first one or two characters of the preset option at the `Insertion point:` prompt. Options prefixed with a P establish a preliminary scale and rotation value to aid in insertion. Then, after the insertion point is selected, the normal prompts are displayed so you can change the preset values. You cannot mix fixed presets, such as Xscale, with preliminary presets, such as PYscale. If you try to mix them, the preliminary presets become fixed, and you will not be reprompted for their values after the insertion.

Continue in the previous TEMP drawing and reinsert the S-FRAME block with a preset scale, as follows:

Block Inserts with Presets

```
Command: Insert
Block name (or ?) <S-FRAME>: Press Enter
Insertion point: S
Scale factor: .625
Insertion point: Drag it and pick a point
Rotation angle <0>: Press Enter
Enter attribute values
Enter form tolerance: %%c.005
```

Your drawing should now resemble figure 13.5.

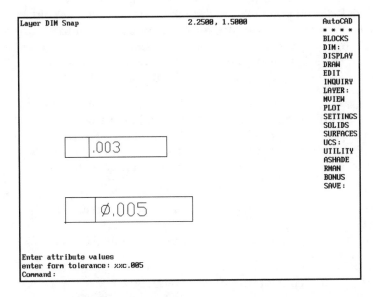

Figure 13.5:
S-FRAME with diameter, inserted with preset scale.

Preset options are a great asset in menu macros which transparently apply preset options, making dragging while in the Insert command easy. This is how the Y14.5 Menu System inserts the GDT symbols.

Editing Attributes

Inserted blocks that contain attributes can be copied, moved, scaled, rotated, and arrayed as a whole. You also can edit any value or parameter of existing attrib entities after insertion.

The *Attedit* (ATTribute EDIT) command enables you to edit attributes, individually or globally, without exploding their block insert. The default setting edits attributes one at a time, enabling you to change value, position, height, angle, style, layer, or color. Global edits are confined to changing value. You can control your selection set by block name, tag name, or attribute value.

To globally edit attributes, respond to the Attedit command's `Edit attributes one at a time? <Y>` prompt with **N**. Global editing is limited to changing the attrib text value itself, not any of the other parameters.

To edit attributes individually, type **Y** or press Enter, for default, at the `Edit attributes one at a time? <Y>` prompt. Use normal object selection to select the attribs (not the blocks), and you can see the `Value/Position/Height/Angle/Style/Layer/Color/Next <N>:` prompt for each. When it prompts, it marks each attribute with an X so you can keep track of which one you are editing. The X stays on the current attrib until you tell it to move on by pressing Enter or **N** (for Next), so you can edit any or all parameters. When editing the text value, you are prompted to `Change or Replace <R>` it.

Global editing or individually changing the text value works like a word processor's global search and replace, prompting you for the `String to change:` and the `New string:` to substitute in the old string's place. If the string to change occurs more than once in a single attribute, only the first occurrence is changed.

You can filter the attributes to be edited whether you are editing text individually or globally. AutoCAD enables you to use wildcard characters (* or ?) to restrict block names, attribute tags, or attribute text values, such as AL*A or R??ROO. The default * specifies all attributes.

Edit the attributes in your feature control frame block, as follows:

Editing Attributes

```
Command: Attedit
Edit attributes one at a time? <Y> N
Global edit of attribute values
Edit only attributes visible on screen? <Y> Press Enter
Block name specification <*>: S-FRAME
Attribute tag specification <*>: TOL*
Attribute value specification <*>: Press Enter
Select Attributes: C
```
Select both attributes using the crossing window
```
2 attributes selected.
String to change: %%c
New string: Press Enter
Command: Press Enter to individually change position and layer
ATTEDIT
Edit attributes one at a time? <Y> Press Enter
Block name specification <*>: Press Enter
```

Editing Attributes—continued

Attribute tag specification <*>: *Press Enter*

Attribute value specification <*>: *Press Enter*

Select Attributes: **C**

Select both attributes using the crossing window

2 attributes selected.

Value/Position/Height/Angle/Style/Layer/Color/Next <N>: **P**

Enter text insertion point: *Drag it and pick a new point*

Value/Position/Height/Angle/Style/Layer/Color/Next <N>: *Press Enter*

Value/Position/Height/Angle/Style/Layer/Color/Next <N>: **L**

New layer: **Text**

Value/Position/Height/Angle/Style/Layer/Color/Next <N>: *Press Enter*

Command: **Erase**

Select objects: **W**

First corner: *Select all entities on the screen using window*

The attributes were updated to reflect the editing, as shown in figure 13.6.

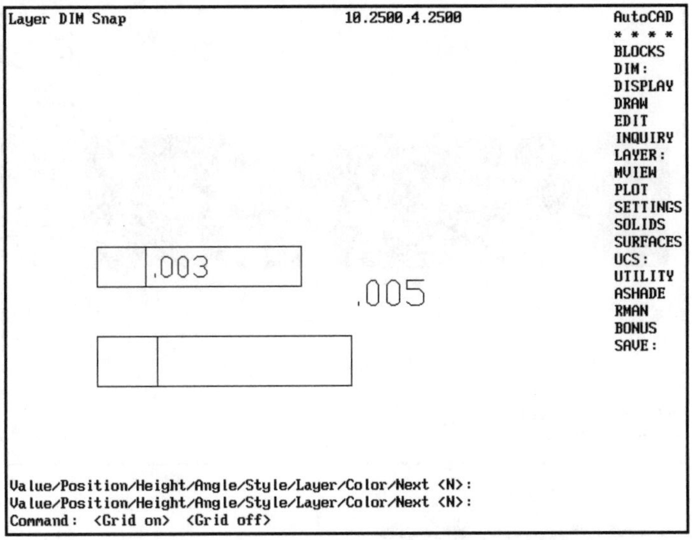

Figure 13.6:
Edited attributes.

When you have normal text information to present and need variable attributes in blocks, it is better to use attributes for both. Text entities within blocks cannot be changed without redefining the block, which would destroy the attributes.

Attribute Editing and Insertion by Dialogue Box

If your system supports dialogue boxes (which require the AUI), you can edit attributes with the Ddatte command.

The *Ddatte* (Dynamic Dialogue ATTribute Edit) command edits attribute string values with a dialogue box (see fig. 13.7). You can edit only one block at a time. It presents the current value and enables you to specify a new value.

The Ddatte command provides a nice visual interface but is limited to selecting a single block and editing all the attribute text values that it contains. It cannot edit other parameters, such as position.

Figure 13.7:
The Ddatte command dialogue box.

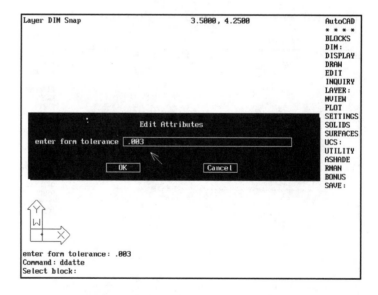

Attribute Entry by Dialogue Box

Attribute information is normally prompted for on the command line during the Insert command. If your system supports AUI and the system variable ATTDIA (attribute dialogue) is set to a non-zero value, however, the same attribute dialogue box that the Ddatte command uses (see fig. 13.7) is utilized instead to enter attribute values during block insertions.

Using the Y14.5—GDT Symbol Library

ANSI Y14.5 and GDT symbols are to be developed according to preferred form and proportion requirements. All figure and symbol proportions are commonly given as a factor of the dimension text height. As described earlier, you could create your symbols for a specific dimension text height (.125, for example), but that would not allow you to use the same symbols set for other dimension text heights. To account for this problem, all the symbols are sized for 1" dimension text height. You then can easily scale your symbols upon insertion to the appropriate dimension text height. If you are using .2 dimensioning text, for example, you simply scale the symbols to .2 in the X and Y axes upon symbol insertion. This automatically adjusts your symbols to the designated text size.

If you do not have the AutoCAD: Drafting and 3D Design Disk, you must use the techniques presented in this section to create and write the remaining symbols to be used for the dimensioning exercises in the next chapter to disk with the Wblock command. The AutoCAD: Drafting and 3D Design Disk's Y14.5 Menu System includes all of the symbols shown in figure 13.8 and more.

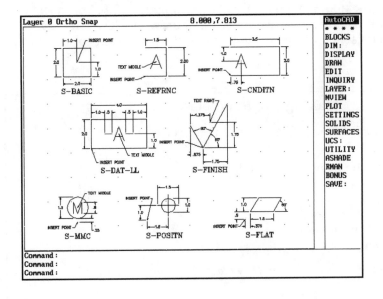

Figure 13.8:
The Y14.5 GDT symbol library.

Refer to table 13.1 to define the attributes in the symbols in figure 13.8. All attributes use the default modes (N for each of the invisible, constant, verify, and preset modes) and text style Romans. Information for the S-FRAME symbol you already made is included.

Table 13.1
Y14.5 GDT Symbols and Attributes

Block Name	Attribute Tag	Att. Prompt	Default	Justification
S-BASIC	(none)			
S-CNDITN	DATUM	Datum	A	Middle
S-DAT-LL	DATUM	Datum	A	Middle
S-FINISH	FINISH	Finish value	(none)	Right
S-FLAT	(none)			
S-FRAME	TOLERANCE	Enter form tolerance	(none)	Left (start point)
S-MMC	(none—letter M is just text)			
S-POSITN	(none)			
S-REFRNC	DATUM	Datum	A	Middle

The insertion points for the above symbols are shown in figure 13.8. You now can make the symbols. If you already have the symbol drawing files, you may skip this exercise. Otherwise, continue in the previous TEMP drawing and follow these steps:

Making the Symbols

 You have the symbol drawing files. Skip this exercise.

 Continue to create the symbols shown in figure 13.8.

```
Command: Layer
```
Freeze TITL- and set layer DIM current*
```
Command: Zoom
All/Center/Dynamic/Extents/ Left/Previous/Vmex/Window/<Scale (X/XP)>:
```
To a height of 10
```
Command: Snap
Snap spacing or ON/OFF/Aspect/Rotate/Style <1.0000>: 0.25
```

◢

Making the Symbols—continued

Command: **Line**

Draw the three sides of the S-CNDITN box

Command: **Attdef**

Define S-CNDITN's DATUM attribute as shown in table 13.1

Command: **Wblock**

Wblock the attribute and lines to filename S-CNDITN with the base point illustrated in figure 13.8

Repeat the process for each of the symbols in figure 13.8 and table 3.1.

Test each symbol by inserting it

Command: **Insert**

Command: **Quit**

You will use these symbols for Chapter 14's geometric dimensioning and tolerancing exercises. If you are not creating the extended Y14.5 symbols set, just read the following section and then skip to the next section.

Creating Parts and Extracting Their Data

Attributes can automate the creation and extraction of information such as part numbers, part descriptions, material, specification numbers, and cost. This information is often found on a drawing's parts list. You will extract a simple parts list from the attribute tags and values attached to a 1/4-20UNC 2A hexagonal head cap screw (hex bolt). A typical parts list follows:

Table 13.2
Extracted Parts List Attribute Information

QTY-REQD	CODE	LENGTH	EST-COST
4	HX01	1.50	.78

It is time-consuming to add attributes, but the ability to extract the information for parts lists and estimates makes it worthwhile. To keep the following exercise simple, use only the QTY-REQD, CODE, LENGTH, and EST-COST attributes to demonstrate a variety of modes, as shown in figure 13.9.

First you will draw a 1/4-20UNC 2A X 1.50 hex bolt and block it with attribute information defining a typical parts list description. Then you will insert it several times and extract the attribute information needed to generate a parts list.

You can easily draw the hex bolt head with the Polygon and Rotate commands.

Figure 13.9:
Bolt head with attribute
tags.

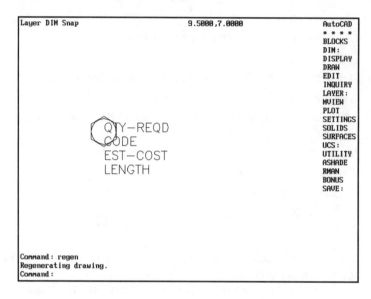

```
Layer DIM Snap                          9.5000,7.0000              AutoCAD
                                                                   * * * *
                                                                   BLOCKS
                                                                   DIM:
                                                                   DISPLAY
                                                                   DRAW
                                                                   EDIT
                                                                   INQUIRY
                                                                   LAYER:
                                                                   MVIEW
                                                                   PLOT
                         QTY-REQD                                  SETTINGS
                         CODE                                      SOLIDS
                         EST-COST                                  SURFACES
                         LENGTH                                    UCS:
                                                                   UTILITY
                                                                   ASHADE
                                                                   RMAN
                                                                   BONUS
                                                                   SAVE:




Command: regen
Regenerating drawing.
Command:
```

The *Polygon* command draws 2D regular (all sides equal) polygons from three to 1,024 sides. The size of the polygon is determined by specifying the radius of a circle in which the polygon is inscribed (inside), or circumscribed (outside), or by specifying the length of one of the polygon's sides. Polygons are closed polylines. Use the Pedit command to edit polygons.

The *Rotate* command enables you to rotate entities around a designated base or pivot point. The rotation angle may be entered as a numeric angle, by picking a point relative to the base point, or by a reference angle option. The reference option enables you to specify the rotation angle relative to a base angle, usually on an existing entity.

You can skip to the insertion and data extraction portion of this sequence if you have the AutoCAD: Drafting and 3D Design Disk, but if you are not familiar with the Invisible, Constant, Verify, and Preset attribute modes, you should follow the entire exercise. Begin a new drawing named TEMP, set your own zoom factor, and follow these steps:

Drawing the Bolt

 You have the HX25-20 file. Start a new TEMP drawing and continue, or you may skip this exercise.

 Begin a new drawing named TEMP and continue.

Command: **Polygon**

Number of sides: **6**

Edge/<Center of Polygon>: *Pick any point*

Inscribed in circle/Circumscribed about circle (I/C): **C**

Radius of circle: **.1875**

Command: **Rotate**

Select objects: **L**

Select objects: **Press Enter**

Base point: **@**

<Rotation angle>/Reference: **90**

Command: **Circle**

3P/2P/TTR/<Center point>: **@**

Diameter/<Radius> **.1875**

Command: **Save**

File<Temp>: *Press Enter*

Attribute Modes

You also need to set the attribute modes and define the attribute tags to be attached to the bolt. These will not be the default visible variable attributes. Remember that an attribute definition has Invisible, Constant, Verify, and Preset modes, which can be on (Y) or off (N). A more complete explanation follows:

- **Invisible.** When off (the default), the attribute value will be displayed on the screen and plotted normally; when on, the inserted attribute is invisible.

- **Constant.** The default, off, creates a variable attribute, prompting for value each time the block is inserted into the drawing. If on, it assigns the attribute a fixed (constant) value for all insertions. A constant attribute cannot be edited after insertion.

- **Verify.** Off, the default, inserts the attributes without user verification; if on, you are prompted to verify each value upon insertion.

- **Preset.** If off, variable attribute values are prompted for during block insertion. If on, prompts are suppressed and the default value will be assigned. This inserts variable attributes as if they were constant attributes, except it allows the values to be edited after insertion. The system variable ATTREQ has the same effect when applied globally to all attributes. If ATTREQ is on, non-preset variable attributes are prompted for during insertion. If ATTREQ is off, the default values are used.

These modes have been set to their off defaults for everything so far. You will see examples of all four modes in the HX25-20 block. The attributes and modes are shown in Table 13.3.

Table 13.3
HX25-20 Bolt Block Attributes

Tag	I C V P	Attribute Prompt	Default	Constant
QTY-REQD	Y N Y N	Quantity required	1	
CODE	Y Y N N	(none)	(none)	HX01
EST-COST	Y N N Y	Estimated Cost	.78	
LENGTH	Y N N N	Length	????	

All of these will be left justified, which is the default setting. You will set the modes listed as each attdef is defined. All are invisible, so the finished drawing will not be cluttered. They could be placed on a separate layer to provide even more control over the visibility and colors.

QTY-REQD is variable, as with the previous attdefs in this chapter, but it also is in Verify mode, so it will prompt for an extra confirmation of value upon insertion. CODE should not change from one insertion to another, so it has a constant value. EST-COST might change, but it is likely to be .78, so it is preset. It inserts without prompting, as a constant would do, but can be changed later by the Attedit command. LENGTH is a simple variable attribute. Its ???? default is a good place holder for values that you may not know upon initial insertion. You can press Enter to skip them, then later replace them with the Attedit command. It is easy to search on ???? for a global update.

Now set modes and define attdefs. To set modes, type **I**, **C**, **V**, or **P** at the attribute modes prompt until the prompt shows the correct combination. Then press Enter to continue. Each time you type **I**, **C**, **V**, or **P**, it toggles the current state of that mode.

Continue in the previous TEMP drawing and follow these steps:

Setting Attribute Modes

Command: **Attdef**

Attribute modes—Invisible:N Constant:N Verify:N Preset:N

Enter (ICVP) to change, RETURN when done: **I**

Attribute modes—Invisible:Y Constant:N Verify:N Preset:N

Enter (ICVP) to change, RETURN when done: **V**

Attribute modes—Invisible:Y Constant:N Verify:Y Preset:N

Enter (ICVP) to change, RETURN when done: *Press Enter*

Attribute tag: **QTY-REQD**

Attribute prompt: **Quantity required**

Default attribute value: **1**

Start point or Align/Center/Fit/Middle/Right/Style: *Pick center of head*

Height <0.1250>: **.125**

Rotation angle <0>: *Press Enter*

Command: *Press Enter*

ATTDEF *(Toggle C and V to set Constant and Verify modes)*

Attribute tag: **CODE**

Attribute value: **HX01**

Start point or Align/Center/Fit/Middle/Right/Style: *Press Enter*

Command: *Press Enter*

ATTDEF *(Toggle C and P to set Constant and Preset modes)*

Attribute tag: **EST-COST**

Attribute prompt: **Estimated cost**

Default attribute value: **.78**

Start point or Align/Center/Fit/Middle/Right/Style: *Press Enter*

Command: *Press Enter*

ATTDEF *(Toggle P to set Preset mode)*

Attribute tag: **LENGTH**

Attribute prompt: **Length**

Default attribute value: **????**

Start point or Align/Center/Fit/Middle/Right/Style: *Press Enter*

Command: **Save**

After you repeat the Attdef command and are prompted for the text by the `Start point or...` prompt, the previous attribute tag is highlighted. If you press Enter at this point, it places the new tag directly below the previous one, as with repeated Text commands. Your drawing should resemble figure 13.9.

Attribute Selection Order

With no more than one attribute, selection order is not a factor when using the Wblock or Block commands. With multiple attributes, however, you should control the order of the prompts upon insertion. You can do this with the order of selection when using the Block or Wblock commands. If you select All by a window or crossing, they will come back in the reverse order of creation because AutoCAD finds more recent entities first. You can plan for this when you create them, or you can select the attdef entities one at a time in the order you choose.

Use the Block command on the bolt and its attributes as follows:

Blocking the Bolt and Its Attributes

```
Command: Block

Block name (or ?): HX25-20

Insertion base point: Pick the center of the head

Select objects: Pick the circle and the polygon

Select objects: Pick each attdef in the order created, top to bottom

Select objects: Press Enter
```

The block is now defined in the current drawing. You will discard this TEMP drawing after you have explored attributes, so write it to disk with the Wblock command if you want to keep it as follows:

Writing the Block to Disk

```
Command: Wblock

File name: HX25-20

Block name: =
```

After you insert the HX25-20 block, its attributes will be controlled by the modes that were set when you defined it.

Invisible, Constant, Verify, and Preset Inserts

Remember, QTY-REQD is variable with Verify mode, CODE is Constant, EST-COST is preset to .78, and LENGTH is a simple variable attribute with a ???? place holder default. Observe the action of these as you insert the block with attributes back into the current drawing.

Continue in the previous TEMP drawing or begin a new drawing named TEMP, set your own zoom factor, and follow these steps:

Inserting the HX25-20 Block Attributes

 Continue in the previous TEMP drawing or begin a new drawing named TEMP.

 Continue in the previous TEMP drawing.

Command: **Insert**

Block name (or ?): **HX25-20**

Insertion point: *Pick point at top left, then press Enter to default scale and rotation*

Enter attribute values

Quantity required <1>: **4**

Length <????>: *Press Enter*

Verify attribute values

Quantity required <4>: *Press Enter*

Command: *Press Enter*

INSERT *(Insert another at middle left with quantity 2 and length 3)*

Command: **Save**

After the block is inserted, the attribute values are invisible (see fig. 13.10). You might want to control attribute visibility for verification and editing, however.

Controlling Attribute Visibility

 When you use invisible attributes, you might need to override the invisibility to check or modify values. The *Attdisp* (ATTribute DISPlay) command globally sets attribute display mode after insertion and overrides the Attdef invisible/visible settings. The default is Normal, which allows the modes set by Attdef to control visibility individually.

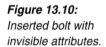

Figure 13.10:
*Inserted bolt with
invisible attributes.*

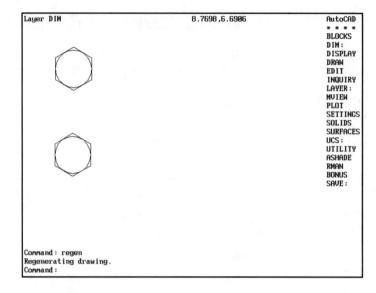

Make the HX25-20 block's attributes visible so you can check and edit them. The Attdisp command toggles the attribute display normal, on, and off. Notice that the values are displayed, not the tags.

Continue in the previous TEMP drawing and follow these steps:

Editing Invisible Attributes

```
Command: Attdisp
Normal/ON/OFF <Normal>: On
Command: Attedit
Edit attributes one at a time? <Y> Press Enter
Block name specification <*>: Press Enter
Attribute tag specification <*>: Press Enter
Attribute value specification <*>: Press Enter
Select Attributes: Pick .78 and ???? values in top left insertion, then press Enter
Value/Position/Height/Angle/Style/Layer/Color/Next <N>: V
Change or Replace? R
New Attribute value: 2.5
Value/Position/Height/Angle/Style/Layer/Color/Next<N>: N
Value/Position/Height/Angle/Style/Layer/Color/Next <N>: V
Change or Replace? <R>: R
Command: Attdisp
Normal/ON/OFF <On>: N
Command: Save
```

Figure 13.11 shows the edited values before you set the Attedit command back to normal.

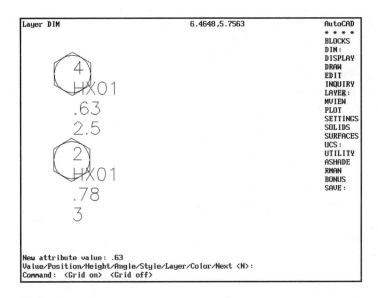

Figure 13.11:
Edited attributes with the Attedit command on.

Setting the Attedit command to off makes all attributes, even normally visible ones, invisible. The Attedit command resets the ATTMODE system variable, which also can be used by the Setvar command to control visibility. With the ATTMODE variable, 0 is off, 1 is normal, and 2 is on.

Extracting Attribute Information

The Attext (ATTribute EXTract) command extracts attributes and writes a file. Databases or spreadsheet programs can process the extracted file for analysis and report generation. This information is formatted into an ASCII text file in one of three possible formats: CDF, SDF, or DXF. CDF is the default format. You can extract all attributes or select certain entities from which to extract attributes.

To make sense of extracted attribute information, you need a way to format the *fields* (items) of data. You are prompted for one of the following output formats when you use the Attext command:

■ **CDF.** (Comma Delimited File). Produces a format which contains one record for each block reference. The data fields are separated by commas, and their width varies with the width of the extracted data. CDF is easy to use with BASIC programs. Additionally, some database packages, such as dBASE III, can read this format directly with an `APPEND FROM...DELIMITED` operation.

■ **SDF.** (Standard Data File). Is considered the standard for input to microcomputer databases. SDF files use spaces to separate and standardize the data fields, usually aligning the data into columns. If the extracted data width exceeds the space allocated in the SDF template, the data will be truncated. SDF is used mostly for FORTRAN programs, for dBASE `COPY...SDF` files, or for dBASE `APPEND FROM...SDF` operations.

■ **DXF.** (Drawing Interchange File). Is AutoCAD's format, and is most commonly used by third-party programs. The Attext command uses a subset of the DXF file format.

Table 13.4
PART-CDF.TXT—Sample CDF Output

'HX25-20', 4,'HX01', 0.63, 2.500
'HX25-20', 2,'HX01', 0.78, 3.000

Table 13.5
PART—SDF.TXT-Sample SDF Output

HX25-20	4HX01	0.63	2.500
HX25-20	2HX01	0.78	3.000

To create a CDF or SDF file, you need to provide a template file for the Attext command to use. (The DXF format is a fixed format, and needs no template.) The following exercise creates a template and extracts the data, but does not process the data further. You need a program such as dBASE III or IV, Lotus 1-2-3, or even a word processor to process the data. Processed data then can be imported back into AutoCAD.

Lotus, for example, might tabulate quantities and generate a bill of materials that would be imported into AutoCAD as text. The use of Lotus and dBASE to import and process data is discussed in *Maximizing AutoCAD Vol. II* (New Riders Publishing).

Working with Template Files

The *template file* is a format instruction list which tells AutoCAD where to put the information in the extracted data file. If you have the AutoCAD: Drafting and 3D Design Disk, you already have the BOLT.TXT template file. Otherwise, you need to create the file shown in table 13.6 as an ASCII text format. You can do so with DOS's EDLIN program editor or with most other text editors or word processors in programming (nondocument) mode. See Appendix A for more information on text files and text editors.

Table 13.6
BOLT.TXT Template File

Tag Name	Output Format
BL:NAME	C011000
QTY-REQD	N004000
CODE	C008000
EST-COST	N008002
LENGTH	N008003

Each line of the template file has two items. The first is the attribute tag name, such as QTY-REQD, which must match exactly. The second defines the output format for that field, such as N004000. The format specification has three parts. The first is the character N or C, which determines if the data is to be treated as a number or a character (alphanumeric). The next three digits define the total field width in characters. The last three digits define the number of characters following the decimal of floating point (real) numbers. If the last three digits are zeros, the number is treated as an integer and any decimal portion is rounded off.

You also can extract information about the block itself, such as BL:NAME for the block's name. Using BL:X, BL:Y, or BL:Z could give you additional information about the block's coordinate position. Other extractable block information includes nesting level, counter number, entity handle, layer, rotation angle, X, Y, and Z scale, and 3D extrusion components. See the *AutoCAD Reference Manual* for details.

Create the above template and extract both a CDF and an SDF file using the BOLT.TXT template. If you do not already have the BOLT. TXT file, create one and then continue in the previous TEMP drawing.

Extracting Attributes

 You have the BOLT.TXT file. Continue in the previous TEMP drawing.

 Create the BOLT.TXT file in table 13.6. Then continue in the previous TEMP drawing.

```
Command: Attext

CDF, SDF, or DXF Attribute extract (or Entities) <C>: C

Template file: BOLT

Extract file name <TEMP>: PART-CDF

2 records in extract file.

Command: Attext

CDF, SDF, or DXF Attribute extract (or Entities) <C>: S

Template file <BOLT>: Press Enter

Extract file name <TEMP>: PART-SDF

2 records in extract file.

Command: Quit
```

You now have produced the two extract files, PART-CDF.TXT and PART-SDF.TXT shown earlier. The PART-SDF file is repeated here (see table 13.7) so you can look at one problem.

Table 13.7
PART-SDF.TXT—Sample SDF Format

HX25-20	4HX01	0.63	2.500
HX25-20	2HX01	0.78	3.000

Notice that the 4 in the first numeric field runs into the HX01 of the CODE field. That happens because numbers are right justified and character fields are left justified. This juxtaposition of numbers does not matter if you are using the extract file as data for a spreadsheet, database, or other program that knows where to start reading each field, but it is a nuisance if you simply want to export a list, format it in your word processor, and print it out. You can add blank columns between fields in the extract file. Just use a dummy tag name in the template. Because the Attext command will not find any attributes for it, it will output as a blank.

Your BOLT.TXT template with an added dummy tag would be as follows:

Table 13.8
BOLT.TXT Template File with Dummy Tag

BL:NAME	C011000
QTY-REQD	N004000
DUMMY	C002000
CODE	C008000
EST-COST	N008002
LENGTH	N008003

An SDF extract using this file would add two blanks between the QTY-REQD and CODE fields, producing the following:

Table 13.9
PART-SDF.TXT with Added Spaces

HX25-20	4	HX01	0.63	2.500
HX25-20	2	HX01	0.78	3.000

 Note Be careful not to use the same (or default) name for both the template and the extract file, or the extract file will overwrite the template.

Summary

This chapter provided you with an efficient and productive symbol library upon which your ANSI Y14.5 dimensioning system can be built. Developing the Y14.5 symbols not only showed you how to create standard symbols but also how to increase your drafting efficiency with "smart" symbols that can be generated accurately and plotted at virtually any drawing scale.

The feature control frame exercise showed you how to add attributes to your symbols to create intelligent text that prompts the user for a feature control tolerance value whenever the feature control frame symbol is inserted. You will find this technique useful for defining attributes whenever you need additional symbols or symbols libraries.

This chapter also showed you how to use attributes to automate the creation and extraction of information such as parts lists and bills of materials. When you added attributes to the hex bolt, you saw how productive it was to export information for analysis and report generation.

Attributes provide tremendous power for annotating your drawings. They add a versatile tool to your drafting tool kit. Remember, however, good data management is necessary for efficient and productive drafting. This also is true for non-graphic data, such as attributes.

Chapter 14 introduces a list of ANSI Y14.5 dimensioning rules and a suggested practical sequence for dimensioning to ANSI standards. You are shown how to use your new Y14.5 symbols to assist you in adding datums, feature control references, and Y14.5 symbols to parts drawings. Chapter 14 also builds upon the drafting techniques you have learned and shows you how to build an assembly drawing from multi-detail subassembly components.

14

APPLYING GEOMETRIC DIMENSIONING AND TOLERANCING

In this chapter:

- Drawing the M-COUPLE in two views
- Following steps and rules for production dimensioning
- Using geometric dimensioning and tolerancing steps

Overview

The purpose of most mechanical drawings is to convey accurate geometric and textual information to those responsible for producing and marketing the object drawn. The purpose of the ANSI Y14.5 geometric dimensioning and tolerancing standards, upon which this chapter is based, is to ensure that all drawings have only one interpretation. The symbols developed in Chapter 13 are used in this chapter to guide you through the geometric dimensioning and tolerancing process in AutoCAD that is necessary to maintain the design intent of your drawings. The exercise in this chapter shows you how to dimension a two-view orthographic part drawing (see figure 14.1) according to the ANSI Y14.5 standards.

Figure 14.1:
The completed M-COUPLE, which you will draw in this chapter.

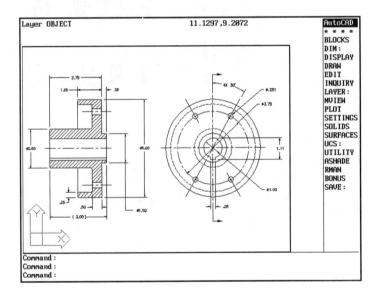

Drawing the M-COUPLE in Two Views

Before you learn to dimension a drawing, you need to draw the M-COUPLE as shown in figure 14.2. If you have the AutoCAD: Drafting and 3D Design Disk, you can skip to the dimensioning section of this chapter. If you do not have the AutoCAD: Drafting and 3D Design Disk, or you want to draw the M-COUPLE for practice, do the following exercise.

First, you will use the *Multiple* command to draw the six concentric circles shown on the right side of the drawing. Multiple is a command modifier that causes any command to repeat. To use the Multiple command to repeat any command in a loop automatically, type **Multiple** at the Command: prompt and then type the command you want to repeat—in this case, the Circle command. To end the command loop and cancel the command, press Ctrl-C. No prompt is issued when you enter the Multiple command. This command is primarily intended for menus and is used in many pull-down menu items.

Drawing the M-COUPLE Front View

Do the following steps to draw the basic front view of the M-COUPLE. At AutoCAD's main menu, begin a new drawing named M-COUPLE. Make this a C-size drawing.

Remember that throughout the exercises in this textbook, you are to press Enter after responding to a prompt.

Drawing the M-COUPLE

Command: **Zoom**

All/Center/Dynamic/Extents/Left/Previous/Window/<Scale (X)>: **Window**

Use the Window option to place a window from to 5,6 to 16,12

Command: **Snap**

Snap spacing or ON/OFF/Aspect/Rotate/Style <1.0000>: *Press F8 to toggle ortho on and type* **0.125**

Command: **Multiple**

Command: **Circle**

3P/2P/TTR/<Center point>: **13,9**

Diameter/<Radius>: **D**

Diameter: **5**

CIRCLE 3P/2P/TTR/<Center point>: **@**

Repeat this sequence for the following diameters: 4.5, 3.75, 2, 1.499, 1

CIRCLE 3P/2P/TTR/<Center point>: **@1.875,0**

Diameter/<Radius>: **.1405**

CIRCLE 3P/2P/TTR/<Center point>: *Press Ctrl-C to exit command*

Drawing the M-COUPLE—continued

Command: **Dim**

Set DIMCEN to 0.0625, use CEN on the hole and restore DIMCEN to -0.1

Command: **Line**

From point:

Draw a center line through the temporary hole (see fig. 14.2)

Command: **Chprop**

Select objects:

Change what property (Color/LAyer/LType/Thickness) ?

Change the 4.5 and 2 diameter circles to layer HL, and then repeat the command to change the 3.75 diameter circle to layer CL, and the center marks to DIM (see fig. 14.3).

Command: **Array**

Rectangular or Polar array (R/P):

Array the hole, center line, and marks. Polar, six times, rotated.

Command: **Erase**

Select objects:

Erase the right and left holes, center marks and lines

Command: **Layer**

?/Make/Set/New/ON/OFF/Color/LType/Freeze/Thaw:

Turn layer DIM off and toggle snap off

Command: **Trim**

Trim the center line circle and lines from within the four holes

Command: **Layer**

?/Make/Set/New/ON/OFF/Color/LType/Freeze/Thaw:

Turn layer DIM on and toggle snap on

Command: **Pline**

From point: *Pick center of 1.0 diameter circle*

Continue with @.13,0 @0,-.61 @-.26,0 and @0,1

Command: **Save**

The basic front view of the coupling is now complete. Your drawing should resemble figure 14.3.

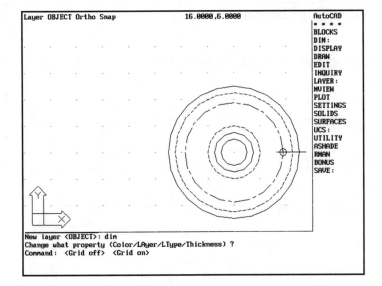

Figure 14.2:
Before arraying holes.

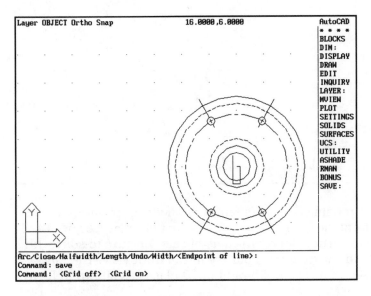

Figure 14.3:
After array, trim, and
rough keyway.

Drawing the M-COUPLE Section View

Now you will trim the keyway and draw the section view by completing the following steps:

Drafting the Section View

Command: **Trim**

Trim both ends of the polyline from within the circle and the circle from within the polyline

Command: **Array**

Rectangular or Polar array (R/P):

The upper right and lower left circles: polar; center 13,9; number of items: 2; angle to fill 30; rotate objects (see fig. 14.4)

Command: **Multiple Fillet**

Figure 14.4:
The trimmed keyway.

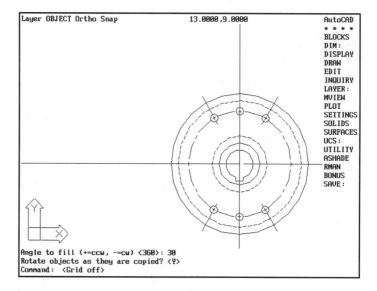

The side view can be drawn using several different methods. Orthographic lines projected over from the front view would create construction lines (see fig. 14.5) which could be trimmed to vertical lines drawn as offsets. Be sure to start with Ortho mode on and snap to the existing geometry in the front view. The Fillet command can now be used to insert .0625 radii in 10 places as shown in figure 14.6.

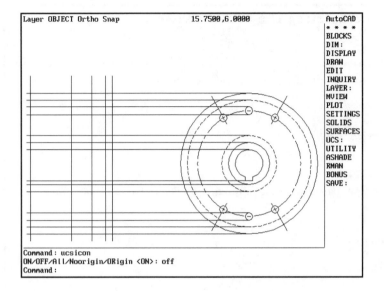

Figure 14.5:
Orthographic lines projected over from the front view.

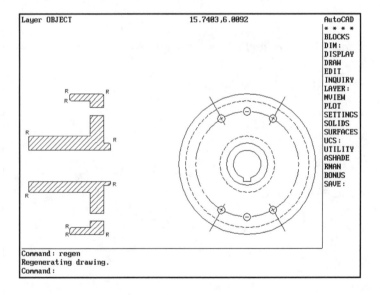

Figure 14.6:
After fillets and crosshatch.

Completing the Section View

```
Command: Hatch
Pattern (? or name/U,style):
```
Pattern ANSI31 at scale 1, rotation 0, and window in all four areas
```
Command: Chprop
Select objects:
```
Change the hatches to layer HATCH
```
Command: Line
From point:
```
Add rest of object lines to section view. Align the keyway top edge using a .Y point filter with Osnap Int.
```
Command: Erase
Select objects: Erase the two construction circles
Command: Layer
?/Make/Set/New/ON/OFF/Color/Ltype/Freeze/Thaw:
```
Set layer CL current
```
Command: Line
From point:
```
Add the center lines shown in figure 14.7. Osnap End for the diagonal.
```
Command: Layer
?/Make/Set/New/ON/OFF/Color/Ltype/Freeze/Thaw:
```
Set layer OBJECT current
```
Command: Dim
Dim: Dimscale
```
Set to 2
```
Dim: Lea
```
Use leader to draw one arrow and lines (no text)
```
Dim: Dimscale
```
Set back to 1 and > to exit
```
Command: Copy
Select objects:
```
Copy the arrow to opposite end
```
Command: Chprop
Select objects:
Change what property (Color/LAyer/LType/Thickness) ?
```
Change the vertical section line to PHANTOM linetype
```
Command: Save
```

The views are now completed and are ready for dimensioning (see fig. 14.7). If you wanted to use these parts in an assembly drawing like the one on the facing page of this chapter, you would write them to disk with the Wblock command before adding the dimensions.

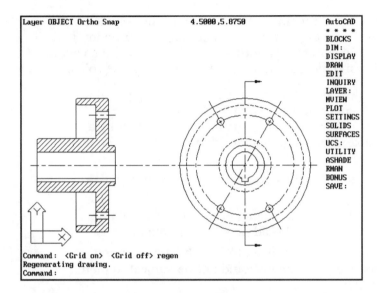

Figure 14.7:
Completed front and section views.

Following Steps and Rules for Production Dimensioning

The following information, although based on the ANSI Y14.5 geometric dimensioning and tolerancing standards, is not intended to be complete or a substitute for the standard.

Size descriptions of engineering drawings should be drawn according to acceptable GDT standards. In the United States, the two most commonly used standards are the American National Standards Institute (ANSI Y14.5M-1982) and the Department of Defense (DOD MIL-STD-8).

The ANSI Y14.5M standards were written for the metric system of measurement. Most U.S. industries using the ANSI Y14.5 adhere to the standards, but substitute the customary U.S. linear unit of decimal inches for metric units. This textbook uses decimal inch units for size descriptions.

Note Geometrics (ANSI Y14.5) do not replace plus and minus dimensioning. Instead, they act together as a joint size description to ensure that a drawing carries with it a single interpretation of production requirements.

Geometric dimensioning and tolerancing is intended to accurately define the engineering intent of a mechanical drawing by describing part function and mating part relationships. To communicate this information, drawings should conform to standard rules of dimensioning. Here are some of those rules:

- All dimensions should have a tolerance, except those specified as reference, maximum, minimum, or commercial stock size. You may apply a tolerance directly to the dimension, indicate it by a general note, or locate it in a supplementary block (title block) of a drawing.

- Dimensions for size, form, and location of features should be as complete as possible.

- Each dimension required to produce an end product should be shown. Reference dimensions should be kept to a minimum.

- Dimensions are selected and arranged to suit the function and mating relationship of a part. They should not be subject to more than one interpretation.

- The drawing should define the part without specifying manufacturing methods. Give only the diameter of a hole, for example, without indicating whether it is to be drilled, reamed, punched, and so on.

- Dimensions should be arranged to give optimum readability. Dimensions should be shown in true profile views with reference to visible (continuous) lines.

- When an overall dimension is specified, one intermediate dimension is omitted or identified as a reference dimension.

- Dimensions are usually placed outside the envelope (outline) of a view. Place dimensions within the outline of a view only if it aids in clarifying the size description.

Using Geometric Dimensioning and Tolerancing Steps

Practice some standard dimensioning steps on the two views of the M-COUPLE. The following seven steps to GDT are a practical sequence for dimensioning AutoCAD drawings according to ANSI standards.

■ Establish dimensioning datum locations

■ Locate holes and slots

■ Locate and size features

■ Give overall sizes

■ Size holes

■ Add feature control references and symbols

■ List notes

The following sections practice these dimensioning steps, building on the dimensioning techniques covered in earlier chapters. You will find dimensioning more complete and less tedious than in earlier chapters, thanks to the use of the Y14.5 symbols you made in Chapter 13.

Pan or zoom as needed throughout the rest of this chapter, using the 'Pan or 'Zoom commands transparently if you are in the middle of a command. Using object snaps liberally in dimensioning helps you keep extension line origins accurate while allowing snap to control the dimension line and text locations for consistency.

If you have the AutoCAD: Drafting and 3D Design Disk, you have a clean drawing of the coupling to use for dimensioning, called D-M-COUP. Otherwise, you need the drawing from the previous exercises.

Establishing Dimensioning Datum Locations

Dimensioning datum locations are selected on the basis of the toleranced features, geometric relationship, and the requirements of the design (design intent). Datums are defined as the theoretically perfect surface, or center lines, from which dimensions originate. These perfect surfaces or center lines are required to ensure manufacturing repeatability. Datums are identified by a datum feature symbol like the one shown in figure 14.8. Each datum is designated by a letter of the alphabet, identified by a dash on each side of the datum letter. All letters of the alphabet may be used to identify a datum except I, O, and Q because these might be mistaken for numerals.

You do not have to draw datum boxes and lines at the time you determine the datum locations, but you will do so in the following exercise. Figure 14.8 shows where the datum surfaces are located on the M-COUPLE.

These features were selected to represent the datum surfaces because of the fit requirements between this and its mating coupling.

Now add the datum lines and symbols. The B datum is associated with a vertical dimension, which you also will add.

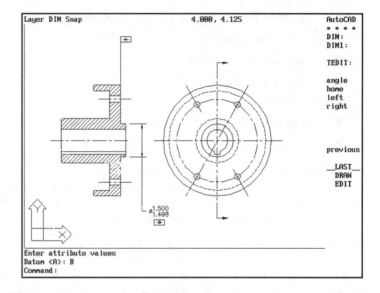

Figure 14.8:
Locating datums.

Adding Datum Lines and Symbols

 Begin a new drawing named M-COUPLE=D-M-COUP

 Continue in the previous M-COUPLE drawing.

Command: **Layer**

?/Make/SetNew/ON/OFF/Color/Ltype/Freeze/Thaw:

Set DIM current and freeze HATCH

Command: **Setvar**

Variable name or ?:

Set LUPREC to 3

Command: **Snap**

Snap spacing or ON/OFF/Aspect/Rotate/Style <1.0000>: **.0625**

Command: **Dim**

Dim: **Dimlim**

Turn on, set DIMTP to 0 and DIMTM to 0.002

Dim: Dimscale

Set the dimscale to 1.0

Dim: **Ver**

Use osnap INT, with %%c<> as text, and then Ctrl-C to exit the Dim command

Adding Datum Lines and Symbols—continued

Command: **Line**

From point:

Draw leaders shown above for the A and B datums

Command: **Stretch**

Select objects to stretch by window...

Select text only with small Crossing window

Toggle ortho off and stretch text to end of leader

Command: **Insert**

Insert the A datum where shown

Block name (or ?): **S-DAT-LL**

Insertion point: **S**

Scale factor: **.125**

Insertion point: *Drag and pick*

Rotation angle : *Press Enter*

Enter attribute values

Datum <A>: *Press Enter*

Command: *Press Enter*

INSERT *Repeat for B datum below dimension text*

Command: **Save**

The resulting dimension and datums are shown in figure 14.8.

Locating Holes and Slots

You next will locate holes and slots in relationship to each other, in chain (CONTINUE), baseline (BASELINE), or polar (ANGULAR) dimensioning form, or from a datum or an origin.

As illustrated in figure 14.9, you will locate the four holes in the front view using a basic polar angular dimension and a diameter dimension on the circular center line. These dimensions are designated as basic dimensions by the placement of basic dimension rectangles around them, using your S-BASIC block. Basic dimensions mean that a size or location is theoretically perfect. No plus or minus tolerance will be attached to these dimensions. It is impossible to repeatedly manufacture any part to absolute perfection, however, so it is necessary to control the location by adding feature control dimensions. You will add feature control dimensions later in this chapter.

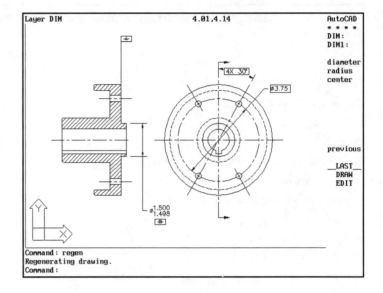

Figure 14.9:

Locating the four holes with basic dimensions.

Continue in the previous M-COUPLE drawing and follow these steps:

Locating Holes

Command: **Setvar**

Set LUPREC to 2

Command: **Dim**

Dim: **Dimlim**

Turn off

Dim: **Dimcen**

Set to 0

Dim: **Dia**

If you have Release 10, Dimension circular center line, enter <> followed by 28 spaces to force text outside. If you are using Release 11, select the proper Dimvar DIMTOFL for this dimension.

Dim: **Ang**

Dimension upper right hole

Select first line: *Pick cutting plane line*

Second line: *Pick center line protruding from hole*

Enter dimension line arc location: *Pick first point on cutting plane line, with pickbox slightly to the right of line*

Locating Holes—continued

Dimension text <30>: **4X <>**

Pad text with extra leading and trailing space to make room for box

Enter text location: *Press Enter*

Command: **Insert**

Block name (or ?): **S-BASIC**

Insertion point: **Nod**

Osnap to node of angular dimension entity (center of text)

of *Pick middle of text*

X scale factor <1> / Corner / XYZ: **.X**

Use .X point filter and Osnap Endpoint to left dimension line to set X scale factor. Use @0,.125 for Y.

Rotation angle <0>: *Press Enter*

Command: *Press Enter*

INSERT *Repeat for diameter dimension (You cannot Osnap Node because of extra spaces)*

Command: **Save**

Locating and Sizing Features

Locate features such as angles, notches (cutouts), rounds, and curves of parts from a datum or from the features' points of origin. Size and dimension the features to clearly describe their characteristics.

When dimensioning curves and rounds, hold the first extension line origin back a bit from the tangent point to give clearance. This is easier than temporarily resetting DIMEXO. Use .X or .Y point filters and object snaps if needed.

To locate and size the features of the M-COUPLE, add the dimensions shown in figure 14.10. Remember to suppress extension lines when clicking on their origins at existing datum or extension lines. To do so, toggle DIMSE1 or DIMSE2 on, or pick the origin at the dimension line's intersection with the datum or existing extension line.

Continue in the previous M-COUPLE drawing and follow these steps:

Locating and Sizing Features

Command: **Setvar**

Variable name or ?: **LUPREC**

Set LUPREC to 3

Command: **Dim**

Dim: **Ver**

Set DIMLIM on, DIMTP to 0.004, DIMTM to 0.006, and dimension the keyway height at first bubble point (see fig. 14.10). Osnap Int at the bottom

Dim: **Hor**

Set DIMTP to 0.002, DIMTM to 0.005, and dimension the keyway width at second bubble point with Int osnaps.

Dim: **Hor**

Set DIMTOL on, DIMTP to 0.005, and dimension the face setback at third bubble point

Command: **Setvar**

Variable name or ?:

Set LUPREC to 2

New value for varname <current>:

Dim: **Hor**

Set DIMTP and DIMTM to 0.02, DIMTAD on, and dimension flange depth at fourth bubble point

Dim: **Exit**

Command: **Stretch**

Select text with small Crossing window

Stretch to left of extension line

Command: **Line**

Add a short leader to the dimension at fourth bubble point

Command: **Dim**

Dim: **Hor**

Turn DIMTAD off and dimension flange face thickness at fifth bubble point

Dim: **Ver**

Dimension flange edge thickness at sixth bubble point

Dim: **Exit**

Command: **Save**

When completed with this exercise, your drawing should resemble figure 14.10.

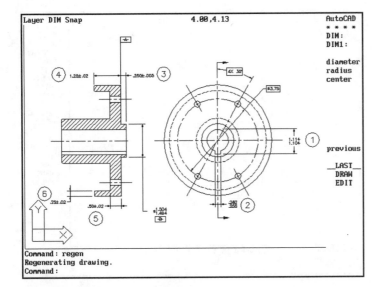

Figure 14.10:
Locating and sizing the M-COUPLE's features.

Giving Overall Sizes

Dimension overall width, height, and depth to clearly describe the size of the part. If possible, place overall sizes between views that share similar dimensions. When overall width or diameter is shared by the front and top views, for example, attach the width dimension to the view which describes the shape in true profile. When finished with this exercise, your drawing should resemble figure 14.11.

To add the overall dimensions shown in figure 14.11 to the M-COUPLE, follow these steps:

Adding Overall Dimensions

Command: **Dim**

Dim: **Hor**

Dimension depth at first bubble point

Dim: **Ver**

Dimension diameter at second bubble point with %%c<> as text

Dim: **Ver**

Set DIMTP and DIMTM to 0.04 and use %%C<> for overall diameter at third bubble point

Dim: **Hor**

Turn DIMTOL off and use (<>) for reference dimension text at fourth bubble point

---

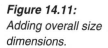

Figure 14.11:
Adding overall size
dimensions.

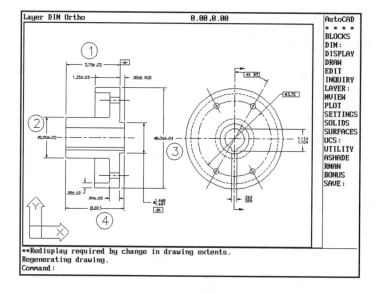

Sizing Holes

Generally, you size holes, counterbores, countersinks, and spotfaces with the
Diameter dimensioning command. Pad the text with leading or trailing spaces if
you need to force the text outside, and extend the leaders to drawing locations
that do not interfere with other dimensions. Locate the dimension text in an
uncluttered area of the drawing, keeping its relationship to the hole obvious. If
the hole is small, as with your four bolt holes, the Diameter dimensioning command omits the dimension line inside the circle. To suppress the center mark,
set DIMCEN to 0. The following exercise will add hole sizes to the drawing as
illustrated in figure 14.12.

Add the hole sizes shown in figure 14.11 to the drawing as follows:

Sizing Holes

Command: **Setvar**

Variable name or ?: **LUPREC**

Set LUPREC to 3

Command: **Dim**

Dim: **DIMCEN**

Set to 0 to turn off, and toggle ortho off

Dim: **DIMTOL**

Turn on, and set DIMTP to 0.015 and DIMTM to 0.002

Sizing Holes—continued

Dim: **Dia**

Dimension upper right hole with text 4X <> at first bubble point. (You may have to zoom in close and toggle snap off to pick it, since the pick point controls the text location.)

Dim: **DIMLIM**

Turn on, set DIMTP to 0.003, and DIMTM to 0

Dim: **Dia**

Dimension circle of keyway hole at second bubble point, and then press Ctrl-C to exit

Command: *Press F9 to toggle on snap*

Command: **Save**

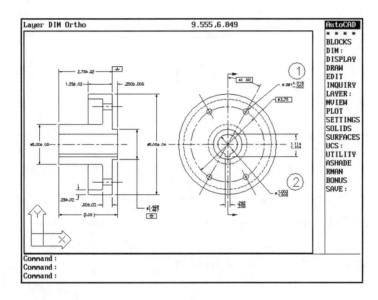

Figure 14.12:
Adding hole sizes to the coupling.

Adding Feature Control References, Symbols, and Finish Marks

Feature control references, symbols, and finish marks ensure that quality control is maintained in manufacturing. Feature control references specify each tolerance zone by a value and by its geometric relationship to the feature. As shown in figure 14.12, the form tolerance of a hole can be controlled by stating that it maintains *position* within a form tolerance zone of .002 at *maximum material condition* to datum -A- and to datum -B-.

Finish marks indicate that a surface is to be machined or finished. The finish mark should be shown only on the edge view of a finished surface. The finish is written in the form of micro inches. One micro inch equals one millionth of an inch (.000001 in.).

Use the symbols shown in figure 14.13 (which you need from Chapter 13 or from the AutoCAD: Drafting and 3D Design Disk) to add the necessary feature control references and symbols. Use the following instructions and illustration 14.14 as a guide to insert the feature control frame and other symbols at the keyway hole dimension:

Figure 14.13:
Y14.5 Symbol Library.

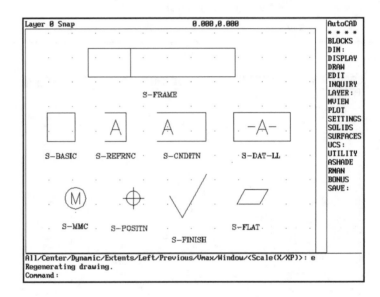

Inserting the Y14.5 Symbols

Command: **Zoom**

All/Center/Dynamic/Extents/Left/Previous/Window/<Scale(X)>:

Zoom in close on the keyway hole's dimension (bubble point 2 of fig. 14.12)

Command: **Insert**

Block name (or ?): **S-FRAME**

Insertion point: **S**

Scale factor: **.125**

Insertion point: *Insert at left (see fig. 14.14)*

Rotation angle : *Press Enter*

Enter attribute values

Enter form tolerance: **%%c.002**

> ### Inserting the Y14.5 Symbol—continueds
>
> Command: *Press Enter*
>
> INSERT *Insert S-POSITN at the same insertion point and 0.125 scale*
>
> Command: *Press Enter*
>
> INSERT *Insert S-MMC and 0.125 scale*
>
> Command: *Press Enter*
>
> INSERT *Insert S-REFRNC and 0.125 scale*
>
> Enter attribute values
>
> Datum <A>: *Press Enter*
>
> Command: *Press Enter*
>
> INSERT *Insert S-CNDITN and 0.125 scale*
>
> Command: *Press Enter*
>
> INSERT *Insert S-MMC in the condition box*
>
> Command: *Press Enter*
>
> *Insert S-FINISH symbols and finish values as illustrated in figure 14.15*
>
> Command: **Save**

The completed feature control frame reference symbol set should resemble figure 14.14.

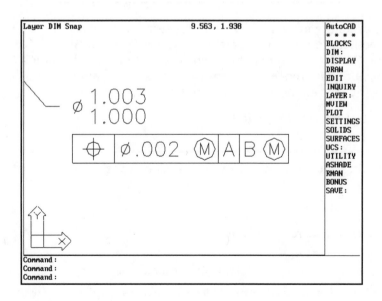

Figure 14.14:
Y14.5 feature control reference with insertion points.

Tip Your snap setting and scales worked out for the insertion points, but often they will not align so well. In such cases, use INT object snaps for the insertions (except S-MMC, which uses NEA).

Refer to figure 14.15 and your Y14.5 Symbol Library to complete the remaining references.

Figure 14.15:
All feature control symbols are added.

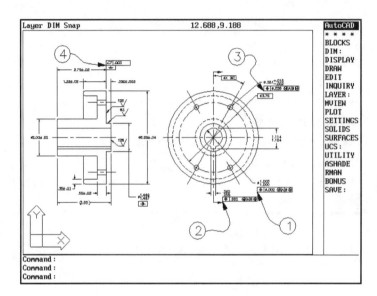

For the upper right hole and keyway width, you could insert S-FRAME (with text %%c.029 and .002 respectively), and you could then insert S-POSITN, S-REFRNC, S-CNDITN, and 2 S-MMC symbols for each. The text of the S-FRAME's Tolerance attribute is the only difference, however, so you can copy and use the Attedit command to edit the keyway hole's feature control frame reference.

Complete the feature control references, as follows:

Completing the Feature Control References

Command: **Copy**

Select objects: **W**

Window all parts of keyway hole's feature control frame

Base point or displacement/Multiple: **M**

Base point: *Pick the lower left corner of frame at first bubble point (see fig. 14.15)*

Second point of displacement: *Pick below keyway width dimension at second bubble point*

▶ **Completing the Feature Control References—continued**

Second point of displacement: *Pick below upper right hole dimension at third bubble point*

Second point of displacement: **Ctrl-C**

Command: **Attedit**

Edit attributes one at a time? <Y> *Press Enter*

Attribute tag specification <*>: *Press Enter*

Attribute value specification <*>: *Press Enter*

Select Attributes: *Pick hole, then keyway width attribute text, then press Enter*

2 attributes selected.

Value/Position/Height/Angle/Style/Layer/Color/Next <N>: **V**

Change or Replace? <R>: *Press Enter*

New attribute value: **%%c.029**

Value/Position/Height/Angle/Style/Layer/Color/Next <N>: *Press Enter*

Value/Position/Height/Angle/Style/Layer/Color/Next <N>: **V**

Change or Replace? <R>: *Press Enter*

New attribute value: **.002**

Value/Position/Height/Angle/Style/Layer/Color/Next <N>: *Press Enter*

Command: **Insert**

Block name (or ?) <S-MMC>: **S-FRAME**

With text .003 at scale 0.125 at fourth bubble point

Command: *Press Enter*

INSERT *Insert S-FLAT in the frame at the same insertion point*

Command: **Save**

Adding to the General Notes

Add general notes as illustrated in the upper right corner of figure 14.16 to convey information pertinent to the part. Use notes when part description lends itself to written, rather than graphic, form. The section profile has 10 radii, for example, all of which are 0.0625. This lends itself to specification by a general note rather than by dimensioning and tolerancing symbols.

You will use an object snap trick to align your new text and match the interline spacing of the existing general notes. You object snap the text start point to the insertion point of the previous text, then enter a blank line to space down one line and begin your real text. After entering the text, use the View command to zoom out to see the entire finished drawing.

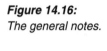

Figure 14.16:
The general notes.

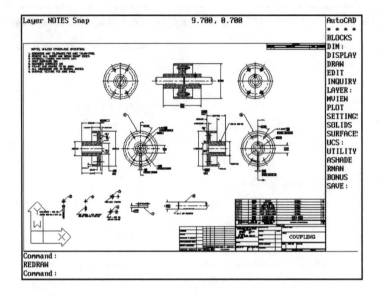

Follow these steps to add to the general notes:

Adding to the General Notes

Command: **Layer**

?/Make/Set/New/ON/OFF/Color/Ltype/Freeze/Thaw:

Thaw layer NOTES and set it current

Command: **Zoom**

All/Center/Dynamic/Extents/Left/Previous/Window/<Scale (X)>:

Zoom to upper left to see existing notes (see fig. 14.16)

Command: **Dtext**

Start point or Align/Center/Fit/Middle/Right/Style: **Ins**

of *Click on last existing line of text*

Height <<0.125>>: *Press Enter*

Rotation angle : *Press Enter*

Text: *Press Spacebar and then press Enter*

Text: **4. ALL FILLETS AND ROUNDS ARE 0.0625 UNLESS OTHERWISE NOTED.**

Text: *Press Enter*

Command: **View**

?/Delete/Restore/Save/Window: **Restore**

► Adding to the General Notes—continued

View name to restore: **BDR**

Command: **Layer**

?/Make/Set/New/ON/OFF/Color/Ltype/Freeze/Thaw:

Thaw TITL*, HATCH, and set TITL-CX current

Command: **Dtext**

Start point or Align/Center/Fit/Middle/Right/Style:

Add the 0.5 high title and any other title block text you want

Command: **End**

The finished M-COUPLE drawing should resemble figure 14.17.

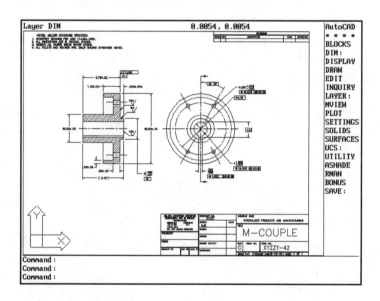

Figure 14.17:
The completed M-COUPLE drawing.

Summary

The exercises in Chapter 14 introduced you to the Multiple command and numerous useful techniques for drafting with AutoCAD. You were provided with a suggested set of steps and rules for production dimensioning. By following the sequence of the seven dimensioning steps, you increase both the dimensioning integrity of your drawings and your own efficiency and productivity.

Plan and perform your dimensioning so that the original intent of the design is maintained throughout the production process. Dimensioning should convey a single interpretation of the size and shape of a part. Misinterpretation of dimensions might result in the manufacture of unusable parts, which can cost a company time, money, and lowered productivity. You can avoid these types of problems by dimensioning your part drawings according to a standard such as ANSI Y14.5.

Chapter 15 introduces you to 3D extrusion drafting. You are shown how to specify an object's geometry in the XY plane and how to specify its thickness in the Z plane. You will find that many parts lend themselves nicely to the technique of extrusion drafting.

15

3D Extrusion Drafting

In this chapter:

- Setting up a prototype for 3D
- Using viewports for simultaneous 2D and 3D views
- Drawing with 3D extrusions
- Shading 3D images
- Solidifying extrusions
- Covering surfaces using the 3Dface command
- Setting up for plotting

Overview

This chapter shows you how to use AutoCAD's extrusion techniques and commands to create three-dimensional drawings with what has, until now, been considered to be two-dimensional entities. An example of what your drawing will look like after completing this chapter's exercises is shown in figure 15.1.

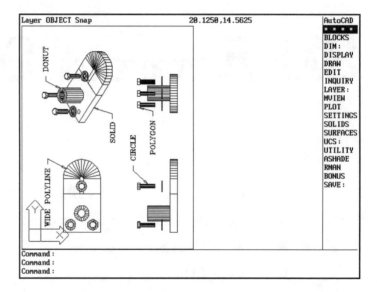

Figure 15.1:
Extruded 3D part.

Two-dimensional entities, such as circles and arcs, are constrained to a single XY plane. Extrusion (sometimes called 2-1/2D) adds thickness to these entities by extruding them in the Z axis. These entities still are essentially two-dimensional, however, because their bases and tops are constrained to the XY plane and all points in the Z axis are perpendicular to their base points.

In other words, you cannot create 3D curves or angles by extrusion. AutoCAD has more complete 3D capabilities which you will explore in later chapters, but for now ease your way into 3D with the extrusion method.

This chapter introduces the THICKNESS system variable, and the Donut, Fill, Hide, Shade, Select, Solid, Pedit, and Vpoint commands. You also will use commands introduced in earlier chapters, such as the Ucs, Vports, Chprop, Offset, and Polygon commands. All of these commands and settings can be applied to most of the familiar entity types to create extruded 3D images.

Extrusions are simple and useful in 3D drafting, enabling you to quickly produce 3D images in rough form. You draw as in 2D, but by manipulating the entity thickness and base elevation, you change 2D entities into 3D. Many parts and objects have geometric characteristics that lend themselves nicely to extrusion drafting. Parts with geometric shapes such as cylinders and rectangular solids may be extruded into realistic-looking 3D geometry. Examples of extrudable entities are shown in figure 15.2.

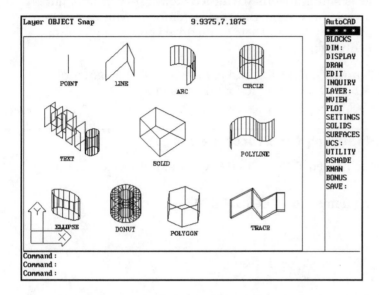

Figure 15.2:
Extruded 3D entities.

You will create a new 3D prototype drawing with viewports and viewpoints set up to show simultaneous 2D and 3D views in the following exercises. You will draw a 3D part with a one-inch thick, bullet-shaped base plate, two holes, a slot, and a hub. You then will add bolts and washers.

Note If you skipped the optional "Setting Up a Scratch View and UCS" section in Chapter 8, call up your existing PROTO-C drawing before continuing and complete it now. If you are using the AutoCAD: Drafting and 3D Design Disk, you already have the PROTO-3D drawing file. You can skip the following steps to create it, or you can go ahead and explore the exercise in a temporary drawing.

Setting Up a Prototype for 3D

You want to retain text styles and most of the settings of your prototype drawing, but the title block material is not relevant to a 3D drawing. If viewed or plotted in 3D, the title block and border would be skewed to an odd angle and would probably obstruct the drawing image. You will erase it.

Viewports, introduced earlier, enable you to view objects in 2D and 3D at the same time. You will want to simultaneously see the top (plan), front, and right side views as well as a 3D view of your drawing, so you will set up four TILEMODE off paper space viewports. Both tiled and untiled viewports enable you to display the four views simultaneously. Untiled viewports can do a little more, however, than tiled viewports. After the part is complete, you can switch to paper space and plot the four views in their untiled viewport configuration. This cannot be done in tiled viewports.

If you are not using the AutoCAD: Drafting and 3D Design Disk, begin a new drawing named PROTO-3D=PROTO-C and follow these steps:

Modifying the Prototype for 3D

 Begin a new drawing named TEMP=PROTO-C, or skip this exercise.

 Begin a new drawing named PROTO-3D=PROTO-C.

Command: **Layer**
?/Make/Set/New/ON/OFF/Color/Ltype/Freeze/Thaw: **T**
Layer name(s) to Thaw: *****
?/Make/Set/New/ON/OFF/Color/Ltype/Freeze/Thaw: *Press Enter*
Command: **Erase**
Select Objects: **C**
Choose everything with Crossing Window
Command: **Ucs**
Origin/ZAxis/3point/Entity/View/X/Y/Z/Prev/Restore/Save/Del/?/<World>: *Press Enter*
Command: **View**
?/Delete/Restore/Save/Window: **Save**
View name to save: **World**
Command: **TILEMODE**
New value for TILEMODE <1>: **0**
Entering Paperspace.
Use MVIEW to insert Modelspace viewports
Regenerating drawing.
Command: **Limits**
ON/OFF/<Lower left corner> <0.0000,0.0000>: **0,0**
Upper right corner <12.0000,9.0000>: **22,17**
Command: **Zoom**
All/Center/Dynamic/Extents/Left/Previous/Vmex/Window/<Scale(X/XP)>: **E**

▶ Modifying the Prototype for 3D—continued

Command: *Press F7 to toggle grid off*

Command: **Mview**

ON/OFF/Hideplot/Fit/2/3/4/Restore/<First Point>: **4**

Fit/<First Point>: **F**

Regenerating drawing.

You now have four identical views, as shown in figure 15.3. Notice that the limited grid area indicates that you are in the World UCS.

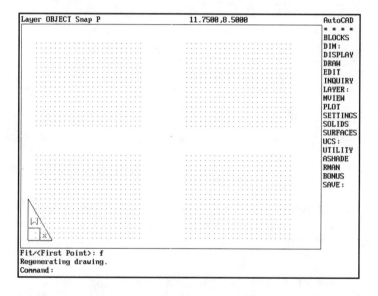

Figure 15.3:
Four views of the drawing.

Using Viewpoints for Simultaneous 2D and 3D Views

The *Vpoint* (Viewpoint) command enables you to determine the direction and angle for viewing a drawing from any point in 3D space. When you issue the command, the drawing is regenerated with a parallel projection from the 3D point that you specify. The original default is the plan view, looking from 0,0,1. The current default is the current viewpoint. You have three ways to define a viewpoint: by entering XYZ values; by supplying an angle in the XY plane and from the XY plane (see fig. 15.4); or by picking a point on the compass icon, using the axes tripod for reference.

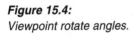

Figure 15.4:
Viewpoint rotate angles.

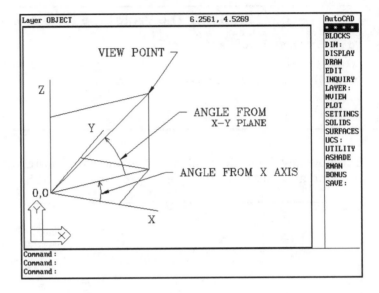

Any point you specify determines only the angle of view, not a viewing distance from the objects. The resulting view is always looking toward 0,0,0 at the *entire* drawing from the specified angle. The objects do not move; only your point of view changes.

When you specify a point's angle, the Vpoint command displays defaults relative to 1.0, such as 0.5000,-0.5000,0.6000. You will find it easier, however, to enter whole numbers, such as 5,-5,6. Either method specifies the same angle. The point for the angle also can be specified by relative points, object snaps, or point filters if desired.

If you use the interactive method of selecting a viewpoint by pressing Enter at the initial prompt, the compass and axes tripod are displayed. You then click on a point on the compass to select a good viewpoint. This method works well for some users but may be confusing to others. The compass represents a flattened *globe*, with its center being the *north pole* (straight down, plan view, viewpoint 0,0,1). The small inner circle represents the *equator* and the outer circle represents the *south pole* (straight up, 0,0,-1). When the compass and tripod are accessed, a small cross (+) represents your cursor. As you move the cursor to the desired location on the compass, the tripod will show the current orientation position dynamically. When you have the orientation you want, click on the point to exit, and AutoCAD will regenerate that viewpoint.

The following exercise provides absolute XYZ points for viewpoints in the right and bottom viewports. If you would rather use one of the other two methods (rotation or compass and tripod) feel free to do so. Any of these methods achieves the same result. The instructions set front, side, and 3D viewpoints in the lower left, lower right, and upper right viewports.

Continue in the previous PROTO-3D or TEMP drawing and follow these steps:

Setting Viewports

Command: **Mspace**

Command: *Click in the lower left viewport to make it active and type* **Vpoint**

Rotate/<View point> <0.0000,0.0000,1.0000>: **0,-1,0**

Regenerating drawing.

Command: **Zoom**

All/Center/Dynamic/Extents/Left/Previous/Vmex/Window/<Scale(X/XP)>: **1XP**

Command: *Click in the lower right viewport and press Enter*

VPOINT Rotate/<View point> <0.0000,0.0000,1.0000>: **1,0,0**

Command: **Zoom**

All/Center/Dynamic/Extents/Left/Previous/Vmex/Window/<Scale(X/XP)>: **1XP**

Command: *Click in the upper right viewport and press Enter*

VPOINT Rotate/<View point> <0.0000,0.0000,1.0000>: **5,-5,6**

Command: **Zoom**

All/Center/Dynamic/Extents/Left/Previous/Vmex/Window/<Scale(X/XP)>: **1XP**

Command: *Click in the upper left (plan) viewport and type* **Zoom**

All/Center/Dynamic/Extents/Left/Previous/Vmex/Window/<Scale(X/XP)>: **1XP**

Command: **Zoom**

Close/Join/Width/Edit vertex/Fit curve/Spline curve/Decurve/Undo/eXit <X>: **W**

First corner: **-1,-1**

Other corner: **10,6**

Command: **End**

Your display should resemble figure 15.5.

The UCS icon is replaced by a broken pencil icon in the bottom two viewports to indicate that point selection will be unpredictable at these angles. The Osnap command and point filtering would be useful in these viewports, but you will use the viewports primarily for observation.

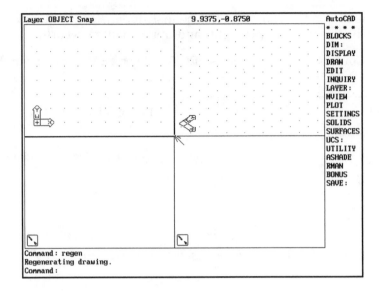

Figure 15.5:
Right viewport with 3D viewpoint.

Drawing with 3D Extrusions

This saved PROTO-3D drawing will be your basic 3D prototype. Now you can begin extruding your 3D part. Three-dimensional extrusions are an extension of 2D, so you will start out in two dimensions and extend into three. Before you draw your part in earnest, do a rough version to see how lines, arcs, and circles act in 3D extrusions.

Begin a new drawing named PART3D=PROTO-3D and follow these steps:

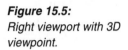

Roughing Out in 2D

Command: **Snap**

Snap spacing or ON/OFF/Aspect/Rotate/Style <1.0000> **0.25**

Command: **Line**

From point: **0,0**

To point:

Draw a 5 x 5 square with lower left corner at 0,0

Command: *Press Enter*

LINE

Draw a two-inch line from first bubble point to second bubble point

Roughing Out in 2D—continued

Command: **Arc**

Center/<Start point>: *Press Enter*

Endpoint: **@0,5**

Command: **Line**

From point: *Press Enter*

Length of line: **2**

Command: **Circle**

3P/2P/TRR/<Center point>:

Draw two 0.275 radius holes at 1,1 and 1,4

Diameter/<Radius>:

Click in the 3D viewport and zoom in closer

Command: **Zoom**

All/Center/Dynamic/Extents/Left/Previous/Vmex/Window/<Scale(X/XP)>: **All**

Click in the upper left viewport to leave it active

As you can see in figure 15.6, your part is rather flat.

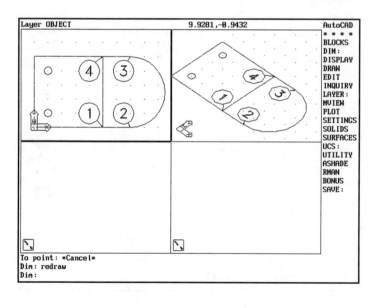

Figure 15.6:
A flat part.

Thickness Makes the Extrusion

To give the part some depth, you need to manipulate its thickness. To make your base plate one inch thick, use the THICKNESS entity property. Just as every entity has a color, linetype, and layer, it also has a thickness. The default thickness is 0, which is why your part looks flat. The Chprop command can change this.

Continue in the PART3D drawing and follow these steps:

Changing Entity Thickness

Command: **Chprop**

Select objects: *Select all entities*

Change what property (Color/LAyer/LType/Thickness) ? **T**

New thickness <0.0000>: **1**

Change what property (Color/LAyer/LType/Thickness) ? *Press Enter*

You now have four views of a wireframe 3D part drawing. The two upper viewports are shown in figure 15.7.

Figure 15.7:
3D part in wireframe.

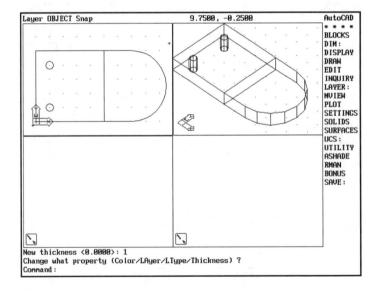

It often is more efficient to use the Chprop command after a part has been drawn, particularly when you are dealing with many different thicknesses. As with most things in AutoCAD, however, thickness can be controlled in other ways. If you use the Setvar command to set the THICKNESS system variable, all subsequent entities will be created with the new default thickness.

Elevation, Thickness, UCSs, and Construction Planes

The XY plane of the current UCS is callled the current construction plane. Thickness is always relative to the current construction plane, which has a default Z elevation of zero. When you designate a thickness, either positive or negative, it will be from the current construction plane.

 The Elev command and the ELEVATION system variable can be used to create a current construction plane with a non-zero Z relative to the current UCS. Also, the Change command changes existing entity thicknesses, and the Elev command resets the THICKNESS system variable.

If your system supports dialogue boxes, you can set the THICKNESS variable with the Ddemodes command or the `Entity Creation...` selection from the `Settings` pull-down menu.

Drawing above and below the WCS Construction Plane

To draw above or below the WCS construction plane, you need to raise the base elevation of entities. Three methods are available:

- Prior to drawing an entity, base elevation can be controlled by setting a UCS with a non-zero Z relative to the WCS. This relocates the current construction plane above or below the WCS XY plane.

- To control base elevation after an entity is created, use the Move or Copy command with a non-zero Z coordinate or offset to raise or lower the entity.

- Specify a non-zero Z coordinate for an entity's first point to establish its base elevation. This works for drawing most types of new entities, and AutoCAD reprompts with an error message when it cannot accept the Z coordinate.

Use the first of these methods with the Donut command to add an extruded hub to your part. You want to draw an extruded entity with a base at the WCS Z axis elevation of one inch, so reset the UCS origin to 0,0,1 relative to the WCS. That will establish the current elevation and construction plane one inch above the WCS.

You also will set a thickness of three inches, which will have its base at this new plane. Remember, if you are in the User Coordinate System (UCS) instead of the World Coordinate System (WCS), the W on the Y axis of the icon disappears. Similarly, the + at the icon's center means that the UCS icon is located at the existing 0,0,0 origin point instead of the lower left-hand corner of the screen.

The *Donut* (or Doughnut) command draws solid filled rings and circles. The donut entities are closed wide polylines. You give an inside diameter value (or two points) and an outside diameter (or two points). The Donut command repeats its `Center of doughnut:` prompt until you cancel or press Enter to exit.

Elevate your UCS, set THICKNESS using the Setvar command, and draw a donut as follows:

Drawing a Thick Donut in an Elevated UCS

Command: **Ucs**

Origin/ZAxis/3point/Entity/View/X/Y/Z/Prev/Restore/Save/Del/?/<World>: **Origin**

Origin point (0,0,0): **0,0,1**

Command: **Thickness**

New value for THICKNESS <0.0000>: **3**

Command: **Donut**

Inside diameter <0.5000>: **1**

Outside diameter <1.0000>: **2**

Center of doughnut: *Pick point at center of square and press Enter to exit*

At this point, use the Zoom All command in the lower left and upper right viewports to see the different views

---

Your drawing should resemble figure 15.8. Now see how it looks with the hidden lines removed.

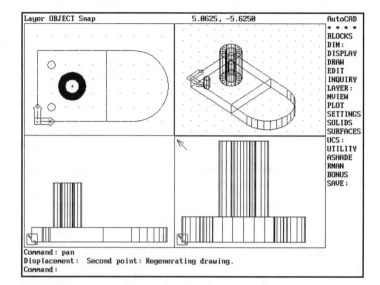

Figure 15.8:
The extruded donut.

Hidden Line Removal

Extruded drawings such as the PART3D drawing are drafted in a 3D mode called *wireframe*. In the wireframe mode, all the lines which make up the drawing are displayed. As the drawing becomes more complex, these lines may confuse, more than explain, an object's shape. To make drawings appear realistic and solid, you can use the Hide command to suppress the lines that would normally be hidden from the current viewpoint.

When you work in 3D, you see the edges of all entities. The *Hide* command calculates solid areas defined by those edges and determines what would be hidden or suppressed from your viewpoint. The Hide command only evaluates circles, polylines (assigned a width), solids, traces, 3Dfaces, meshes, and extruded edges of entities assigned a thickness as opaque surfaces. Extruded circles, polylines (assigned a width), solids, and traces also are considered solid entities, having top and bottom faces.

Only the current viewport will show the hidden lines removed. Set the 3D viewport current and use the Hide command. The *nnn* notation equals the number of vectors processed.

> ### Removing the Hidden Lines
>
> Command: **Hide**
>
> Regenerating drawing.
>
> Removing hidden lines: **nnn**

The 3D image in the upper right viewport is much clearer, as shown in figure 15.9.

Figure 15.9:
Part with hidden lines removed.

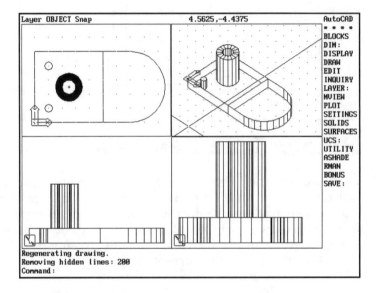

 The Hide command is used frequently in the following exercises. If you are working on a slow machine, you may want to avoid using it to save time.

Hidden Line Removal Speed

The cylindrical hub, a polyline created by the Donut command, appears quite solid, but the base created with lines and arcs is open, with no top or bottom. Before you make your part more solid, explore the Hide command further.

The Hide command takes geometrically more time as a drawing becomes more complex because it must compare every line to every other line in the drawing.

You can increase the speed of hidden line removal by displaying only the part of your drawing you wish to hide. AutoCAD hides only the entities displayed in the current viewport, so you can save time by zooming in to what you want to see.

Turning layers off does not help; they are still considered as if visible. Entities on frozen layers are ignored by the Hide command, however. A fast computer also will help.

Hiding and Plotting

Using the Hide command in the drawing editor does not affect the plot. You are informed of the current plot-hide setting at the beginning of the plot dialogue: whether hidden lines will or will not be removed. You can change the setting by responding affirmatively to the `Do you want to change anything? <N>` prompt. You will be asked if you want to `Remove hidden lines?` near the end of the plot dialogue. If you plot with hidden lines removed, AutoCAD uses the same process as it does on screen, and it takes about the same amount of time, plus the normal plot time.

Where Do Hidden Lines Go?

The Hide command does not actually remove lines from a drawing. It only suppresses their display.

You also have the option of displaying hidden lines as if on another layer. This enables you to control their color and linetype. To do so, create a layer (or layers) with a name that corresponds to the layer name of the entities to be hidden. Such layers are named with the prefix HIDDEN attached to the original layer name, such as HIDDENOBJECT for the OBJECT layer. Then when you execute the Hide command, the hidden lines that would otherwise be suppressed are temporarily drawn on the HIDDEN-prefixed layer.

This Hide option does not create new entities, just temporary lines that can be displayed or suppressed by turning the HIDDEN-prefixed layer on and off. If such a layer exists and is on during plotting, those lines will be plotted according to the settings for its layer. Although you cannot edit these temporary lines, you can use the layer settings to control the on/off, color, and linetype properties. Thus, you can view or plot drawings with hidden lines in the colors and linetypes of your choosing.

Shading 3D Images

The *Shade* command is quite similiar to the Hide command; the difference is that the Shade command enables you to produce a shaded image of your drawing. The shaded image is generated using one light source which is located directly behind the current viewpoint. This procedure simulates the AutoShade 2.0 Quick Shade command.

Shaded images can only be displayed on the screen; you cannot plot them. One way to capture a shaded image for later use, however, is with the Mslide (Make Slide) and Vslide (View Slide) commands, which are discussed in Appendix C of the instructor's guide and are defined in the AutoCAD command list appended to this book.

Shade Options

AutoCAD provides several options for the Shade command. The SHADEDGE system variable 0—3, controls these options. The following list describes these settings:

- **<0>.** Creates shaded faces with no edge highlighting. This option requires a 256-color display with the standard AutoCAD 256-color map.

- **<1>.** Creates shaded faces with edges highlighted in the display background color. Requires a 256-color display.

- **<2>.** Creates simulated hidden-line rendering. Polygons are shaded with black centers and the color of visible edges is determined by the entities color.

- **<3>.** Creates faces that are not shaded, but are drawn in their entity color. Hidden faces are not displayed, and visible edges are traced in the background color. This is the SHADEDGE default value.

Shading Reflection and Ambient Light—SHADEDIF

When the SHADEDGE system variable is set for 0 or 1, it shades the faces based on the angle the faces form with the viewpoint, and the percentage of diffuse reflection and ambient light. These light factors are set by the system variable SHADEDIF.

The default for the reflection and ambient light (SHADEDIF) is 70. This designates that 70% of the light is diffuse reflection from the light source and 30% is ambient light. The SHADEDIF variable may be set from 0—100. The higher the setting, the higher the contrast.

Shade your 3D drawing and see how it looks. Make sure your upper right viewport is current and type **Shade** at the Command: prompt. Your part now should be shaded, as shown in figure 15.10.

Note   You will use the Shade command again later in the chapter, but if you would like to use it more often, follow each Hide command with a Shade command.

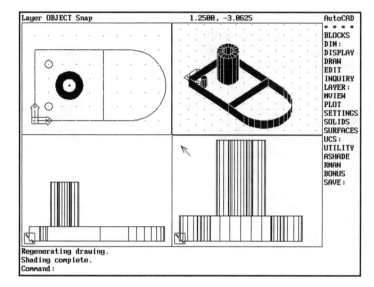

Solidifying Extrusions

As you saw earlier, lines and arcs extrude similar to fences, not to solid objects fully enclosing a 3D space. They are suitable for some images, but generally you need to use entities that will have a top and bottom enclosure when extruded. These solid entities include circles, traces, wide polylines (including those generated by the Donut command), and the solid entity itself.

The *Solid* command draws solid filled areas or extruded volumes. If the Fill command (or system variable FILLMODE) is set to *on* (1), the solid is displayed filled. These areas can be triangular or quadrilateral (four sided).

You enter points in a triangular or bow tie order to get a triangle or quadrilateral. The first two points are the endpoints of a starting edge; the next point defines the cornerpoint of a triangle; at the Fourth point: prompt, you can press Enter to close the triangle or enter a fourth point to define a quadrilateral. The command repeats the third and fourth point prompts, adding on new solids with the previous third and fourth points as new first and second points, until you press Enter at the Third point: prompt or cancel it.

The *Fill* command, an on/off toggle command, controls whether polylines, solids, and traces are displayed and plotted as filled, or if only the outline is displayed and plotted. In either case, they will hide as usual. The default setting is *on*.

If you drew a solid over the square's lines, it would be hard to select the lines to later erase them. You could erase them first, but when drawing complex 3D objects you often need construction lines to draw to. The Select command provides an easy way to erase construction lines.

The *Select* command enables you to pick entities to retain as a selection set. At the next entity selection prompt, use the Previous option to reselect the retained set. You can create the selection set with standard object selection. The Select command is often used in menu macros.

Select the square of lines, replace them with a solid, erase them, and turn off the Fill command. Then invoke the Hide command again to see the difference in solidity.

Continue in the previous PART3D drawing, click in the upper left viewport, and follow these steps:

Using Select, Solid, and Fill

Command: **Ucs**

Origin/ZAxis/3point/Entity/View/X/Y/Z/Prev/Restore/Save/Del/?/<World>: **World**

Command: **Setvar**

Variable name or ?: **Thickness**

New value for THICKNESS <3.0000>: **1**

Command: **Select**

Select objects: *Pick all four lines of the square*

Command: **Solid**

First point: *Pick lower left corner of square*

Second point: *Pick lower right corner of square*

Third point: *Pick upper left corner of square*

Fourth point: *Pick upper right corner of square*

Third point: *Press Enter*

Command: **Erase**

Using Select, Solid, and Fill—continued

```
Select objects: P

Select objects: Press Enter

Command: Fill

ON/OFF <On>: Off

Command: Regen

Command: Click on the upper right viewport to make it active and type Hide

Command: Save
```

Your drawing now should resemble figure 15.11.

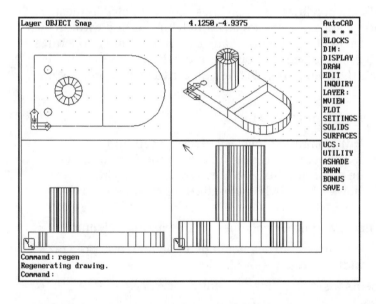

Figure 15.11:
Part with solid base.

The part looked a bit too solid before the regeneration, obscuring the donut and circles. New entities are drawn with the current Fill setting, but a regeneration is required before it affects existing entities. As you saw when you turned Fill off, the Hide command does not care if Fill is *on* or *off*.

Note A conflict results from having Fill *off* for drawing solids and polylines in 3D work and having Fill *on* for drawing wide polyline borders in 2D work. You can resolve this by plotting 2D and 3D portions separately, on the same sheet, with Fill set appropriately for each. You will explore AutoCAD's full 3D entities, which can represent solid volumes without being affected by Fill, in later chapters.

Editing Polylines with the Pedit Command

Now you need to complete the curved portion of the base, which is supposed to have a slot in it. You can salvage your existing geometry by turning it into a wide polyline.

The *Pedit* command enables you to make various changes to existing polylines, to convert lines and arcs into polylines, and to add lines, arcs, and polylines to other existing polylines.

The Pedit command edits 2D polylines, 3D polylines, and 3D polygon meshes. Editing 3D polylines and meshes is a subset of 2D polyline editing with its own set of prompts. Two basic sets of editing functions exist. The first set operates on the entire polyline; the second set lets you edit individual vertices. The default response is X to exit the command. The default for the vertex editing option is N for next vertex.

The main level Pedit options are the following:

- **Close/Open.** The Pedit command toggles between open and closed. Close adds a segment (if needed) and joins the first and last vertices to create a continuous polyline. When the polyline is open, the prompt shows `close`; when closed, the prompt shows `open`.

- **Join.** Adds arcs, lines, and other polylines to an existing polyline.

- **Width.** Sets a single width for all segments of a polyline, overriding any individual widths already stored.

- **Edit vertex.** Presents a set of options for editing vertices.

- **Fit curve.** Creates a smooth curve through the polyline vertices.

- **Spline curve.** Creates a curve using polyline vertices as control points. The curve usually will not pass through the polyline vertex points.

- **Decurve.** Undoes a Fit or Spline curve back to its original definition.

- **Undo.** Undoes the most recent editing function.

- **eXit.** The default, <X>, takes you out of Pedit and returns you to the `Command:` prompt.

To edit individual segments or vertices within a polyline, select the edit vertex option to get into the edit vertex subcommands. The first vertex of the polyline will be marked with an X, which shows you what vertex you are editing. Move the X by pressing Enter (or N, for next) until you get the vertex you want to edit.

Editing options include:

- **Next/Previous.** Gets you from one vertex to another by moving the X marker to a new current vertex. Next is the default.

- **Break.** Splits or removes segments of a polyline. The first break point is the vertex where you invoke the Break option. Use Next/ Previous to get to another break point. Go performs the break. (Using the Break command is usually more efficient than using a Pedit Break unless curve or spline fitting is involved.)

- **Insert.** Adds a vertex at a point you specify after the vertex currently marked with an X. This can be combined with the Break command to break between existing vertices.

- **Move.** Changes the location of the current vertex to a point you specify.

- **Regen.** Forces a regeneration of the polyline so you can see the effects (such as width changes) of your vertex editing.

- **Straighten.** Removes all intervening vertices from between the two vertices you select, replacing them with one straight segment. It also uses the Next/Previous and Go options.

- **Tangent.** Enables you to specify a tangent direction at each vertex to control curve fitting. The tangent is shown at the vertex with an arrow, and can be dragged or entered from the keyboard.

- **Width.** Controls the starting and ending width of an individual polyline segment.

- **eXit.** Takes you out of vertex editing and back to the main Pedit command.

You will use the Pedit command to convert the lines and arc into a polyline. Then use the Offset command to offset the polyline to the inside. The offset distance will be half of the polyline width that you will use when you widen the polyline with the Pedit command to form the slot.

 This operation is somewhat complicated. If it helps to Undo the following operation after its completion and try it again, you should do so.

Continue in the previous PART3D drawing and follow these steps:

Forming the Slot with Pedit

Command: **Pedit**

Select polyline: *Pick one of the two straight lines, in any viewport*

Entity selected is not a polyline

Do you want to turn it into one? <Y> *Press Enter*

Close/Join/Width/Edit vertex/Fit curve/Spline curve/Decurve/Undo/eXit <X>: **J**

Select objects: *Pick the arc and the other line*

2 segments added to polyline

Close/Join/Width/Edit vertex/Fit curve/Spline curve/Decurve/Undo/eXit <X>:
Press Enter

Command: **Offset**

View is not plan to UCS. Command results may not be obvious. *(You get this message if not in plan view. It will be obvious enough in this case.)*

Offset distance or Through <Through>: **1.125**

Select object to offset: *Pick any point on the polyline*

Side to offset? *Pick any point inside the polyline*

Select object to offset: *Press Enter*

Command: **Erase**

Select objects:

Erase the original polyline

Command: **Pedit**

Select polyline: **L**

Close/Join/Width/Edit vertex/Fit curve/Spline curve/Decurve/Undo/eXit <X>: **W**

Enter new width for all segments: **2.25**

Close/Join/Width/Edit vertex/Fit curve/Spline curve/Decurve/Undo/eXit <X>:
Press Enter

Command: **Hide**

Command: **Save**

The resulting polyline slot is shown in figure 15.12.

That completes the basic volume of your part. Ignore the square end of the slot, which should be round. The two round holes, represented by circles, also are inadequately shown. An extruded circle appears as a solid cylinder, not as an empty hole. And no matter what entity you use for the holes, it will not open up a hole in the face of the solid base. Better tools for dealing with these are shown in the following chapters, although they are more complex to use.

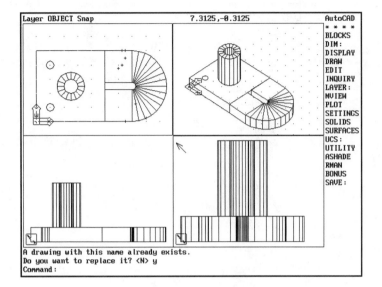

Figure 15.12:
Slot formed by polyline.

Extruding a Hexagon Bolt

Now add bolts to the part as you look more closely at extruding circles. The bolts in this exercise are drafted in a simplified style. Leaving the threads off the bolts will help keep the exercise brief. To create the extruded bolt shank with the Circle command, change the THICKNESS variable and use point filters to set the base elevation. The bolt head's base, generated by the Polygon command, is positioned by establishing a new UCS origin at the top of the shank.

Click in the upper left viewport to make it active and follow these steps:

Extruding a Bolt

Command: **Setvar**

Variable name or ?: **Thickness**

New value for THICKNESS <3.0000>: **2**

Command: **Circle**

3P/2P/TTR/<Center point>: **.XY**

of *Pick center of lower left hole*

(need Z): **3**

Diameter/<Radius>: **.25**

Extruding a Bolt—continued

```
Command: UCS
Origin/ZAxis/3point/Entity/View/X/Y/Z/Prev/Restore/Save/Del/?/<World>: Origin
Origin point <0,0,0>: Cen
of Pick top of bolt shaft extruded circle in 3D viewport
Command: Zoom
All/Center/Dynamic/Extents/Left/Previous/Vmex/Window/<Scale(X/XP)>: Zoom in on
bolt in upper right 3D viewport
Command: Setvar
Variable name or ?: Thickness
New value for THICKNESS <2.0000>: 0.34375
Command: Polygon
Number of sides: 6
Edge/<Center of polygon>: @
Inscribed in circle/Circumscribed about circle (I/C): C
Radius of circle: .375
Command: Hide
```

As you can see, the top of the bolt head is not closed, as shown in figure 15.13.

Figure 15.13:
The open bolt head.

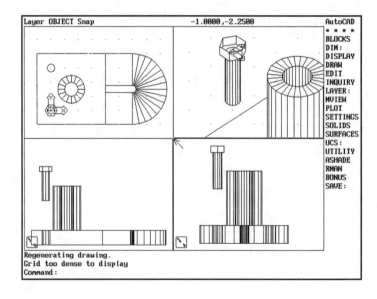

The Polygon command creates a zero-width polyline, so you could close it by drawing the polygon with half the desired radius (0.1875), using the Pedit command to make its width equal to the real desired radius (0.375). This is similar to the technique you used to create the earlier slot.

Covering Surfaces with the 3Dface Command

Another technique, shown below, is to use the 3Dface command to close the top and then copy the bolt to the other hole and slot.

The *3Dface* command defines individual three-corner or four-corner 3Dface entities, similar to solid entities or individual facets of polygon meshes.

Shapes defined by either three-corner or four-corner points are called 3Dfaces. You can define nonplanar faces by varying the Z coordinates for the corner points, but only faces with coplanar Z coordinates will hide other entities. You can construct 3dfaces with visible or invisible edges.

Unlike the Solid command, which requires that points be entered in a criss-cross fashion, 3Dface points are entered in a natural clockwise or counterclockwise fashion. To draw a three-sided face, press Enter at the `Fourth point:` prompt. For convenience in entering groups of faces, the command repeatedly prompts for additional third and fourth points after the first set of prompts. It uses the previous third and fourth points as the first and second points of each subsequent face and terminates when you press Enter at the `Third point:` prompt. When entering groups of faces, enter the points two by two, in an S pattern. Groups of faces with invisible common edges are good for defining complex surfaces.

3Dfaces may be created with visible or invisible edges. AutoCAD enables you to designate any number of edges as invisible. A 3Dface with invisible edges is called a phantom because it cannot be seen or selected. You can hide lines behind it with the Hide command, however. To define an invisible edge, enter an I before clicking on the first vertex of that edge.

Sometimes you need to display invisible edges to determine where the 3Dfaces are positioned or to edit them. The SPLFRAME variable controls the display of invisible edges. When SPLFRAME is set to zero (the default), invisible edges are not displayed. When set to a non-zero value such as 1, all invisible edges are displayed.

Close the bolt head with the 3Dface command. Make sure that the top-right viewport is current and follow these steps using figure 15.14 as a guide:

Closing the Bolt Head with 3DFace

```
Command: Zoom
All/Center/Dynamic/Extents/Left/Previous/Vmex/Window/<Scale(X/XP)>:
```
Zoom in on bolt head
```
Command: Osnap
Object snap modes: INT
Command: 3Dface
First point: Pick first point
Second point: Pick second point
Third point: Press I and pick third point
Fourth point: Pick fourth point
Third point: Pick fifth point
Fourth point: Pick sixth point
Third point: Press Enter
Command: Setvar
Variable name or ?: SPLFRAME
New value for SPLFRAME <0>: 1
Command: Regen
Command: Undo
Auto/Back/Control/End/Group/Mark/<number>: 2
REGEN SETVAR Regenerating drawing.
Command: Osnap
Object snap modes: NON
```

Your drawing should resemble figure 15.15 after you are finished with this exercise.

Now create one washer with the Donut command, and then copy both the bolt and washer to the other hole and slot as follows:

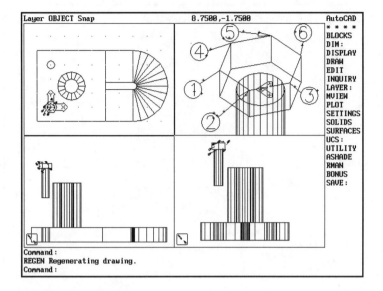

Figure 15.14:
*Pick points for 3Dface
with invisible edges.*

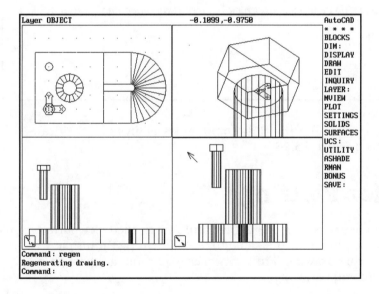

Figure 15.15:
*3Dfaces with SPLFRAME
on.*

Creating the Washer and Copying

```
Command: Zoom
All/Center/Dynamic/Extents/Left/Previous/Vmex/Window/<Scale(X/XP>: P
Command: Ucs
Origin/ZAxis/3point/Entity/View/X/Y/Z/Prev/Restore/Save/Del/?/<World>: Origin
Origin point <0,0,0>: 0,0,-3
Command: Setvar
Variable name or ?: Thickness
New value for THICKNESS <.34375>: .109
Command: Donut
```
Make a washer at lastpoint @
```
Inside diameter <0.5000>: .562
Outside diameter <1.0000>: 1.375
Command: Copy
Select objects: Copy the bolt and washer to the other hole and slot
```
Select entities in front, side, or 3D viewports and pick base and displacement points in plan view
```
Command: Hide
Command: Shade
Command: Save
```

Your 3D part is now complete. After the Hide command was invoked, the drawing should have resembled figure 15.16.

Setting Up for Plotting

One advantage of using paper space mode is that multiple untiled viewports (and their contents) can be plotted at the same time. You can plot multiple views simultaneously for this drawing. First, however, you must go through a few more steps to prepare your drawing.

Checking Scale and Alignment of Views

You can control the display of each viewport independently. As a result, different magnification (zoom) factors can be set in each viewport.

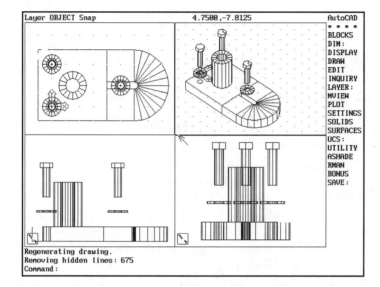

Figure 15.16:
Completed part with
hidden lines removed.

At the beginning of the exercise, you set the zoom position of the plan viewport to Left -1,-1 and the magnification to 1XP. This set your screen position for orthographic alignment and scale to 1 times the paper space scale (which is full) or full scale.

If your views are not properly aligned or scaled, use the Zoom command with Left option to set the window corner at -2,-2,-3 and the size to 1XP. The orthographic views are scaled 1"=1" relative to the paper space scaler.

Setting Up ANSI Drawing Sheets

AutoCAD provides an AutoLISP routine for setting up the drawing screen and various parameters. The routine, Mvsetup, may be used with TILEMODE *on* or *off*. You have used this productive routine in TILEMODE *on* to set up various unit types, drawing scales, and drawing sheet sizes, in previous chapters. With TILEMODE *off*, the Mvsetup routine provides an even richer supply of drafting tools.

Using Mvsetup with TILEMODE Off

When TILEMODE is *off*, Release 11's Mvsetup routine can be used to insert one of a predefined group of ANSI titleblocks sizes A–E and create a set of viewports entities within the title block. The routine also enables you to specify a global scale factor. This scale factor is defined as a ratio between the scale of the title block in paper space and the drawing scale in model space.

When you invoke the Mvsetup routine with TILEMODE *off*, the following options are presented:

■ **Align.** Enables you to pan the view in a viewport so that it aligns with a designated base point in another viewport.

■ **Create viewports.** Enables you to create the following Mview viewport layout options: Std. Engineering sets up a four-viewport configuration similiar to the one you set up in this exercise (top view, front view, right side view, and 3D view).

■ **Scale viewports.** Sets the scale for selected viewports for a ratio between the scale of the border in paper space and the scale of the drawing entities displayed in the selected viewports.

■ **Title block.** Provides the following options: `Delete objects/ Origin/Undo/<Insert title block>:`. The Insert title block option creates the following paper/output size viewport entities: None, ANSI-V Size, ANSI-A Size, ANSI-B Size, ANSI-C Size, ANSI-D Size, ANSI-E Size, and Arch/Engineering (24x36).

Use the Mvsetup routine to create a D-Size ANSI drawing sheet and title block for your PART3D drawing in paper space. Some of the following prompts and screen messages may not appear depending on your program's settings.

Using the MVSETUP Routine

```
Command: Pspace
Command: Layer
?/Make/Set/News/ON/OFF/Color/Ltype/Freeze/Thaw: ON
Layer name(s) to turn On: TITL-OT
?/Make/Set/News/ON/OFF/Color/Ltype/Freeze/Thaw: Press Enter
Command: Click on BONUS, next, and MVSETUP on screen menu
Align viewports/Create viewports/Scale viewports/Title block/Undo: T
Delete objects/Origin/Undo/<Insert title block>: Press Enter
Delete current paperspace setup? <N>: Press Enter
Specify a new origin point for this sheet? <N>: Press Enter
Available paper/output sizes:
0: None
1: ANSI-V Size
2: ANSI-A Size
```

Using the MVSETUP Routine—continued

```
3: ANSI-B Size

4: ANSI-C Size

5: ANSI-D Size

6: ANSI-E Size

7: Arch/Engineering (24 x 36)

Add/Delete/Redisplay/<Number of entry to load>: 5

Create a drawing named ansi-d.dwg? <Y>: N

Align viewports/Create viewports/Scale viewports/Title block/Undo: Press Enter

Available Metaview viewport layout options:

0: None

1: Single

2: Std. Engineering

3: Array of Viewports

Add/Delete/Redisplay/<Number of entry to load>: 0
```
Press F1 to toggle back to the graphics screen.

Now move the four original viewports to a good location within the new sheet, as follows:

Moving the Four Viewports

```
Command: Move

Select objects: Pick four original viewport frames

Select objects: Press Enter

Base point of displacement: 0,0

Second point of displacement: 2,2.5

Command: Zoom

All/Center/Dynamic/Extents/Left/Previous/Vmex/Window/<Scale(X/XP)>: All
```

Your drawing now should display the new D-Size border and title block, as shown in figure 15.17.

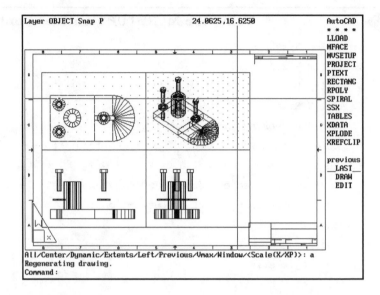

Figure 15.17:
The D-size title block is created.

The borders and title blocks used in the Mvsetup routine are created through an AutoLISP routine if designated border drawings do not exist. If you prefer to have the routine insert one of your own custom sheets you must name the sheet(s) ANSI-A.DWG, ANSI-B.DWG, and so on. These drawings must be placed in a directory specified by the ACADPREFIX variable.

Note Make sure that the directory specified by the ACADPREFIX variable is in the AutoCAD file path. The variables ACAD and ACADCFG can be set to include the ACADPREFIX directory.

Freezing Viewport Frames for Plotting

Because paper space viewport frames are defined as entities, you can change their properties to control them as needed. In this case, you want to freeze the four original viewport frames as follows:

Freezing Pspace Viewport Frames

Command: **Chprop**

Select objects: *Pick the four frames*

4 selected, 4 found.

Select objects: *Press Enter*

Change what property (Color/LAyer/LType/Thickness) ? **LA**

New layer <0>: **Const**

Change what property (Color/LAyer/LType/Thickness) ? *Press Enter*

Command: **Layer**

?/Make/Set/New/ON/OFF/Color/Ltype/Freeze/Thaw: **F**

Layer name(s) to Freeze: **CONST**

Your drawing should resemble figure 15.18 and is now ready to plot from paper space.

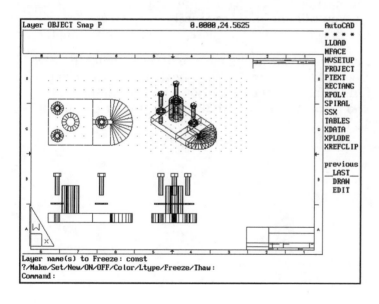

Figure 15.18:
Ready to plot from paper space.

Summary

In this chapter, you set up and used a 3D prototype drawing which you will use again in Chapter 16. As you developed PROTO-3D, you set AutoCAD's viewports, UCSs, and viewpoints so that you could simultaneously view your part drawing in two dimensions and in three. You also were introduced to AutoCAD's tools for extrusion drafting which, although limited to 2-1/2 dimensions, provide an easy method for roughing out many 3D parts.

The PART3D entities were displayed in wireframe mode when first extruded. Three-dimensional wireframe drawings are useful when describing relatively simple parts, but as a part's 3D geometry becomes complex, hidden lines should be removed to display a more realistic-looking 3D image. Although it might be time-consuming to process hidden lines, you can control layers and views to efficiently hide selected parts of the drawing.

Some entities lend themselves quite well to extrusion drafting, appearing in a solid-looking form. Circles, traces, and wide polylines, for example, show a top and a bottom when they are extruded. These 2-1/2 dimension extrusions are useful in a drafter's tool kit. You will find that they nicely complement AutoCAD's full 3D capabilities, which you will explore in the following chapter.

Chapter 16 shows you how to use 3D surfacing tools to develop comprehensive 3D drawings in the User Coordinate System (UCS). You will be guided through the development of a part in surface 3D and then shown how to capture and display 2D orthographic and auxiliary views, and 3D perspective or parallel projection views, from your 3D drawings.

16

3D WIREFRAME AND MESH MODELING

In this chapter:

- The User Coordinate System
- Drawing the construction envelope
- 2D and 3D polylines
- 3D polygon mesh surfaces
- Surfaces of revolution—Revsurf
- Tabulated surfaces—Tabsurf
- Polygon faces—Pface

Overview

Three-dimensional drafting often is the most effective way to describe a shape. Isometric, oblique, orthographic, and perspective drawings are often used to communicate designs to individuals with little or no technical drafting experience. Traditionally, 3D drafting has been an addition to the standard engineering drawings necessary for manufacturing. AutoCAD, however, enables you to reverse the process and efficiently draft parts in three dimensions, and then capture engineering drawing views from the 3D database. In this chapter, you will create a 3D surface model, as illustrated by figure 16.1, that will be used to create Chapter 17's multi-view drawing.

Figure 16.1:
Four views of the angle support.

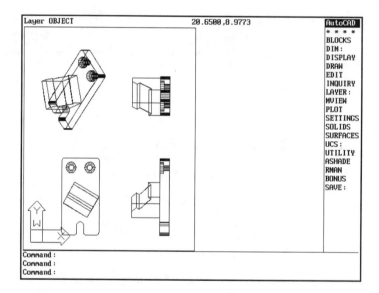

AutoCAD's 3D goes well beyond 2-1/2D extrusions by using two main elements: a group of commands that creates full 3D entities, and manipulation of the User Coordinate System (UCS). The UCS offers an efficient way to develop geometry in 3D space. Unlike the traditional, fixed World Coordinate System (WCS), the UCS is specifically designed to be re-oriented to enable drafting in any position or angle. This enables so-called 2D (or 2-1/2D) entities to be placed anywhere in space.

Full 3D means that any of an entity's coordinate points can exist anywhere in space. Points, lines, and 3D polylines are full 3D entities. Three-dimensional polylines are just like 2D polylines, except that they cannot have width or arc segments. They cannot be curve fit, but they can be spline fit. Points, lines, and

3D polylines are useful for construction lines and wireframe drawings, but surfaces are needed to represent real objects.

The concept behind surface modeling is to create drawings of virtually any shape which, when viewed with hidden lines removed, appear realistic. This chapter introduces you to the useful surface modeling techniques available through AutoCAD's 3D surface entities: the 3Dmesh and 3Dface.

The 3Dface, introduced in the previous chapter, is simply a three-corner or four-corner surface created by the 3Dface command. Meshes are more complex. A mesh resembles a face, a single surface with three or four corner points, but it actually is a special form of polyline, called a *3D polygon mesh*. A mesh is an array of faces with up to 256x256 vertices. Using a mesh enables you to define multi-faceted surfaces — such as tabulated surfaces, ruled surfaces, surfaces of revolution, and edge-defined surfaces — as single entities.

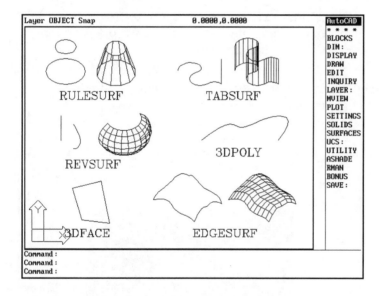

Figure 16.2:
Typical 3D surfaces and entities.

AutoCAD's 3D polygon mesh tools can surface model virtually any part. In this chapter, you will draw a realistic 3D image of an angle support, using lines and polylines to rough it out and the Rulesurf, Tabsurf, Revsurf, and 3Dface commands to surface it.

The User Coordinate System

The key to getting around in 3D is the UCS. You can set the UCS to an unlimited number of positions or orientations, each of which can be saved and restored.

You have used the UCS only as a means of shifting your coordinate system for ease of coordinate entry in 2D so far. The current UCS position determines where points are entered. You can relocate the UCS more dramatically than you have so far, shifting its origin and rotating its axes by any distance or angle about any of the X, Y, or Z axes. The UCS may be positioned in one of several ways, such as with the Origin, 3point, and X,Y,Z rotation options. Use whichever method you prefer. Often, 3point is used with object snap for accurate positioning.

You can enter points within the UCS as if you were working in the WCS Cartesian coordinate system, creating 3D drawings from 2D entities at any point or angle in space. You can do this because 2D entities are created in the current construction plane, which is the XY plane of the current UCS. Although full 3D entities and commands can be used regardless of the current UCS, setting specific UCSs can make coordinate entry seem easier and more logical.

The Settings pull-down menu includes two items to simplify setting UCSs. You can select UCS Options... to view an icon menu of preset UCS orientations or UCS Control... to activate the Dducs dialogue box.

The *Dducs* (Dynamic Dialogue User Coordinate System) command displays dialogue boxes that control the User Coordinate System. You also can use it to create or rename a UCS.

Figure 16.3:
UCS Control dialogue box.

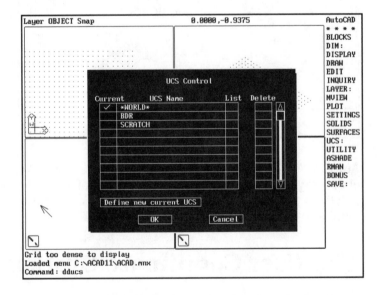

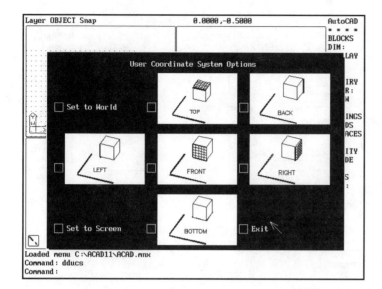

Figure 16.4:
UCS Options icon menu.

The UCS icon is an on-screen indicator of your current UCS orientation. The UCS icon can be set to move to the new origin or it can remain in the lower left corner of the viewport. It is better to have the UCS icon located at the origin in most 3D drafting.

The plus sign (+) on the UCS icon, as shown in figure 16.5, means that the icon is located at the origin of the current UCS. You can set it to display at the origin by setting the Ucsicon command, but when that would cause it to fall off the screen, it omits the plus sign and shifts to the screen's lower left corner.

You might not be sure from which angle you are viewing your drawing at times. When you view your drawing from above (positive Z), the UCS icon displays a box at its base. When you view your drawing from below (negative Z), the box is removed.

As you move the UCS to establish new drafting planes, you will need to develop an efficient method for managing your 3D drawings. As you are introduced to 3D construction drafting techniques, you will learn how to manipulate, save, and restore UCSs.

3D Techniques for the Angle Support

Three primary techniques will be used to draw the angle support shown in figure 16.1:

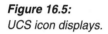

Figure 16.5:
UCS icon displays.

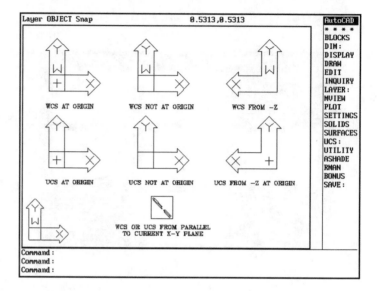

1. Rough it out by drawing a temporary 3D construction envelope on the CONST layer. The construction envelope is the rough perimeter form of the part. It provides points and lines to orient and snap to as you draw the detailed part.

2. Use UCSs liberally, reorienting our current UCS (and its construction plane) to various points, lines, and planes of the construction envelope.

3. Draw portions of the part in the SCRATCH UCS. Although the angle support is not a complex part, 3D images often get so dense you cannot see points to object snap to. By drawing simple portions in a SCRATCH UCS and then moving them into their real locations in the WCS, you sidestep this complexity. You will find this building block drafting technique increasingly useful as you continue with the 3D modeling and design techniques.

Drawing the Construction Envelope

The purpose of construction drafting is to develop a framework to guide you in drawing the part and in setting UCS positions. Using the uncluttered envelope framework to position UCSs is easier than trying to position them on the geometry of the developing part, and more flexible than trying to set up and recall named UCSs for every possible case encountered.

You need two envelopes, one for the angle base and one for the angle bracket. You will draw the envelopes with lines rather than with extruded entities so you can avoid obscuring other entities to come and keep your object snaps straight-forward. Lines also provide the right type of entities to guide some of the 3D commands you will use later.

If you have the AutoCAD: Drafting and 3D Design Disk, you have the completed envelope (see fig. 16.6) in a drawing named ENVELOPE.DWG. If you are comfortable using the Line, Copy, UCS, Rotate, and Vpoint commands in 3D to set up viewports, and doing object snapping in 3D, you can skip to the section on the Tabsurf command and drafting with polylines, where you begin developing the angle base profile.

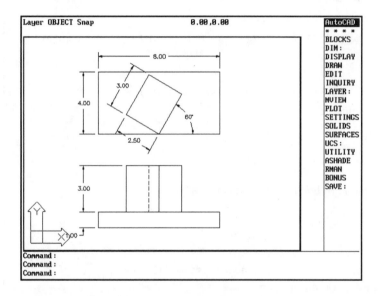

Figure 16.6:
Dimensioned construction envelope.

Begin the ANGLE drawing with the PROTO-3D prototype from Chapter 15 or from the AutoCAD: Drafting and 3D Design Disk. You will set the current layer to CONST and draw a 4"x8" rectangle for the part's base. After you draw the rectangle, copy it one inch up, in the positive Z axis direction, to make the top. Then you draw lines connecting the two rectangles to form the sides. To locate the starting points and endpoints of these lines, set a running Osnap command Intersect.

Begin a new drawing named ANGLE=PROTO-3D. Click in the upper left (plan) viewport to make it active and follow these steps:

Drawing the Envelope with 3D Lines

Command: **Layer**

?/Make/Set/New/ON/OFF/Color/Ltype/Freeze/Thaw:

Set CONST current

Command: **Snap**

Snap spacing or ON/OFF/Aspect/Rotate/Style <1.0000>: **0.25**

Command: **Line**

From point: *Draw a 4"x8" rectangle with lower left corner at 3,3,0*

Command: **Copy**

Select objects: *Select all four lines*

<Base point or displacement>/Multiple: **0,0,1**

Second point of displacement: *Press Enter, then click in the upper right (3D) viewport to make it active*

Command: **Zoom**

All/Center/Dynamic/Extents/Left/Previous/Window/<Scale (X)>: **W**

Zoom in close in upper right viewport

Command: **Osnap**

Object snap modes: **END**

Command: **Line**

From point: *Draw a vertical line at each of the four corners*

Command: **Osnap**

Object snap modes: **NON**

Command: **Zoom**

All/Center/Dynamic/Extents/Left/Previous/Window/<Scale (X)>: **W**

Zoom each of the viewports to match figure 16.7

Command: **Vports**

Save/Restore/Delete/Join/SIngle/?/2/<3>/4: **Save**

Save to name 3D

Command: **UCS**

Origin/ZAxis/3point/Entity/View/X/Y/Z/Prev/Restore/Save/Del/?/<World>: **Origin**

Set Origin to lower left corner of base (3,3,0)

You probably noticed that the last four lines you drew were vertical. In Release 10 and later, line entities are full 3D, with their endpoints anywhere in space, so the former 3Dline command is no longer needed. Lines and coordinates default to the current UCS Z elevation of zero, but you used the Osnap command to force the upper endpoints to the copied rectangle.

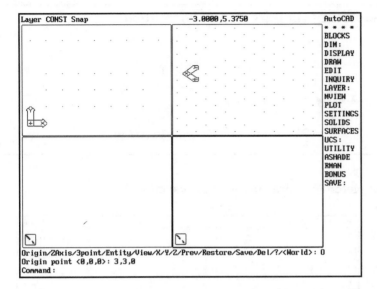

Next, draw a 2.5"x3" rectangle to represent the overall form of the angle bracket which sits on top of the base. You will draw this rectangle in its finished location by setting an elevated and skewed UCS, but you also could draw the rectangle in the current UCS and move and rotate it into position. After you draw the rectangle, copy it three inches up and draw lines connecting the two rectangles as before.

First, however, you must set the UCS in two steps: offsetting the origin and rotating it about the Z axis as follows:

Completing the Envelope

Command: **UCS**

Origin/ZAxis/3point/Entity/View/X/Y/Z/Prev/Restore/Save/Del/?/<World>: **Origin**

Set the Origin to 4,0,1

Command: *Press Enter*

UCS

Origin/ZAxis/3point/Entity/View/X/Y/Z/Prev/Restore/Save/Del/?/<World>: **Z**

Rotation angle about Z axis <0.0>: **60**

Command: Line

From point: *Draw a 2.5"x3" rectangle with lower left corner at the UCS origin*

Command: **Copy**

Select objects: *Copy it up with displacement 0,0,3*

> ### Completing the Envelope—continued
>
> Command: **Osnap**
>
> Object snap modes: **INT**
>
> Command: **Line**
>
> From point: *Draw the four verticals in the 3D viewport*
>
> Command: **Osnap**
>
> Object snap modes: **NON**

The envelope is now complete. Your drawing should resemble figure 16.8.

Figure 16.8:
Completed base and top envelope.

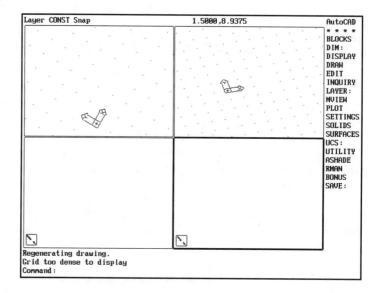

Now move your construction framework to the SCRATCH UCS, where you will do most of the work. This technique keeps the current "real" area of the drawing clear for assembling the parts as you create them.

2D and 3D Polylines

You draw the profile of the base with AutoCAD's Pline and Pedit commands.

Polyline entities can be 2D or 3D, or even 3D meshes, created by the Pline, 3Dpoly, and mesh family of commands. All are polyline entities if you list them. The primary difference between the 2D and 3D polylines is that 3D polylines consist only of zero-width straight line segments anywhere in space, while 2D polylines are a connected sequence of line and arc segments with any widths, but restricted to a single plane. Because all of their segments can be treated and manipulated as one entity, both types are commonly used to define profiles from which to generate surface meshes. The following exercise uses 2D polylines to generate the base profile, from which a surface is projected with the Tabsurf command.

Developing the Angle Base Profile

You draw the inside radius for the base's notch with the Arc mode of the Pline command, which enables you to generate a single continuous polyline made up of straight and arc segments. In Arc mode, you can drag a polyline arc by its endpoint. To continue the polyline with straight segments, use the Line option. Arc mode always draws each arc tangent to the previous arc or line segment, unless you specify a different starting direction with the Direction option. Here are the Arc mode options:

Arc/Close/Halfwidth/Length/Undo/Width/<Endpoint of line>:

After you draw the polyline, you can use the Fillet command to radius all of the outside corners in one operation. You can draft the base in either of the top viewports, although you will find it easier to draw in the upper left 2D plan viewport.

Continue in the previous ANGLE drawing, or begin a new drawing named ANGLE=ENVELOPE, and follow these steps:

Drawing the Angle Base Profile

  Continue in the previous ANGLE drawing or begin a new drawing named ANGLE=ENVELOPE.

  Continue in the previous ANGLE drawing.

Command: **Layer**

?/Make/Set/New/ON/OFF/Color/Ltype/Freeze/Thaw: **Set**

Set current layer to OBJECT

Command: **UCS**

Origin/ZAxis/3point/Entity/View/X/Y/Z/Prev/Restore/Save/Del/?/<World>: **World**

Command: **Snap**

Snap spacing or ON/OFF/Aspect/Rotate/Style/ <1.0000>: **0.125**

Command: **Pline**

From point: *Pick lower left corner of base at first bubble point (see fig. 16.9)*

► **Drawing the Angle Base Profile—continued**

```
Current line-width is 0.00
```
Arc/Close/Halfwidth/Length/Undo/Width/<Endpoint of line>: *Polar point @1.625<90*

Arc/Close/Halfwidth/Length/Undo/Width/<Endpoint of line>: *Polar point @1<0 at second bubble point*

Arc/Close/Halfwidth/Length/Undo/Width/<Endpoint of line>: **A**

Angle/CEnter/CLose/Direction/Halfwidth/Line/Radius/Second pt/Undo/Width/<Endpoint of arc>: *Drag and pick polar point @0.75<90 at third bubble point*

Angle/CEnter/CLose/Direction/Halfwidth/Line/Radius/Second pt/Undo/Width/<Endpoint of arc>: **L**

Angle/CEnter/CLose/Direction/Halfwidth/Line/Radius/Second pt/Undo/Width/<Endpoint of arc>: *Finish tracing the base and close the last segment*

Command: **Fillet**

Polyline/Radius/<Select two objects>: **R**

Enter fillet radius <0.000> **.25**

Command: *Press Enter*

FILLET Polyline/Radius/<Select two objects>: **P**

Select 2D polyline: *Pick base profile*

Command: **Save**

Your drawing should resemble figure 16.10.

All of the angled vertices of the base profile were filleted in one operation. To fillet individual corners, select two segments instead of using the Polyline option, but they both must be segments of the same polyline.

3D Polygon Mesh Surfaces

Now that you have a profile curve, you can generate a surface. AutoCAD's primary surface entity is the 3D polygon mesh. Mesh vertices are designated by:

- M (column) vertices
- N (row) vertices

You can create a mesh using the 3Dmesh command by inputting each vertex coordinate by row and column. That gets tedious, however, for all but the simplest surfaces.

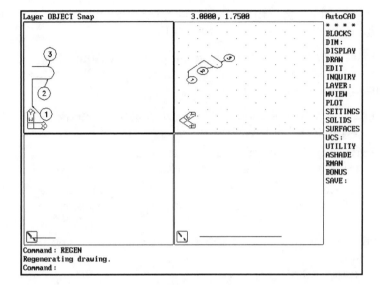

Figure 16.9:
Drawing the polyline arc notch.

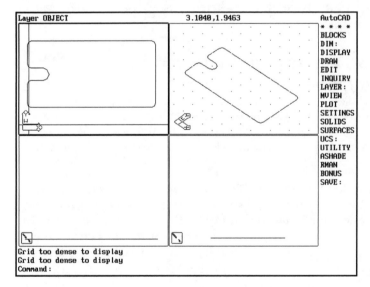

Figure 16.10:
The completed polyline base.

Command

The *3Dmesh* command creates three-dimensional polygon meshes. Give the mesh size and specify the vertices as 2D or 3D points, starting with vertex (0,0) and ending with vertex (M,N). Three-dimensional meshes act like 3Dfaces fused together, and they are treated as one entity. The meshes are created open. Close the mesh by editing it with the Pedit command.

The Pedit command can be used to close or open meshes, move vertices, and to smooth meshes in a manner similar to spline or curve fitting.

The 3Dmesh command is intended primarily for automated use by AutoLISP programs. For manual use, AutoCAD has concentrated the power of 3D meshes into five efficient 3D polygon mesh commands. These are:

- **Pface (Polygon Face).** Constructs a general polygon mesh, defined by vertices and faces composed of those vertices.

- **Rulesurf (Ruled Surfaces).** Generates a ruled surface between two defining curves such as polylines, arcs, or circles.

- **Tabsurf (Tabulated Surfaces).** Projects a defining curve at some distance and angle in space. The top and bottom remain open and parallel.

- **Revsurf (Revolution Surface).** Revolves a defining curve about some axis. The Revsurf command is most often used to create holes, cylinders, cones, domes, and spheres.

- **Edgesurf (Edge-Defined Coons Surface Patch).** Surfaces an area bounded by four adjoining edges.

Controlling Mesh Density (Surface Tabulation)—Surftab

All of these surfacing commands operate in the same general manner, using existing entities to define their edges, profiles, axes, and directions. The surfaces are generated between, or project from, existing entities, leaving them unchanged.

The mesh density is controlled by the SURFTAB1 and SURFTAB2 system variables. The higher the SURFTAB setting, the denser and more accurate the mesh, and the longer it takes to regenerate and hide. If you are not concerned about generating extremely realistic 3D polygon meshes, or if you want to keep your workstation's performance as fast as possible, keep the SURFTAB values reasonably small.

SURFTAB1 sets the distance for the development of "tabulation" lines in the direction of revolution. SURFTAB2 sets the distance for the development of "tabulation" lines if the selected path curve is a line, arc, circle, or spline-fit polyline.

Tabulated Surfaces—Tabsurf

Tabulated surfaces generate a 3D polygon mesh that is defined by a path curve and a direction vector. The path curve (also known as the *directrix*) can be a selected line, arc, circle, 2D polyline, or 3D polyline. The direction vector (also known as the *generatrix*) can be a selected line, 2D polyline, or 3D polyline. The direction vector defines the direction and length along which the path curve is projected. If a polyline is selected as the direction vector, it is interpreted as if it was a single segment from its first to its last vertex.

 The *Tabsurf* command generates a 3D polygon mesh by projecting an entity (path curve) through space along a direction vector.

Tabulated surfaces have no intermediate vertices along the direction vector. One half of the mesh vertices are placed along the curve path and the other half are offset along parallel curve paths the length and direction of the direction vector. In other words, there are two vertices in the M direction, along the direction vector, by N vertices along the path curve. The system variable SURFTAB1 defines the 3D mesh density of the tabulated surface in the N direction. (Note that SURFTAB1 and SURFTAB2 do not correspond to M and N as you might assume.) The tabulation lines are omitted in straight segments, so the SURFTAB1 setting only affects curves.

Extending the Base with Tabsurf

Leave SURFTAB1 set to 6, its default, and select the polyline profile as your path curve. For the direction vector, use one of the corner lines of the envelope. Select the corner line near its lower end because it is interpreted from the end-point nearest its pick point to the opposite endpoint.

Continue in the previous ANGLE drawing and generate the base as follows:

Generating the Base with Tabsurf

Command: **Tabsurf**

Select path curve: *Pick the polyline base*

Select direction vector: *Pick one of the one-inch verticals, near its bottom*

The result (see fig. 16.11) resembles an extruded entity, with parallel top and bottom, but the "extrusion" need not be perpendicular to the base entity.

After the tabulated surface has been generated, review it. If the polygon mesh needs fewer or more tabulations, you can erase (or undo) the tabulated surface, reset the variable SURFTAB1, and try it again.

Figure 16.11:
Envelope with base after invoking the Tabsurf command.

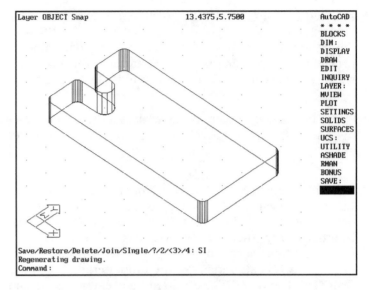

```
Layer OBJECT Snap                    13.4375,5.7500              AutoCAD
                                                                * * * *
                                                                BLOCKS
                                                                DIM:
                                                                DISPLAY
                                                                DRAW
                                                                EDIT
                                                                INQUIRY
                                                                LAYER:
                                                                MVIEW
                                                                PLOT
                                                                SETTINGS
                                                                SOLIDS
                                                                SURFACES
                                                                UCS:
                                                                UTILITY
                                                                ASHADE
                                                                RMAN
                                                                BONUS
                                                                SAVE:

Save/Restore/Delete/Join/SIngle/?/2/<3>/4: SI
Regenerating drawing.
Command:
```

Surfaces of Revolution—Revsurf

The angle base contains two drill holes and spotfaces. You will create them with the Revsurf command, defining the wall profile and revolving it about a center axis. First, however, you need to draw the axis and profile with a line and a polyline. Use a temporary UCS and the Trim and Pedit commands to accurately define the profile polyline.

Follow these steps:

Setting Up for Revsurf

Command: **Line**

From point: *Draw a center line from 10,4,-1 to 10,4,2*

Command: **Copy**

Select objects: *Copy the center line twice, with displacements of @.2625,0 and @.5625,0*

Command: **Line**

From point:

To point: *Draw a line through the three lines, from 10,4,.625 to 11,4,.625*

Setting Up for Revsurf—continued

Command: **Chprop**

Select objects: *Pick the center line (see fig. 16.12)*

Change what property (Color/LAyer/LType/Thickness) ? **Layer**

Change the center line to layer CL

Click in the lower left viewport to make it active

Command: **Chprop**

Select the extruded polyline on the base

Change what property (Color/LAyer/LType/Thickness)? **LA**

New layer <Object> **NOTES**

Now turn off the layer NOTES. This will help keep the drawing area uncluttered

Command: **Zoom**

All/Center/Dynamic/Extents/Left/Previous/Window/<Scale(X)>:

Zoom in on the lines

Command: **UCS**

Origin/ZAxis/3point/Entity/View/X/Y/Z/Prev/Restore/Save/Del/?/<World>: **3** *(see fig.16.12)*

Origin point <0,0,0>: **END**

of *Pick bottom of center line*

Point on positive portion of the X-axis <11.0000,4.0000,-1.0000>: **END**

of *Pick bottom of right line*

Point on positive-Y portion of the UCS X-Y plane <10.0000,5.0000,-1.0000>: **END**

of *Pick top of center line*

Command: **Trim**

Select cutting edge(s)...

Select objects: *Select all lines in lower left viewport*

Select object to trim: *Pick all four ends above and below base envelope lines*

Select object to trim: *Pick four ends to remove inside envelope*

Select object to trim: *Press Enter*

Command: **Pedit**

Select polyline: *Select one trimmed line and use the Join option to join all three*

Command: **Save**

The ready-to-surface hole setup should resemble figure 16.13.

Figure 16.12:
3Point UCS set for the Revsurf command.

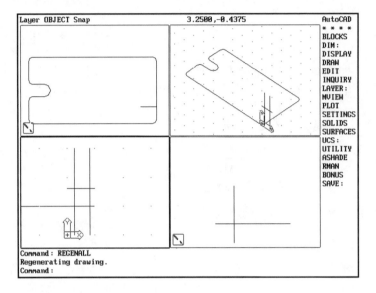

Figure 16.13:
Trimmed lines to generate the Revsurf command.

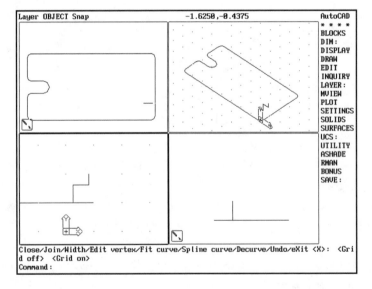

Now you can use the Revsurf command to generate a hole. The Revsurf command generates a 3D polygon mesh by revolving an entity or curved path profile around a selected axis.

The *Revsurf* (Revolution Surface) command generates a 3D polygon mesh by revolving a profile path curve around a selected axis.

Right Hand Rule—Direction of Rotation

The direction of rotation is not important for a full-circle surface, but you need to know how to visualize it for partial circular surfaces. The direction of rotation or revolution can be visualized by using the right hand rule.

Using your right hand, extend your thumb along the axis of revolution. With the thumb pointing toward the end of the axis line which is furthest from the pick point, curl your fingers. Your fingers will point in the direction of the rotation.

The axis of rotation defines the M direction (controlled by SURFTAB1) and the path curve defines the N direction (controlled by SURFTAB2). The SURFTAB2 setting is ignored by straight segments, but controls the density of tabulation lines for curved segments.

Using Figure 16.14 as a guide, try two SURFTAB1 settings as you revolve the hole profile about its center line:

Drawing Holes with Revsurf

Command: **Revsurf**

Select path curve: *Pick the polyline profile*

Select axis of revolution: *Pick the center line*

Start angle <0>: *Press Enter*

Included angle (+=ccw, -=cw) <Full circle>: *Press Enter*

Command: **U**

Command: **Setvar**

Variable name or ?: **SURFTABL**

New value for varname <Surftab1>: **16**

Command: *Type* **Revsurf** *and repeat, as above*

Command: **Zoom**

All/Center/Dynamic/Extents/Left/Previous/Window/<Scale(X)>: **2.5**

Zoom to a scale of 2.5 in the lower left viewport

Command: **UCS**

Origin/Zaxis/3point/Entity/View/X/Y/Z/Prev/Restore/Save/Del/?/<World>: *Press Enter*

▶ **Drawing Holes with Revsurf—continued**

Restore the World coordinate system

Command: **Copy**

Select Objects: **Last**

Copy last with a displacement of 0,2

Command: **Save**

The trade-off between speed and precision, as demonstrated by the two
SURFTAB1 settings, is a constant factor in 3D drafting.

Figure 16.14:
Revsurf and holes.

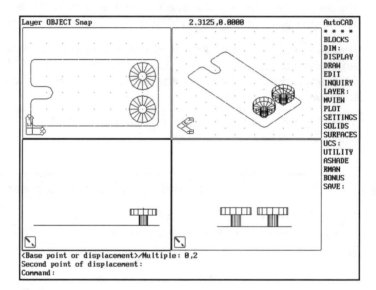

Tabulated Surfaces—Tabsurf

You can use the same technique used for the angle base to generate the angle
bracket, although in this case you need to work in a UCS that is perpendicular
to the WCS. The UCS 3point option can set your UCS on the left front face of
the angle bracket profile. It would be easier, however, to work if your view was
perpendicular to this UCS as if the left front of the bracket was your plan view.
It can be tricky to calculate the viewpoint needed for this view. Fortunately,
AutoCAD can help with the Plan command.

A *Plan* view is a viewpoint of 0,0,1 in the selected UCS. It can be applied to the current UCS, a previously saved UCS, or to the WCS.

Now orient your UCS to the bracket's left front and set your plan view to it. Continue in the previous ANGLE drawing, click in the lower left viewport to make it active, then follow these steps:

Setting Up the UCS and Plan View for Tabsurf

Command: **UCS**

Origin/ZAxis/3point/Entity/View/X/Y/Z/Prev/Restore/Save/Del/?/<World>: **3**

Use Endpoint option of the Object Snap command to set a 3point UCS: establish the origin at the first bubble point, pick on X axis at second bubble point, and pick on Y axis at third bubble point

Click in the upper left viewport to make it active

Command: **Plan**

<Current UCS>/Ucs/World: *Press Enter*

Regenerating drawing.

Command: **Zoom**

All/Center/Dynamic/Extents/Left/Previous/Window/<Scale(X)>: *Zoom in close, as shown in figure 16.15*

Command: **UCS**

Origin/ZAxis/3point/Entity/View/X/Y/Z/Prev/Restore/Save/Del/?/<World>: **Save**

Save to name LSIDE

Command: **View**

?/Delete/Restore/Save/Window: **Save**

Save to name LSIDE

Your upper left viewport should match figure 16.15. (You will notice some interference from the real objects at the left side.)

Now it is a simple matter to draw a polyline for the end profile. Overlap the ends, and then use the Trim and Pedit commands to close it accurately. Click in the upper left viewport to make it active before following these steps:

Figure 16.15:
*UCS plan to left side for
Tabsurf command.*

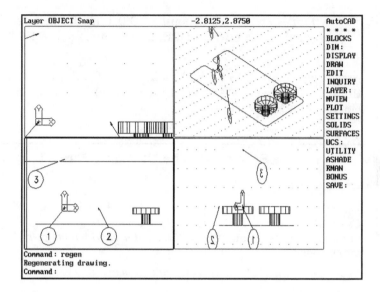

Projecting the End Profile Polyline Using TABSURF

Command: **Pline**

From point: *Osnap Int to upper left corner of angle envelope*

Current line-width is 0.0000

Arc/Close/Halfwidth/Length/Undo/Width/<Endpoint of line>:

*Continue with points: @0,-3   @2.5,0   @0,1.25   @0.375<-135   @1.75<135   @0.375<45
and @1<135. (see fig. 16.16)*

Command: **Trim**

Select cutting edge(s)...

Select objects:

Select object to trim: *Trim off part of polyline above angle envelope*

Command: **Pedit**

Select polyline: *Pick the polyline*

Close/Join/Width/Edit vertex/Fit curve/Spline curve/Decurve/Undo/eXit <x>: **Close**

Close the polyline with the Close option

Command: **Tabsurf**

Select path curve: *Pick the polyline*

Select direction vector: *Pick the upper right front edge of the envelope at the first
bubble point*

Projecting the End Profile Polyline Using TABSURF—continued

Command: **UCS**

Origin/ZAxis/3point/Entity/View/X/Y/Z/Prev/Restore/Save/Del/?/<World>: **Restore**

Restore World coordinate system and click in the upper right viewport to make it active

Command: **Vports**

Save/Restore/Delete/Join/SIngle/?/2/<3>/4: **SI**

Turn off layer CONST and turn on layer NOTES to see entire drawing with the base

Use the Chprop command to change the base back to the object layer

Command: **Hide**

Command: **Save**

The part's basic profile is now complete. Your drawing should resemble figure 16.17.

The *Rulesurf* (Ruled Surface) command generates a 3D polyline mesh depicting the ruled surface between two entities. The two entities can be points, lines, arcs, circles, 2D polylines, or 3D polylines. If one boundary, such as a circle or closed polyline, is closed, then the other boundary must be either a point or be closed. A point can be used with any entity. Figure 16.18 shows examples of ruled surfaces.

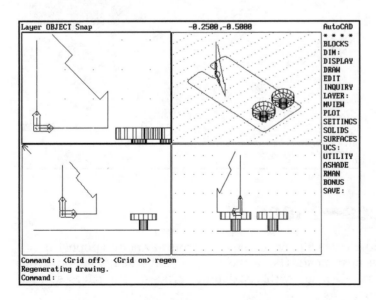

Figure 16.16:
Polyline before invoking the Trim and Pedit commands.

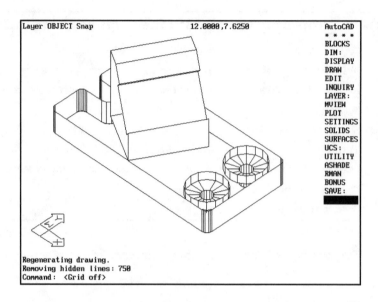

Figure 16.17:
Tabsurf with hide in single viewport.

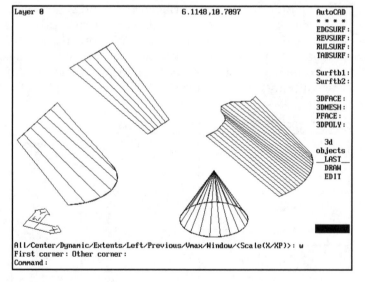

Figure 16.18:
Examples of ruled surfaces.

Polygon Faces—Pface

The *Pface* command creates a polygon mesh of arbitrary points (topography). This is called a *rat nest mesh*. Using the Pface command helps you avoid making unnecessary 3D faces with coexistent vertices. This saves storage space as well as time.

You can enter an unlimited number of Pface vertices in 2D or 3D space. The vertices also can be designated at any distance from each other.

The Pface command works well for surfacing planar as well as non-planar polygons. In the case of the left side of the angle bracket, you have a planar surface without interior geometry (such as holes, notches, and so on).

Making Invisible Edges on Pfaces

You can create invisible edges on Pfaces like those used on 3Dfaces in the previous chapter. To create invisible Pface edges, enter a negative number as a response to the `Face N, vertex N:` prompt line. For example, the following negative numbers:

```
Face 5, vertex 5: -5
Face 6, vertex 6: -6
```

would create an invisible edge between vertex 5 and 6.

Close the left side of the angle bracket with the Pface command. No invisible edges are necessary. Follow these steps:

Closing Irregular Shapes with Pface

Command: **Vports**

Save/Restore/Delete/Join/SIngle/?/2/<3>/4: **Restore**

Restore 3D click in the lower left viewport to make it active

Command: **UCS**

Origin/ZAxis/3point/Entity/View/X/Y/Z/Prev/Restore/Save/Del/?/<SCRATCH>: **Restore**

Restore LSIDE

Command: **Vports**

Save/Restore/Delete/Join/SIngle/?/2/<3>/4: **SI**

Restore SIngle

Command: **Layer**

?/Make/Set/New/ON/OFF/Color/Ltype/Freeze/Thaw: **Freeze**

Freeze layer CONST to suppress clutter

Command: **Osnap**

Object snap modes: **INT**

Command: **Pface**

Closing Irregular Shapes with Pface—continued

```
Vertex 1: Pick first bubble point  (see fig. 16.19)
Vertex 2: Pick second bubble point
Vertex 3: Pick third bubble point
Vertex 4: Pick fourth bubble point
Vertex 5: Pick fifth bubble point
Vertex 6: Pick sixth bubble point
Vertex 7: Pick seventh bubble point
Vertex 8: Pick eighth bubble point
Vertex 9: Press Enter

Face 1, vertex 1: 1
Face 1, vertex 2: 2
Face 1, vertex 3: 3
Face 1, vertex 4: 4
Face 1, vertex 5: 5
Face 1, vertex 6: 6
Face 1, vertex 7: 7
Face 1, vertex 8: 8
Face 1, vertex 9: Press Enter
Face 2, vertex 1: Press Enter

Command: Hide
```

The above sequence surfaced the left side of the angle bracket as shown in figure 16.20.

Figure 16.19:
Pick points for Pface.

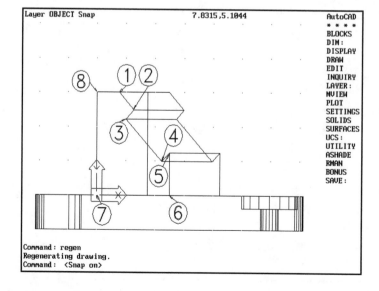

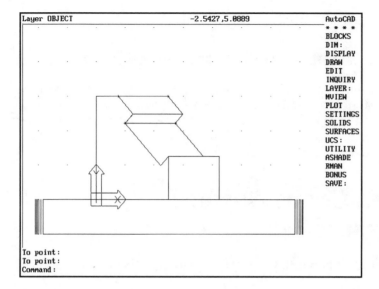

Now copy the left side to create the right side as follows:

Copying the Left Side to the Right

Command: **Osnap**

Object snap: **NON**

Command: **Copy**

Select objects: **Last**

Base point or displacement/Multiple:

Displacement 0,0,-3

Command: **UCS**

Origin/ZAxis/3point/Entity/View/X/Y/Z/Prev/Restore/Save/Del/?/<World>: *Press Enter*

Restore World

Command: **Vports**

Save/Restore/Delete/Join/SIngle/?/2/<3>/4: **Restore**

Restore viewport 3D

Command: **Hide**

Command: **Save**

Now the sides of the bracket are closed.

Closing the Base's Top and Bottom — Optional

Closing the base's top and bottom is slightly complicated because of the more complex edge and the two holes. Divide the surface to define a square around the holes that can be filled. You also can create a quarter-pie set of faces for the typical large and small radii, and then copy and mirror them to the rest. This technique leaves you easy-to-fill rectangular areas.

Edge Defined Coons Surface Patch—Edgesurf

Another surface generating command, Edgesurf, is not often used in mechanical drafting.

The *Edgesurf* command generates a 3D polygon mesh by approximating a Coons surface patch from four adjoining edge entities. Each edge can be a line, arc, or open polyline, anywhere in 3D space. The endpoints of the edge entities must touch, combining to form a closed path. You can pick the edges in any order. The first edge or entity selected defines the M direction (controlled by SURFTAB1) of the mesh. The two edges that touch the M edge define the N direction (controlled by SURFTAB2).

The *Edgesurf* command fills the area inside its boundaries with an interpolated bicubic surface patch, which is mathematically correct but probably not the actual contour you would program a machine tool to cut. Examples of boundary sets and their generated surfaces are shown in figure 16.21.

Experiment with the Edgesurf command. You might find it useful for approximating surfaces that fill irregular areas.

Challenge Exercise—Optional

Put a hole through the angled and back faces of the angle bracket which are now completely closed. See the multi-view angle support illustrated by figure 17.1 to get an idea of what the bracket hole should look like.

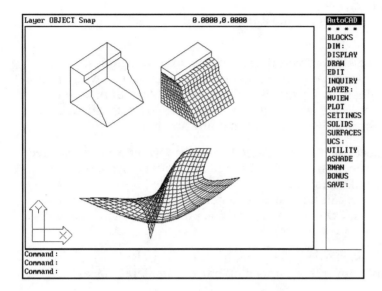

Examples of the Edgesurf command.

To add this bracket hole, use RULESURF to generate a hole between a circle drawn on the back face of the angle bracket and a corresponding ellipse on the inclined front face.

Tip Instead of drawing in the middle of the faces, it is easier to draw centered on the previous polyline at the left edge, using it as an axis line. Also, to avoid twist between the circle and ellipse, treat both the circle and ellipse as polylines.

Working in the LSIDE UCS, draw the circular ellipse and then use two lines to project the polyline circle center and top quadrant points from the back onto the inclined plane to define the top and center of the ellipse.

Use the Rotate command to rotate the ellipses into the planes of the back and inclined front faces. Use the UCS ZAxis option to set up for the inclined face ellipse rotation. Now use RULESURF to generate a polygon mesh between the circle and ellipse. In order to replace the obscuring front and back faces of the resulting mesh with a series of smaller facets, experiment with the Pface command.

Summary

This chapter introduced you to the tools you need for 3D surface drafting and design. You can see how being able to quickly and accurately manipulate the

User Coordinate System (UCS) is the most important feature for efficient 3D performance.

The angle support exercise showed you three fundamental techniques for 3D drafting: developing and using a construction envelope; orienting, saving, and restoring a UCS; and using a scratch UCS and a building-block approach to drawing. These three techniques work together to provide you with an efficient and productive method for surface modeling virtually any part.

This chapter also developed the 3D wireframe techniques which were presented in Chapter 15, and introduced AutoCAD's three-dimensional polygon mesh tools. These tools include 3D meshes, polygon meshes, ruled surfaces, tabulated surfaces, surfaces of revolution, and edge-defined Coons surface patches. As you saw in the exercises, 3D meshes can be used to surface model virtually any 3D shape or part.

Some parts might require surface modeling with 3D faces. Both 3Dfaces and Pfaces are versatile tools, convenient for closing hard-to-model surfaces.

You might want to create and surface model specific shapes, and then save them in a 3D surface modeled library. Geometry such as the drill and spotface, developed in this chapter, provide you with a good example of a useful 3D library drawing. Try expanding the 1x1 block technique presented in Chapter 13 to a 1x1x1 technique.

You will view a 3D part, capture the views, insert them into an engineering drawing, and dimension them with geometric dimensioning and tolerancing techniques in the next chapter.

17

3D MANIPULATIONS

In this chapter:

- Creating orthographic and parallel projection views from 3D objects
- Viewing 3D drawings using the Dview command
- Using paper space to compose a multi-view drawing
- Removing unused blocks, layers, linetypes, shapes, and styles with the Purge command
- Controlling layer visibility in paper space viewports
- Adding dimensions in 3D views

Overview

This chapter shows you how to create a multi-view drawing from the previous chapter's surface model. To build the multi-view drawing, develop the model first in 3D, then create orthographic views to accurately communicate the design concept. Release 10 users employ the block-insertion method and Release 11 users utilize paper space viewports to create the multi-view drawing.

The multi-view drawing is created using Release 10 by inserting several blocks from Chapter 16's ANGLE SUPPORT into a drawing which then can be traced, annotated, and dimensioned. Each block views the original 3D drawing from one of the orientations needed for the multi-view drawing. These are the plan, front, and 3D (parallel projection) views in Chapter 16's viewports and an auxiliary view which is the same as Chapter 16's LSIDE orientation.

Using a combination of the Wblock (or Block), UCS, and Insert commands enables you to combine multiple views in a single drawing. Using the Wblock or Block command to insert blocks is relative to the UCS that is current when the commands are executed. To create blocks for multiple views, you simply orient the UCS to each desired view and block the object in that orientation. Multiple blocks from different orientations can be inserted into a single UCS, maintaining the orientations that they were blocked with.

In Release 11, the multi-view drawing is created in paper space by viewing the 3D model through paper space viewports. Each viewport contains an orthographic view of the 3D angle support. Blocks of the angle support are not needed to show the orthographic views simultaneously. The finished multi-view drawing appears exactly the same as the block-insertion method (see fig. 17.1).

 Note   All illustrations in Chapter 17 show the optional hole in the angle bracket that was an optional exercise at the end of Chapter 16.

Creating Orthographic and Parallel Projection Views

The orientations needed for the blocks (Release 10) or viewports (Release 11) can be achieved in one of several ways. You can set the UCS first and then use the Plan command to orient the view, but that requires zooming in after invoking the Plan command. You can use the Vpoint command to orient the view and then set the UCS to match, but the Vpoint command is sometimes awkward for odd angles.

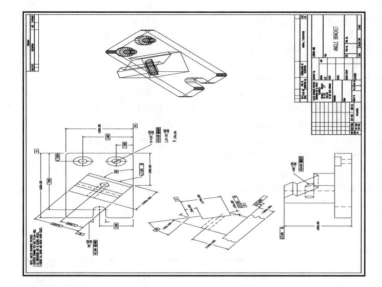

Figure 17.1:
The multi-view angle support drawing.

The best approach is to orient the view with the Dview command, then set the UCS to match. The Dview command is a fast, powerful, interactive command for controlling views. You can use it to: examine several different views without a screen regeneration; view the drawing from different angles, directions, and distances; put your drawing in perspective view; hide lines; work with subsets of the entire drawing's entities; and clip foreground or background portions of the drawing. You will use the Wblock command and various orientations to explore the features of the Dview command.

Viewing 3D Drawings Using the Dview Command

The *Dview* (Dynamic view) command enables you to view a drawing in much the same way a cameraman moves around a set, taking shots from different distances, angles, and magnifications. Unlike the Vpoint command which only offers a few ways to set the viewing angle, the Dview command offers a rich set of options to achieve any angle or magnification in a single step.

The Dview command enables you to dynamically drag and rotate the 3D model with the aid of slider bars. You can display a perspective view of the model and toggle back and forth between parallel and perspective views. The Dview command is similar to the concept of using a camera to view a target. You can set a camera point, target point, lens length, and position front and back clipping planes. The default is parallel (not perspective) projection.

The Dview command uses the same names and terms used in cinematography, such as when references are made to panning and zooming the camera. You can establish the line of sight used to view your drawing by setting a camera or a target option, for example, or by setting two points. The camera comes equipped with zoom lenses. Unlike real cameras, this one has no distortion and only goes into perspective mode when the Distance option is used. Clipping may be used to show cut-away or sectional views, and the camera may be twisted to any angle, even turned upside down—something the Vpoint command cannot do.

Most of the Dview options accept input from the Dview slider bars (see fig. 17.2) as well as typed input.

Figure 17.2:

A Dview command slider bar.

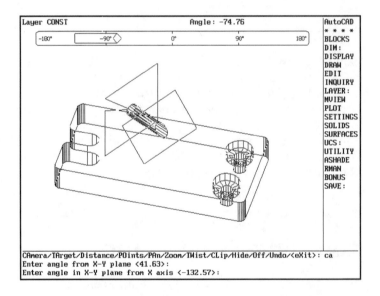

The slider bars provide a way to interactively drag and pick numeric values such as scale, distance, or magnification. A slider bar looks like a ruler with a moving diamond anchored at the current setting. As you move your cursor along the bar, the indicator diamond slides with it, the coords display is replaced by a dynamic display of the equivalent input value, and the Dview command image updates as quickly as it can keep up.

In some options, the bar displays other values to guide you. The values shown on the slider bar are not the same as the input values. The Distance option, for example, accepts typed input in drawing units, but shows 1X, 4X, and 16X as guide values (relative to the current view) along the slider bar.

Picking with the slider bar is quick and intuitive, but not precise. When you want precise values, use the slider bar to approximate the result you want and then use the keyboard to input the precise number. The values on the slider bar vary with the Dview command options, which are as follows:

- **CAmera.** Rotates the camera angle around the target point by entering angles or using the slider bars. Rotation is the same as the Vpoint command Rotate option: you enter the angle *up* from the current XY plane, then the angle from the X axis *in* the XY plane. This rotates the camera around the existing target point.

- **TArget.** Rotates the target angle relative to the existing camera point. This is the opposite of the CAmera option.

- **Distance.** Moves the camera along the existing line-of-sight angle, toward or away from the target point. When you select distance, perspective viewing (mode) is automatically turned on. To simply enlarge or shrink the view, use the Zoom option. When perspective viewing is on, the UCS/WCS icon is replaced by a perspective icon. Slider bar marks are labeled 0X, 1X, up to 16X, meaning that value times the current distance. See the Off option for turning perspective off.

- **POint.** Enables you to relocate the camera and target points using XYZ coordinates, with object snaps if needed. No slider applies, but a rubber band to the target point aids in specifying the camera point. Perspective mode is temporarily disabled during point specification if it was active.

- **PAn.** Repositions the drawing without changing magnification. Without perspective, it works like the normal Pan command and you can enter or pick points. In perspective mode, the perspective shifts as you pan and you must pick the points. No slider applies, but you can drag the image as you pick the second point.

- **Zoom.** With perspective on, Zoom enables you to set the camera's lens length in millimeters by entering a value or using the slider bar. With perspective off, it works like the Zoom command's Center option except that magnification is by scale factor instead of view height, and the value by input or slider is in terms of the *n*X-type scale factor.

- **TWist.** Enables you to twist the view around the current line of sight. You can enter a value in degrees counterclockwise, or you can drag it with a rubber band from the view center to the crosshairs. When dragging, the angle displays on the status line.

- **CLip.** Sets front and back clipping planes, such as you would use to see a section through an object. The cutting planes are placed perpendicular to the line of sight at the designated position be-

tween the camera and target (or beyond the target if a negative
back clip is specified). Clip options include Back, Front, and Off.
Perspective automatically turns the front clip on, with the plane at
the camera's position unless you place it in front of the camera.
This default prevents objects behind the camera from appearing in
perspective.

- **Hide.** Removes hidden lines on the current Dview command selection set. This enables you to examine the effects of hide on selected portions of the drawing.

- **Off.** Turns off perspective mode.

- **Undo.** Undoes the last Dview command. You can repeatedly undo, back to the beginning of the command.

- **eXit.** Ends and exits the Dview command. After exiting, the current drawing is regenerated in the new view. Cancel instead of exiting if you want to redisplay the drawing as it was before you entered the Dview command.

Experiment with the Dview command's features. If your drawing seems to disappear, it probably is off the screen, or it is zoomed so far in or out that it appears as blank space or a dot.

The Dview command uses normal object selection, but if you have no objects selected, it uses a house-shaped icon to indicate orientation during Dview option settings. You also can create your own icon by making a one-unit-sized 3D block named DVIEWBLOCK.

The `Dview Options` selection from the `Display` pull-down menu shows an icon menu, with the frequently-used Camera, Pan, and Zoom options, as shown in figure 17.3.

Using the Dview Camera

You will use the Dview command to view the back side of the angle support and to establish the views needed for your multi-view drawing's blocks. After you choose the Dview command's selection set, you can speed up performance by selecting only as many entities as you need to represent the objects you wish to manipulate. Avoid selecting curves, text, and meshes because they slow things down considerably. Exclude the holes of the angle support, for example, by using the object selection Remove mode after windowing the entire drawing.

To get started, edit the ANGLE drawing completed in Chapter 16. If you have the AutoCAD: Drafting and 3D Design Disk, skip this exercise.

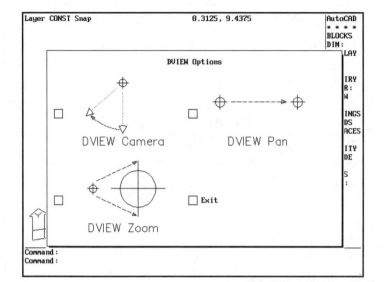

Figure 17.3:
The Dview options icon menu.

Setting Up the ANGLE Drawing

 You are already set up. Skip to the next exercise.

 Edit an existing drawing named ANGLE.

```
Command: UCS
Origin/ZAxis/3point/Entity/View/X/Y/Z/Prev/Restore/Save/Del/?/<World>: Press
Enter
Command: Vports
Save/Restore/Delete/Join/SIngle/?/2/<3>/4: R
?/Name of viewport configuration to restore: 3DSI
Regenerating drawing.
Command: Chprop
Select objects: C
First corner: 7,-1.25
Other corner: 5,13
88 found
Select objects: Press Enter
Change what property (Color/LAyer/LType/Thickness) ? LA
New layer <OBJECT>: CONST
```

Setting Up the ANGLE Drawing—continued

```
Change what property (Color/LAyer/LType/Thickness) ? Press Enter

Command: Layer

?/Make/Set/New/ON/OFF/Color/Ltype/Freeze/Thaw: T

Layer name(s) to Thaw: *

?/Make/Set/New/ON/OFF/Color/Ltype/Freeze/Thaw: ON

Layer name(s) to turn On: *

?/Make/Set/New/ON/OFF/Color/Ltype/Freeze/Thaw: Press Enter

Regenerating drawing.

Command: Zoom

All/Center/Dynamic/Extents/Left/Previous/Vmax/Window/<Scale(X/XP)>: A

Regenerating drawing.

Command: Erase

Select objects: Erase the construction envelope

Command: Zoom

All/Center/Dynamic/Extents/Left/Previous/Vmax/Window/<Scale(X/XP)>: P

Regenerating drawing.
```

The entire angle support should be visible on the CONST layer as shown in figure 17.4:

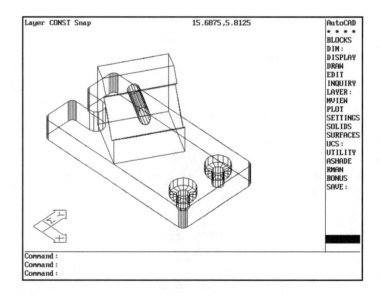

Figure 17.4:
Prepared 3D angle support.

Now use the Camera option sliders to rotate the camera around the target and view the back of the angle support from a bird's-eye view, with a Hide option. Then use Camera again to set a top view and write it to file T-TOP using the Wblock command. The T- prefix designates temporary blocks. Release 11 users can skip the steps that create the blocks for the block-insertion method.

Begin a new drawing named ANGLE=DV-ANGLE if you have the AutoCAD: Drafting and 3D Design Disk. Otherwise, continue in the ANGLE drawing and follow these steps:

Applying Dview Camera and Hide

 Begin a new drawing named ANGLE=DV-ANGLE

 Continue in the previous ANGLE drawing.

```
Command: Dview
Select objects: C
First corner: 7,-1.25
Other corner: 5,13
88 found
Select objects: R
Remove objects: 4.25,7.25
1 selected, 1 found, 1 removed
Remove objects: 9.5,6.5
1 selected, 1 found, 1 removed
Remove objects: 9.5,4.5
1 selected, 1 found, 1 removed
Remove objects: Press Enter
CAmera/TArget/Distance/POints/PAn/Zoom/TWist/CLip/Hide/Off/Undo/<eXit>: CA
Enter angle from X-Y plane <40.32>: Drag angle to about 35 degrees and the coords
display and pick
Enter angle in X-Y plane from X axis <-45.00>: Drag angle to about 135 degrees
and pick
CAmera/TArget/Distance/POints/PAn/Zoom/TWist/CLip/Hide/Off/Undo/<eXit>: H
Removing hidden lines: 375
CAmera/TArget/Distance/POints/PAn/Zoom/TWist/CLip/Hide/Off/Undo/<eXit>: CA
Enter angle from X-Y plane <35.13>: 90
```

Applying Dview Camera and Hide—continued

Enter angle in X-Y plane from X axis <135.08>: **0**

CAmera/TArget/Distance/POints/PAn/Zoom/TWist/CLip/Hide/Off/Undo/<eXit>: *Press Enter*

Regenerating drawing.

Command: **Wblock** *(Release 10 only)*

File name: **T-TOP**

Block name: *Press Enter*

Insertion base point: **3,3**

Select objects: **C**

First corner: **2.75,2.75**

Other corner: **11.25,7.25**

88 found

Select objects: *Press Enter*

Command: **Oops** *(Release 10 only)*

Command: **Save**

File Name <ANGLE>: *Press Enter*

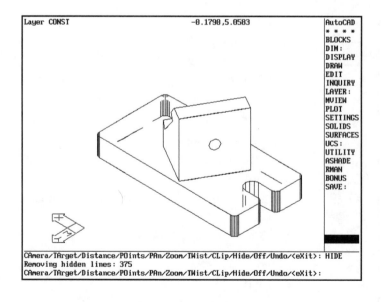

Figure 17.5:
The back dynamically viewed with Hide.

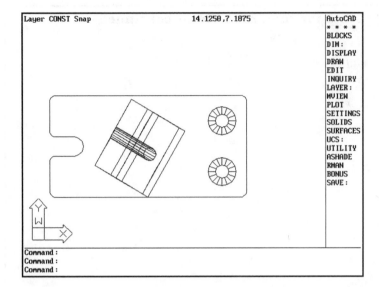

Figure 17.6:
Top view for T-TOP 2H.

Using the Dview Points Option

The Target option is used in exactly the same manner as Camera, except that the angles are opposite. Another difference is that the target moves instead of the camera. The Points option works like the Vpoint command, except that you can set the target point instead of having to look through point 0,0,0. Use Points to set new target and camera points to display a front view.

Continue in the previous drawing and follow these steps:

Setting Points for the Front View

Command: **Dview**

Select objects: **C**

First corner: **2.75,2.75**

Other corner: **11.25,7.25**

88 found

Select objects: *Press Enter*

CAmera/TArget/Distance/POints/PAn/Zoom/TWist/CLip/Hide/Off/Undo/<eXit>: **PO**

Enter target point <8.0752, 5.4248, 1.4578>: **7,3,0**

Enter camera point <8.0752, 5.4248, 10.7315>: **7,0,0**

CAmera/TArget/Distance/POints/PAn/Zoom/TWist/CLip/Hide/Off/Undo/<eXit>: *Press Enter*

Setting Points for the Front View—continued

Regenerating drawing.

Command: **UCS** *(Release 10 only)*

Origin/ZAxis/3point/Entity/View/X/Y/Z/Prev/Restore/Save/Del/?/<World>: **V**

Command: **Wblock** *(Release 10 only)*

File name: **T-FRONT**

Block name: *Press Enter*

Insertion base point: **3,0**

Select objects: **C**

First corner: **2.75,-.25**

Other corner: **11.25,4.25**

88 found

Select objects: *Press Enter*

Command: **Oops** *(Release 10 only)*

Release 10 users need to use the UCS View option to align the UCS to the current view so you can write the block to disk relative to the view.

The auxiliary view needed to show the profile of the angle bracket is nearly the same, but aligned to the left face. You can use the Points option by using the Osnap command to move the target and camera points to opposite sides of the inclined front face.

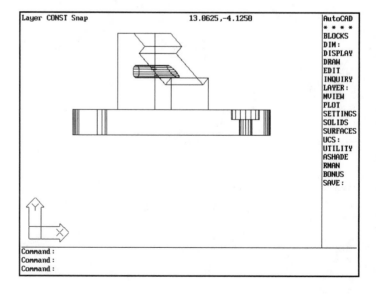

Figure 17.7:
Front view for T-FRONT.

Continue in the previous ANGLE drawing and follow these steps:

Osnapping Points for the Auxiliary View

```
Command: Dview

Select objects: C

First corner: 2.75,-.25

Other corner: 11.25,4.25

88 found

Select objects: Press Enter

*** Switching to the WCS ***

CAmera/TArget/Distance/POints/PAn/Zoom/TWist/CLip/Hide/Off/Undo/<eXit>: PO

Enter target point <7.0000, 3.0000, 0.0000>: INT

of Pick at first bubble point

Enter camera point <7.0000, 0.0000, 0.0000>: INT

of Pick at second bubble point

CAmera/TArget/Distance/POints/PAn/Zoom/TWist/CLip/Hide/Off/Undo/<eXit>: Press
Enter

*** Returning to the UCS ***

Regenerating drawing.

Command: UCS

Origin/ZAxis/3point/Entity/View/X/Y/Z/Prev/Restore/Save/Del/?/<World>: V

Command: Wblock (Release 10 only)

File name: T-AUX

Block name: Press Enter

Insertion base point: INT

of Pick at third bubble point

Select objects: C

First corner: -1,-.125

Other corner: 8,4.25

88 found

Select objects: Press Enter

Command: Oops (Release 10 only)

Command: Save

File name <ANGLE>: Press Enter
```

The current UCS was not the WCS, so the Dview command temporarily switched into the WCS during input. You normally think of views in terms of the WCS, so it is used during input unless the WORLDVIEW system variable is set to zero. The default is 1.

Your drawing should now resemble figure 17.9.

Figure 17.8:
Pick points for Dview points.

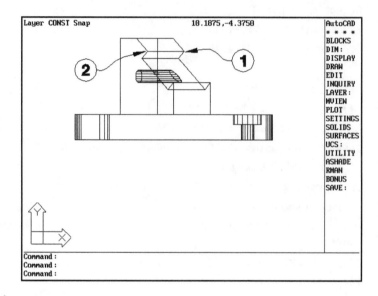

Figure 17.9:
Auxiliary view for T-AUX.

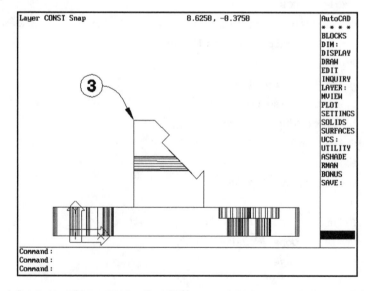

The last view you need to write to disk is the 3D view. Play around with perspective on the way there.

Using Dview Distance, Pan, and Zoom

The Distance option puts the Dview command and your drawing into perspective mode until you return to normal with the Off option. When you exit the Dview command in perspective mode, you are limited. The Pan, Zoom, and Sketch commands are prohibited. Other commands can be used, but you cannot pick points or use the Osnap command in a perspective viewport. The solution is simple. Just enter points from the keyboard or use multiple viewports and pick in a non-perspective viewport. Object selection works normally right in perspective.

Set perspective with an initial distance of 24 and pan as shown in figures 17.10 and 17.11. Then, still in perspective, adjust the camera angle and zoom in on it.

Continue in the ANGLE drawing and follow these steps:

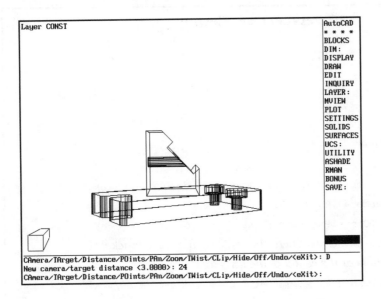

Figure 17.10:
Perspective distance at 24.

Figure 17.11:
Perspective centered with Pan option.

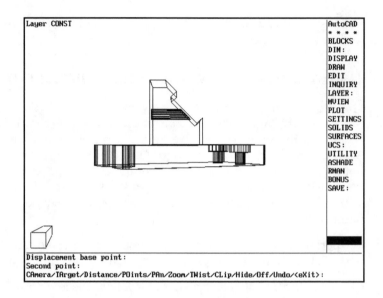

```
Layer CONST                                                    AutoCAD
                                                               * * * *
                                                               BLOCKS
                                                               DIM:
                                                               DISPLAY
                                                               DRAW
                                                               EDIT
                                                               INQUIRY
                                                               LAYER:
                                                               MVIEW
                                                               PLOT
                                                               SETTINGS
                                                               SOLIDS
                                                               SURFACES
                                                               UCS:
                                                               UTILITY
                                                               ASHADE
                                                               RMAN
                                                               BONUS
                                                               SAVE:




Displacement base point:
Second point:
CAmera/TArget/Distance/POints/PAn/Zoom/TWist/CLip/Hide/Off/Undo/<eXit>:
```

3D Perspective Viewing

Command: **Dview**

Select objects: **C**

First corner: **-1,-.25**

Other corner: **8,4.25**

88 found

Select objects: *Press Enter*

*** Switching to the WCS ***

CAmera/TArget/Distance/POints/PAn/Zoom/TWist/CLip/Hide/Off/Undo/<eXit>: **D**

New camera/target distance <3.0000>: **24**

CAmera/TArget/Distance/POints/PAn/Zoom/TWist/CLip/Hide/Off/Undo/<eXit>: **PA**

Displacement base point: *Pick a point near the center of the angle bracket*

Second point: *Pick a point near the center of the screen*

CAmera/TArget/Distance/POints/PAn/Zoom/TWist/CLip/Hide/Off/Undo/<eXit>: **CA**

Enter angle from X-Y plane <-0.00>: *Drag angle slider to about 41 and pick*

Enter angle in X-Y plane from X axis <-120.00>: *Drag angle slider to about -132 and pick*

CAmera/TArget/Distance/POints/PAn/Zoom/TWist/CLip/Hide/Off/Undo/<eXit>: **Z**

Adjust lenslength <50.000mm>: *Drag to lens slider to about 60mm and pick*

3D Perspective Viewing—continued

CAmera/TArget/Distance/POints/PAn/Zoom/TWist/CLip/Hide/Off/Undo/<eXit>: *Press Enter*

*** Returning to the UCS ***

Regenerating drawing.

Command: **Save**

File name <ANGLE>: *Press Enter*

The perspective is still active after exiting the Dview command. If you pan to re-center it after getting the perspective the way you want it, the pan will alter the vanishing point.

Your drawing now should resemble figure 17.13.

You do not want a perspective for your multi-view drawing, so turn it off and adjust your 3D view with the Pan and Camera options. With perspective off, you can pan freely.

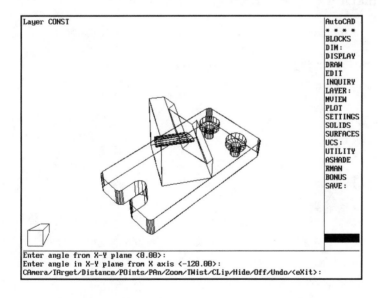

Figure 17.12:
Perspective improved with camera option.

Figure 17.13:
Perspective zoomed.

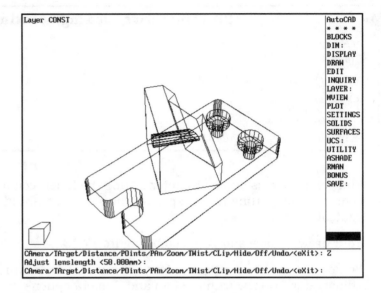

Adjusting and Wblocking a 3D Dview

Command: **Dview**

Select objects: **C**

First corner: *Pick a point below and left of the angle bracket*

Other corner: *Pick a point above and right of the angle bracket*

88 found

Select objects: *Press Enter*

*** Switching to the WCS ***

CAmera/TArget/Distance/POints/PAn/Zoom/TWist/CLip/Hide/Off/Undo/<eXit>: **O**

CAmera/TArget/Distance/POints/PAn/Zoom/TWist/CLip/Hide/Off/Undo/<eXit>: **PA**

Displacement base point: **6,6**

Second point: **8.5,8**

CAmera/TArget/Distance/POints/PAn/Zoom/TWist/CLip/Hide/Off/Undo/<eXit>: **CA**

Enter angle from X-Y plane <41.63>: **52**

Enter angle in X-Y plane from X axis <-132.57>: **-135**

CAmera/TArget/Distance/POints/PAn/Zoom/TWist/CLip/Hide/Off/Undo/<eXit>: *Press Enter*

*** Returning to the UCS ***

Regenerating drawing.

Command: **Setvar** *(Release 10 only)*

Adjusting and Wblocking a 3D Dview—continued

```
Variable name or ?: SPLFRAME
New value for SPLFRAME <0>: 1
Command: Regen (Release 10 only)
Regenerating drawing.
Command: UCS (Release 10 only)
Origin/ZAxis/3point/Entity/View/X/Y/Z/Prev/Restore/Save/Del/?/<World>: V
Command: Wblock (Release 10 only)
File name: T-3D
Block name: Press enter
Insertion base point: -3,3
Select objects: C
First corner: -3,3
Other corner: 6,11
252 found
Select objects: Press Enter
Command: Quit
Really want to discard all changes to drawing? Y
```

You drawing now should resemble figure 17.14.

Release 10 users have all your needed views for the multi-view drawing in individual drawing files. Release 11 users now know how to set up the orthographic views for the paper space viewports. Quit the ANGLE drawing and get ready to assemble the multi-view drawing. Release 11 users can skip ahead to the "Creating a Multi-View Drawing in Paper Space" section. The AutoCAD command prompts and figures from this point to the "Creating a Multi-View Drawing in Paper Space" section are for Release 10.

Inserting Captured Blocks

You will create a multiple view engineering drawing of the angle support in this part of the exercise. This drawing will consist of the front and top orthographic views, one auxiliary view, and the 3D parallel projection view. You will insert these previously saved views of the angle support into a D-size title sheet and use them as tracing templates to create a proper set of 2D views.

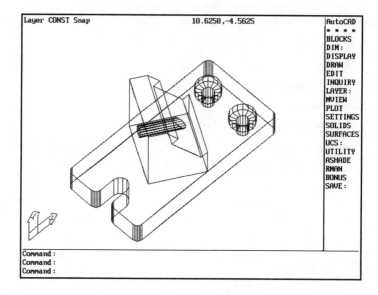

Figure 17.14:
3D view for T-3D.

Allow plenty of room for dimensioning between each view when you place the blocks onto the D-size sheet. CAD drafting often requires substantial amounts of dimensioning space. The exact spacing between the blocks is not critical, but the alignment is. When developing an orthographic drawing, the views must align. You can use the Snap and Osnap commands and point filters to align them during or after insertion so that shared dimensions, such as width, height, and depth, are common in each view. In this exercise, snap will be sufficient.

Use the PROTO-D drawing from the AutoCAD: Drafting and 3D Design Disk or from Chapter 12, and the T-TOP, T-FRONT, T-AUX, and T-3D files you wrote to disk in this chapter. You will insert all of the blocks except T-AUX at their default 1:1 scale and 0 rotation angle. T-AUX must be aligned with the skewed bracket in the top view. To align it, set a temporary UCS before inserting.

Begin a new drawing named M-ANGLE=PROTO-D and follow these steps:

Inserting the Views

```
Command: View

?/Delete/Restore/Save/Window: R

View name to restore: BDR

Command: Snap

Snap spacing or ON/OFF/Aspect/Rotate/Style <0.1250>: .5

Command: Insert
```

Inserting the Views—continued

```
Block name (or ?): T-TOP
Insertion point: 7,14
X scale factor <1> / Corner / XYZ: Press Enter
Y scale factor (default=X): Press Enter
Rotation angle <0>: Press Enter
Command: UCS
Origin/ZAxis/3point/Entity/View/X/Y/Z/Prev/Restore/Save/Del/?/<World>: 3
Origin point <0,0,0>: INT
of 9,14
Point on positive portion of the X-axis <9.8349,14.2500,1.0000>: INT
of
Point on positive-Y portion of the UCS X-Y plane <9.3349,15.1160,1.0000>: INT
of
Command: Insert
Block name (or ?) <T-TOP>: T-AUX
Insertion point: 0,-3
X scale factor <1> / Corner / XYZ: Press Enter
Y scale factor (default=X): Press Enter
Rotation angle <0>: Press Enter
Command: UCS
Origin/ZAxis/3point/Entity/View/X/Y/Z/Prev/Restore/Save/Del/?/<World>: P
Command: Insert
Block name (or ?) <T-AUX>: T-FRONT
Insertion point: 7,1.5
X scale factor <1> / Corner / XYZ: Press Enter
Y scale factor (default=X): Press Enter
Rotation angle <0>: Press Enter
Command: Insert
Block name (or ?) <T-FRONT>: T-3D
Insertion point: 21,7
X scale factor <1> / Corner / XYZ: Press Enter
Y scale factor (default=X): Press Enter
Rotation angle <0>: Press Enter
```

When you have inserted the four blocks and are satisfied with their positions, your drawing should resemble figure 17.15.

Figure 17.15:
The blocks are inserted.

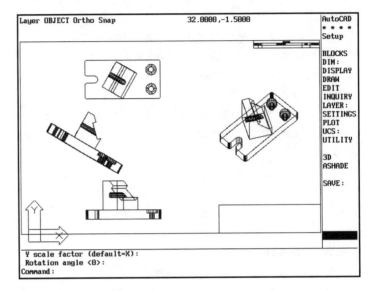

Editing the Views into 2D

Before dimensioning, you need to trace the angle support views to create 2D drawings. Because the angle support was developed in 3D, it includes details (such as the curves and holes) that become confusing in 2D. It generally is easiest to trace over such images than to try to edit them into an acceptable 2D form.

Tracing the blocks is actually very quick and easy because the geometry is already there. You do not have to enter coordinates or calculate distances; just use the object snaps on everything. You can use point filters to align to adjacent views if necessary.

You want the new entities you create to all be in the XY plane of the WCS (or your BDR UCS), with Z coordinate values of zero. But object snaps normally snap many of these points to non-zero Z coordinates. They would appear correct, but it would not really be a proper drawing and might complicate dimensioning and the appearance of linetypes. You could override the Z coordinates with point filters, but an easier way exists for Release 10 users. The FLATLAND system variable makes AutoCAD act like it did before it became full 3D, locking all so-called 2D entities (including lines) to the WCS XY plane. Turn FLATLAND on before you begin to trace the top view.

Note If you did not add the optional bracket hole to the angle bracket in Chapter 16, ignore the following sections set off with [square brackets].

Editing the Top View

```
Command: Zoom
All/Center/Dynamic/Extents/Left/Previous/Window/<Scale(X)>: W
First corner: 6.5,13.5
Other corner: 15.5,18.5
Command: Snap
Snap spacing or ON/OFF/Aspect/Rotate/Style <0.5000>: .0625
Command: Setvar
Variable name or ?: FLATLAND
New value for FLATLAND <0>: 1
Command: Pline
From point: 7,14
Current line-width is 0.0000
Arc/Close/Halfwidth/Length/Undo/Width/<Endpoint of line>: @8<0
Arc/Close/Halfwidth/Length/Undo/Width/<Endpoint of line>: @4<90
Arc/Close/Halfwidth/Length/Undo/Width/<Endpoint of line>: @8<180
Arc/Close/Halfwidth/Length/Undo/Width/<Endpoint of line>: @1.625<-90
Arc/Close/Halfwidth/Length/Undo/Width/<Endpoint of line>: @1<0
Arc/Close/Halfwidth/Length/Undo/Width/<Endpoint of line>: A
Angle/CEnter/CLose/Direction/Halfwidth/Line/Radius/Second pt/Undo/Width/
<Endpoint of arc>: @.75<-90
Angle/CEnter/CLose/Direction/Halfwidth/Line/Radius/Second pt/Undo/Width/
<Endpoint of arc>: L
Arc/Close/Halfwidth/Length/Undo/Width/<Endpoint of line>: @1<180
Arc/Close/Halfwidth/Length/Undo/Width/<Endpoint of line>: C
Command: Fillet
Polyline/Radius/<Select two objects>: R
Enter fillet radius <0.0000>: .25
Command: Fillet
Polyline/Radius/<Select two objects>: P
```

Editing the Top View—continued

```
Select 2D polyline: L

6 lines were filleted

1 was parallel

Command: <Snap off> <Ortho off> Osnap

Object snap modes: END,INT

Command: Circle

3P/2P/TTR/<Center point>: 2P

First point on diameter: 13.4,17

Second point on diameter: 14.5,17

Command: Circle

3P/2P/TTR/<Center point>: 2P

First point on diameter: 13.7,17

Second point on diameter: 14.3,17

Command: Circle

3P/2P/TTR/<Center point>: 2P

First point on diameter: 13.4,15

Second point on diameter: 14.5,15

Command: Circle

3P/2P/TTR/<Center point>: 2P

First point on diameter: 13.7,15

Second point on diameter: 14.3,15
```

[Command: **Circle**] *(Ignore square bracket lines if you did not add the optional bracket hole.)*

```
[3P/2P/TTR/<Center point>: 2P]

[First point on diameter: 10.8,15.8]

[Second point on diameter: 11.28,15.57]
```

Toggle snap on

```
Command: Line

From point: 8.875,15.25

To point: @2.9<60

To point: @2.48<331

To point: @3<240

To point: C

Command: Line

From point: 9.5,14.875
```

Editing the Top View—continued

```
To point: @3<60
To point: Press Enter
Command: Line
From point: 9.75,14.75
To point: @3<60
To point: Press Enter
Command: Line
From point: 9.9375,14.625
To point: @3<60
To point: Press Enter
Command: Line
From point: 10.75,14.125
To point: @3<60
To point: Press Enter
[Command: Line] (Ignore square bracket lines if you did not add the optional bracket hole.)
[From point: PER]
[to 10,17.125]
[To point: TAN]
[to 11.25,15.875]
[To point: Press Enter]
[Command: Line]
[From point: PER]
[to 9.25,16]
[To point: TAN]
[to 11,15.4375]
[To point: Press Enter]
Command: Osnap
Object snap modes: NON
Command: Chprop
Select objects: 9.8125,16.125
1 selected, 1 found.
Select objects: 10.1875,16.5
1 selected, 1 found.
Select objects: 10.75,16.5625
```

Editing the Top View—continued

```
1 selected, 1 found.
Select objects: Press Enter
Change what property (Color/LAyer/LType/Thickness) ? LA
New layer <OBJECT>: HL
Change what property (Color/LAyer/LType/Thickness) ?
Command: Erase
Select objects: 9.9375,16.375
1 selected, 1 found.
Select objects: Press Enter
Command: Redraw
Command: End
```

When you have edited the view to your satisfaction, remove the 3D block drawing. Remember that you can save the temporary T-TOP drawing on the disk if you want. Your drawing should now resemble figure 17.16.

Figure 17.16:
The edited top view.

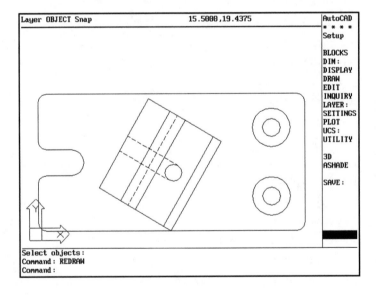

Purging Blocks, Layers, Linetypes, Shapes, and Styles

The T-TOP block is no longer in use in the M-ANGLE drawing, but it remains in the drawing database. It can be deleted.

The *Purge* command removes unused blocks, layers, linetypes, shapes, and styles to save file space and increase drawing loading speed. This command must be executed at the start of a drawing editor session before any drawing or editing commands are given. Purge prompts you for confirmation before it removes each item.

Purge the T-TOP block. Edit an existing drawing named M-ANGLE and follow these steps:

Purging Blocks

Command: **Purge**

Purge unused Blocks/LAyers/LTypes/SHapes/STyles/All: **B**

Purge block T-TOP? <N> **Y**

Command: **End**

Cleaning Up the 3D View—Optional

The 3D view is acceptable as a wireframe, although the 3D polygon mesh holes are a bit densely detailed. You can accept it as is (see fig. 17.17), or use one of the following alternatives:

- **Wireframe Option.** If you want to edit the view into a better wireframe, you can trace over it in a similar manner to the upper view. Use the Ellipse command to trace the holes and slot. It then will be necessary to break the ellipse to properly create the slot end. Or, instead of tracing over the part completely, you can salvage part of it by returning to Mspace and exploding the block. Then, for example, you could redraw the holes with ellipses and lines and erase the meshes of the holes. You may need to work in various UCSs for the best effect using this technique.

Figure 17.17:
3D wireframe view as is.

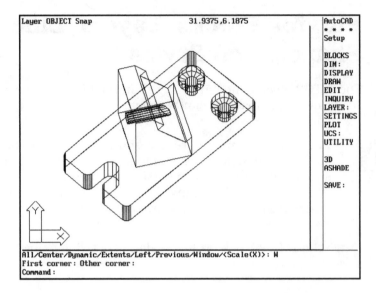

```
Layer OBJECT Snap                          31.9375,6.1875        AutoCAD
                                                                 * * * *
                                                                 Setup

                                                                 BLOCKS
                                                                 DIM:
                                                                 DISPLAY
                                                                 DRAW
                                                                 EDIT
                                                                 INQUIRY
                                                                 LAYER:
                                                                 SETTINGS
                                                                 PLOT
                                                                 UCS:
                                                                 UTILITY

                                                                 3D
                                                                 ASHADE

                                                                 SAVE:


All/Center/Dynamic/Extents/Left/Previous/Window/<Scale(X)>: W
First corner: Other corner:
Command:
```

- **Hide Option.** You can use the Hide command or plot the drawing with hidden lines removed, but it is not very practical. The command will take a very long time to consider all the irrelevant lines in the border, 2D views, and dimensioning. You have two alternatives: the DXB method, or plotting the 3D view separately from the rest of the drawing, but on the same sheet. Briefly, the DXB method involves configuring AutoCAD for an ADI plotter with the DXB option, then plotting the view to a file with hidden lines removed. The DXB file is then imported into the drawing with the Dxbin command. Both of these alternatives are discussed in detail in the book, *Inside AutoCAD* (New Riders Publishing).

Completing the 2D Front and Auxiliary Views—Optional

If you want to fully complete the M-ANGLE drawing, trace over the front and auxiliary views in the same manner as the upper view. When completed, the traced views should appear similar to those in figure 17.19.

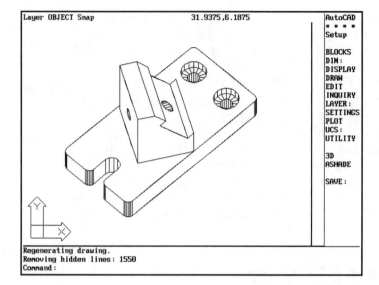

Figure 17.18:
3D view with Hide.

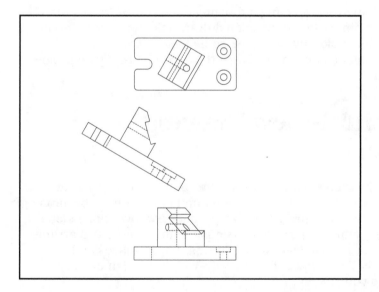

Figure 17.19:
Optional: Completed front
and auxiliary views.

■ **Front View.** Zoom in, make sure FLATLAND is on (1), set object snap to INT, END, turn snap off, and use the Line command to draw everything but the optional bracket hole. You may have to zoom in closer in some areas. After the lines are drawn, zoom in on the optional hole and draw two ellipses, connected by two lines.

To get the ellipse for the optional hole on the inclined face correct, you will have to trace it with 16 polyline segments and use the Pedit command's Fit Curve option on it. Then erase the block and invoke the Redraw command. Use the Chprop command to move hidden lines to layer HL, and then save the drawing.

■ **Auxiliary View.** Zoom to see the view and align the UCS with the Entity option. Use the Dview command's Twist option, zoom to align it to the screen (30 degrees), and zoom in close. Use lines with FLATLAND on and object snaps INT and END to trace it all. Zoom in closer, or zoom out and align with other object snaps and point filters on the upper view if needed. Erase the T-AUX block and use the Redraw command to cleanup the screen. Restore view BDR and UCS BDR. End the drawing and reload to purge the now unused blocks, then save the drawing.

Dimensioning 2D Views

There is nothing special about completing a drawing constructed in this manner. The views are now ordinary two-dimensional drawings. You can add geometric tolerancing and dimensioning using the same techniques covered in earlier chapters. Or you might want to do it with the Y14.5 Menu System. The completed dimensioning is shown in figure 17.1.

Creating a Multi-View Drawing in Paper Space

Release 11 adds a new drawing environment to AutoCAD called paper space. Model space is the three-dimensional drawing environment you have been using up to this point to construct your drawings. Paper space is a two-dimensional environment for adding certain types of dimensions, adding notes, and arranging views of your model for drawing within or plotting. Paper space can be thought of as an infinitely large sheet of paper with which you can open viewports that look onto your model.

Paper space viewports have some additional features over their model space counterparts. They can be any size, they do not have to touch (be tiled), and they can overlap one another. In addition, paper space viewports are like any other entity. This means that the viewport can be edited, copied, have color, and be assigned a layer. Also, the Vplayer (View Port LAYER) command allows each viewport to control what layers are visible or frozen within itself.

The Command Set for Paper Space Viewports

There are three primary commands and one system variable that use viewports in paper space. The TILEMODE system variable, when set to 0 (off) enables paper space. The Mview command makes paper space viewports, as well as performs other functions. To enter model space, use the Mspace command and to return to paper space, use the Pspace command.

Begin a new drawing named M-ANGLE=PROTO-D, then enable paper space, setup the border, and create four paper space viewports. Notice that three of the viewports overlap.

Creating Viewports in Paper Space

Command: **Layer**

?/Make/Set/New/ON/OFF/Color/Ltype/Freeze/Thaw: **T**

Layer name(s) to Thaw: *****

?/Make/Set/New/ON/OFF/Color/Ltype/Freeze/Thaw: *Press Enter*

Regenerating drawing.

Command: **Zoom**

All/Center/Dynamic/Extents/Left/Previous/Vmax/Window/<Scale(X/XP)>: **A**

Regenerating drawing.

Command: **Block**

Block name (or ?): **BDR-D**

Insertion base point: **-1,-1**

Select objects: **C**

First corner: **-.25,-.25**

Other corner: **32.25,20.25**

129 found

Select objects: *Press Enter*

Command: **TILEMODE**

New value for TILEMODE <1>: **0**

Entering Paper space.

Use Mview to insert model space viewports

Regenerating drawing.

Command: **Limits**

Reset Paper space limits:

ON/OFF/<Lower left corner> <0.0000,0.0000>: *Press Enter*

Creating Viewports in Paper Space—continued

Upper right corner <12.0000,9.0000>: **34,22**

Command: **Zoom**

All/Center/Dynamic/Extents/Left/Previous/Vmax/Window/<Scale(X/XP)>: **A**

Regenerating drawing.

Command: **Insert**

Block name (or ?): **BDR-D**

Insertion point: **0,0**

X scale factor <1> / Corner / XYZ: *Press Enter*

Y scale factor (default=X): *Press Enter*

Rotation angle <0>: *Press Enter*

Command: **Explode**

Select block reference, polyline, dimension, or mesh: *Pick anywhere on the BDR-D block*

Command: **Layer**

?/Make/Set/New/ON/OFF/Color/Ltype/Freeze/Thaw: **F**

Layer name(s) to Freeze: **????-CX,SPEC-OT**

?/Make/Set/New/ON/OFF/Color/Ltype/Freeze/Thaw: **N**

New layer name(s): **FRZ-VP,FRZ-BASE,FRZ-HOLES,FRZ-FACES,DIM-TOP,DIM-AUX,DIM-FRONT,TR-TOP,TR-AUX,TR-FRONT**

?/Make/Set/New/ON/OFF/Color/Ltype/Freeze/Thaw: **C**

Color: **Red**

Layer name(s) for color 1 (red) <OBJECT>: **DIM***

?/Make/Set/New/ON/OFF/Color/Ltype/Freeze/Thaw: **C**

Color: **Cyan**

Layer name(s) for color 4 (cyan) <OBJECT>: **TR***

?/Make/Set/New/ON/OFF/Color/Ltype/Freeze/Thaw: **S**

New current layer <OBJECT>: **FRZ-VP**

?/Make/Set/New/ON/OFF/Color/Ltype/Freeze/Thaw: *Press Enter*

Command: **Mview**

ON/OFF/Hideplot/Fit/2/3/4/Restore/<First Point>: **4,11.5**

Other corner: **20.75,20.75**

Regenerating drawing.

Command: **Mview**

ON/OFF/Hideplot/Fit/2/3/4/Restore/<First Point>: **4.5,6.5**

Creating Viewports in Paper Space—continued

```
Other corner: 14.75,14

Regenerating drawing.

Command: Mview

ON/OFF/Hideplot/Fit/2/3/4/Restore/<First Point>: 4,1.5

Other corner: 17,6.75

Regenerating drawing.

Command: Mview

ON/OFF/Hideplot/Fit/2/3/4/Restore/<First Point>: 21.5,7

Other corner: 30.5,17.25

Regenerating drawing.

Command: Save

File name <M-ANGLE>: Press Enter
```

Your drawing should now show the border in paper space and four paper space viewports (see fig. 17.20).

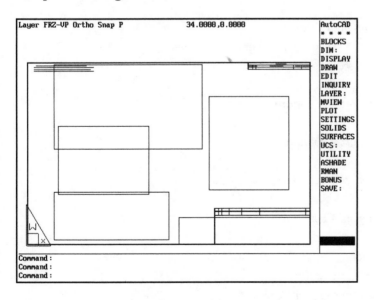

Figure 17.20:
Four paper space
viewports.

The next step in creating a multi-view drawing in paper space is to insert the angle bracket in model space and set up the various views of your model. Each view is created exactly the same as earlier in the chapter. This time, however, you need to be concerned with the scale of the object in each viewport. Because the model is small enough to be plotted at 1:1 scale on a D-size sheet, set the zoom scale in each viewport to the scale of paper space. The Zoom command's XP option scales the view to paper space.

Setting Up Views of the Model

Command: **Mspace**

Make viewport 1 current

Command: **UCS**

Origin/ZAxis/3point/Entity/View/X/Y/Z/Prev/Restore/Save/Del/?/<World>: **W**

Command: **Insert**

Block name (or ?): **ANGLE**

Insertion point: **0,0**

X scale factor <1> / Corner / XYZ: *Press Enter*

Y scale factor (default=X): *Press Enter*

Rotation angle <0>: *Press Enter*

Select Bonus, next, and MVSETUP

Loading C:\ACAD11\MVSETUP.LSP — Please wait.

C:MVSetup loaded.

Type **MVS** *or* **Mvsetup** *to set up your drawing*

MVSetup, Version 1.00b, (c) 1990 by Autodesk, Inc.

Align viewports/Create viewports/Scale viewports/Title block/Undo: **S**

Select the viewports to scale:

Select objects: *Pick viewport 1 boundary*

1 selected, 1 found

Select objects: *Pick viewport 2 boundary*

1 selected, 1 found

Select objects: *Pick viewport 3 boundary*

1 selected, 1 found

Select objects: *Pick viewport 4 boundary*

1 selected, 1 found

Select objects: *Press Enter*

Set zoom scale factors for viewports.

Interactively/<Uniform>: *Press Enter*

Enter the ratio of paper space units to model space units...

Number of paper space units. <1.0>: *Press Enter*

Number of model space units. <1.0>: *Press Enter*

Align viewports/Create viewports/Scale viewports/Title block/Undo: *Press Enter*

Setting Up Views of the Model—continued

Make viewport 1 current

Command: **Zoom**

All/Center/Dynamic/Extents/Left/Previous/Vmax/Window/<Scale(X/XP)>: **L**

Lower left corner point: **0,0**

Magnification or Height <9.2500> : **Press Enter**

Regenerating drawing.

Make viewport 2 current

Command: **Zoom**

All/Center/Dynamic/Extents/Left/Previous/Vmax/Window/<Scale(X/XP)>: **L**

Lower left corner point: **0,0**

Magnification or Height <7.5000> : *Press Enter*

Regenerating drawing.

Make viewport 3 current

Command: **Zoom**

All/Center/Dynamic/Extents/Left/Previous/Vmax/Window/<Scale(X/XP)>: **L**

Lower left corner point: **0,0**

Magnification or Height <5.2500> : *Press Enter*

Regenerating drawing.

Make viewport 4 current

Command: **Zoom**

All/Center/Dynamic/Extents/Left/Previous/Vmax/Window/<Scale(X/XP)>: **L**

Lower left corner point: **0,0**

Magnification or Height <10.2500> : *Press Enter*

Regenerating drawing.

Command: **Dview**

Select objects: **3,4**

1 selected, 1 found

Select objects: *Press Enter*

CAmera/TArget/Distance/POints/PAn/Zoom/TWist/CLip/Hide/Off/Undo/<eXit>: **CA**

Enter angle from X-Y plane <90.00>: **52**

Enter angle in X-Y plane from X axis <-90.00>: **-135**

CAmera/TArget/Distance/POints/PAn/Zoom/TWist/CLip/Hide/Off/Undo/<eXit>: *Press Enter*

Regenerating drawing.

Command: **Zoom**

All/Center/Dynamic/Extents/Left/Previous/Vmax/Window/<Scale(X/XP)>: **C**

Setting Up Views of the Model—continued

Center point: **7.5,5.5**

Magnification or Height <10.2500> : *Press Enter*

Make viewport 2 current

Command: **Dview**

Select objects: **L**

1 found

Select objects: *Press Enter*

CAmera/TArget/Distance/POints/PAn/Zoom/TWist/CLip/Hide/Off/Undo/<eXit>: **PO**

Enter target point <5.1471, 3.7500, 2.0000>: **END**

of **7.1793,6.2892**

Enter camera point <5.1471, 3.7500, 3.0000>: **END**

of **5.6478,3.6909**

CAmera/TArget/Distance/POints/PAn/Zoom/TWist/CLip/Hide/Off/Undo/<eXit>: *Press Enter*

Regenerating drawing.

Make viewport 3 current

Command: **Dview**

Select objects: **L**

1 found

Select objects: *Press Enter*

CAmera/TArget/Distance/POints/PAn/Zoom/TWist/CLip/Hide/Off/Undo/<eXit>: **PO**

Enter target point <6.5896, 2.6250, 2.0000>: **7,3,0**

Enter camera point <6.5896, 2.6250, 3.0000>: **7,0,0**

CAmera/TArget/Distance/POints/PAn/Zoom/TWist/CLip/Hide/Off/Undo/<eXit>: *Press Enter*

Regenerating drawing.

Command: **UCS**

Origin/ZAxis/3point/Entity/View/X/Y/Z/Prev/Restore/Save/Del/?/<World>: **V**

Command: **Pan**

Displacement: **7,0**

Second point: **@2.25<270**

Regenerating drawing.

Command: **UCS**

Origin/ZAxis/3point/Entity/View/X/Y/Z/Prev/Restore/Save/Del/?/<World>: **P**

Command: **Save**

File name <M-ANGLE>: *Press Enter*

The orthographic views should now appear similar to figure 17.21.

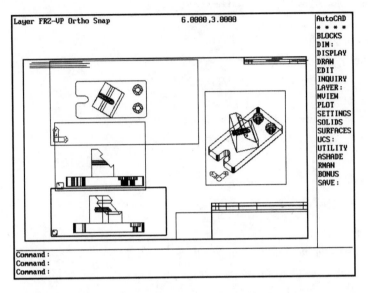

Figure 17.21:
The set up orthographic views.

Surfaces shared between views are only dimensioned once. It is important for orthographic views to line up with each other so dimensions can be read properly. The next step shows you how to use the Mvsetup command to align views across viewports.

Aligning Geometry in Paper Space Viewports

Make viewport 1 current

Command: **Pan**

Displacement: **3,3**

Second point: **@1.6441<351**

Command: **Mvsetup**

MVSetup, Version 1.00b, (c) 1990 by Autodesk, Inc.

Align viewports/Create viewports/Scale viewports/Title block/Undo: **A**

Angled/Horizontal/Vertical alignment/Rotate view/Undo? **V**

Basepoint: **END**

of **4.875,4.25**

Other point: **END**

of *Pick bubble point 1 (see fig. 17.22)*

Angled/Horizontal/Vertical alignment/Rotate view/Undo? **R**

Aligning Geometry in Paper Space Viewports—continued

```
Specify in which viewport the view is to be rotated.
Basepoint: END
```
of *Pick bubble point 2 (see fig. 17.22).*
```
Angle from basepoint: -30
*** Switching to the WCS ***
*** Returning to the UCS ***
Angled/Horizontal/Vertical alignment/Rotate view/Undo? A
```
Make viewport 1 current
```
Basepoint: END
```
of **4.875,4.25**

Make viewport 2 current
```
Other point: END
```
of *Pick bubble point 2 again*

Specify the distance and angle to the new alignment point

in the current viewport where you specified the basepoint
```
Distance from basepoint: 4
Angle from basepoint: 240
Angled/Horizontal/Vertical alignment/Rotate view/Undo? Press Enter
Align viewports/Create viewports/Scale viewports/Title block/Undo: Press Enter
Command: Save
File name <M-ANGLE>: Press Enter
```

All the orthographic views are aligned as seen in figure 17.22.

Note Once the views are scaled and aligned, do not pan or zoom in any viewport. Pans and zooms should be done while in paper space.

Next, prepare the model for indicating hidden lines and breaks. Because the model was made from 3Dfaces, some of the lines that appear solid are actually made up of short line segments. These short line segments need to be frozen and replaced with solid lines. Also, the entire base does not need to be shown in the auxiliary view, so it can be shown broken on either end. This is done by tracing a portion of the base and then freezing the base in the auxiliary view. The holes are frozen in all views except the 3D view and need to be traced. The Vplayer command will be used later to choose which layers are visible in individual viewports.

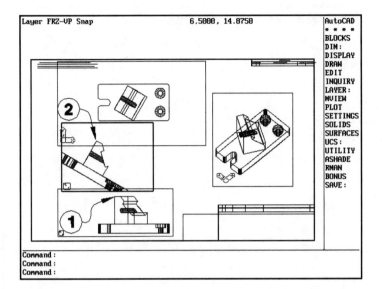

Prepare for Tracing

Command: **Explode**

Select block reference, polyline, dimension, or mesh: **5.5,7**

Command: **Chprop**

Select objects: **W**

First corner: **9.125,3.25**

Other corner: **10.75,6.75**

2 found

Select objects: **5.875,5.375**

[1 selected, 1 found] *(Ignore square bracket lines if you did not add the optional bracket hole.)*

[Select objects: *Press Enter*]

Change what property (Color/LAyer/LType/Thickness) ? **LA**

New layer <OBJECT>: **FRZ-HOLES**

Change what property (Color/LAyer/LType/Thickness) ? *Press Enter*

Command: **Chprop**

Select objects: **W**

First corner: **2.75,2.75**

Other corner: **11.25,7.25**

88 found

Select objects: **R**

Remove objects: **C**

Prepare for Tracing—continued

```
First corner: 4.625,3.125
Other corner: 10.625,6.75
61 found, 61 removed
Remove objects: Press Enter
Change what property (Color/LAyer/LType/Thickness) ? LA
New layer <OBJECT>: FRZ-BASE
Change what property (Color/LAyer/LType/Thickness) ? Press Enter
Command: Pspace
Command: Zoom
All/Center/Dynamic/Extents/Left/Previous/Vmax/Window/<Scale(X/XP)>: W
First corner: 11.125,4.5
Other corner: 13.125,4.875
Regenerating drawing.
Command: Mspace
Command: UCS
Origin/ZAxis/3point/Entity/View/X/Y/Z/Prev/Restore/Save/Del/?/<World>: V
Command: Chprop
Select objects: C
First corner: 5.7261,3.2099
Other corner: 6.3211,3.2343
4 found
Select objects: C
First corner: 6.3529,3.2031
Other corner: 7.1805,3.2382
5 found (2 duplicate)
Select objects: Press Enter
Change what property (Color/LAyer/LType/Thickness) ? LA
New layer <OBJECT>: FRZ-FACES
Change what property (Color/LAyer/LType/Thickness) ? Press Enter
Command: UCS
Origin/ZAxis/3point/Entity/View/X/Y/Z/Prev/Restore/Save/Del/?/<World>: P
Command: Pspace
Command: Zoom
All/Center/Dynamic/Extents/Left/Previous/Vmax/Window/<Scale(X/XP)>: P
Regenerating drawing.
Command: Save
File name <M-ANGLE>: Press Enter
```

Now you are ready to trace portions of the model and learn how to use Vplayer to control layer visibility in individual viewports. Place the traced geometry on the TR- layers. The traced top entities go on the TR-TOP layer, the traced auxiliary view entities go on the TR-AUX layer, etc. When you are done tracing the top, zoom out and notice that the traced entities appear in all viewports. Then use the Vplayer command to freeze the TR-TOP layer in viewports two, three, and four.

Tracing 3D Geometry

Command: **Zoom**

All/Center/Dynamic/Extents/Left/Previous/Vmax/Window/<Scale(X/XP)>: **W**

First corner: **3.75,11.25**

Other corner: **21,21**

Regenerating drawing.

Command: **Mspace**

Command: LAYER

?/Make/Set/New/ON/OFF/Color/Ltype/Freeze/Thaw: **S**

New current layer <FRZ-VP>: **TR-TOP**

?/Make/Set/New/ON/OFF/Color/Ltype/Freeze/Thaw: *Press Enter*

Command: **Osnap**

Object snap modes: **END**

Command: **Circle**

3P/2P/TTR/<Center point>: **2P**

First point on diameter: **9.375,6**

Second point on diameter: **10.625,6**

Command: **Circle**

3P/2P/TTR/<Center point>: **2P**

First point on diameter: **9.75,6**

Second point on diameter: **10.25,6**

Command: **Circle**

3P/2P/TTR/<Center point>: **2P**

First point on diameter: **9.375,4**

Second point on diameter: **10.625,4**

Command: **Circle**

3P/2P/TTR/<Center point>: **2P**

First point on diameter: **9.75,4**

Second point on diameter: **10.25,4**

[Command: **Pspace**] *(Ignore square bracket lines if you did not add the optional bracket hole.)*

[Command: **Zoom**]

▶ **Tracing 3D Geometry—continued**

[All/Center/Dynamic/Extents/Left/Previous/Vmax/Window/<Scale(X/XP)>: **W**]

[First corner: **10.875,15.625**]

[Other corner: **13.25,17.125**]

[Regenerating drawing.]

[Command: **Mspace**]

[Command: <Snap off> **Circle**]

[3P/2P/TTR/<Center point>: **2P**]

[First point on diameter: **7.194,4.91**]

[Second point on diameter: **6.938,4.47**]

[Command: **Line**]

[From point: **Tan**]

[to *Pick anywhere on the circle*]

[To point: **5.75,5.75**]

[To point: *Press Enter*]

[Command: **Line**]

[From point: **Tan**]

[to]

[*Toggle snap off*]

[To point: **5.4821,5.3014**]

[To point:]

[*Toggle snap on*]

[Command: **Pspace**]

[Command: **Zoom**]

[All/Center/Dynamic/Extents/Left/Previous/Vmax/Window/<Scale(X/XP)>: **P**]

[Regenerating drawing.]

Command: **Vplayer**

?/Freeze/Thaw/Reset/Newfrz/Vpvisdflt: F

Layer(s) to Freeze: **FRZ-HOLES,FRZ-FACES**

All/Select/<Current>: **S**

Select objects: **4,17.75**

1 selected, 1 found

Select objects:

?/Freeze/Thaw/Reset/Newfrz/Vpvisdflt:

Regenerating drawing.

Command: **Mspace**

Command: **Line**

From point: **5.75,3.75**

Tracing 3D Geometry—continued

```
To point: @2.8771<60
To point:
Command: Chprop
Select objects: L
1 found
Select objects: 6,5.625
1 selected, 1 found
Select objects: 5.75,5.125
1 selected, 1 found
Select objects:
Change what property (Color/LAyer/LType/Thickness) ? LT
New linetype <BYLAYER>: HIDDEN
Change what property (Color/LAyer/LType/Thickness) ?
Command: Pspace
Command: Zoom
All/Center/Dynamic/Extents/Left/Previous/Vmax/Window/<Scale(X/XP)>: P
Regenerating drawing.
Command: Layer
?/Make/Set/New/ON/OFF/Color/Ltype/Freeze/Thaw: S
New current layer <TR-TOP>: TR-AUX
?/Make/Set/New/ON/OFF/Color/Ltype/Freeze/Thaw:
Command: Vplayer
?/Freeze/Thaw/Reset/Newfrz/Vpvisdflt: F
Layer(s) to Freeze: TR-TOP
All/Select/<Current>: S
Select objects: 14.75,8
1 selected, 1 found
Select objects: 17,6
1 selected, 1 found
Select objects: 23.5,8
1 selected, 1 found
Select objects:
?/Freeze/Thaw/Reset/Newfrz/Vpvisdflt: F
Layer(s) to Freeze: FRZ-BASE
All/Select/<Current>: S
Select objects: 14.75,8
1 selected, 1 found
```

Tracing 3D Geometry—continued

```
Select objects:
?/Freeze/Thaw/Reset/Newfrz/Vpvisdflt:
Regenerating drawing.
```

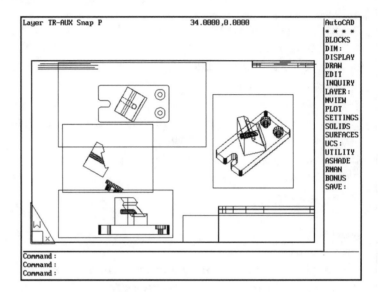

Figure 17.23:
The 3D-traced top.

Dimensioning a 3D View

Dimensioning a 3D view sometimes is required for assembly instructions and exploded parts drawings. You will apply angular, diameter, and horizontal dimensions to the 3D view of the angle support. The actual dimensioning commands work exactly as you are accustomed to in 2D work, but some preparation is required before you can use them. There are two problems to consider.

First, some dimensioning commands expect to find certain kinds of entities. The Diameter or Radius dimension commands, for example, expect you to select circles or arcs. But your 3D object is made up of 3D meshes and 3Dfaces—not lines, 2D polylines, arcs, and circles — so you must add dimensionable entities before dimensioning at times. Be sure the drawing is in the appropriate UCS for each entity when added and use object snaps to make sure the added entities align with the existing 3D geometry.

Second, you must align UCSs to the entities being dimensioned when you dimension them. Dimensions are 2D entities and are generated in the current UCS. If the current UCS is not coplanar with the entity being dimensioned, you actually will dimension the entity's projection into the UCS, not its true size. An aligned dimension in the WCS object snapped to the 2.5-inch front left baseline of the angle support, for example, would come out 2.468 in the T-3D view you wrote to disk earlier. To perform dimensioning on a 3D part, the UCS must be properly positioned to align the dimensions to the part.

Draw an angular dimension between the baseline of the angle bracket and the angle base. First set the UCS, then dimension it. You will need either the T-3D drawing used earlier in this chapter or the D-3D drawing from the AutoCAD: Drafting and 3D Design Disk.

Follow these steps to draw an angular dimension between the baseline of the angle bracket and the angle base:

Angular Dimensioning in 3D

 Begin a new drawing named DIM-3D=D-3D.

 Begin a new drawing named DIM-3D=T-3D.

```
Command: SPLFRAME
New value for SPLFRAME <1>: 0
Command: LUPREC
New value for LUPREC <4>: 3
Command: Regen
Regenerating drawing.
Command: UCS
Origin/ZAxis/3point/Entity/View/X/Y/Z/Prev/Restore/Save/Del/?/<World>: 3
Origin point <0,0,0>: NEA
to .188,4.125
Point on positive portion of the X-axis <1.197,4.114,-1.945>: NEA
to @2<38
Point on positive-Y portion of the UCS X-Y plane <-0.422,4.899,-1.945>: NEA
to @3.5<137
Command: Dim1
Dim: ANG
Select arc, circle, line, or RETURN: Press Enter
Angle vertex: INT
of 3.75,0
```

Angular Dimensioning in 3D—continued

First angle endpoint: **@3<180**

Second angle endpoint: **INT**

of **@2.5<150**

Enter dimension line arc location: **.875,.875**

Dimension text <30>: *Press Enter*

Enter text location: **@**

Your drawing should resemble figures 17.24 and 17.25.

To do a diameter dimension, you first need to draw a circle over the counter-sunk hole, which is made of a 3D polygon mesh. The current UCS will work for this.

Continue in the previous drawing and follow these steps:

3D Diameter Dimensioning

Command: **Zoom**

All/Center/Dynamic/Extents/Left/Previous/Vmax/Window/<Scale(X/XP)>: **W**

First corner: **5.375,.625**

Other corner: **9.75,.625**

Command: **Circle**

3P/2P/TTR/<Center point>: **2P**

First point on diameter: **INT**

of **6.188,1**

Second point on diameter: **INT**

of **7.313,1**

Command: **Dim1**

Dim: **Dia**

Select arc or circle: **7.063,.563**

Dimension text <1.125>: **<>** *Followed by 6 spaces*

Enter leader length for text: **7.875,-.5**

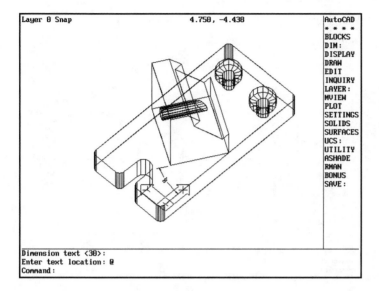

Figure 17.24:
Completed angular dimension in 3D.

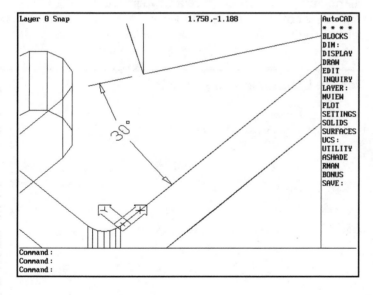

Figure 17.25:
Detail of angular dimension.

Figure 17.26:
Completed diameter
dimension.

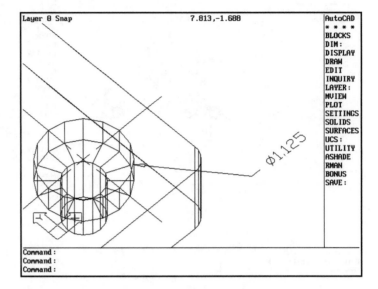

Horizontal and vertical dimensioning likewise require a properly oriented UCS. But you do not need to create new entities unless you want to use the entity option. Dimension the height of the bracket at its back left edge, as follows:

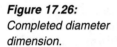

Vertical Dimensioning in 3D

```
Command: Zoom
All/Center/Dynamic/Extents/Left/Previous/Vmax/Window/<Scale(X/XP)>: P
Command: UCS
Origin/ZAxis/3point/Entity/View/X/Y/Z/Prev/Restore/Save/Del/?/<World>: 3
Origin point <0,0,0>: INT
of 3.063,3.813
Point on positive portion of the X-axis <4.057,3.848,0.000>: INT
of @2.542<330
Point on positive-Y portion of the UCS X-Y plane <3.557,4.714,0.000>: INT
of 2.366<44
Command: Dim1
Dim: VER
First extension line origin or RETURN to select: INT
of 0,3
Second extension line origin: INT
```

Vertical Dimensioning in 3D—continued

of **0,0**

Dimension line location: **-.5,1**

Dimension text <3.000>: *Press Enter*

Command: **End**

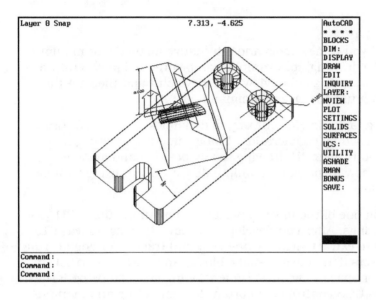

Figure 17.27:
Completed 3D vertical dimension.

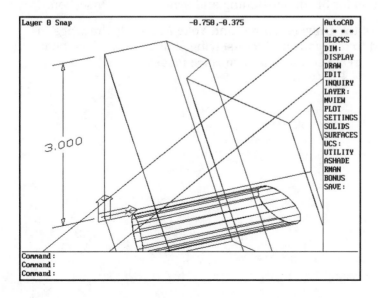

Figure 17.28:
Detail of vertical dimension.

You can use the same techniques to complete the rest of the part if you want. The process is to set your UCS, add entities if needed, and dimension normally. Be careful with your object snaps, because groups of 3D faces with invisible edges have many little unseen intersections between them. You also can add the appropriate Y14.5 symbols. The same principal applies for inserting symbols; the UCS position controls the block insertion.

Summary

This chapter introduced you to new tools and alternative methods for manipulating 3D drawings. A 3D drawing, for example, can be oriented in several ways. You can set the UCS and then use plan view; use viewpoint and then set the UCS to match; or you can use the Dview command.

The Dview command is a fast and efficient way to dynamically view your drawing without the delay caused by regeneration. Using camera-like terms, it enables you to drag and rotate your 3D drawing to any position and angle in full 3D space. You also saw how to view and manipulate your 3D drawing with perspective vanishing points.

This chapter showed you one of the most important 3D manipulations: 2D view extraction from 3D drawings. After you develop a 3D part drawing, Release 10 users can create blocks to extract virtually any view and trace it for engineering drawings. Release 11 users don't have to make blocks and only have to set up the proper views in paper space viewports. Dimensioning also can be performed on 3D drawings. Just as UCS control is important for generating and manipulating 3D geometry, so it is for 3D dimensioning and symbol block insertion.

The 3D Surface Models of the Universal Joint and Yoke Assembly drawings in Chapter 18 are designed to test your problem-solving skills. You will see how AutoCAD can be used to create sophisticated surface models.

18

ADVANCED 3D SURFACE MODELING

In this chapter:

- Modeling the U-joint cap
- Modeling the yoke
- Modeling the U-joint
- Creating a 3D exploded illustration

Overview

You have seen how AutoCAD can be used to make realistic-looking 3D geometry, but it is capable of modeling objects much more complicated than the ones you have built so far. This chapter explores AutoCAD's capabilities at a more sophisticated level. By using AutoCAD's 3D polygon mesh commands to create 3D meshes, you can construct three-dimensional models of surprising complexity and realism, such as the universal joint and yoke assembly shown in figure 18.1.

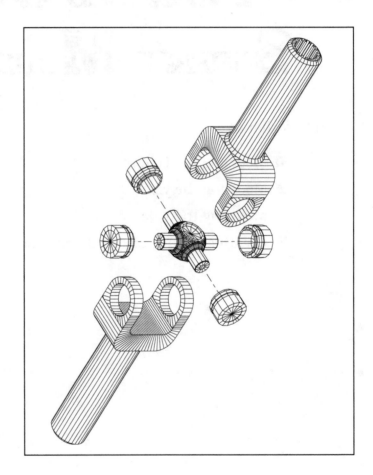

Figure 18.1:
Optional: Universal joint and yoke assembly.

The following instructions do not provide the command sequences necessary to walk you through the construction of this model. They give you an outline to follow and leave the details for you to work out on your own. It can be done more than one way, so you may find techniques you prefer to those presented. Don't hesitate to experiment. Using these instructions, your ingenuity, and the techniques and commands you already have learned, you should be able to complete this exercise and test your problem-solving skills.

Build each part of the universal joint and yoke assembly separately, and then combine all the pieces into a final composite drawing. This not only helps to keep file sizes manageable but also causes displays to generate faster and lines to be hidden sooner as you work on individual parts.

The construction envelope technique introduced earlier helps you visualize the parts you are drawing. The envelope also provides convenient object snap points for the basic shape of the part being drawn.

You should work in the predefined UCS and viewports, both named SCRATCH, in the PROTO-3D prototype drawing. This enables you to create 3D geometry in one portion of 3D space, within a construction envelope. Rotate finished portions of each part 180 degrees about the origin into clean space in the WCS to move them out of the way for subsequent commands and to allow easy selection for blocking.

Use the predefined viewports and align the UCS to aid in the following steps. Make all profiles and path curves on the CONST layer and switch when necessary to create finished meshes on the OBJECT layer. Remember to define blocks on layer 0 for future flexibility.

Modeling the U-Joint Cap

Begin with the Revsurf command and build one U-joint cap, write it to disk, insert it into the final drawing, and array it into place for the other three caps.

Begin a new drawing named 3D-CAP=PROTO-3D. Use figure 18.2 as a guide to draw the profile of the cap section as a polyline.

Set the system variable SURFTAB1 to 16. Execute the Revsurf command. Select the profile polyline for the path curve, the center line for the axis of rotation, and 360 degrees of included angle. You can experiment with other SURFTAB1 and SURFTAB2 settings by erasing the mesh, changing the variables, and running the Revsurf command again to see the results. Your finished cap should resemble figure 18.2.

If necessary, mirror the completed cap so that the open end is pointing in the positive Z direction of the SCRATCH UCS, and move the center of the cap and center line to 0,0. Save the cap and center line to a file named B-CAP with the Wblock command using 0,0,0 as the insertion point. This part of the drawing should look like figure 18.2 after you complete these steps. When you are finished, end the drawing and continue.

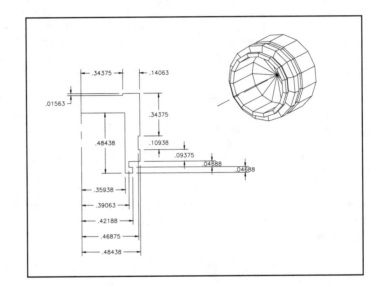

Figure 18.2:
The cap profile and modeled cap.

Modeling the Yoke

Now draw the drive shaft yoke using the Rulesurf, Tabsurf, and Edgesurf commands and a construction envelope. Mirror and rotate the yoke later to create a second.

Use figure 18.3 as a guide for drawing the construction envelope of the yoke. Manipulate the UCS to the three planes when necessary. When the envelope is complete, set the UCS parallel to the circles where the yoke is attached to the spline shaft.

Use the two inner circles of the construction envelope for the inner and outer boundaries of the splines, creating one complete spline profile. Draw a line from the center past the second circle and polar array it 28 times about the center. Draw a polyline with Int object snaps as shown in figure 18.4. The polyline is shown wide for clarity and should be drawn with a width of zero. Array the single polyline spline 14 times about the center point. Use the Pedit command to join the 14 splines into one polyline. Copy the spline polyline to the other end of the shaft center line and use the Tabsurf command to finish the 3D spline.

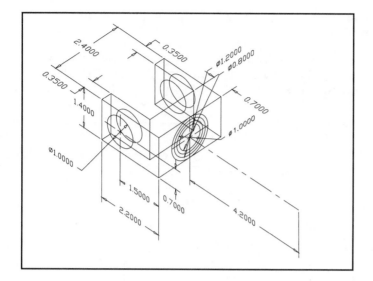

Figure 18.3:
The yoke construction envelope.

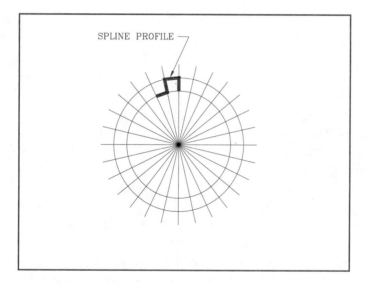

Figure 18.4:
Spline to be arrayed.

Change the third construction circle to the Object layer and use the Tabsurf command to create the shaft by passing first the spline path curve along the 4.2-inch center line, and then the third circle only 4.1 inches along the center line. These leave room for a 0.1-inch chamfer between the outside surface of the shaft and the inside edge of the splines.

Build the chamfer at the end of the shaft and the weldment between the yoke and shaft with the Revsurf command. Use 3Dface to close the end of one spline and array it around the shaft. The completed yoke and shaft should appear similar to the one in figure 18.5.

Use the Fillet command to radius the edges of the yoke to the dimensions shown in figure 18.5. With lines, "close off" one ear of the yoke from the body at the point where the ears intersect the arcs that the Fillet command created.

Figure 18.5:
Yoke size description.

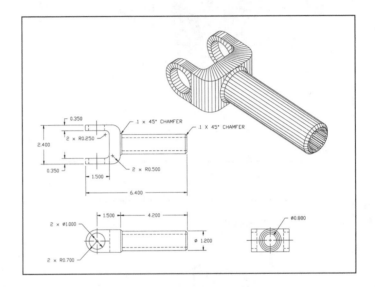

Join the arcs and lines of one side of one ear into a polyline and copy it to the other side of the same ear. With the Rulesurf command, click on the two polylines and then the two circles, making one ear. Copy it to the other side of the yoke.

Join the arcs and lines on either the top or bottom of the yoke body into a co-planar polyline, and use the Tabsurf command to pass this path curve along one of the 1.4-inch construction lines to model the curved surfaces of the yoke body.

Join the arcs and lines at the other side of the yoke body into two polylines and two lines on the same plane. One polyline will include two arcs and one line forming the inside curved edge of the yoke, and the other polyline will include two short line segments, two arcs, and one longer line segment that form the outer curved edge of the yoke. The remaining two lines are the intersection of the yoke body and the two ears. With these four entities, use the Edgesurf command to close the yoke body top and bottom that were left open by the tabulated surfaces you made in the last step.

Write the yoke and shaft to a file named B-YOKE with the insertion point at the end of the shaft's center, and end this drawing.

Modeling the U-Joint

With the cap, yoke, and shaft complete, all that remains is the U-joint. This part, however, requires more analytical skills than the previous parts.

Begin a new drawing UJOINT=PROTO-3D. Use the dimensions shown in figure 18.6 to draw the U-JOINT's arm profile and center line.

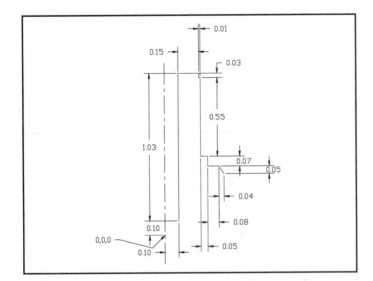

Figure 18.6:
U-JOINT arm profile.

Sweep the profile 360 degrees around the center line with the Revsurf command.

Use the Array command and the polar option to replicate the entity around a center point so that the circumference of each surface of revolution is tangent to the adjacent one.

Draw the hub center with a 0.1-inch relief by constructing a polyline and revolving the polyline around a center line of the cross with the Revsurf command. Ensure that the hub center is perpendicular and tangent to the four 3D meshes created in the last step. Mirror the hub center to the back side of the U-joint.

Refer to figure 18.8 to enclose one of the remaining eight openings of the U-joint with the Edgesurf command. Compare the curve of the patch with other viewpoints. Use construction lines to divide the triangular opening into three sections, coinciding at the center of the opening. Patch one of these sections and array it about center point.

Figure 18.7:
Universal joint with hidden lines removed.

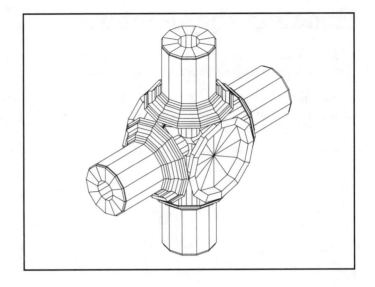

Figure 18.8:
Coons surface patch.

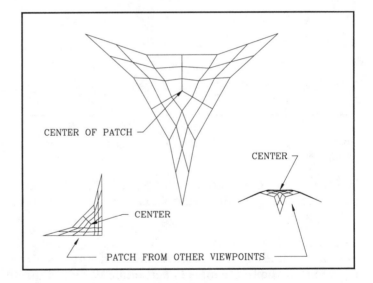

Mirror and array the resulting surface patches into position over the other openings. Your completed U-joint should resemble figure 18.7.

Use the Wblock command to save the U-joint to a file named B-UJOINT, with a convenient insertion point and end the drawing.

Creating a 3D Exploded Illustration

Now bring each of the pieces completed thus far into one exploded assembly illustration as shown in figure 18.9. Removing the hidden lines from this drawing will take a considerable amount of time, so plan appropriately.

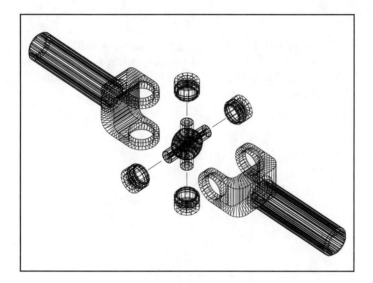

Figure 18.9:
Complete assembly in wireframe.

Begin a new drawing named EXPILL=PROTO-3D. Insert the B-YOKE block first and align it as necessary to provide room both for the other parts and for mirroring the yoke 180 degrees.

Mirror the yoke to produce its counterpart on the opposing side of the U-joint and rotate the new yoke 90 degrees along its center line to accommodate the alternating U-joint arms.

Insert the CAPBLK block and align it between and below the two B-YOKE blocks.

Use the Array command with the polar option to array one cap into four, using the centerline of the yoke shaft as the center point.

Insert the B-UJOINT block at the center of the B-CAP array, making sure to align it carefully with the caps and yokes.

Now you can view the finished assembly from various angles with the Dview, Hide, and Shade commands, and plot it. The finished assembly is shown in figure 18.9 in wireframe, and at the beginning of this chapter in figure 18.1 with hidden lines removed.

This completes the instructions for the advanced 3D surface modeling exercise. You have explored some powerful 3D surface modeling tools.

Summary

This chapter tested your 3D surface modeling and problem-solving skills. AutoCAD may be used to construct sophisticated 3D models such as the universal joint and yoke assembly. If you tackled this exercise, you enhanced your 3D modeling skills beyond the general level.

DOS, BATCH FILES, AND TEXT EDITORS

This appendix describes common DOS (Disk Operating System) operations and AutoCAD file-handling procedures to help you manage the AutoCAD program and drawing files. If you need additional information on DOS commands or syntax, refer to your DOS reference manual.

Working with Files

DOS refers to program or data information as *files*. You can think of a file as an individual document in your office's file cabinet. The folder that holds a number of related documents is the *subdirectory*, and the file cabinet itself is like the hard drive where the files and subdirectories are stored.

Each file requires a unique name, called a *file name*, that distinguishes it from the many other files in the computer system. A file name can consist of up to eight characters, with an optional three-character extension following a period. AutoCAD drawing files, for example, use the extension DWG. Some keyboard characters, however, are invalid for use in file names, including " / \ [ ] : | + = ; , and . (period).

When specifying files for DOS operations, you often can save keystrokes and operate on several groups of files at one time by using the question mark and asterisk wild-card characters. The question mark (?) wild card substitutes for a single character, whereas the asterisk (*) wildcard substitutes for multiple characters. Table A.2 shows examples on how to use wild card characters.

Table A.2
Wild Card Characters

Characters	Function
PART?.DWG	Finds all DWG files beginning with PART, followed by any single character
PART*.DWG	Finds all DWG files beginning with PART, followed by any other characters
???.DWG	Finds all DWG files that have three-character file names
*.DWG	Finds all DWG files
PART*.*	Finds all files that begin with PART
.	Finds all files

Using DOS Directory Commands To Manage Files and Directories

Computer systems can access an unlimited number of files. You can organize the files on your disk into meaningful groups, called *subdirectories*. Subdirectories are organized in a tree-type structure similar to the AutoCAD menu hierarchy.

The *root directory* of a disk is the basic level of DOS. You can think of the directory as a tree in which the elements of the directory branch downward. The topmost entry on the directory tree is the root directory. The root directory holds up to 512 files and subdirectories, and usually is where you store only the basic files the system needs to start up. You should store all other files in organized subdirectories, making it easier to find files for both you and DOS.

Subdirectories, which use the same naming conventions as files, can hold as many files as disk space allows. The directory you are working in is known by DOS as the *current* subdirectory. DOS remembers the last subdirectory you were in on the other drives in your system. If you are in the C:\ACAD subdirectory, for example, iand you change to a new directory in a different drive specification by entering D:\SHOP, DOS remembers (as stored in memory) the last directory you were in. You may, therefore, return to the ACAD subdirectory simply by entering C: and DOS returns you to C:\ACAD.

Navigating through Directories (DIR)

The DIR command lists all or specified files contained in a subdirectory. Table A.2 shows how to use the DIR command, as well as the different switches and options available to it.

Table A.2
The DIR Command Options

Command	Function
C:\>> **DIR**	Displays a list of the files in the current directory or subdirectory
C:\>> **DIR A:*.DWG**	Displays a list of all drawing files in the root directory of the disk in drive A
C:\>> **DIR \ACAD-DWG**	Displays a list of all files in the subdirectory named ACAD-DWG
C:\>> **DIR /P**	Displays a directory list one screen page at a time for easier viewing
C:\ACAD-DWG>> **DIR *.DWG /P**	Displays a directory list of all DWG files in the ACAD-DWG subdirectory one screen page at a time
C:\>> **DIR /W**	Displays a directory list in a wide list format

Creating Directories (MD or MKDIR)

The MD or MKDIR command creates a new directory in the root directory, or a subdirectory in an existing directory. You can make as many directories as you want, but each must have a different name. This name cannot be the same as a file name in the current directory. Table A.3 shows how to use the MD command, as well as the options available to it.

Subdirectories can be nested; that is, a directory can have subdirectories of its own, and they can have further nested subdirectories. In the ACAD-DWG\JOHN example in table A.3, for example, the JOHN directory is nested in the subdirectory named ACAD-DWG.

Table A.3
The MD Command Options

Command	Function
`C:\>> MD ACAD-DWG`	Makes a subdirectory named ACAD-DWG in the current directory
`C:\>> MD ACAD-DWG\JOHN`	Makes a subdirectory named JOHN in ACAD-DWG, the parent subdirectory
`C:\>> MD B:\DAVE`	Makes a subdirectory named DAVE in the root directory of drive B

Changing Directories (CD or CHDIR)

The CD or CHDIR (change directory) command is used to make another directory the current directory. This is similar to putting one folder away and taking out another. You must, however, follow the directory tree structure (close the open folder) by first changing to a subdirectory's parent directory (the directory "above" the current directory) when traversing a file tree. It is not possible, in current versions of DOS, to jump across subdirectories in a single operation. The CD command also can be used to display the name of the current subdirectory.

Table A.4
The CD Command Options

Command	Functions
`C:\>> CD \ACAD`	Makes the ACAD subdirectory the current directory
`C:\APPS\CAD\>> CD ACAD`	Makes the ACAD subdirectory, located in the parent CAD subdirectory, current
`C:\ACAD>> CD \`	Makes the root directory current
`C:\>> CD B:\ACAD-DWG`	Makes the ACAD-DWG subdirectory of disk drive B: current, while the current drive remains unchanged
`C:\APPS\CAD\>> CD C:\APPS\CAD\`	Displays the directory name

Saving AutoCAD Drawing Files in Subdirectories

You can save AutoCAD drawings in any existing subdirectory during an AutoCAD session in three ways. You can specify the subdirectory with the file name when you use the Save command in AutoCAD as follows:

```
Enter name of drawing:          Places ARM in subdirectory
\DRAWINGS\ARM                   named DRAWINGS
```

Or, you can change the directory in the Save dialogue box by clicking on the directory name. After clicking inside the box, you may edit the subdirectory name or delete the existing name and enter a subdirectory name when you want the file saved.

Finally, you can specify the subdirectory with the file name when you begin a new drawing as follows:

```
Save file name <<PIN>>:          Places PIN in the subdirectory
\JOHN\PIN                        named JOHN
```

Using Path Commands

A *path* is one or more directories that must be "opened" to reach a specified file. In \DRAWINGS\ARM.DWG and \APPS\CAD\PIN.DWG, for example, \DRAW-INGS and \APPS\CAD are the *path names*. Path names must be separated from file names by backslashes.

The PATH command in DOS specifies a set of paths that DOS searches for executable files (such as COM, EXE, and BAT files). The path name `PATH C:\;C:\DOS;C:\ACAD`, for example, tells DOS to first look in the root directory of drive C, then in the C:\DOS directory, and finally in the C:\ACAD directory when given a command or program name to execute at the DOS command prompt. The path usually is specified in the AUTOEXEC.BAT file.

Removing Directories (RD or RMDIR)

The RD or RMDIR (remove directory) command removes a subdirectory from a disk. A subdirectory cannot be removed if it contains files or other subdirectories. You first must delete all files and remove all subdirectories, and then make the subdirectory's parent directory current before you can remove the subdirectory. To remove a subdirectory named DRAWINGS from the root directory, for example, enter the following:

```
C:\>> RD \DRAWINGS
```

Using DOS File Commands

The following DOS commands are commonly used on files. DOS is not case-sensitive; that is, you can input commands from the keyboard in uppercase, lowercase, or mixed case.

Disk drives are referred to as the *source drive* (from which information is transferred from) and the *target drive* (from which information is transferred to).

Copying Files (COPY)

The COPY command copies files from one disk or directory to another. When copying AutoCAD drawings or backup files, you must include the file extension or appropriate wild cards.

When you copy a file to a destination that contains an existing file with the same name, the file at the destination is overwritten by the new file, without any warning. Table A.5 shows how to use the COPY command, as well as the options and switches available to it.

Table A.5
The COPY Command Options

Command	Function
`C:\>> COPY PART.DWG B:`	Copies the drawing file named PART from the current subdirectory to the target disk in drive B
`C:\>> COPY *.* A:`	Copies all files from the current directory in drive C to the target disk in drive A
`C:\>> COPY A:*.*`	Copies all files from a source disk in drive A to the current drive and directory
`C:\>> COPY *.DWG A:/V`	Copies all .DWG files from the current subdirectory of drive C to the target disk in drive A and verifies the copy
`C:\>> COPY \JOHN\ PART.DWG A:`	Copies the drawing file named PART from the JOHN subdirectory to the target disk in drive A
`C:\>> COPY PART.DWG A:LATCH.DWG`	Copies the drawing file named PART to the target disk in drive A and renames the file LATCH.DWG

Comparing Files (COMP)

You can use the COMP (compare files) command, which has the same syntax as COPY command, to verify critical files. COMP is a better test than COPY's /V option. To compare all the drawing files for consistency in the current directory with all the drawing files on the disk in drive A, for example, enter the following command:

```
C:\>> COMP *.DWG A:*.DWG
```

Deleting Files (DEL)

The delete command deletes a specified file. Table A.6 shows how to use the DEL command, as well as the options available to it.

Table A.6
The DEL Command Options

Command	Function
C:\>> **DEL PART.DWG**	Deletes the drawing file PART from the current subdirectory
C:\>> **DEL \ACAD-DWG\ARM.DWG**	Deletes the drawing file ARM from the ACAD-DWG subdirectory
C:\>> **DEL A:*.BAK**	Deletes all backup files from the disk in drive A
C:\ **DEL \ACAD-DWG**	Deletes entire ACAD-DWG subdirectory

If you specify a subdirectory name without specifying a file name, the DEL command deletes all the files in that subdirectory. Also, DEL*XYZ.* is equivalent to *.* and deletes all files in the current directory. The asterisk wild card represents all characters to the right, until it encounters a period or the end of the file name. When you delete an entire drive or directory, DOS prompts you with Are you sure? Y/N?. Before you answer Y, be sure that you want to delete the drive or directory you have indicated.

Renaming Files (REN)

The REN (rename file) command renames a designated file with a new file name. When you use this command, be sure to include correct file extensions, such as DWG, so that AutoCAD is able to read the files. Table A.7 shows how to use the REN command, as well as the options available to it.

Table A.7
REN Command Options

Command	Function
C:\>> **REN PIN.DWG BLOCK.DWG**	Renames the drawing file named PIN to the new drawing file named BLOCK
C:\>> **REN ARM.BAK ARM.DWG**	Renames the backup file named ARM to the drawing file named ARM

Using DOS Disk Commands

The DOS disk contains a valuable set of programs that make it easier to perform various operating system functions. Each of these programs is given a specific file name which corresponds to its function (to the extent that eight characters allow). Many of these programs also enable you to specify various operating parameters. You, for example, follow the DISKCOPY program name with disk drive parameters which tell you the system where to copy from and to (that is, DISKCOPY A: B:).

Changing the Default Drive

When you change the default drive, it is similar to looking in another file cabinet. You can change to any drive configured in your system. To change to drive A when you are in drive C, for example, enter C:\>> **A:**. To change back to drive C, enter A:\>> **C:**.

Checking Disks (CHKDSK)

The CHKDSK (check disk) command checks the file integrity of available drives or individual files, and reports memory allocations. Table A.8 shows how to use the CHKDSK command, as well as the options and switches available to it.

Lost clusters are leftover pieces of files that may be recovered into a readable file named in the form FILEnnnn.CHK. The nnnn parameter is a sequential number for each file written. Once the lost clusters are converted into readable files, you can look at them to determine if they contain any useful information. If not, remove them from the disk. Do not use this option with AutoCAD's Shell command. You should use the CHKDSK command periodically to maintain free disk space.

Table A.8
CHKDSK Command Options

Command	Function
C:\>> CHKDSK	Checks the files on drive C and reports the current memory allocation
C:\>> CHKDSK D:	Checks the files on drive D and reports the current memory allocation
C:\>> CHKDSK /F	Checks the default drive and fixes any errors it finds (chains of lost clusters)

Copying Floppy Disks (DISKCOPY)

The DISKCOPY command enables you to copy a source disk to a target disk. DISKCOPY copies all the files from the source disk and, if necessary, formats the target disk in the process. DISKCOPY works for copying floppy disks only. Table A.9 shows how to use the DISKCOPY command.

Table A.9
DISKCOPY Command Options

Command	Function
A:\>> DISKCOPY A: B:	Copies all files from drive A to drive B
A:\>> DISKCOPY A: A:	Copies a disk onto another disk in a single drive system

You are prompted when to insert the source (original) disk and when to insert the destination (copy) disk into the A: disk drive. It may be necessary that you alternate the disks a number of times (depending on how many files are on the source disk). After the copying is complete, DOS prompts you if you want to make any additional copies.

Comparing Floppy Disks (DISKCOMP)

The DISKCOMP command, which uses the same syntax as DISKCOPY, verifies critical files on floppy disks. To compare all the drawing files in the current directory with all the drawing files on drive A, for example, enter the following:

    C:\>> DISKCOMP A: B:

Formatting Disks (FORMAT)

The FORMAT command initializes a disk so that files can be written to it. The format process also checks a disk for bad tracks, which are created during the manufacturing process. New disks must be formatted before you use them.

When you format a disk that has files stored on it, all the files are deleted. Although DOS V3.0 and later versions make it more difficult than earlier versions to accidently format a disk and destroy all existing data, be careful when you use this command. Table A.10 shows how to use the FORMAT command.

Table A.10
FORMAT Command Options

Command	Function
C:\DOS>> **FORMAT A:**	Formats the disk in drive A
A:\>> **FORMAT B:**	Formats the disk in drive B (the disk in drive A must contain a copy of the format program)

Creating a Bootable Disk Using the FORMAT /S Command

The FORMAT /S (format with system) command creates a *bootable disk*. A bootable disk is used to boot up the computer when it is turned on. You do not need to format AutoCAD drawing disk or other data diskettes with the /S switch. To format a disk in drive A and copy the operating system (DOS) files to disk, use the following command:

    C:\DOS>> **FORMAT A:/S**

Formatting with Volume Labels (FORMAT /V)

The FORMAT /V (format with volume label) command labels drawing disk for file management purposes. To format a disk in drive A and to apply a volume label (name) to it, enter the following command. The volume label displays when other DOS commands are used on it.

    C:\DOS>> **FORMAT A: /V**

Displaying Directory Trees (TREE)

The TREE command displays the directory structure of a specified drive. If no drive is specified, the default drive's directory tree is shown. Table A.11 shows how to use the TREE command.

Table A.11
TREE Command Options

Command	Function
C:\>> **TREE**	Displays the directory structure on drive C
C:\>> **TREE A:**	Displays the directory structure on drive A

Setting Environment Variables (SET)

The SET command sets program-specific DOS environment variables to values that can affect the way that program performs. Some programs use this method for controlling memory allocation, directory usage, and other program execution options. See the *AutoCAD Installation and Performance Guide* for more information on how AutoCAD uses the SET command.

Creating Batch Files

The concept of *batch processing* comes from the mainframe computer world in which extremely large batches of records or transactions are processed over-night. A personal computer *batch file* is a simple text file containing one or more DOS commands that execute one at a time as if you type them at the DOS prompt. Batch processing provides you with an easy way to program and execute many frequently used DOS commands to manipulate files, directories, and programs. Batch files are named with up to eight characters and the DOS extension BAT.

A batch file is executed by the DOS command processor similar to the way it executes programs. When a command is entered at the DOS prompt, DOS first checks to see if it is an internal DOS command, such as DIR or COPY, and then *searches* the directories contained in the current path for files with the extensions COM, EXE, and BAT). A batch file can be suspended by pressing the Ctrl-Break or Ctrl-C.

Batch files can use replaceable *parameters*, which are types of variables. In this way, one batch file can perform the same operations on different files, directories, or drives. A replaceable parameter is a character string that follows the batch file (or command or program) name on the DOS command line. OLDFILES, \NEWFILES, and X:, for example, are parameters to the QUENCH command or batch file in the following line:

```
C:\>> A:QUENCH OLDFILE \NEWFILES X:<F20>.
```

Up to ten replaceable parameters can be used with one batch file before it is expanded using the SHIFT command. Ten parameters should be sufficient for all but the most elaborate needs.

Parameters can be used within the batch file. DOS substitutes the parameters you specify on the command line after a batch file name for corresponding variables within the batch file. These variables are specified by the names %0 - %9. In the preceding batch file, QUENCH.BAT, DOS would substitute the value of the drive letter and batch file name for %0, OLDFILE for %1, \NEWFILES for %2, and X: for %3, and so on up to %9. You would use the names %0-%9 within the batch file when referencing information to be supplied by the user in the preceding order. See Appendix B for examples of how these are used in a batch file to begin AutoCAD.

Similar to the way menu macros automate AutoCAD, batch files can automate DOS. Batch files can execute other batch files, display messages, repeat DOS commands for groups of files, branch to specified sections in the batch file, perform conditional execution of commands, and test for the successful execution of other programs. This gives the DOS user plenty of power and makes working with DOS much easier. For a further explanation of batch file features, consult your DOS reference manual.

Understanding the Automatic Executing .BAT File (AUTOEXEC.BAT)

When you turn on a DOS-based computer, the command processor searches for an AUTOEXEC.BAT file in the root directory of the disk it was started from. An example of an AUTOEXEC.BAT file that can be used for automatically running AutoCAD is described in Appendix B.

Selecting Text Editors

A text editor is the easiest way to create batch and other text files. Any good text editor works as long as it creates "pure" ASCII files that include the ASCII <ESCAPE> character. It also must be able to merge files and enable you to turn word wrap off. Norton's Editor, for example, includes this, as well as the following recommended features:

- Contains editing options such as move, block copy, delete, undelete, search and replace, and is capable of merging files

- Uses little disk space and memory

- Loads, saves, and exits quickly

- Handles large files, saves files to another name, and compares files for differences

- Has line and column counter display, can jump to a designated line number, and has a row mode

- Has word wrap (no automatic carriage returns)

If you have doubts about your DOS editor's capability to produce ASCII files, test it with the following steps.

1. With your text editor, create a few screens full of text. Save the file to the name TEST.TXT and exit to DOS.

2. Enter the following command. Your text should scroll on-screen.

    `C:\>> ` **`COPY TEXT.TXT CON`**

3. Delete the file by entering `C:\>> ` **`DEL TEXT.TXT`**.

Your text editor is okay if after you entered **COPY TEXT.TXT CON** the screen showed text identical to what you typed in your editor. The screen should not have shown extra ^L, åÇäÆ characters, or smiling faces. If any garbage appeared on screen, especially at the top or bottom of the copy, then your text editor is not suitable, or is not configured correctly for ASCII output. If you have this problem and you want to create your own ASCII files, it will be necessary to find another text editor that will do the job correctly.

B

Systems, Setup, Memory, and Errors

AutoCAD can be used on many different workstation configurations. As the number of AutoCAD-supported workstations increases, so does the number of available options. This book was developed on a 386-based computer using AutoCAD Release 11—DOS 386; however, the exercises and text in this book can be used with any of the computers that support AutoCAD.

Using AutoCAD on DOS-Based, Unix-Based, and Other Systems

The 16-bit IBM-AT and compatibles and the 32-bit Intel 80386 microprocessor-based computers that run PC-DOS or MS-DOS operating systems are the most widely used systems for microcomputer-based designing and drafting. The IBM 386-based machines (which are up to four times faster than the IBM-AT) have become the main micro-CAD platform.

Engineering workstations, such as the SUN 3, SPARCstation, and 386i, are becoming popular AutoCAD industrial drafting and design platforms. These computers run a variety of 32-bit micro-processors, from the Intel 80386, to the Motorola 68020 and 68030, to specialized RISC processors. They use UNIX, which is a multitasking operating system that is not limited to the current 640K RAM (Random Access Memory) constraints of MS-DOS. These UNIX platforms are powerful, flexible, and fast, but the UNIX operating system is more complex than MS-DOS.

AutoCAD also has been ported to Xenix 386, a type of UNIX that runs AutoCAD on 386-based AT compatibles much faster than the DOS version.

AutoCAD also is available for several other hardware and operating system combinations. These include IBM's OS/2 (Operating System/2), the Macintosh II, DEC VMS, and Apollo AEGIS. Although the operating systems and user environments of these platforms differ substantially, AutoCAD looks and performs nearly identically on each one. AutoCAD's binary file format enables access to files between these systems without the need for file conversion.

Understanding the General System Components

In addition to a processor, your computer needs a math co-processor and sufficient RAM to run AutoCAD. The math co-processor should match the processor in type and speed. RAM requirements vary with the operating system. DOS requires at least 640K, but you can increase AutoCAD's performance by increasing the RAM from 1M to 4M (megabytes). Other operating systems need between 2M and 8M of RAM. DOS 386, for example, requires 2M of RAM—640K conventional memory and 1M of extended memory. See the *AutoCAD Installation and Performance Guide* for more information and performance tips.

Your computer also needs a hard disk with at least 20M of space for DOS and up to 100M for UNIX, depending on your flavor of UNIX. If you do not have a large amount of RAM, a fast hard disk access time (less than 30 milliseconds) will noticeably improve AutoCAD's performance.

A typical micro-CAD workstation also needs input and output devices. The absolute minimum is a mouse and a video graphics display. Options include a digitizer tablet and a plotter or printer. The components of the CAD workstation vary in their general appearance, but their functions remain the same. A typical configuration is shown in Chapter 1.

Setting Up AutoCAD in a DOS Environment

DOS, either PC DOS or MS-DOS, is a collection of programs for operating your computer. These programs process commands to manage files, information, and input/output devices. DOS enables the computer to communicate with its hardware. You need DOS to set up your AutoCAD environment. Although AutoCAD performs well under DOS, it is continually fighting a 640K RAM limit imposed by MS-DOS. MS-DOS is written to address up to 640K of RAM directly. Because AutoCAD is a very large program and its drawing files can be large, AutoCAD must swap portions of program code, drawings, and temporary files in and out of this 640K. When this happens, AutoCAD writes temporary disk files, slowing the performance of the system considerably. One way to avoid this problem is to add *extended* or *expanded* RAM to the workstation.

Using Extended and Expanded Memory

DOS runs in the first 640K of RAM, which is the memory space that is common to all PCs. 80286 and 80386 computers also may contain *extended memory*, which is RAM that is in the address space above 1M. XT-type computers have no provisions for extended memory, but can be enhanced with *expanded memory*. Expanded memory is RAM that exists in a separate address space and is accessed through an area of the conventional memory address space between 640K and 1M. AT-type computers and 386 ATs may contain extended memory, expanded memory, or both.

To get around the memory limitations of DOS, you can enhance your workstation by adding extended or expanded memory. Unless you also need expanded memory for other programs, extended memory is preferable for AutoCAD. AutoCAD can use extended or expanded memory as *extended I/O page space* to substitute for swapping data to disk. Extended I/O page space is a temporary storage area. AutoCAD accumulates changes in I/O page space and places them to disks in "chunks." This greatly increases AutoCAD's performance. See the *AutoCAD Installation and Performance Guide* and the README.DOC file for information on installation and setting DOS environment variables to control this additional memory.

AutoLISP is the AutoCAD programming language used by the *AutoCAD: Drafting and 3D Design Disk's* Y14.5 menus, by many third-party programs, and even by several items on the standard AutoCAD menu. AutoLISP also competes for DOS's limited 640K of memory, using up to 128K of it. Using Extended AutoLISP (Release 10), you can load AutoLISP into extended (but not expanded) RAM. This technique prevents AutoLISP from running out of RAM, as well as speeds it up by eliminating swapping. Extended AutoLISP also uses about 80K less of the 640K RAM than normal AutoLISP, freeing up more memory for the rest of AutoCAD. See the *AutoCAD Installation and Performance Guide* for more information.

Loading DOS Programs on a Hard Disk

This book assumes that the computer you are using has a hard disk installed and formatted and that the hard disk contains the DOS system files needed to boot DOS from the hard disk. This means that when you turn on the computer (with the floppy disk drive empty), the C> or C:\> DOS command prompt appears. In addition to system files, DOS includes utility programs, which are external commands, such as FORMAT and DISKCOPY. These utilities usually are stored in a subdirectory named C:\DOS. A path setting of C:\DOS tells the DOS command processor where to find these utility programs.

This book also assumes that you are familiar with directories, subdirectories, and the following DOS commands:

- **DIR.** Lists files and subdirectories
- **COPY.** Copies files
- **COMP.** Compares files
- **DISKCOPY.** Copies diskette
- **DISKCOMP.** Compares diskette
- **FORMAT.** Formats (prepares) disk for data
- **MD.** Makes directory (subdirectory)
- **CD.** Displays current directory
- **CD *name*.** Changes to directory name

If you do not have a directory on your path that contains the DOS utility files, make a subdirectory and copy the DOS files into it from the DOS disk. The path is one of several settings made by two files, the *CONFIG.SYS* and *AUTOEXEC.BAT* files, that the computer reads when it starts up. You need to verify several settings in these files and modify them if necessary. You can modify them using the DOS EDLIN text editor or any other text editor, such as Norton's Editor, that produces ASCII files without control characters or word processor format codes. Most word processors have an ASCII non-formatted or non-document mode. This book assumes that you have a program editor available. If you do not have an ASCII editor available, or if you are not sure that your editor is suitable, see Appendix A for information on selecting and testing text editors. Appendix A also shows an alternative COPY CON method for creating text files.

If you are unfamiliar with these DOS concepts and commands, see Appendix A and your DOS manual for more information. You then can refer to this appendix for tips on troubleshooting problems.

The CONFIG.SYS File

The CONFIG.SYS file installs device drivers that tell the computer how to talk to devices, including RAM disks, expanded memory, and some disk drives and video cards. It also includes instructions that improve your system's performance and increase your environment space for customization.

The CONFIG.SYS file must be located in the root directory so it is read automatically when your computer boots up. Unless you need to modify it or reconfigure it, you may never even know that a CONFIG.SYS file exists. To do the exercises exactly as they are written in this book, you need a CONFIG.SYS file that contains the following lines. If you have a CONFIG.SYS file, check and modify it if needed. If you do not have one, create one making sure that the following lines are used.

```
BUFFERS=32
FILES=24
SHELL=C:\COMMAND.COM /P /E:512
```

The BUFFERS= line allocates more RAM to hold your recently used data. You should use a number between 20 and 48. The FILES= line allocates more RAM to keep recently used files open. This reduces directory searching and increases data access speed. The SHELL= line ensures adequate space for DOS environment variables. The /E:512 is for DOS 3.2 or 3.3. Substitute /E:32 for DOS 3.1 or 3.0.

The SHELL= and FILES= lines are required to give enough environment and file space for this textbook's setup. The numbers for FILES= and BUFFERS= are minimal, and larger values may improve disk performance even more. Larger values, however, decrease the RAM available for AutoCAD and other functions, so you may have to compromise, particularly if you get Out of RAM error messages when you use AutoCAD or if you cannot load AutoLISP.

The AUTOEXEC.BAT File

The AUTOEXEC.BAT file is a DOS batch file that automatically sets up your system when you turn the computer on. At their simplest, DOS batch files are lines of commands that are executed as if typed at the DOS command prompt. Like CONFIG.SYS, AUTOEXEC.BAT must be in the root directory. Examine your AUTOEXEC.BAT file. For this textbook, your AUTOEXEC.BAT should contain the following lines:

```
PROMPT $P$G
PATH C:\;C:\DOS;
```

The PROMPT PG command causes the DOS prompt to display your current directory path, such as C:\ACAD> instead of C>. By displaying the path in the DOS prompt, you are constantly informed as to your current directory, or your location in the directory tree. Without the path display, you may log into the wrong directory and have difficulty finding your files later.

The PATH command is essential for automatic directory access to programs and DOS commands. The C:\ root and C:\DOS paths are needed for this book's setup. Each path is separated by a semicolon. If your DOS files are in a different directory, substitute your directory name. You should use the path setup that is specific to your DOS setup. Your path may contain additional directories.

If your AUTOEXEC.BAT does not include prompt and path lines, edit or create the file in your root directory.

 The CONFIG.SYS and AUTOEXEC.BAT changes do not take effect until you reboot your computer. To reboot your computer, either press Ctrl-Alt-Del or turn off your computer and then turn it back on.

Setting Up AutoCAD

The AutoCAD program comes on several floppy disks. The program disks (except for the sample drawings and programs on the Bonus Disk) must be copied onto your formatted hard disk to run AutoCAD.

Creating a Subdirectory for AutoCAD

The best method for managing a hard disk is to keep your root directory small and to organize your data and program files in some logical order. One approach is to keep your AutoCAD files in a subdirectory named ACAD, using the DOS MD command. Once you create the new subdirectory, make ACAD the current directory by using the DOS CD command. The following steps create and make ACAD the current directory:

```
C:\> MD \ACAD
C:\> CD \ACAD
C:\ACAD>
```

If you do not already have AutoCAD copied to and configured in your ACAD directory, do so now. See your *AutoCAD Installation and Performance Guide* for complete instructions on how to configure AutoCAD for your specific system. Once you have the AutoCAD program files in the ACAD subdirectory of your hard drive, the files remain there when you turn the computer off.

Configuring AutoCAD

After you start AutoCAD for the first time, the program informs you that it has not been configured. It automatically displays a series of configuration menus to help you configure your system to run AutoCAD. Step through the configuration menus and menu options as they are presented and select the hardware devices that make up your workstation. If you have any difficulty with this process, see the *AutoCAD Installation and Performance Guide* for more information. If you use an ADI device driver, see the manufacturer's instructions.

Starting AutoCAD

If you have just installed and configured AutoCAD, start the program now by changing to the ACAD directory and typing **ACAD** to execute the program, as in the following:

```
C:\>> CD \ACAD
C:\ACAD>> ACAD
```

Assuming your AutoCAD program directory is named ACAD, you can start AutoCAD from any directory by typing **\ACAD\ACAD**. If your AutoCAD program directory is not ACAD, substitute your AutoCAD directory name in place of the first ACAD. Also, if the path statement in your AUTOEXEC.BAT file includes C:\ACAD, just type **ACAD**. For an AutoCAD directory set up as ACAD11, for example, type **\ACAD11\ACAD** and press Enter at the DOS prompt.

Once AutoCAD is configured and you start the program, the main menu appears on-screen. The main menu enables you to create new drawings or to edit existing drawings, plot drawings, install (configure) AutoCAD. The main menu also gives you several utility options from which to choose.

 If you are installing AutoCAD for the first time, refer to Chapters 1 and 2 for hardware and menu options.

If you want to test your AutoCAD configuration, turn to Chapter 3 and begin the first drawing exercise.

Setting Up for *AutoCAD: Drafting and 3D Design*

Once AutoCAD is configured correctly, you need to set it up to use the AutoCAD with this textbook. The textbook's exercises and the optional disk are designed so that you can work through the book's exercises without interfering with your normal AutoCAD setup and workflow. To avoid potential conflict, set up a separate directory and AutoCAD configuration for the textbook exercises.

The following example shows how to create the D3D-ACAD subdirectory using the DOS CD and MD commands:

```
C:\ACAD>> CD \
C:\>> MD D3D-ACAD>
C:\>> CD D3D-ACAD
C:\D3D-ACAD>>
```

Creating the D3D-ACAD Subdirectory in a UNIX Environment

On a UNIX system, create the D3D-ACAD subdirectory in your home directory. Throughout the textbook, you need to substitute appropriate UNIX commands and paths for the DOS commands and paths shown. Table B.1 shows UNIX commands and the DOS equivalent commands.

Table B.1
DOS and UNIX Commands

DOS	UNIX	Purpose
CD \	cd ~	Change to root (DOS) or home (UNIX) directory
MD \D3D-ACAD	mkdir ~/d3d-acad	Make book's directory
DIR *filename*	ls -l filename	List directory for filename
DIR *.	ls -d */	List directories

Some UNIX systems may vary from these examples. Depending on your system, AutoCAD may be installed in /usr/acad, /files/acad, or ~acad directories. Check with your UNIX system administrator if you are not sure how AutoCAD is set up.

DOS does not care whether file names are in upper or lowercase; however, UNIX file names are case-sensitive and usually are lowercase. If you use UNIX, input your file names in lowercase letters.

Installing the AutoCAD: Drafting and 3D Design Disk

Besides saving you typing and drawing set-up time, the optional disk provides starting drawings for the chapter exercises. This enables you to bypass material and jump into the book at the place you want. If you do not have the AutoCAD: Drafting and 3D Design disk, see the back of the book for ordering information.

Before installing the drawing files on your hard disk, make a backup copy of the disk using the DISKCOPY command in DOS. Store the original disk in a safe place, and use your copy as the working disk. Do the following instructions to load the AutoCAD: Drafting and 3D Design Disk onto your hard disk. First, you need to change to the D3D-ACAD subdirectory and insert your working disk in drive A. Next, type the following command at the DOS prompt to load the files into the subdirectory. The files list on-screen as they are copied.

```
C:\D3D-ACAD>> A:D3D-LOAD
```

In addition to drawing files for the book's exercises, the AutoCAD: Drafting and 3D Design disk contains the Y14.5 menu files with drafting symbols, macros, and AutoLISP routines. These are installed and explained in Chapter 12.

To install the AutoCAD: Drafting and 3D Design Disk on a UNIX system, you can install the files on the DOS system first. Then copy the files by disk or across the network (if you are on a network) into the ~D3D-ACAD directory.

Copying the AutoCAD Configuration and Overlay Files

Before using AutoCAD with *AutoCAD: Drafting and 3D Design*, copy the configuration file from your AutoCAD program subdirectory to the D3D-ACAD subdirectory. By using the D3D-ACAD subdirectory, the Y14.5 program files are kept from interfering with your existing AutoCAD configuration and files as you work through the exercises in the textbook. To copy the configuration files, use the CD command in DOS to change to the D3D-ACAD directory, and then copy the files using the COPY command, as follows:

```
C:\>> CD\D3D-ACAD
C:\D3D-ACAD>> COPY \ACAD\ACAD.CFG
```

 The preceding example assumes your hard disk is drive C and that ACAD is your AutoCAD subdirectory name. If yours is different, substitute your drive letter or subdirectory name.

Automating AutoCAD Startup Using ACAD.BAT

The ACAD.BAT batch file contained on the AutoCAD: Drafting and 3D Design disk is used to start AutoCAD as you use the drawing files for this book. ACAD.BAT avoids conflicts with your current AutoCAD setup and keeps the drawing files out of the ACAD directory.

The ACAD.BAT file is a batch file similar to the AUTOEXEC.BAT batch file. Individual batch files like ACAD.BAT can be executed to run multiple commands and settings at the DOS prompt with a single command. Batch files are particularly useful for setting up and starting programs. ACAD.BAT loads and runs the AutoCAD program, saving you from having to type in loading instructions each time you run AutoCAD.

The following shows how to create the ACAD.BAT file and lists the functions of each command line. ACAD.BAT automates loading and starting AutoCAD, telling AutoCAD where to find its support and configuration information. It also makes the D3D-ACAD directory the default directory for storing your drawing files.

Creating the ACAD.BAT File

Command entry	Function
SET ACAD=\acad	Sets the support variable
SET ACADCFG=\D3D-ACAD	Sets the configuration variable
CD\D3D-ACAD	Changes to \D3D-ACAD subdirectory
\acad\ACAD %1 %2	Starts AutoCAD
SET ACAD=	Deletes variables upon exiting from AutoCAD
SET ACADCFG=	Deletes variables upon exiting from AutoCAD
CD\	Changes back to the root directory

The \acad\ACAD %1 %2 line runs AutoCAD from the current directory, in this case \D3D-ACAD. The %1 %2 entries in a batch file tell DOS that two command line parameters may follow the ACAD command when the batch file is executed.

Use your ASCII text editor to edit the ACAD.BAT if necessary. See Appendix A if you need help with text editors.

Testing ACAD.BAT

You can start an AutoCAD session for this book from any directory on your hard drive by typing **\ACAD**. The batch file changes the directory to D3D-ACAD and the AutoCAD program displays the main menu.

Creating a Default ACAD.DWG

You can prepare a temporary prototype drawing so that your initial AutoCAD sessions are set to the default settings. When you begin a new drawing, AutoCAD looks for a drawing called ACAD.DWG. AutoCAD uses this drawing to establish the default working environment for your new drawing. Your prototype drawing should be the same as when you took AutoCAD out of the box and booted up the program for the first time. To make sure this is true, you need to create a new ACAD.DWG in your D3D-ACAD directory.

The following exercise creates the prototype drawing. The equal sign following the drawing name tells AutoCAD to make the ACAD.DWG with its original default settings. When you end the session, the prototype drawing is added to the D3D-ACAD subdirectory. You do not need to create the ACAD.DWG file unless the original has been edited. You also do not need to have ACAD.DWG in the current directory unless the original has been removed from the ACAD directory. AutoCAD looks for this file in the current directory and then in the directory from which AutoCAD was loaded.

Creating a Prototype Drawing

Enter selection: **1**	Starts a new drawing
Enter NAME of drawing: **ACAD=**	Displays the drawing editor
Command: **End**	Saves the drawing and exits to the main menu

---

Note   If you have not just installed and configured ACAD, your initial drawing setup may be configured to some other drawing. If you are not sure that it is set to ACAD.DWG, then check it now and change it to \D3D-ACAD\ACAD if needed. To do so, chose item 5 in the main menu to reconfigure AutoCAD, then choose item 8 in the configuration menu and specify \D3D-ACAD\ACAD as the prototype file of your initial drawing setup.

If you have any problems configuring or setting up, see the *AutoCAD Installation and Performance Guide* or Appendix A of this textbook.

Automating AutoCAD with a UNIX Script

The syntax and process of creating the UNIX equivalent of the ACAD.BAT file depends on your particular system environment. Consult your system administrator or refer to the *AutoCAD Installation and Performance Guide* for syntax. UNIX users can omit all memory settings, such as ACADFREERAM and LISPHEAP; however, ACAD and ACADCFG need to be set. You also need to add the appropriate entries to change directories and to start up AutoCAD.

C

AUTOCAD COMMAND LIST

The following is a list of the commands available in AutoCAD. Each command name is followed by a brief description of its action and the primary prompts it generates. For a more detailed description of AutoCAD commands, see the *AutoCAD Reference Guide*. For a thorough coverage of the AutoCAD commands from a tutorial approach, see *Inside AutoCAD, Special Edition* (New Riders Publishing).

Selecting Objects in AutoCAD

When you use AutoCAD's editing commands, AutoCAD prompts you to select the objects that you want the command to operate on. You can pick a point on-screen using the crosshairs, or you can use one of the following options:

- **Multiple.** Enables you to select multiple objects simultaneously
- **Last.** Selects the last object created
- **Previous.** Selects all the objects in the previous selection set
- **Window.** Selects all objects within a window, which you specify
- **Crossing.** Selects all the objects that are within or crossing the borders of a window, which you specify
- **Box.** Selects objects in the same manner as a Window if you place the box's second corner to the right of the first corner; selects ob-

jects in the same manner as a Crossing window if you place the box's second corner to the left of the first corner

- **Auto.** Enables you to select single entities by picking; selects objects in the same manner as the Box option if you pick a blank area of the screen

- **Single.** Selects a single object

- **Add.** Enables you to add nonselected entities to an existing selection set

- **Remove.** Enables you to remove selected entities from an existing selection set

- **Undo.** Undoes the last option

AutoCAD selects objects in the order that they are added to the drawing database. If you pick the intersection of two objects, for example, the newest of the two objects is selected.

Picking Points Using Coordinates

As you just learned, AutoCAD enables you to pick points using the crosshair cursor and various options. AutoCAD also enables you to pick points using coordinates that you type in. AutoCAD uses three types of coordinates: absolute, relative, and polar. When you use *absolute coordinates* to pick a three-dimensional point in AutoCAD, you specify the point in the X,Y,Z format, which defines a point in the Cartesian coordinate system. You specify *relative coordinates* by their distance in the X,Y,Z directions from the last point you selected. Relative coordinates take basically the same format as absolute coordinates (that is, three numbers separated by commas), but also use the @ symbol as a prefix. The @ or "at" symbol tells AutoCAD that the following point is to be positioned in relation to the last point drawn.

Polar coordinates are entered in the form *@distance<angle*, when *distance* and *angle* are values measured from the last point selected. If the Z coordinate is omitted, the current Z elevation is assumed. Polar coordinates have effect only in the X and Y axes.

AutoCAD provides a filter method to build a coordinate by using any combination of the X,Y, or Z components of an existing entity. Filters enable you to specify the coordinate values you want to extract from a coordinate pair or triple. The filter is invoked by preceding the coordinate letter(s) with a period (such as .X or .YZ) when prompted for a point. The remaining coordinate components are then prompted for and can be supplied by filtering or numerical means.

AutoCAD Commands

The following commands that are shown with a leading apostrophe (') can be executed *transparently* from within another command. Entered this way, the current command is suspended and the transparent command executes. After the transparent command completes its function, the original command is resumed. When executed from the command prompt, the apostrophe is not needed.

Aperture

The Aperture command controls the size of the target box located in the middle of the crosshairs during object snap selection. You can change the size in pixels of the aperture box. The default setting is 10 pixels for most displays. The setting is half the height of the box, or the number of pixels above or below the crosshairs.

```
Object snap target height (1-50 pixels) <10>
```

Arc

The Arc command draws any segment of a circle that is greater than one degree and less than 360 degrees. Except for the three-point option, arcs are constructed in a counterclockwise direction. An arc or line can be continued from the last point of the last arc or line by defaulting its `Start point:` or `From point:` prompts; that is, by pressing Enter at these prompts. The default is three-point arc construction, but you can use several other methods.

```
Center/<Start point>:
```

Area

The Area command enables you to calculate an area by picking a series of points or by selecting entities, such as circles and polylines. In addition to the area, you also are given the perimeter and line length or circumference of the selected object. You can keep a running total as you add and subtract areas. The default picks points to define the area.

```
<First point>/Entity/Add/Subtract:
```

Array

The Array command copies selected entities in rectangular or polar patterns. A rectangular array prompts for the number and spacing of rows and columns.

A polar array prompts for center point, number of copies to make, the angle to fill with the copies, and whether or not to rotate each copy. By dragging a rectangle at the `Unit cell...` prompt, you can show AutoCAD the X and Y spacing for rectangular arrays.

```
Rectangular or Polar array (R/P):
```

Attdef

The Attdef (ATTribute DEFinition) command defines the way attribute text is prompted for and stored. Attributes are saved in blocks that can contain additional entities. Mode toggles are provided for Invisible, Constant, Verify, and Preset options.

```
Attribute modes  —  Invisible:N  Constant:N  Verify:N
Preset:N
Enter (ICVP) to change, RETURN when done:
```

Attdisp

The Attdisp (ATTtribute DISPlay) command controls attribute visibility after insertion of the block that includes the attribute. Attdisp overrides the Attdef invisible/visible settings. The default is Normal, which defaults to the setting at which the attributes were created.

```
Normal/ON/OFF <Off>:
```

Attedit

The Attedit (ATTribute EDIT) command enables you to edit attributes individually or globally. The default setting edits attributes one at a time, enabling you to change value, position, height, angle, style, layer, or color. Global edits are confined to changing value. You can control your selection set by block name, tag name, or attribute value.

```
Edit attributes one at a time? <Y>
```

Attext

The Attext (ATTribute EXTract) command extracts attribute data from your drawing. This information is formatted into an ASCII text file in one of three possible formats: CDF, SDF, or DXF. CDF is the default format. You can extract all attributes, or you select certain entities from which extract attributes.

```
CDF, SDF, or DXF Attribute extract (or Entities) <C>:
```

Axis

The Axis command creates ruler marks, or ticks, on the lower and right side of your screen. These marks are used as visual drawing aids. The Snap option sets the mark spacing equal to the current snap value. Aspect controls unequal horizontal and vertical tick values. The default setting is Off with a default value 0.0000.

```
Tick spacing(X) or ON/OFF/Snap/Aspect:
```

Base

The Base command specifies the insertion base point to insert a drawing into another drawing. By default, every drawing file has a base point of 0,0,0, relative to which it is inserted into other drawings.

```
Base point <0.0000,0.0000,0.0000>:
```

Blipmode

The Blipmode command toggles blips on and off. The default is On.

```
ON/OFF <On>:
```

Block

The Block command defines a group of entities as a block within the current drawing. (Use the Insert command to insert blocks into your drawing.) You define a block by choosing an entity selection set that is deleted from the current drawing and stored as a block definition in the drawing. (The Oops command restores the entities.) You are prompted for a block name and insertion base point. The base point is a reference point relative to which the blocks are inserted and scaled. Such blocks can be inserted only in a drawing where they have been defined, although AutoCAD can insert other drawings as blocks as well.

```
Block name (or ?):
Insertion base point:
```

Break

The Break command enables you to split or erase portions of lines, arcs, circles, 2D polylines, and traces. When you select an object to break, the default assumes your pick point also is your first break point.

```
Select object:
Enter second point (or F for first point):
```

Chamfer

The Chamfer command creates a beveled edge for intersecting lines and contiguous segments of a 2D Polyline. Chamfer trims or extends two lines or polyline segments at specified distances from their intersection or vertex point and creates a new line to connect the trimmed ends. You can chamfer an entire polyline at once using the Polyline option. Chamfer requires two distance values, in which the first distance value is applied to the first selected line and the second distance to the second line. The default distances are 0.

```
Polyline/Distances/<Select first line>:
```

Change

The Change command enables you to modify existing entities. You can change the endpoints of lines, in which the nearest endpoint is pulled to the change point. You can respecify the center and radius of circles. You can enter new text or you can enter new values for any Text or Attdef option. You also can enter a new origin or rotation angle for a block insert. If you select multiple entities, you are prompted for each. After you use the Change command, you might have to regenerate the screen to see the revisions.

```
Properties/<Change point>:
```

Chprop

The Chprop command redefines the layer, color, linetype, and 3D thickness properties of existing entities. Use the Chprop command rather than the Change command to change entity properties.

```
Change what property (Color/LAyer/LType/Thickness) ?
```

Circle

The Circle command is used to draw circles. The default method uses a center point and radius to create the circle. If Dragmode is set to on or auto (the default), you can determine the size of the circle by dragging the circle on-screen. AuotCAD also enables you to construct circles by selecting three points on the circumference, by selecting two points and a diameter of the circle, or by drawing a circle tangent to two existing entities.

```
3P/2P/TTR/<Center point>:
```

Color

The Color command controls the color of new entities, overriding the default layer color. To change the color of existing entities, use the Chprop command. To control layer colors, use the Layer command. Use a color number or name to set a new color. You also can set the current entity color using the 'Ddemodes dialogue box. The default setting is Bylayer.

```
New entity color <BYLAYER>:
```

Copy

The Copy command creates a replica of an entity or selection set anywhere in 2D or 3D space. The command uses standard object selection. The original entity or selection set remains unchanged. You can show and drag displacement by picking two points or by using an absolute XY displacement value. The Multiple option enables you to repeat the Copy command for a specified selection set.

```
<Base point or displacement>/Multiple:
Second point of displacement:
```

Dblist

The Dblist command displays a list of properties of all entities in the database of the current drawing.

Ddatte

The Ddatte (Dynamic Dialogue ATTribute Edit) command edits attribute string values using a dialogue box. You can edit only one block at a time. It presents the current value and enables you to specify a new value.

```
Select block:
```

'Ddemodes

The Ddemodes (Dynamic Dialogue Entity creation MODES) dialogue box shows the current settings for layer, color, linetype, elevation, and thickness. You can change any of these variables. When you select the layer, color, and linetype settings a dialogue box appears on-screen.

'Ddlmodes

The Ddlmodes (Dynamic Dialogue Layer MODES) command presents a dialogue box to control layer options. The options include setting the current layer, creating new layers, renaming layers, and modifying layer properties, such as color, linetype, on/off, freeze, and thaw.

'Ddrmodes

The Ddrmodes (Dynamic Dialogue dRawing MODES) command controls the settings of the following drawing aids using a dialogue box: snap, grid, axis, ortho, blips, isoplane, and isometric mode.

Dducs

The Dducs (Dynamic Dialogue User Coordinate System) command displays dialogue boxes that control the User Coordinate System. You also can use Dducs to create or rename a UCS. The default setting is *WORLD*.

Delay

The Delay command is used in scripts to pause execution of the script primarily for the display of slides. The delay parameter is specified in approximately 1 microsecond increments, depending on the hardware used.

Dim/Dim1

The Dim command activates the dimensioning mode. The `Command:` prompt changes to `DIM:`, and only the subcommands associated with dimensioning are active. The Exit command or pressing Ctrl-C redisplays the `Command:` prompt. Dim1 activates the dimension mode for a single command and then returns you to the `Command:` prompt.

```
DIM:
```

Dist

The Dist (distance) command determines the distance between two points.

```
First point:
Second point:
```

Divide

The Divide command marks an entity into equal length segments. You can divide lines, circles, arcs, and polylines. The divided entity is not physically separated; point entities or blocks are placed as markers at each division point.

```
Select object to divide:
<Number of segments>/Block:
```

Donut

The Donut (or Doughnut) command draws solid filled rings and circles. The donut entities are closed wide polylines. To draw donuts in AutoCAD, you select an inside diameter value (or two points) and an outside diameter (or two points). AutoCAD prompts you with Center of doughnut: until you press Ctrl-C or press Enter to exit the command.

```
Inside diameter <0.5000>:
Outside diameter <1.0000>:
Center of doughnut:
```

Dragmode

The Dragmode command controls dynamic dragging of objects during their creation or editing. It has the following three states:

```
ON/OFF/Auto <Auto>:
```

Dtext

The Dtext (Dynamic TEXT) command prompts for the same text justification parameters as the Text command; however, Dtext draws the text characters on the screen as you type them, and enables you to enter multiple lines of text. Dtext displays a rectangular character box to show where the next character is placed.

```
Start point or Align/Center/Fit/Middle/Right/Style:
```

Dview

The Dview command is a display tool for viewing 3D models in space. Dview is similar to the Vpoint command. In Dview, however, you can dynamically drag and rotate the 3D model with the aid of slide bars. You also can display a per-

spective view of the model and toggle back and forth between parallel and perspective views. The Dview command is similar to the concept of using a camera
to view a target. You can set a camera point, target point, lens length, and position front and back clipping planes. The default is for parallel projection.

```
Select objects:
CAmera/TArget/Distance/POints/PAn/Zoom/TWist/CLip/Hide/Off/
Undo/<eXit>:
```

Dxbin

The Dxbin command enables you to import binary drawing interchange files,
which can be created by external programs, including AutoShade. If AutoCAD is
configured with an ADI plotter, the DXB file output option can be selected,
which creates a file with a DXB extension. The DBX file format is described in
the AutoCAD manual.

```
DXB File:
```

Dxfin/Dxfout

The Dxfin and Dxfout commands are used to create and import DXF (Drawing
Interchange Format) files for analysis by other programs or translation to other
CAD programs. The DXF file is an ASCII text file.

```
File name <default>:
Enter decimal places of accuracy (0 to 16)/Entities/Binary
<6>:
```

Edgesurf

The Edgesurf command generates a 3D polygon mesh by approximating a
Coons surface patch from four adjoining edge entities. Each edge can be a line,
arc, or open polyline, anywhere in 3D space. The endpoints of the edge entities
must touch, combining to form a closed path. You can pick the edges in any
order. The first edge or entity selected defines the M direction (controlled by
Surftab1) of the mesh. The two edges that touch the M edge define the N direction (controlled by Surftab1).

```
Select edge 1:
Select edge 2:
Select edge 3:
Select edge 4:
```

Elev

The Elevation command sets the elevation and extrusion thickness of entities you construct. The elevation is the object's base value on the Z plane. The extrusion thickness (negative or positive) is its height above or below the base elevation. The elevation setting only affects those entities whose Z value is not given. The default is <0.0>. You also can set the elevation and thickness with the Ddemodes Dialogue Box.

```
New current elevation <0.0000>:
New current thickness <0.0000>:
```

Ellipse

The Ellipse command constructs ellipses. The default setting creates an ellipse using an axis defined by the endpoints; the other axis distance is defined as half the length of the first axis.

```
<Axis endpoint 1>/Center:
```

End

The End command saves the drawing file and exits to AutoCAD's main menu. The old drawing file becomes the new BAK file.

Erase

The Erase command deletes entities from the drawing. The Oops command is used to restore the last entity erased.

```
Select objects:
```

Explode

The Explode command converts the selected block, polyline, dimension, hatch, or mesh into its component entities.

```
Select block reference, polyline, dimension, or mesh:
```

Extend

The Extend command lengthens the endpoints of a line, open polyline, and arc to a boundary edge. Boundary edges include lines, circles, arcs, and polylines.

You can have more than one boundary edge, and an entity can be both a boundary edge and an entity to extend.

```
Select boundary edge(s)...
Select objects:
```

Files

The Files command activates the file utilities menu. It provides an alternative to DOS (or your operating system) for managing your files.

Fill

The Fill command controls the solid fills of polylines and solids. The default setting is on.

```
ON/OFF <On>:
```

Fillet

The Fillet command creates an arc with a predefined radius between any combination of lines, circles, and arcs. Fillet extends or trims entities as needed to draw the specified arc. A single polyline can be filleted at selected vertices, or globally at all vertices; a single polyline cannot be filleted with other entities. An arc entity is inserted at the preset fillet radius. The default fillet radius is 0, which causes the entities or segments to be extended or trimmed to their intersection point.

```
Polyline/Radius/<Select two lines>:
```

Filmroll

The Filmroll command produces a file containing a description of the entities that can be processed into fully shaded renderings using AutoShade. The filmroll file also contains camera, lighting, and scene descriptions that are created in the drawing using AutoShade tools. AutoShade is a separate program by Autodesk.

```
Enter the filmroll file name <drawing.name>:
```

'Graphscr

The Graphscr command switches the display screen to graphic mode.

Grid

The Grid command is a drawing aid that displays dots at any user-defined increment. It helps you to keep the space you are working in and the size of your drawing entities in perspective. Grid dynamically toggles off and on, as well as accepts numeric values. The default settings are 0.0000 and Off.

```
Grid spacing(X) or ON/OFF/Snap/Aspect <0.00>:
```

Handles

The Handles command assigns a unique label to every drawing entity. This label is in hexadecimal format and is stored in the drawing database. It is used to access entities with AutoLISP or external programs. The default setting is Off.

```
Handles are disabled.
ON/DESTROY:
```

Hatch

The Hatch command cross-hatches or pattern-fills an area defined by a boundary. The boundary must be continuous and closed, formed by any combination of lines, arcs, circles, polylines, or 3Dfaces. The hatch patterns available are defined in a file named ACAD.PAT. You also can specify the spacing and angle for parallel or cross-hatched continuous lines. By default, the Hatch command creates a block with a hidden name and inserts it. The default pattern creates a block with a hidden name and inserts it. If you precede the pattern name with an asterisk, such as *name, the hatch is drawn with individual line entities. You also can choose one of the following styles of hatching for nested boundaries: Normal, Outermost, or Ignore. Hatching is defined and generated relative to the XY axes and plane of the current UCS.

```
Pattern (? or name/U,style):
```

'Help or '?

Help lists available commands and provides specific information about the operation of individual commands. The apostrophe prefix causes the command to be transparent and therefore executes within another command.

```
Command name (RETURN for list):
```

Hide

The Hide command removes hidden lines.

ID

The ID command identifies the absolute XYZ coordinates of any selected point.

```
Point:
```

Igesin/Igesout

The Igesin and Igesout commands produce or import IGES (Initial Graphics Exchange Standard) files for translation to or from other CAD programs.

```
File name:
```

Insert

The Insert command inserts an image of a block definition into the current drawing. You pick the insertion point, XYZ scale values, and the rotation angle. The insertion point is relative to the block's base point. The default X scale factor is 1, and the Y scale defaults to equal the X scale. By specifying a negative scale factor, AutoCAD mirrors the image along that axis. Rotation angle defaults to 0. If you preface the block name with an asterisk, such as *Front, AutoCAD inserts a copy of each individual entity in the block's definition. This often is referred to as insert* (insert-star) or a *block (star-block).

```
Block name (or ?):
Insertion point:
X scale factor <1> / Corner / XYZ:
Y scale factor (default=X):
Rotation angle <0>:
```

Isoplane

The Isoplane command enables you to draw in isometric mode. Ctrl-E toggles to the next isoplane. When you draw isometrically, the grid and crosshairs are displayed isometrically. The default is the left plane. You also can set the isoplane using the Ddrmodes dialogue box.

```
Left/Top/Right/<Toggle>:
```

Layer

The Layer command controls layers, which act as transparent drawing overlays. You can create an unlimited number of layers and give them names up to 31 characters long. You can set any layer active (current), turn layers on (visible) or off (invisible), freeze or thaw layers, and control their colors and linetypes. When a layer is frozen, it is disregarded by AutoCAD and is not plotted, calculated, or displayed. You draw on the current layer. The default settings for new layers are white with continuous linetype. You also can control layers using the Ddlmodes dialogue box.

```
?/Make/Set/New/ON/OFF/Color/Ltype/Freeze/Thaw:
```

Limits

The Limits command determines your drawing area or boundaries, which are defined by the absolute coordinates of the lower left and upper right corners. The Limits command enables you to modify these values or turn limits checking on and off. The default settings are from 0,0 to 12,9 with limits checking off. With limits checking turned off, you can draw outside the limits. With limits checking on, you can continue some entities outside the limits, but cannot begin to draw an entity outside the limits.

```
ON/OFF/<Lower left corner> <0.0000,0.0000>:
Upper right corner <12.0000,9.0000>:
```

Line

The Line command draws straight line segments. You can enter 2D or 3D points by entering a starting point at the `From point:` prompt and endpoints at successive `To point:` prompts. AutoCAD presents the `To Point:` prompt until you press Enter, the Spacebar, or Ctrl-C until you can close of series of lines by using the C (Close) option; the U option undoes the last segment. The previous line or arc created can be continued by typing Pre at the first prompt, or by pressing Enter or the Spacebar.

```
From point:
To point:
```

Linetype

The Linetype command assigns linetypes to entities, loads linetype definitions stored in library files, and creates new linetype definitions. You can assign a linetype to an entity directly (explicitly), so that its linetype is independent of the linetype assigned to the layer or indirectly (implicitly) by assigning the linetype BYLAYER, which is the default linetype assignment. You also can set linetype using the 'Ddemodes dialogue box. The default setting is Bylayer.

```
?/Create/Load/Set:
```

List

The List command provides information on selected entities within a drawing. This command lists layer assignment, the XYZ position relative to the current UCS, color, and non-default linetypes.

```
Select objects:
```

Load

The Load command loads new shape library files (SHX files) into the current drawing or to list previously loaded library files.

```
Name of shape file to load (or ?):
```

Ltscale

The Ltscale (LineType SCALE) command determines the dash and space settings for linetypes in a drawing. All linetypes (except continuous) are multiplied by the Ltscale. After you change the linetype scale, you need to regenerate the drawing to make the changes visible. The default setting is 1.0000.

```
New scale factor <1.0000>:
```

Measure

The Measure command marks an entity at predetermined segment lengths. You can measure lines, circles, arcs, and polylines. The entity is not physically separated; point entities or blocks are placed as markers at each segment point.

```
Select object to measure:
<Segment length>/Block:
```

Menu

The Menu command loads a new menu file (MNU) into the current drawing that defines the actions performed by selections from the screen, tablet, pull-down, icon, button, and auxiliary menus. The default menu is ACAD.

```
Menu file name or . for none <acad>:
```

Minsert

The Minsert (Multiple INSERT) command inserts multiple copies of blocks in rectangular array patterns. The command has the same prompts as the Insert command for insertion point, XY scaling, and rotation angle, as well as prompts for rows and columns.

```
Number of rows (---) <1>:
Number of columns (||||) <1>:
```

Mirror

The Mirror command creates mirror images of a selected group of entities across a mirror line. When you mirror the entities, you can keep or delete them depending on the drawing. The default keeps the original objects. The MIRRTEXT system variable controls the mirroring of text.

```
Select objects:
First point of mirror line:
```

Move

The Move command moves an entity or selection set to a new drawing location anywhere in 2D or 3D space.

```
Base point or displacement:
Second point of displacement:
```

Mslide

The Mslide command creates a "slide" file (SLD), which is a snapshot of the active viewport. This file can be viewed using the Vslide command.

```
Slide file <drawing name>:
```

Multiple

Multiple is a command modifier, which, when placed in front of any command, automatically repeats that command in a loop. Multiple, however, does not repeat command modifiers or parameters. To end the command loop, press Ctrl-C. No prompt is issued after you enter the Multiple command.

Offset

Offset enables you to copy an entity parallel to itself, once you establish an off-set distance. You can offset a line arc, circle, or polyline by giving an offset distance, or picking a point through which the offset line is to pass.

```
Offset distance or Through <Through>:
```

Oops

The Oops command restores the last entity or group of entities deleted by the most recent Erase command.

Ortho

Ortho, which is a toggle command, constrains your drawing lines, polylines, and traces to horizontal and vertical lines. Ortho mode controls the angle at which you pick the second point in many drawing and editing commands. The default setting is off.

```
ON/OFF <Off>:
```

Osnap

The Osnap (Object SNAP) command enables you to preset one or more running object snap modes. The default setting is off, or NONe. You can override a running mode by entering a different transient object snap mode or modes when a point is requested. The Status command displays the current running osnap mode.

```
Object snap modes:
```

'Pan

Pan, which is a transparent command, enables you to scroll around the screen without altering the current zoom ratio. It is similar to repositioning paper on a drafting board to access a different drawing part. You do not physically move entities or change the drawing limits; you move your display window across the drawing. The default setting provides a displacement in relative coordinates.

```
Displacement:
Second point:
```

Pedit

The Pedit command edits 2D polylines, 3D polylines, and 3D polygon meshes. When you edit 3D polylines and meshes, which are subsets of 2D polyline editing, AutoCAD issues different sets of prompts for each. Two basic sets of editing functions are available under the Pedit command. The first set operates on the entire polyline; the second set enables you to edit individual vertices. The default response is X, which exits the command. The default for the vertex editing option is N for next vertex.

```
Close/Join/Width/Edit vertex/Fit curve/Spline curve/
Decurve/Undo/eXit <X>:
Next/Previous/Break/Insert/Move/Regen/Straighten/
Tangent/Width/eXit <N>:
```

Plan

The Plan command provides a plan view of the drawing, defined as a view point of 0,0,1 in the selected UCS. Plan can be applied to the current UCS, a previously saved UCS, or to the WCS.

```
<Current UCS>/Ucs/World:
```

Pline

The Pline command draws 2D polylines. A polyline is a series of line and arc segments that are interconnected because they share the same vertices and are processed as single entities. After entering the first point at the From point: prompt, you can continue in line mode or arc mode. Each mode has its own set of prompts. A polyline also can have a constant width or taper. To edit polylines, you can use Pedit as well as most of the regular edit commands.

```
Arc/Close/Halfwidth/Length/Undo/Width/<Endpoint of line>:
Angle/CEnter/CLose/Direction/Halfwidth/Line/Radius/Second
pt/
Undo/Width/<Endpoint of arc>:
```

Plot

The Plot command directs a drawing to a plotter or to a plot file. If you plot from the main menu, you are prompted for the name of the drawing file you want to plot. If you plot from within the drawing, AutoCAD assumes you want to plot the current drawing. Only layers that are on and thawed are plotted.

```
What to plot—Display, Extents, Limits, View or Window <D>:
```

Point

The Point command creates a point entity at the coordinates chosen that can be snapped to with the Osnap NODe option.

```
Point:
```

Polygon

The Polygon command draws 2D polygons, which are objects composed of lines of equal lengths. The number of sides ranges from three to 1,024. The size of the polygon is determined by specifying the radius of a circle in which the polygon is either inscribed (inside) or circumscribed (outside), or by specifying the length of one of the polygon's sides. Polygons are closed polylines. Use the Pedit command to edit polygons.

```
Number of sides:
Edge/<Center of Polygon>:
Inscribed in circle/Circumscribed about circle (I/C):
```

Prplot

Prplot directs a drawing to a printer plotter, such as a dot matrix or laser printer. If you plot from the main menu, you are prompted for the name of the drawing file you want to plot. If you plot from within the drawing, AutoCAD plots the current drawing. Only layers that are on and thawed are plotted.

```
What to plot — Display, Extents, Limits, View or Window <D>:
```

Purge

Purge is used to eliminate unused blocks, layers, linetypes, shapes, and styles from the current drawing. This reduces the file's size and the number of object names displayed as lists by commands or displayed for selection by dialogue boxes. The Purge command can be used only before the first command is entered in a drawing session that alters the current drawing's database.

```
Purge unused Blocks/LAyers/LTypes/SHapes/STyles/All:
```

Qtext

The Qtext (Quick TEXT) command sets a mode that causes the screen to draw boxes in place of text strings and attributes. This saves time when redrawing or regenerating the screen. The box or rectangle is the height and approximate length of the text string. The default setting is Off.

```
ON/OFF <Off>:
```

Quit

The Quit command terminates the drawing editor and discards all edits made in the current drawing session.

```
Really want to discard all changes to drawing?
```

Redefine

The Redefine command enables you to substitute AutoCAD's built-in commands with your own commands created in AutoLISP or provided by external commands in the ACAD.PGP file. A built-in command is invoked by prefixing the command name with a period. A built-in command must be undefined before it can be redefined.

```
Command name:
```

Redo

The Redo command reverses the previous U or Undo command. This command must be used immediately after the U or Undo command.

'Redraw/Redrawall

Redraw cleans up the current viewport. Redrawall cleans up all viewports. Blips are removed and any entities or parts of entities that seem to have disappeared during editing are redrawn. Grid dots are redrawn if the grid is on. You can get the same effect by pressing F7 or Ctrl-G twice.

Regen/Regenall

The Regen command causes the current viewport to be regenerated (recalculated and redrawn). The Regenall command regenerates all viewports. When a drawing is regenerated, the data and geometry associated with all entities is recalculated. Regen and Regenall are not transparent commands. You can cancel a regeneration by pressing Ctrl-C.

Regenauto

Regenauto enables you to control some screen regenerations. Some changes, such as block redefinitions, linetype scale changes, or redefined text styles, require regenerations before they are made visible. Sometimes, particularly when making multiple changes, you do not want to wait for these regenerations. You can set Regenauto off and use the Regen command to regenerate the screen when you are ready to view the results.

```
ON/OFF <On>:
```

Rename

Rename enables you to rename existing blocks, layers, linetypes, styles, UCSs, views, and viewports.

```
Block/LAyer/LType/Style/Ucs/VIew/VPort:
Old <MI>(object)<D> name:
New <MI>(object)<D> name:
```

Resume

The Resume command returns control of AutoCAD to a script that has been interrupted by keyboard input or error.

Revsurf

The Revsurf (REVolution SURFace) command generates a 3D polygon mesh by revolving a selected profile path curve around a selected axis.

```
Select path curve:
Select axis of revolution:
Start angle <0>:
Included angle (+=ccw, -=cw) <Full circle>:
```

Rotate

The Rotate command enables you to rotate entities around a designated base or pivot point. The rotation angle can be entered as a numeric angle, by picking a point relative to the base point or by using a reference angle option. The reference option enables you to specify the rotation angle relative to a base angle, usually on an existing entity.

```
<Rotation angle>/Reference:
```

Rscript

The Rscript command is used within a script to replay the script from the beginning, thereby creating a continuous loop.

Rulesurf

The Rulesurf (RULEd SURFace) command generates a 3D polyline mesh depicting the ruled surface between two entities. The two entities can be points, lines, arcs, circles, 2D polylines, or 3D polylines. If one boundary, such as a circle or closed polyline, is closed, then the other boundary must be a point or be closed. A point can be used with any another entity.

```
Select first defining curve:
Select second defining curve:
```

Save

The Save command writes drawing changes made since the drawing was last saved or ended to the disk file, but remains in the drawing editor. A drawing can be saved under another name, enabling you to save several versions of a drawing, thus documenting the stages of its development or creating alternate versions of a final drawing.

```
File name <drawing name>:
```

Scale

The Scale command changes the size of existing entities. The entities are scaled relative to the base point selected. The same scale factor is applied to the X and Y axes. You can enter a numerical scale factor or use the Reference option to pick a reference and new length. A numerical scale factor is the default choice.

```
Base point: <Scale factor>/Reference:
```

Script

The Script command creates a script file that automates routine tasks. A script executes until a keystroke is input from the keyboard, a command error occurs, or the end of the script file is encountered.

```
Script file <drawing name>:
```

Select

The Select command enables you to pick entities to retain as a selection set. At the next entity selection prompt, use the Previous option to reselect the retained set. You can create the selection set using the standard object selection. Select often is used in menu macros.

```
Select objects:
```

'Setvar

The Setvar command retrieves and modifies system variables. Most system variables also are modified through AutoCAD commands. A few system variables are read-only, and cannot be modified. Type **?** for a list of all variables.

```
Variable name or ? <default>:
```

Shape

The Shape command is used to insert shapes into the current drawing at user-specified parameters. This command also lists the available shapes for the drawing.

```
Shape name (or ?):
Starting point:
Height <1.0>:
Angle <0>:
```

Sh/Shell

Sh suspends the drawing editor and enables you to execute DOS internal commands from within AutoCAD. After you press Enter at the OS Command: prompt, an appended right angle bracket (C:\>>) is shown. Type **Exit** to return to the AutoCAD drawing editor. The Shell command suspends the drawing editor and enables you to execute DOS external commands and other programs. Type **Exit** to return to the AutoCAD drawing editor at the point where you left it.

```
OS Command:
C:\>>
```

Sketch

The Sketch command enables you to draw freehand using the mouse or pointing device.

```
Record increment <current>:
Sketch.  Pen eXit Quit Record Erase Connect.
```

Snap

The Snap command enables you to move the crosshairs at any defined increment. You can modify the increment value and turn the setting on and off. It may be rotated to any user specified angle and given unequal X and Y increment values. The default setting is 1.0000 and off.

```
Snap spacing or ON/OFF/Aspect/Rotate/Style <1.0000>:
```

Solid

The Solid command draws solid areas or extruded volumes. If the Fill command (or system variable FILLMODE) is set to on (1), the solid is displayed filled. These areas can be triangular or quadrilateral (four sided). The first two points are the endpoints of a starting edge; the next point defines the corner point of a triangle. At the Fourth point: prompt, you can press Enter to close the triangle or enter a fourth point to define a quadrilateral. The command repeats the third and fourth point prompts, adding on new solids with the previous third and fourth points as new first and second points, until you press Enter at the Third point: prompt or cancel the command.

```
First point:
Second point:
Third point:
Fourth point:
```

Status

The Status command, when entered at the Command: prompt, gives you current information on drawing limits, extents, the drawing aids settings, and some system information. When entered in Dim mode, it provides the current state of dimensioning variables.

Stretch

The Stretch command enables you to extend (or shrink) certain entities by selecting them with a crossing window and picking a base and new point of displacement. You can stretch lines, arcs, traces, solids, polylines, and 3D faces. Entity endpoints that lie inside the crossing window are moved, those outside the crossing window remain fixed, and the lines or arcs crossing the window are stretched. Entities that are defined entirely within the crossing window (all endpoints, vertices, and definition points) are moved. The definition point for a block or shape is its insertion base point; for a circle, the center point; for text, the lower left corner.

```
Select objects to stretch by window...
Base point:
New point:
```

Style

The Style command enables you to create new text styles, modify existing styles, and obtain a list of defined styles. The style name is arbitrary; you can use up to 31 characters to name a style. Various appearance attributes are used to create unique text styles. A style definition includes the name of a text font file. Several styles can be derived from a single font file. Font files use the SHX extension.

```
Text style name (or ?) <ROMANC>:
```

Tablet

The Tablet command is used to calibrate a digitizer to input an existing paper drawing, to configure the digitizer for up to four tablet menu areas and a screen pointing area, and to toggle the tablet between a pointing mode and a digitizing mode. The tablet must be on to digitize drawings.

```
Option (ON/OFF/CAL/CFG):
```

Tabsurf

The Tabsurf (TABulated SURFace) command generates a 3D polygon mesh by projecting an entity (path curve) through space along a direction vector.

```
Select path curve:
Select direction vector:
```

Text

The Text command enables you to enter text in your drawing one line at a time. Unlike the Dtext command, Text does not dynamically show your text characters on the screen as you enter them. Several justification options can be specified. Text places the text string after you input the text.

```
Start point or Align/Center/Fit/Middle/Right/Style:
```

'Textscr

The Textscr command flips the display screen to text mode. Textscr has no effect in a dual screen configuration.

Time

The Time command displays the following parameters: current date and time; date and time the current drawing was created; date and time the drawing was last updated; and the current amount of time in the drawing editor. AutoCAD enables you to set the timer at elapsed intervals.

```
Current time:
Drawing created:
Drawing last updated:
Time in drawing editor:
Elapsed timer:
Timer on.
Display/ON/OFF/Reset:
```

Trace

The Trace command enables you to draw solid lines of a specified width. AutoCAD automatically miters the corners of adjacent trace segments entered during the same command.

```
From point:
To point:
To point:
```

Trim

The Trim command makes it possible for you to clip entities that cross a boundary or cutting edges. Entities such as lines, arcs, circles, and polylines can act as boundary edges and as objects to trim.

```
Select cutting edge(s)...
Select object to trim:
```

U/Undo

The U and Undo commands enable you to step back through your drawing, reversing previous commands or groups of commands. The Undo command keeps track of the previous commands in a temporary file. The temporary file then is cleared at the end of each drawing session or when you plot the drawing. The U command undoes a single preceding command or a group of previous commands. Undo offers additional controls.

```
Auto/Back/Control/End/Group/Mark/<number>:
```

Ucs

The UCS (User Coordinate System) command enables you to redefine the location of 0,0 and the direction of X,Y. The default UCS is the WCS (World Coordinate System). You can set your user coordinate system using the UCS command or the Dducs dialogue box.

```
Origin/ZAxis/3point/Entity/View/X/Y/Z/Prev/Restore/Save/Del/
?/<World>:
```

Ucsicon

The Ucsicon marker graphically displays the origin and viewing plane of the current UCS. The default setting for the icon is on and Noorigin, which displays at the lower left corner of the screen. The Origin option displays at 0,0,0.

```
ON/OFF/All/Noorigin/ORigin <ON>:
```

Units

The Units command controls the format and display for the input of coordinates, distances, and angles. You specify the system of units, the precision, the system of angle measurement, the precision of angle display, and the direction of angles.

'View

The View command enables you to save, name, and restore the current display or a windowed area. The view name can be up to 31 characters.

```
?/Delete/Restore/Save/Window:
```

Viewres

The Viewres command controls fast zooms and the display resolution of arcs, circles, ellipses, polyline arcs, and linetypes. The default setting is for fast zooms with a resolution factor of 100 percent. Fast zoom enables most zooms and pans to operate at redraw speed rather than regeneration speed.

```
Do you want fast zooms? <Y>
Enter circle zoom percent (1-20000) <100>:
```

Vpoint

The Vpoint (ViewPOINT) command enables you to determine the direction and angle for viewing a drawing by selecting a 3D viewpoint. The command regenerates the drawing with a parallel projection from the 3D point that you specify. The original default is the plan view, looking from 0,0,1. The current default is the current viewpoint. You can define a viewpoint in one of three ways: by entering XYZ values; by providing an angle in the XY plane and from the XY plane; or by picking a point on the compass icon, using the axes tripod for reference.

```
Rotate/<View point> <0.0000,0.0000,1.0000>:
Enter angle in X-Y plane from X axis <270>:
Enter angle from X-Y plane <90>:
```

Vports

The Vports command enables you to divide your screen into several viewing areas. Each viewport can display a different view of your drawing. Each viewport contains its own drawing display area and can have independent magnification, viewpoint, snap, grid, viewres, ucsicon, dview, and isometric settings. You can use the Zoom, Regen, and Redraw commands in each viewport. DOS-based systems enable you to define up to four viewports at any one time. Other systems enable you to define up to sixteen.

```
Save/Restore/Delete/Join/Off/?/2/<3>/4:
```

Vslide

The Vslide command displays the contents of a slide file (SLD) in the current viewport. A slide contained within a slide library created by the Slidelib utility program also can be viewed. The viewport is returned to its original state using the Redraw command.

```
Slide file <drawing name>:
```

Wblock

The Wblock (Write BLOCK) command writes a drawing, a selection set, or a block definition to disk as a new drawing file (not a block definition). AutoCAD prompts for a file name, and then a block name. A * specifies the entire drawing. If you press Enter or the Spacebar at the prompt for the block name, AutoCAD prompts for an insertion point and a selection set.

```
File name:
Block name:
Insertion base point:
```

'Zoom

The Zoom command magnifies (zooms in) or shrinks (zooms out) the display in the current viewport. The command does not physically change the size of the drawing; rather, it enables you to view a small part of the drawing in detail or look at a greater part with less detail. Entering a value followed by an X specifies the magnification of the zoom relative to the current display — 5X, for example, magnifies the viewport five times. A number alone specifies the magnification relative to the entire drawing. Several other methods of specifying the desired magnification are provided.

```
All/Center/Dynamic/Extents/Left/Previous/Window/<Scale(X)>:
```

3Dface

The 3Dface command creates shapes defined by either three or four corner points entered in circular fashion. You can define nonplanar faces by varying the Z coordinates for the corner points; however, only faces with co-planar Z coordinates hide other entities. You can construct 3dfaces with visible or invisible edges.

```
First point:
Second point:
Third point:
Fourth point:
```

3Dmesh

The 3Dmesh command creates three-dimensional polygon meshes. You can give the mesh size, as well as specify the vertices as 2D or 3D points by starting with vertex (0,0) and ending with vertex (M,N). 3D meshes act like 3Dfaces fused together and are treated as one entity. The meshes are created open. You can close the mesh by editing it using the Pedit command.

```
Mesh M size:
N size:
Vertex (0, 0):
```

3Dpoly

The 3Dpoly command creates 3D polylines that have straight line segments and no width.

```
First point:
Close/Undo/<Endpoint of line>:
```

Using the AutoLISP 3D Programs

In addition to AutoCAD's built-in 3D polygon mesh commands, the AutoLISP language contains many 3D construction and editing programs. Each object construction program creates a single 3D polygon mesh. These programs are supplied on the AutoCAD distribution disks labeled Support and Bonus.

 The AutoCAD Bonus disk is sent only to AutoCAD customers who mail in their registration cards.

Once the program files are in your AutoCAD directory, you can use them during your drawing sessions. The 3D object construction programs are accessed by selecting 3D Construction from the Draw pull-down menu, or by selecting 3D Objects from the 3D screen submenu. Other selections must be executed from the AutoCAD command line. The following programs are documented in the *AutoLISP Programmer's Reference*; those relevant to the concepts covered in this book are briefly discussed here.

Axrot

The Axrot command is the same as the Rotate command, but it is implemented in 3D space.

```
Select objects:
Axis of rotation X/Y/Z:
Degrees of rotation: <0>:
Base point <0,0,0>:
```

Box

The Box command draws a 3D rectangular box or cube to your specifications parallel to the current XY plane.

```
Corner of box:
Length:
Cube/<Width>:
Rotation angle about Z axis:
```

Chface

The Chface command enables you to move individual 3D face vertices.

```
Select entity to change:
1/2/3/4/Undo/Display/<Select vertex>:
```

Cl

The Cl command draws a pair of center lines through an existing circle or arc. The lines are drawn parallel to the circle and on the layer CL.

```
Select arc or circle:
Radius is nnnn
Length/<Extension>:
```

Cone

The Cone command builds a cone from the dimensions and segments you enter.

```
Base center point:
Diameter/<radius> of base:
Diameter/<radius> of top <0>:
Height:
Number of segments <16>:
```

Dome or Dish

The Dome and Dish commands create the top or bottom half of a sphere from a center point and dimension. You can specify the number of segments in both directions.

```
Center of dome:
Diameter/<Radius>:
Number of longitudinal segments <16>:
Number of latitudinal segments <8>:
```

Edge

The Edge command highlights invisible 3D face edges for selection.

```
Display/<Select edge>:
```

Mesh

The Mesh command offers a simpler method of creating planar 3D meshes than does the 3Dmesh command. You need only specify four corner points in clockwise or counterclockwise fashion, and the mesh M and N sizes.

```
First corner:
Second corner:
Third corner:
Fourth corner:
Mesh M size:
Mesh N size:
```

Project

The Project command is used when you create 2D engineering drawings from 3D models. It creates 2D lines, arcs, circles, polylines, solids, and point entities in the current UCS from their 3D counterparts. 3D meshes, polyline width, and extrusion information are not supported.

Pyramid

The Pyramid command draws a three- or four-sided pyramid with the sides meeting in an apex, flattened top, or ridge.

```
First base point:
Second base point:
Third base point:
Tetrahedron/<Fourth base point>:
Top/<Apex point>:
Ridge/Top/<Apex point>:
```

Slot

The Slot command (not available in Release 11) constructs a 3D slot or hole, then uses 3D faces with invisible edges to form a rectangular outline around the slot or hole on the top and bottom surfaces.

```
Hole or Slot? H/S <S>:
First center point of slot:
Slot radius:
Second center point of slot:
Depth:
```

Sphere

The Sphere command constructs a sphere as one polygon mesh.

```
Center of sphere:
Diameter/<radius>:
Number of longitudinal segments <16>:
Number of latitudinal segments <16>:
```

Torus

The Torus command builds a toroidal polygon mesh, or 3D doughnut, by drawing a tube around a center point.

```
Center of torus:
Diameter/<radius> of torus:
Diameter/<radius> of tube:
Segments around tube circumference <16>:
Segments around torus circumference <16>:
```

Wedge

The Wedge command creates a wedge-shaped polygon mesh that starts from a corner point.

```
Corner of wedge:
Length:
Width:
Height:
Rotation angle about Z axis:
```

3Darray

The 3Darray command is equivalent to the Array command but is implemented in 3D space. The term *levels* is used to describe the Z element of rectangular arrays. Polar arrays are restricted to a single level rotated from the current XY plane.

```
Select objects:
Then for Rectangular arrays:
Rectangular or Polar array (R/P):
Number of rows (---) <1>:
Number of columns (||||) <1>:
Number of levels (...) <1>:
Distance between rows (---):
Distance between columns (||||):
Distance between levels (...):
Or for Polar arrays:
Number of items:
Angle to fill <360>:
Rotate objects as they are copied? <Y>:
Center point of array:
Second point of axis of rotation:
```

INDEX

— B —

— D —

— G —

— H —

— S —

— T —

New Riders Puts You on the Cutting Edge of Computer Information!

You'll Find All You Need To Know
About Graphics
with Books from New Riders!

New Riders Covers
All Your Operating Systems Needs!

Maximizing MS-DOS 5

New Riders Publishing

This all-new book/disk set is designed to provide the most practical instruction for today's busy computer user. It includes task-oriented, practical examples and provides DOS-related discussion of networking, Windows, and DOS-Shell task-switching environments. Features a comprehensive command reference and bonus disk with macros, batch files, and utilities.

Through DOS 5

1-56205-013-3, 700 pp., 7⅜ x 9¼
$34.95 USA

Inside SCO/UNIX

New Riders Publishing

This tutorial/reference presents everything you need to get started and use the UNIX operating system for everyday tasks! You'll learn how to increase your UNIX proficiency and also find a comprehensive command reference.

SCO Xenix 286, SCO Xenix 386, SCO UNIX/System V 386

1-56205-028-1, 600 pp., 7⅜ x 9¼
$29.95 USA

Maximizing Windows 3

Jim Boyce

This is the complete guide to maximizing the Windows environment—complete with a companion disk! Covering all aspects of customizing Windows installations, the text includes valuable tips and tricks for memory and disk efficiency. Also covered are advanced techniques on networking, data exchange, icons, ToolBook, and third-party enhancement.

Windows 3.0

1-56205-002-8, 704 pp., 7⅜ x 9¼
$39.95 USA

To Order, Call:
(800) 428-5331 OR (317) 573-2500

Networking Is Easy
with Books from New Riders!

Inside LAN Manager

Don Baarnes

Here is the perfect introduction to practical end-user and system administration skills! The text covers standard and enhnaced DOS workstation features as well as OS/2 workstation features. You'll also find tips on customizing your network environment. Includes discussion on LAN Manager's domains, multiple servers, and internetworking capabilites.

Latest Version

1-56205-023-0, 700 pp., 7³⁄₈ x 9¹⁄₄

$34.95 USA

Inside Novell Netware

Michael Day

This is a comprehensive tutorial/reference for end-users wanting to get the most power from their network operating system. You'll find complete coverage of both command-line and menu-driven utilities as well as installation and system management information.

Novell NetWare 286 & 386

1-56205-022-2, 700 pp., 7³⁄₈ x 9¹⁄₄

$29.95 USA

To Order, Call:
(800) 428-5331 OR (317) 573-2500

Add to Your New Riders Library Today
with the Best Books for the Best Software

Yes, please send me the productivity-boosting material I have checked below. Make check payable to New Riders Publishing.

❏ **Check enclosed.**

Charge to my credit card:

❏ **VISA**   ❏ **MasterCard**

Card # _____

Expiration date: _____

Signature: _____

Name: _____

Company: _____

Address: _____

City: _____

State: _____ ZIP: _____

Phone: _____

The easiest way to order is to pick up the phone and call 1-800-541-6789 between 9:00 a.m. and 5:00 p.m., EST. Please have your credit card available, and your order can be placed in a snap!

Quantity	Description of Item	Unit Cost	Total Cost
	Inside CorelDRAW!, 2nd Edition	$29.95	
	AutoCAD 3D Design & Presentation*	$29.95	
	Maximizing Windows 3 (Book-and-Disk set)	$39.95	
	Inside AutoCAD, Special Edition (for Releases 10 and 11)*	$34.95	
	Maximizing AutoCAD: Volume I (Book-and-Disk set) Customizing AutoCAD with Macros and Menus	$34.95	
	AutoCAD for Beginners	$19.95	
	Inside Autodesk Animator*	$29.95	
	Maximizing AutoCAD: Volume II (Book-and-Disk set) Inside AutoLISP	$34.95	
	Inside AutoSketch, 2nd Edition*	$24.95	
	AutoCAD Reference Guide, 2nd Edition	$14.95	
	AutoCAD Reference Guide on Disk, 2nd Edition	$14.95	
	Inside CompuServe (Book-and-Disk set)	$29.95	
	Managing and Networking AutoCAD*	$29.95	
	Inside AutoCAD, Release 11, Metric Ed. (Book-and-Disk set)	$34.95	
	Maximizing MS-DOS 5 (Book-and-Disk set)	$34.95	
	Inside Generic CADD*	$29.95	
	Inside Windows	$29.95	
	AutoCAD Bible	$39.95	
	*Companion Disk available for these books	$14.95 ea.	

❏ **3½″ disk**

❏ **5¼″ disk**

Shipping and Handling: See information below.		
TOTAL		

Shipping and Handling: $4.00 for the first book and $1.75 for each additional book. Floppy disk: add $1.75 for shipping and handling. If you need to have it NOW, we can ship product to you in 24 to 48 hours for an additional charge, and you will receive your item overnight or in two days. Add $20.00 per book and $8.00 for up to three disks overseas. Prices subject to change. Call for availability and pricing information on latest editions.

New Riders Publishing • 11711 N. College Avenue • P.O. Box 90 • Carmel, Indiana 46032
1-800-541-6789   **1-800-448-3804**
Orders/Customer Service   **FAX**

To order: Fill in the reverse side, fold, and mail

BUSINESS REPLY MAIL
FIRST CLASS PERMIT NO. 6008 INDIANAPOLIS, IN

POSTAGE WILL BE PAID BY ADDRESSEE

NEW RIDERS PUBLISHING

P.O. Box 90

Carmel, Indiana 46032